Third Edition

Write It

A Process Approach to College Essays with Readings

Linda Strahan
*University of California,
Riverside*

Kathleen Moore
University of California

D1501835

Kendall Hunt
publishing company

Cover image © Shutterstock, Inc.

Kendall Hunt
publishing company

www.kendallhunt.com
Send all inquiries to:
4050 Westmark Drive
Dubuque, IA 52004-1840

Printed in the United States of America

10 9 8 7 6 5 4 3 2 1

Contents

Part 2:   WRITING ASSIGNMENTS   49

Acknowledgments

We want to acknowledge the University Writing Program faculty and TAs at the University of California, Riverside, for their contributions to this new edition. We are particularly indebted to the classroom instructors, whose exemplary teaching of the lessons in this book and whose careful assessments of the needs of their students have directly influenced much of this text. *Write It* has changed and grown because of you. In particular, warm thanks to Benedict Jones for his tenacious editing of the manuscript—the book has been improved because of his careful work—and for his contribution of a diagnostic test to Part 1. Thanks also go to Albert Anthony for his contributions to the new case study in Part 3.

Deep appreciation goes to the reviewers who offered us many good suggestions that ultimately improved this new edition.

We are indebted to the Kendall Hunt team whose skills and support made this book possible. We especially thank our editor Elizabeth Klipping and our project coordinator Amanda Smith for their endless patience and professionalism, their impressive problem-solving skills, and their consistent attention to detail.

Wayne Stauffer
Houston Community College Southeast

Dr. Danika Brown
University of Texas, Pan American

Deborah Harris
Loyola Marymount University

Roberta Barki
UTSA

Jeanine Bator
Yakima Valley Community College-Grandview Campus

Jill Darley-Vanis
Clark College

Susan Kay
Cascadia Community College

David Hurst
College of the Sequoias

Rebecca Hess
La Sierra University

Candice Rai
University of Washington, Seattle

Sarah Trombly
Austin Community College

Amy Shank
Wenatchee Valley College

Jefferson Hancock
Cabrillo College

Carrie Bailey
Clark College

Becky Villarreal
Austin Community College

Amy Hundley
Merced College

Foreword

Engineers tell us that they spend half of their time on the job writing reports, proposals, and job-related messages to their colleagues. Much of that work is "writing on demand," which must be completed rapidly, accurately, and in a way that helpfully addresses the requirements of the task. In many walks of life, the ability to respond quickly in writing, doing that work in a way that truly addresses the issue at hand, is what eventually distinguishes the rising professional, entrepreneur, craftsman, teacher, and civic leader, as well as the effective employee. Writing on demand also prepares us to speak in job-related settings. It readies us to formulate and express our thoughts in spoken words that others find useful, informative, and persuasive.

Your work in this course will improve your chances of thriving at the University, which holds in high esteem the ability to compose thoughts with dispatch, accuracy, relevance, and verve. Your preparation will help you become a better reader, for good writers see more when they read. Conversely, the more you learn to read attentively, the better the writer you will become. What you learn in this class will also help you articulate your ideas and express yourself in aspects of your life that have little to do with the world of work or academics. A trained proficiency in writing and reading will give you greater access to the ideas and experiences of others.

Your lecture class, your workshop sessions, and your online studies will prepare you to succeed in this class and prepare you for Freshman English. You will need to be patient as well as dedicated; many students need more than one quarter to become proficient writers. Remember that the goal of this book is to help all students reach proficiency as quickly as possible. We look forward to seeing you in Freshman English.

Professor John Briggs
Director of the University Writing Program
University of California, Riverside

Preface

This book will introduce you to a form of academic writing that you will meet in many of your college classes across the disciplines. Each section of the book presents and gives you practice with a range of writing strategies that guide you through the writing process and show you how to use each stage to maximize its benefits. These strategies will help you gain the confidence and understanding you need to write effective academic essays. Students, especially those majoring in disciplines other than English, sometimes see introductory college writing courses as unnecessary and unimportant. However, you will be asked to read critically and give written responses in many of your college courses, and your professors will take for granted your ability to do these things. If you work through this book carefully, we believe that you will develop a process for writing that will allow you to effectively complete any college writing assignment you are likely to see that asks you to respond to an idea.

Producing a successful essay can be a daunting task because it requires not one but a series of skills: focused reading, critical thinking, careful analysis, marshaling of evidence, drafting, and editing. *Write It* offers exercises to guide you through each stage in the production of an essay, allowing you the opportunity to practice each skill, one stage at a time. While the book goes through the writing process step by step, remember that writing is always a recursive activity, and when you begin a paper, you may not always begin at step one with your topic and proceed in a linear way, one step at a time, to proofreading. *Write It*, however, must examine the steps in the writing process sequentially, beginning with a reading and a follow-up writing prompt, and continuing right through prewriting, drafting, and rewriting using a peer review. As you move through the guiding exercises *Write It* provides, new ideas will come to you. Don't set these discoveries aside but carry them forward into the remaining exercises. As you relate old and new information, you will explore each assignment's topic from several angles so that your ideas will build on one another. In this way the steps, though done in isolation, will come together in a unified perspective. The organization of this book is intended to help you come to see essay building as a process rather than a formula, the stages as necessary steps to internalize until each becomes an intuitive part of writing itself.

Because no writers—in the real world or in the classroom—write in a vacuum, *Write It* provides readings and tasks for students to address. In each of six writing assignment sections, you are first asked to attend to a reading selection and respond to a writing topic about that reading. The reading selection and writing topic are followed by structured writing tasks that help you develop and organize your ideas in order to answer that question in a successful way. *Write It* guides you through each stage in the process; you meet each unit's central reading and then move through a sequence of prewriting exercises, such as "Questions to Guide Your Reading," "Opinion and Working Thesis Statement," "Planning and Drafting Your Essay," and a peer draft review form, that will help you develop, revise, and edit your essay. Each section also includes a series of related readings that lead you to consider the topic of each assignment in a larger context and to participate in an exchange of ideas about the topic each assignment unit addresses. You will also find class discussions and homework activities that reinforce grammar, comprehension, and critical thinking skills. Following the assignment units is a section that contains student essays, and you will be able to read and evaluate the essays other students have written in response to a few of the reading selections' writing topic. This process encourages you not just to become a writer of college essays but also to become a reader and writer in college. As you participate in the exchange of ideas with others in the academic community, you will both shape and be shaped by that community. Your experiences are unique to you, and your writing will reflect the knowledge you've accumulated from those experiences as you engage with others in defining the world in which we all live.

HERE IS HOW TO USE THIS SKILL-BUILDING BOOK

Write It is presented in three parts.

Part 1: BASIC INFORMATION that will give you a good foundation for completing the reading and writing assignments in your English classes. Included in Part 1 are the following:

- Steps for a thoughtful reading of an essay
- An annotated reading
- Avoiding plagiarism and copyright infringement
- A suggested structure for an essay that responds to another writer's work
- Two alternative essay structures
- An introduction in an argument essay
- Guidelines for writing a directed summary
- Strategies for developing your ideas
- Writing a paragraph that supports your thesis statement
- Transitions
- Conclusions
- Logical fallacies
- Ten steps for careful editing of common writing errors
- A scoring rubric
- Tips for budgeting your time in a timed writing exam
- Using your handbook
- Diagnostic tests
- Sentence skills assessments

Part 2: SIX ASSIGNMENT UNITS that contain a central essay to read and analyze and a writing assignment to respond to with your own essay. For each of these, the book will lead you through the writing process as you:

- Read for comprehension and learn to recognize and evaluate a writer's argument.
- Develop your own position and supporting evidence.
- Organize your ideas into an effective essay structure.
- Revise and edit for coherence and clarity.
- Incorporate supplemental readings to expand and broaden the scope and complexity of your essay response.
- Participate in class discussion activities.
- Complete homework activities.

Part 3: FOUR CASE STUDIES that provide examples of students' writing to highlight strategies other students have used to construct essays. This section gives you an opportunity to practice applying criteria from the scoring rubric to evaluate others' essays. By evaluating the writing of others, you will become better at evaluating your own.

The step-by-step lessons in this skill-building workbook will provide you with a strong foundation for good writing. The book's techniques have been widely tested and proven successful. In a recent survey on our campus, students credited the lessons in this book for their success in their first college writing class. We are confident that this book will work for you, too.

Basic Information

How to Use Part 1

The particular argument essay that you will study in *Write It*—one that responds to the essay of another writer—will help you gain practice in critically analyzing issues, formulating logical arguments, and persuasively expressing your opinions by using the conventional rules of written English and a conventional essay structure. The thesis-centered essay is the most commonly assigned essay format in college. Its purpose is to persuade, and its formal parts are established by convention and provide a structure for presenting an argument. These parts include an introduction that orients the readers to the essay's subject, a thesis statement that presents the argument, the body paragraphs that develop and support the argument, and a conclusion that closes the essay.

Part 1 is designed to be used as a writing reference section, as it gives you a basic set of directions for writing within the argument essay's conventional format. The section gives you an overview of the process of essay writing and contains the following information:

Strategies for Comprehension

> How to do a thoughtful reading
>
> Guidelines for annotating an essay

Goals When Drafting

> An overview of the essay's structure
>
> Suggestions for writing the introduction and a well-developed thesis statement
>
> Guidelines for writing a directed summary
>
> A basic structure for writing supporting paragraphs

Some ways to use transitions
Options for writing a conclusion

Help with Revising and Editing

Ten steps for careful editing
Using a scoring rubric to critique an essay

Some Additional Resources

Tips for writing a timed essay
Guidelines for using a handbook
Diagnostic exercises for checking grammar skills

As you can see, Part 1 of this book contains guidelines for all of the essay's parts to help you work within the essay's conventional structure. The information in Part 1 is organized around the stages of the writing process and includes guidance on building each of the conventional essay parts that come together to form the essay's overall structure. Spend some time with these pages before moving to Part 2, where you will be asked to put them into practice. As you engage with the writing assignments in Part 2 and use the stages of the writing process to develop an essay within a particular writing context, you will want to turn back to Part 1 for guidance.

Steps for a Thoughtful Reading of an Essay with an Example

In order to respond appropriately to a reading selection you will have to spend some time reading and analyzing the reading selection's argument and supporting material. Here are some guidelines to help you develop sound strategies for understanding. You will need to understand the reading selection before you can discuss its argument and respond with an argument of your own.

In our everyday lives, we read on a daily basis. We live in a literate society, so we read things like signs, emails, and menus without much effort and without thinking about them very much. In an academic setting, however, reading becomes an activity that requires effort and thought. Use the steps below to ensure that your reading is focused and productive.

1. **Consider the title given to the material you are to read.**

   It should suggest a particular topic or topics to you. Think about what you already know about the topic. Think about what else you need to know about the topic in order to have an informed opinion about it. Look at the wording of the title again and try to determine from it the author's opinion of the topic or his or her reason for writing about the topic.

2. **Learn about the author.**

   If biographical information about the author is presented with the reading, look for biographical information that may have influenced the content and perspective of the reading. Sometimes, you can better evaluate a writer's argument by taking into account his or her level of expertise or personal connection to the subject of the essay.

3. **Read through the material once quickly.**

   This first rapid reading gives you an overview of the subject, the author's attitude toward the subject, and the nature of the supporting evidence that the reading contains.

4. **Read again to identify the thesis.**

   For your second reading, you need a pen or a highlighter as well as your eyes. Your first task on the second reading is to find and mark the thesis. The thesis states the author's position on the topic. Often, it is contained in a single sentence, but, in some cases, it takes several sentences to make clear the point of the work. There are times when the author does not state his or her thesis explicitly, but, having read through the essay once, you should be able to state it, and you might want to note it in the margin.

5. **Read slowly and methodically through the rest of the material.**

   Each paragraph has a topic sentence. It expresses the main point of the paragraph. The topic sentence is usually found at the beginning of the paragraph, but it can be anywhere within the paragraph. You should note the point (or topic sentence) of each paragraph as you work through your second reading. The remainder of the paragraph contains evidence to support the topic sentence. During this reading, it is your job to evaluate this evidence for its logic and validity. It is useful for future reference to make comments in the margins regarding the strength and weakness of the paragraph's evidence.

6. **Read again for review.**

   Now that you have thought through the ideas and evidence supporting the ideas in your reading, read the whole thing again. Watch for any anomalies, statements, or points that don't fit with your overall understanding of the material. If you find any, take time to determine whether the material is an authorial error or a misreading on your part. You may find that you need to go back to Step 4 and begin working through the reading again. Once you are certain that your reading is accurate, you are prepared to discuss, summarize, and respond to the reading with your own essay.

Look over the following essay and notice the way that one writer used Write It's *guidelines to underline main ideas and make notations in the margins. These notes help identify the essay's argument and supporting details.*

Leadership: Facing Moral and Ethical Dilemmas

Essay

THE CENTER FOR BUSINESS AND ETHICS AT LOYOLA MARYMOUNT UNIVERSITY

Last year in the U.S. alone 257 public companies with $258 billion in assets declared bankruptcy. This was a huge increase over the previous year's record of 176 companies with $95 billion. This year will certainly be worse in terms of big companies going bust. Big Fortune 500 companies aren't expected to collapse.

Outlining of the problem

Taking a look at what went wrong and why these companies failed reveals moral and ethical shortcomings. There are other obvious factors that contribute to a company's demise. A bad economy, financial risks that don't pay off, accounting manipulations that seemed smart at the time, loss of competitive advantage, and rapidly changing market preferences are undeniably strong negative factors. But to truly understand, one must look deeper, into the very hearts and souls of the leaders who guide corporate responsibility. One must look at the moral and ethical stance of an organization and the role of leadership in creating a culture of values.

Thesis statement

Restatement of the thesis

September 11th was a tragedy that brought harsh consequences for many businesses. One can blame terrorism. But the recent rash of bankruptcies is more frightening in that we brought this on ourselves. True, one can point fingers at the CEO's in charge. There is no doubt there were some who were in a position to know when to jump ship before the rest of us.

In 1986, the space shuttle Challenger exploded, causing the death of seven astronauts. A subsequent investigation of the culture at NASA revealed important lessons. There was not one single error that occurred, and neither did the managers intentionally commit wrongdoing. Yet it could have been prevented. The errors were years in the making. NASA engineers noticed damage to the crucial O-rings, yet they repeatedly convinced themselves the damage was acceptable. One analyst described it as "an incremental descent into poor judgment." The culture at NASA was extremely success-oriented. They had hired the best of the best, and had highly complex and sophisticated performance goals. The pressure to succeed gradually mounted until minor violations of standards became standard. Nothing looked wrong until it was all over.

The culture at Enron was very similar. They hired the brightest from graduate schools. Success was rewarded and non-performers shunned. The emphasis was on the numbers and immediate success rather than on long term values. There was a gradual descent into poor judgment, denial, greed, deceit, ego, wishful thinking, poor communications, and lax oversight. But it was apparent only in retrospect. No one noticed at the time, as everyone was immersed in the culture. The question to ask is not how did this happen at Enron, but how is it happening in one's own organization right now? Where are the corporate standards being violated? As a leader, in what ways is one contributing to a loosening of ethical and moral values? What does one need to do to improve organizational integrity?

Ethical and professional dilemmas are not new. In the past, people relied more on religious doctrine to guide standards; however, evil carried out in the name of religion has shaken confidence in religious traditions. These are difficult times in terms of people's ability to know what is the right thing to do and still

Comparison to emphasize the seriousness of the situation

Example: 1986 space shuttle explosion that resulted from managerial/engineering errors in judgment

Example: Enron's culture of denial, deceit, etc.

remain successful in their professions. Is business ethics an oxymoron?

We seem to accept that modern businesses have morality and ethics different from social traditions. Robert Jackall (1997) suggests that the modern bureaucracy has created a "society within a society" in which there is a set of ethical standards that may be consistent with those of the larger society. This might help explain how certain corporate leaders could do what they did and still look themselves in the mirror. Our current capitalistic society goes along with these special societies, as long as they are successful. Enron was touted as one of the most innovative organizations five years in a row by *Fortune* magazine. Only when there is a collapse do people cry "foul."

In America, the Protestant work ethic at one time formed the basis of good business relationships. A person's word was his bond, and business could be counted on with a handshake. Personal integrity and reputation mattered. But in business, there is also a "dog eat dog" mentality. To the victor go the spoils. Somehow, when it comes to business, there is such an emphasis on success that morals and ethics take a back seat.

The larger an organization, the more complex the strategy and operations, the easier it becomes to stretch standards and change the numbers to reflect what is desired, rather than what is. Meeting the numbers seems more desirable than sticking to reality. Besides, one might reason that "reality" or "truth" is really just a question of which version, which perspective. Here's the way one cynical executive put it: "Let's be honest. We lie and our colleagues lie to us. That's how human beings operate. People prefer to tell each other what they want to hear . . . I don't need perfect people, I need successful people who can think for themselves and get the job done. If they need to tell a little white lie, I can live with that."

Explanation for the changing definition of business ethics.

Reference to authority to explain the modern ethical standard of corporations.

Comparison of modern business ethics to Protestant work ethic.

Restatement of explanation and a quotation for impact.

Avoiding Plagiarism and Copyright Infringement

You may be aware of the requirement that all work you turn in for credit must be your own, but sometimes students inadvertently commit plagiarism because they are unclear about what constitutes plagiarism or infringement of copyright laws. Review the following definitions and rules and check to see that your own paper meets all the requirements of intellectual and academic honesty.

Copyright refers to the legal ownership of published material. Any writing—a play, an essay, a pamphlet, a website—is the intellectual property of the person who wrote it. If, in your paper, you borrow that property by quoting, summarizing, or paraphrasing, you must give credit to the original author. The *fair use* laws allow you to borrow *brief passages* without infringing on copyright, but you must credit the source and document it properly. Your handbook will show you the correct form to use for each and every source.

Plagiarism occurs when students make poor choices and turn in another student's work as their own. Institutions of higher learning have strict policies regarding this type of plagiarism, and the consequences for this action can be significant. Plagiarism may also be committed by oversight; a student may have forgotten where he or she found the particular material or even that the material was not his or her own. It is important during your research that you include all the source information in your notes so that you will not accidentally commit plagiarism and be held accountable for it.

Remember to acknowledge the following:

> *Ideas*—any idea or concept that you learned elsewhere that is not common knowledge
>
> *Words and Phrases*—exact reproduction of another author's writing
>
> *Charts/Tables/Statistics/Other Visuals*—other forms of work done by an author
>
> *Your Own Work*—work of your own, done for a different assignment or purpose

Intellectual property is the result of work done by a person with the head rather than the hands; nevertheless, the result of that work still belongs to the person who did it. If a carpenter made a chair, that chair is owned by its maker. You would consider taking that chair an act of theft. Try to think of printed material as a similar object and show that property the same respect you would any other. By doing so, you will avoid plagiarism and copyright infringement.

Read the following essay written by a college freshman for a composition course. Do you find her argument compelling? Why or why not? What position would you take if you were asked to write an essay on plagiarism?

Plagiarism: A Crime to Be Prevented

Essay

Vicki Xiong

Plagiarism is an ugly word; it is an ugly act to be caught in—to have next to your name. No matter how ugly the word, students all across America continue to resort to its tempting "benefits." With the modern advent of the World Wide Web, and the accessibility of the home computer, the act of plagiarism has become an easier crime to commit. Growing up, children are taught that stealing is wrong; plagiarism is indeed just that, wrong—for it is the stealing of another's idea(s). The only way to combat the outbreak of plagiarism is through prevention. Prevention of plagiarism is our best hope in securing the honors of academia in the years to come.

Plagiarism is when someone represents someone else's creative or academic work, whether all of it or part of it, as one's own. There are several forms of plagiarism. It can be an omission, where someone fails to acknowledge or give credit to the creator of words, pictures, or ideas. Or, it can be a case where a person uses someone else's ideas and gives credit, but invents the source.

Study after study has continued to show that plagiarism is a growing epidemic. Students, when surveyed anonymously, overwhelmingly admit without any reservation to having relied on plagiarism to complete their assignments. Many people have studied this growing problem, and some think that as many as 95% of today's students plagiarize with little hesitation.

Plagiarism is a problem because it harms all parties involved—the plagiarizer, fellow classmates, and even the entire student body. The plagiarizer, taking part in academic dishonesty, makes a conscious decision to cheat not only those involved but himself or herself as well. The logic is simple. The workload (assignments, tests, quizzes, projects, etc.) of a course is designed to aid students in learning the basic fundamentals of the course. When cheating is practiced, the student robs himself or herself from the true learning experience, and thus loses the chance of absorbing the knowledge that might have been drawn upon for future reference.

Likewise, fellow classmates are harmed as well (especially in the college setting). When classes are graded on a curve, it is unfair to the diligent students who dedicate time and effort to do their best only to be deprived of the full benefit of the curve, as the cheaters set the curve with their added advantage. As students learn that some are plagiarizing to improve their grades, they lose faith in the integrity of the school and may decide that they have to plagiarize, too, in order to compete. As long as plagiarism is allowed to go on with little, if any, penalty, students will eventually lose their belief that colleges are honorable institutions and that going to one is a privilege.

On the large scale, society is harmed as well. Society is harmed when plagiarizers don't get caught. When plagiarizers are praised for their work, when they get the promotion, or when they get accepted into a professional school based on their supposed merit, they are rewarded for their dishonesty. Society is harmed when incapable, lazy people get by on their cheating ways and, when push comes to shove, are unable to perform their job to the best of their abilities because they cheated themselves from the basic training that schooling was supposed to provide. Plagiarism benefits no one. Yet it is an ever-growing problem in our constantly advancing society, where lust after the newest gadgets and tools will lead them to continue to live dishonestly to get what they want. This is not one of the lessons college graduates should be learning.

Unfortunately, academic dishonesty and plagiarism are not foreign issues in our present-day academia, but so far little has been done to stop it. On the contrary, the act of plagiarism has become a means of survival in the hostile and aggressive realities of higher education. As college admissions and professional school admissions continue to become more and more competitive, students will only be drawn more to the temptations of cheating. Little is done by campus authority figures to combat this. They should discuss the harmful effects of plagiarism and offer alternative choices for students who are struggling and under pressure to succeed. Many times, students plagiarize because their friends all do and they just haven't thought about the seriousness of what they're doing. If this problem was discussed more openly, these students might make different choices. When students are caught plagiarizing, professors are usually lenient. They seem unwilling to confront students who cheat. As long as professors and others in authority remain unconcerned about their students relying on plagiarism to complete their assignments, it will continue to grow and eventually it will destroy the integrity of higher education.

Educators should make a commitment, and join forces with other fellow educators across America in the fight against plagiarism.

Teachers should make it a duty to teach all students what plagiarism is, and to drill the ethical consequences of plagiarism into each and every student before they enter college. The conditioning should start as soon as students enter grade school. In the first grade, little lessons on cheating should be taught, and as students progress from grade school, to middle school, to high school, each year, lessons in cheating, academic dishonesty and plagiarism should be reiterated in more detail and observed under a stricter set of guidelines. The common excuse of "I was never taught that" will instantly be eliminated, as all students will be informed from an early age. The repercussions of plagiarism should be on a no-tolerance basis. If students are assured that when caught, they will be punished to the maximum, this will undoubtedly stimulate a fear and thus draw students away from the lure of dishonesty and cheating. Teachers and professors, alike, must be firm on implementation of the consequences when occurrences do happen; they must carry out the punishment—not just let it go with a warning. Then they will become the role models for students that they should be.

In addition to annual lessons on plagiarism, teachers at the high school level should also spend time teaching students ways to manage time. This will directly aid in the lowering of the overwhelming shock students often experience upon entering college and will hopefully decrease the temptation of resorting to academic dishonesty. At the same time, teachers should teach students to think for themselves—allowing them to explore the possibilities of their imaginations. Assignments and projects should not be so strictly constrained—confined by guideline after guideline. In contrast, assignments should encourage students to think outside of the box; this will enable them to practice creative thinking and, in turn, will reduce dependency on other people's thoughts and ideas as they build confidence in their own ideas. In essence, teachers should teach students to think, not to regurgitate.

Plagiarism is a serious problem that is rapidly growing. Its appeal has drawn in students from all walks of life. The act of plagiarism is no laughing matter. It must be taken seriously. Our actions will eventually catch up with us. Excuses will eventually run out. Educators should not put off lessons in plagiarism, but begin the conditioning as soon as possible—for prevention is our best bet in ending today's academic dishonesty crisis.

A Suggested Structure for an Essay That Responds to Another Writer's Work

The structure of a thesis-centered essay is established by convention. That is, the thesis essay format has an introduction that contains the thesis statement, followed by body paragraphs that support it, and a conclusion that gives closure to the essay.

An Introduction That Contains

> an introductory sentence that introduces the reading selection's title, author, and subject.
>
> a summary of the reading selection that includes an answer to the writing topic.
>
> your THESIS STATEMENT in response to the writing topic.

Body Paragraphs That Include

> a topic sentence that gives the paragraph's central point, one that supports your thesis statement.
>
> concrete evidence, explained so that it supports the central point and the thesis statement.

A Conclusion That Gives

> a reminder of the reading selection's argument and your argument.
>
> a sense of closure for the essay.

Two Alternative Essay Structures

Although it is most common in an argumentative essay to place the thesis early, usually toward the end of the first paragraph, there are alternative structures that can be used in an argument essay. Each of the two essay examples in this section contains a clear thesis statement, but neither thesis can be found at the beginning of the essay. The first essay uses what we call the "hourglass structure," and the second uses what we call the "funnel structure."

The Hourglass Structure

One alternative structure for an essay places the thesis statement somewhere in the middle of the essay. Here is a diagram of this type of essay.

An Introduction That Contains

> an anecdote that is related to the subject of the essay.
>
> a hint about the author's position on the subject.

Body Paragraphs That Include

> topic sentences.
>
> concrete evidence that supports the writer's position.
>
> further examples that support the writer's position.
>
> A THESIS STATEMENT.

More Body Paragraphs That Include

> topic sentences.
>
> concrete evidence that supports the writer's position.
>
> added examples that support the writer's position.

A Conclusion That Gives

> a reminder of the writer's position.
>
> a sense of closure for the essay.

With the hourglass structure, writers ask readers to read a fair portion of the essay before they come to the essay's central point. Writers begin talking about a subject, offering assertions, anecdotes, and observations whose significance is not yet clear. These assertions and observations are meant to create a path to the central point—stated in a thesis statement—followed by more corroborating assertions and observations.

Writers might use this structure when their thesis is controversial and, rather than risk losing readers who disagree right up front, they draw them in by offering material more widely agreed upon and accessible. You will want to notice when a writer uses an alternate essay structure because it will help you to identify the argument and the linking ideas that support it.

Read "The Early Bird Gets the Bad Grade" and locate the thesis statement. Then locate the parts of the hourglass structure as shown in the diagram above for an essay that places its thesis in the center of the essay. Why do you think the writer used the hourglass structure to present her argument?

The Early Bird Gets the Bad Grade

Essay

NANCY KALISH

Nancy Kalish is the coauthor of The Case Against Homework: How Homework Is Hurting Our Children and What We Can Do About It.

It's Monday morning, and you're having trouble waking your teenagers. You're not alone. Indeed, each morning, few of the country's 17 million high school students are awake enough to get much out of their first class, particularly if it starts before 8 a.m. Sure, many of them stayed up too late the night before, but not because they wanted to. Research shows that teenagers' body clocks are set to a schedule that is different from that of younger children or adults. This prevents adolescents from dropping off until around 11 p.m., when they produce the sleep-inducing hormone melatonin, and waking up much before 8 a.m. when their bodies stop producing melatonin. The result is that the first class of the morning is often a waste, with as many as 28 percent of students falling asleep, according to a National Sleep Foundation poll. Some are so sleepy they don't even show up, contributing to failure and dropout rates.

Many of our presidential candidates have been relatively silent on how they plan to save our troubled education system. For those still searching for a policy that might have a positive impact, here's an idea: stop focusing on testing and instead support changing the hours of the school day, starting it later for teenagers and ending it later for all children. Indeed, no one does well when they're sleep-deprived, but insufficient sleep among children has been linked to obesity and to learning issues like attention deficit/hyperactivity disorder. You'd think this would spur educators to take action, and a handful have.

In 2002, high schools in Jessamine County in Kentucky pushed back the first bell to 8:40 a.m., from 7:30 a.m. Attendance immediately went up, as did scores on standardized tests, which have continued to rise each year. Districts in Virginia and Connecticut have achieved similar success. In Minneapolis and Edina, Minnesota, which instituted high school start times of 8:40 a.m. and 8:30 a.m. respectively in 1997, students' grades rose slightly and lateness, behavioral problems, and dropout rates decreased.

Later is also safer. When high schools in Fayette County in Kentucky delayed their start times to 8:30 a.m., the number of teenagers involved in car crashes dropped, even as they rose in the state.

So why hasn't every school board moved back that first bell? Well, it seems that improving teenagers' performance takes a back seat to more pressing concerns: the cost of additional bus service, the difficulty of adjusting after-school activity schedules, and the inconvenience to teachers and parents.

But few of these problems actually come to pass, according to the Center for Applied Research and Educational Improvement at the University of Minnesota. In Kentucky and Minnesota, simply flipping the starting times for the elementary and high schools meant no extra cost for buses. Nor have after-school jobs and activities been affected as anticipated. And though team practices and matches might have to start a bit later, student participation has usually stayed the same. Some districts have even witnessed improved performance from better-rested athletes.

Of course, when school starts later, it has to end later. But instead of viewing this as a liability, we should see it as an opportunity to extend the day even further until 5 p.m. or later, not just for high school students but for those in elementary and middle school as well.

It would help working parents if their children were on the same basic schedule. But there are other reasons to start and end school at a later time. According to Paul Reville, a professor of education policy at Harvard and chairman of the Massachusetts Board of Education, "Trying to cram everything our 21st-century students need into a 19th-century six-and-a-half-hour day just isn't working." He says that children learn more at a less frantic pace, and that lengthening the school day would help "close the achievement gap between disadvantaged students and their better-off peers." Massachusetts has opened more than a dozen "expanded learning time" schools, which add about three hours to the school day. Students spend additional time on subjects like math and English, but also enjoy plentiful art, music, physical education and recess—all of which are being slashed at many schools.

Also, why not make sure there's built-in time for doing homework? That way, children could get their work done at school where professionals can help them, freeing them to spend time with their families when they do get home.

So if candidates want the parent vote, here's a wake-up call. Stand up for an educational policy that allows students' real needs—rather than outdated time constraints—to dictate how and when our children learn best.

The Funnel Structure

Another alternative structure for an argument essay is one that places its thesis somewhere within the conclusion of the essay. Here is a diagram of this type of essay structure.

An Introduction That Contains

> Either:
>
> an anecdote
>
> an example
>
> a summary of the topic
>
> information related to the topic

Body Paragraphs That Include

> topic sentences
>
> other anecdotes that point toward a particular position on the subject.
>
> facts, statistics, or other information that point toward a particular position on the subject.
>
> further examples that point toward a particular position on the subject.
>
> concrete evidence that points toward a particular position on the subject.

A Conclusion That Gives

> a clear statement of the author's THESIS.
>
> a sense of closure for the essay.

With the funnel structure, writers pile up the evidence piece by piece but do not draw the significance of this evidence until the end. Writers might use this structure to draw attention to the reasonableness of their argument to a hostile audience, to lead an uninformed audience to form the writer's desired conclusion on an issue, or simply to prepare readers to accept a surprising conclusion. Read "When Volunteerism Isn't Noble" and locate the thesis statement. Then use the diagram above to see how this essay's parts are organized. Why do you think this writer chose the funnel structure for her argument?

When Volunteerism Isn't Noble

Essay

LYNN STEIRER

Lynn Steirer was a student at a community college when she wrote this essay. It was published on the op-ed page of The New York Times *in 1997.*

Engraved in stone over the front entrance to my old high school is the statement, "No Man Is Free Who Is Not Master of Himself." No surprise for a school named Liberty.

But in 1991, the Bethlehem school board turned its back on the principle for which my school was named when it began requiring students to perform community service or other volunteer work. Students would have to show that they had done 60 hours of such service, or they would not receive their high school diploma.

That forced me to make a decision. Would I submit to the program even though I thought it was involuntary servitude, or would I stand against it on principle? I chose principle, and was denied a diploma.

Bethlehem is not alone in requiring students to do volunteer work to graduate. Other school districts around the country have adopted such policies, and in the state of Maryland, students must do volunteer work to graduate.

Volunteerism is a national preoccupation these days. Starting Sunday, retired General Colin Powell, at President Clinton's request, will lead a three-day gathering in Philadelphia of political and business leaders and many others. General Powell is calling for more people to volunteer. That is a noble thought.

But what President Clinton has in mind goes far beyond volunteering. He has called for high schools across the country to make community service mandatory for graduation—in other words, he wants to *force* young people to do something that should be, by its very definition, voluntary.

That will destroy, not elevate, the American spirit of volunteerism. I saw firsthand how many of my classmates treated their required service as a joke, claiming credit for work they didn't do or exaggerating the time it actually took.

Volunteering has always been important to me. As a Meals on Wheels aide and a Girl Scout, I chose to give hundreds of hours to my community, at my own initiative. While my family and I fought the school's mandatory service requirement, I continued my volunteering, but I would not submit my hours for credit. Two of my classmates joined me in this act of civil disobedience. At the same time, with the assistance of the Institute for Justice, a Washington legal-policy group, we sued the school board.

As graduation neared, a school official pulled me aside and said it was not too late to change my mind. That day, I really thought about giving in. Then he asked the question that settled it for me. "After all," he said, "what is more important, your values or your diploma?" I chose to give up my diploma, eventually obtaining a graduate equivalency degree instead. The courts decided against us and, unfortunately, the Supreme Court declined to hear our case. The school has continued the program.

Volunteering is important. But in a country that values its liberty, we should make sure that student "service" is truly voluntary.

An Introduction in an Argument Essay

Use the guidelines below to help you shape an introduction appropriate for your paper. Be sure to look back at the introduction once your draft is completed because you may want to revise it after you have worked through your ideas more systematically and are more likely to understand your argument better than when you began to draft. For this reason, many writers draft their introduction after they have written their body paragraphs.

The introduction is often the most difficult part of an essay to draft. A paper's opening creates a first impression for readers, and deciding how to begin can be difficult. The introduction should do three things: capture readers' attention, set the stage for the paper's argument, and present the thesis statement. Length is also an important consideration: an introductory paragraph should be only as long as necessary to provide a context for the argument that the paper will develop. Too much detail or background information will bog down your introduction and leave readers feeling confused or rushed along. Save the details for the paper's body.

Customarily, the last sentence of the introduction is the **thesis statement**. A strong thesis statement is essential to developing, organizing, and writing a successful persuasive paper. An essay isn't successful simply because its grammar is correct, or because it has an introduction, a set of body paragraphs, and a conclusion. These components must have a thesis statement to tie them together and give them significance. The thesis statement is an important part of the introduction because it unifies the essay and gives it its purpose. Including it at the end of the introduction ensures that readers clearly understand the paper's purpose at the outset.

The essays you will do in *Write It* follow the same format, and the introduction for each essay assignment will be effective if you follow these steps:

Introduce the reading selection by giving the author's first and last name and the selection's title.

Give a directed summary of the reading selection(see next page).

Present your thesis statement (be sure it answers the writing topic question).

Hints

- **Don't offer a flat explanation of what you will cover in the paper:**
  "This essay will discuss…," for example.
- **Avoid clichés:**
  "It is certainly true that love is blind."
- **Avoid meaningless platitudes:**
  "People often find it difficult to get along with others in this world."
- **Do not resort to overly broad statements:**
  "Since the beginning of time humans have tried to live peacefully."

Guidelines for Writing a Directed Summary

Writing a successful summary of a reading selection can be challenging because it requires a thorough understanding of the reading's argument and supporting material. Before attempting to summarize a reading, be sure to spend time analyzing it using the "Steps for a Thoughtful Reading of an Essay."

The summary guidelines we give are based on a specific type of writing assignment. In other words, *Write It* works solely with a particular type of writing assignment—one that asks you to read another writer's essay and respond to that essay's argument in an essay of your own. With this kind of writing assignment, you will be required to write a focused summary of a particular aspect of the assigned reading selection. That focus will be determined by the writing topic question that follows the reading selection. The summary you write will be limited in scope to the aspect set forward in the writing topic question. The directed summary will also set the context and terms of the argument you will have to address in your response.

A directed summary is a summary that requires a specific answer. The goal is not necessarily to summarize an entire essay but to summarize those parts of the essay relevant to the writing topic question. To write a directed summary that is complete and correct, follow the steps below:

Preparation

Step 1: Carefully read through the reading selection and the writing topic questions that follow it.

Step 2: Underline the key terms in the first question.

Step 3: Locate in the essay the specific sentences that provide information relevant to answering the first question.

Step 4: Decide on the answer to that question. Be sure to provide a thorough response.

Writing

Step 1: In or near the opening sentence, include the title of the essay (in quotation marks) and the full name of the author (after the first mention, the author should be referred to by last name only).

Step 2: Use direct quotation, when appropriate, to emphasize the answer the author provides to the question.

Step 3: In your own words, fully answer the first question in the writing topic.

Step 4: Explain this answer using support found in the essay.

Hints

- Do not include minor details or points.
- Do not insert your own opinions or ideas and attribute them to the author.
- Do not ordinarily include examples.

Strategies for Developing Your Ideas

Students often say that they know *how* to write an essay—that is, they know it should have an introduction, thesis statement, supporting body paragraphs, and a conclusion—but they don't have anything to write *about*. They don't know what to say and they can't think of any experiences they have had that they can use. Consider using the techniques below for exploring your thoughts and finding strategies that work whenever you are faced with a challenging writing assignment.

Time is the crucial element here. It takes time to think carefully and systematically about a subject. You will have to focus your thoughts and have patience in order for your mind to work, to develop insights that go beyond surface impressions and quick, easy judgments. You should do much of your thinking in writing—this aspect is very important. Writing your thoughts down will give them definition and clarity.

If you find yourself without good ideas about a subject, try these strategies. You might not use all of them for any given assignment. Instead, look them over and choose those that seem most promising for the particular piece of writing you are developing:

1. *Focus*: Write down the subject of the reading selection that you want to explore; a simple word or phrase may be enough.

2. *Response*: Look over the selection again (and the reading and summary questions you have answered) and list its ideas. Write down

   a. any questions and/or doubts you have about these ideas, and a list of your reasons;

   b. any points the writer makes that you find persuasive, and the reasons you find them convincing;

   c. your thoughtful impression of the reading selection;

   d. a final conclusion about the selection's argument, its weaknesses, its strengths.

Hint

Your responses here do not have to be polished. Allow yourself to write freely, putting down all ideas that come to you. You will sort them out later.

---

3. *Reflection*: Now you need some data, some basic observations from your own experience that you can examine and use to draw conclusions or insights. First write down, in a rough list, any personal memories you have that seem to relate to the subject you are writing on. Do a few minutes of freewriting to explore these memories. Try some *focused freewriting*, where you keep the essay's general subject in mind but write down everything that you can, even things you roughly associate with the subject. Stay with it until you feel you have something substantial, something your readers will find thoughtful and compelling.

   If you need more structure, try using these general guidelines for each incident:
   a. Begin by simply recounting what you remember: make it as brief as possible but don't omit anything that seems important.

b. Now expand your thinking: try to speculate about the importance of the memory and its relevance to the subject you are exploring.

c. Look over what you have written: underline the ideas that seem to you to be important. Think about the way they relate to the reading selection's ideas. How are your ideas like the selection's? How are they different?

d. Take note: consider any judgment words in your freewriting, such as "sometimes," "always," "seems to," "might mean," "only when," "but if."

These will help you formulate the position you want to take in your thesis statement.

4. ***Expansion***: Keep the subject in mind and write down any relevant experiences you can think of from the world at large. Do you know of any examples from books, the news, movies, and your cultural awareness in general? Freewrite for each example that comes to mind.

5. ***Reconsideration***

a. First, begin by simply recounting the event or text, summarizing its main elements as briefly as you can without omitting important elements.

b. Now, move beyond the basic facts and try to explore the implications of each for the subject. What thoughts come to mind as you reflect on the event or text? What do those thoughts suggest about the subject? Take your freewriting as far as you can for each event or text you listed.

c. Then, look over all that you have written. Underline the ideas that seem to you to be important. Try to explain in writing how they relate to the reading selection's ideas. How are they like the reading selection's? How are they different?

d. Finally, look for the judgment words. These will help you formulate the position you want to take in your thesis statement. What seems to be your strongest feeling about the subject, the one most dominant in your freewriting?

6. ***Shape***: Consider what you have underlined and the judgment words you found. What significance do they have once you consider them all together? What do they "add up to"?

a. Group parts of your freewriting together. Find some main ideas that you came back to two or three times using different experiences, examples, or texts. Try to identify all of the main ideas you find, and write out the connection between them and the underlined portions of your freewriting.

b. Explore the parts you underlined and the implications you noted by asking yourself the following questions:

- Which parts seem important, and why?

- How do the lists you made fit together, or what do they add up to?

- Do any parts of your freewriting contradict other parts, or do parts have similar ideas?

- What do either the contradictions, or the similarities, suggest?

c. Identify the ideas that you feel strongly about. Write about the reasons why they are important and the way they relate to the subject you are exploring.

Hint

Sometimes it is too restrictive to think in terms of "for or against" the reading selection's subject. There are often more than two positions on a topic, and disagreeing with the position taken in the reading selection may mean that, while the selection's ideas may be sound, the conclusions drawn are not as convincing, in your mind, as the conclusions you want to draw.

Hint

Your goal is to uncover what you know and develop it so that you can show your readers how you arrived at your main ideas and how your ideas led to your thesis statement.

Once you've done some freewriting and located important topics and supporting details, you have the foundation pieces to create an outline.

Writing a Supporting Paragraph for Your Thesis Statement

The body paragraphs make up the largest part of an essay, and each paragraph should develop one important point in support of the thesis statement. Paragraphs should be unified around a central point and should contain concrete evidence that clarifies and supports that central point. Readers need concrete evidence as examples that help them to understand your ideas. Therefore, body paragraphs usually open with a topic sentence, and include evidence, a discussion of the evidence, and an explanation of how the paragraph's subject matter connects to your thesis claim.

Writing a well-developed paragraph can be easy once you understand the paragraph's conventional structure. Here is a useful mnemonic device that will help you construct well-developed body paragraphs:

Remember the 4Cs:
Controlling idea sentence
Corroborating details
Careful description of the details' relevance
Connection to the thesis statement

Once you determine your thesis statement, you can develop your supporting paragraphs using the following guidelines:

Controlling idea sentence

First, write a topic sentence that announces the point you want to make in the paragraph.

Corroborating details

Then, think of specific examples that will help you explain and prove the point.

Careful description of the details' relevance

Now, carefully explain how each example proves the point you are making in the paragraph.

Connection to the thesis statement

Be sure to connect your examples and explanation to the position you have taken in your thesis statement. Tell your reader what the paragraph's point and examples have to do with your argument.

Here's an example: Thesis: The violence on television desensitizes viewers to violence and can ultimately lead to a thoughtless and uncaring society.

Controlling idea sentence for a paragraph supporting the thesis statement
Write a sentence stating the point you want to make in the paragraph:
After seeing casual violence repeatedly on television, viewers come to see real-life violence in terms of entertainment rather than real human tragedy.

Corroborating details
Think of some examples that will show that people see violence in terms of entertainment rather than real tragedy:

- the pause in traffic flow whenever there is an accident on the freeway because people want to look
- news reporting today spends time primarily reporting on acts of violence in society, etc.

Careful description of the details' relevance
Explain how these examples show that people see violence in terms of entertainment rather than real-life tragedy.

Connection to the thesis statement
Explain how we can understand this view of violence as an indication of society's growing lack of thought and care (paragraph's controlling idea), and how this is a direct result of television violence (tie to thesis statement).

Here is a sample body paragraph from a student paper on George Orwell's *Down and Out in Paris and London*. See if you can follow the 4Cs paragraph development.

The paper's thesis statement: In *Down and Out in Paris and London*, George Orwell shows the poor not as criminals but as people with no options.

(*Controlling Idea/Topic Sentence*) Orwell's novel shows that poverty ultimately degrades character because the poor cannot afford ethics. (*Corroborating details*) As a *plongeur* at Hotel X, Orwell is forced to exist in an environment where almost anything goes, and he has to adapt in order to be accepted and keep his job. He recounts how, even to be hired for work, he must lie about his intentions. He is told by his friend Boris that "a *plongeur* can[not] afford a sense of honour," and so the narrator hides the fact that he intends to "break his contract" with the hotel by walking away as soon as his job at the Auberge is available. He says that later he realizes how "foolish it had been to have any scruples" because the hotels do not act honorably toward their employees, and the system seems to be "every man for himself." Orwell also tells of thieves among the staff, and of how the doorkeeper regularly robs him of his wages. (*Careful Description of the Details' Relevance*) The social order of the workers at the Hotel X operates openly by dishonesty and drunkenness, and Orwell cannot avoid joining this order if he wants to earn money to live. (*Connection to the Thesis Statement*) Given a choice between honor and the necessities of life, the poor in the novel often seem to have little choice but to do whatever is necessary to earn their keep. Dignity and honor are luxuries that they cannot always afford.

Transitions

Connect or Correct

Essays need transitions to link the ideas in individual sentences to each other and to tie paragraphs together. Transitions are the words or phrases that help relate thoughts and ideas to each other. Without transitions, sentences are merely lists, and paragraphs can seem disconnected from each other.

Transitions link concepts in one of two ways: they can signal that individual sentences or paragraphs extend a train of thought (***connect***), or they can predict for the reader that whatever follows will change the direction of thought (***correct***). Careful use of transitions improves the overall coherence of your essay.

There are a number of categories of transitional words that ***connect*** sentences and paragraphs. Here are some of the kinds of transitions and some examples of words and phrases that ***connect***:

1. *time*—afterward, later, meanwhile, next, now, suddenly, then
2. *continuation*—also, finally, furthermore, in addition, secondly
3. *reasons*—for this reason, in order to, to that end
4. *examples*—for example, for instance, to illustrate, to show that
5. *assertion*—in fact, indeed, to tell the truth
6. *repetition*—as already noted, in other words
7. *similarly*—in the same way, likewise
8. *space*—here, near, opposite

Here are some kinds of transitions and some examples of words and phrases that ***correct***:

1. *alternative*—besides, not, or
2. *contrast*—however, in contrast, on the other hand, to the contrary

Smooth transitions between sentences and paragraphs can be achieved in other ways besides the use of particular transitional words and phrases. Some other ways to link ideas and thoughts are as follows:

1. *repetition*—repeating a word or phrase from the previous sentence or paragraph in the new construction
2. *parallelism*—using a similar structure in consecutive sentences or paragraphs. In other words, begin paragraphs with very similar sentences or sentences noticeably similar in structure. Within a paragraph, repetition of sentence structure can be used for emphasis and to draw attention to connected ideas.

Conclusions

Any essay that includes discussion of more than one point, idea, or example requires a conclusion. Without a conclusion, the reader has no sense of closure, no certainty that you have come to the end of your argument. It is important that you let the reader know that your essay is complete, not because you have run out of things to say or time to say them, but because you have fully explored and supported your thesis. The conclusion of the essay is also the place for you to impress upon the reader the importance of considering your ideas.

The conclusion's primary purpose is to provide closure for your essay, but there are several effective ways to accomplish that goal. Consider the strategies below so as to be able to call on the most appropriate one for every essay you write.

A good conclusion accomplishes two tasks:

1. It makes the reader aware of the finality of your argument.
2. It leaves the reader with an understanding of the significance of your argument.

Hint

Check to see that the conclusion of your essay fulfills the promise suggested by your introduction.

Writing the conclusion of your essay will offer you many choices and many challenges. You may choose a simple, formal ending, or you may choose to be somewhat creative and less conventional. Familiarize yourself with the possibilities below, and then decide which works best for your particular essay:

TYPES OF CONCLUSIONS

Brief Summary	"In conclusion …"
	"To summarize briefly …"
Significance of Subject	"All these matters need to be understood because …"
Most Important Point	"Lastly, remember that …"
Request for Action or Opinion	"X must be changed …"
Useful Quotation	"In the words of …"
Emotional Statement	an outcry, appeal, or plea such as "Let's all move to…" or "Please…"
Interesting Anecdote	a short relevant story
Directive	"In the future" or "From now on"

Logical Fallacies

A writer's job is to provide as much evidence and support for his or her thesis as possible. It is important, however, that the arguments a writer offers to defend that thesis are sound. If some of the arguments the writer presents are illogical or unfair, the writer will undermine his or her own position and lose credibility with readers.

Arguments that lack reason or justice are called *fallacies*. Fallacies are simply false arguments. Often, a writer's enthusiasm for his or her own position will lead the writer to make assertions that cannot be proven by the evidence at hand or cause the writer to make claims that are false. The best way to guard against spurious arguments is to become familiar with some of the most common types of fallacies and learn to recognize them in your own writing and the writing of others.

Fallacies fall into two categories. The first category contains unethical arguments. These arguments attempt to manipulate the reader emotionally or attack the opposing position in some way that is unjust. Here are some examples of fallacies that are manipulative or unfair:

1. *Ad hominem*—using a personal attack on the person rather than the argument itself

    example: The members of the Glee Club are a bunch of prima donnas, so, of course, they would oppose spending money to chart a bus instead of using cars to go to Disneyland for Senior Ditch Day.

2. *Birds of a feather*—using guilt by association to blame the person for actions of friends or family

    example: John Smith's sister has a drug problem, so even though he is a qualified nurse, he shouldn't be trusted in a job that requires him to administer prescribed narcotics to dying patients.

3. *Sob story*—using a sad situation or dramatic case to manipulate the readers' emotions

    example: José Cortez was the only member of his family to survive a horrific plane crash, so he is the best candidate for mayor of our town.

The majority of fallacies are illogical because the thinking behind their arguments is flawed; the conclusions offered by these fallacies follow neither inductive nor deductive reasoning. Here are some examples of false reasoning:

1. *Circular reasoning*—restating the same argument in other words instead of giving evidence or proof

   example: The President has thought a lot about health care, so his plan is the most well-thought-out plan available.

2. *Post hoc, ergo propter hoc* (Latin for "after this, therefore because of this")—assuming because one event follows another, the first is caused by the second

   example: Saturday night, Eun Hee went to the movies with her girlfriends, and on Sunday, her boyfriend Jun Ho broke up with her. Jun Ho ended his relationship with Eun Hee because she went out with her friends.

3. *False dichotomy*—assuming an either/or choice so that the writer's position seems the only correct one

   example: Either we eradicate the pit bull breed altogether or children playing outside will not be safe from dog attacks.

4. *Hasty generalization*—basing a conclusion on limited evidence

   example: My dog leaves the carrots in his bowl when I give him my leftover beef stew. Therefore, dogs do not eat vegetables.

5. *False authority*—citing a source that has no validity in terms of the subject

   example: Li'l' Hound, a popular rapper, took his mother to Mexico for expensive cancer drug treatments unapproved by the FDA, so the medicine must really work.

Proofreading Your Essay for Mistakes in Grammar and Mechanics

Students often feel that their work is completed once they have revised their rough draft by honing the content and arguments it contains, but they should still do a sentence-level examination to eliminate any errors in their sentences. Frequently, errors in the rough draft are overlooked during the revision process because writers are focused on idea development and structure. Any writer should review one last time for grammatical, mechanical, and spelling errors. While word processing programs can be helpful in finding some mistakes, computers are limited in this area. It is, therefore, the writer's responsibility to proofread and edit before printing out a final draft.

Examine the following ten errors commonly made by writers. Becoming familiar with these errors will help you to avoid them.

1. Underline the verbs and then
   - check to see that they agree with their subjects. (For help, consult a handbook.)
   - make sure you have used the correct verb tense. (For help, consult a handbook.)
   - when possible, change "to be" verbs (is, are, was, etc.) to action words.

     Flat: Gloria Watkins is a good writer.

     Active: Gloria Watkins writes brilliantly.

2. Mark sentences that contain informal language or slang. Rewrite them using more formal language.

   No: Kids' fairy tales are, like, really great to hear when you're a kid.

   Yes: We all enjoyed listening to fairy tales when we were young.

3. Circle all the pronouns in your draft and then
   - check to be sure that the noun they refer to is clear; if it isn't, change the pronoun to a noun.
   - be sure that the pronouns agree with their referent.

     No: Even though a person may witness an accident, they will not be able to remember exactly what happened.

     Yes: Even though a person may witness an accident, he or she will not be able to remember exactly what happened.

4. Identify sentences close to one another in the paper that use the same word two or more times (ignoring common words such as "the" or "to"). Eliminate the repetition by
   - looking for synonyms to replace repeated words.
   - seeing if you can combine two sentences into one and eliminate repetition that way.

5. To vary the pace of your sentences, try changing the construction of three or four of your sentences. For example, you can reorder the word(s) or turn sentences into clauses.

   Every culture has its own celebrations and rituals to mark special days.

   Celebrations and rituals mark special days in every culture.

   A writer might revise a paper several times before he or she submits it for a class.

   Before submitting a paper for a class, a writer might revise it several times.

6. Be sure there are no commas joining two complete sentences. For each comma splice, use one of the following methods to correct the error:

   Comma splice error: Barbara decided to run for public office, however, she knew the odds were against her winning.

   • Change the comma to a semicolon.

     Barbara decided to run for public office; however, she knew the odds were against her winning.

   • Change the comma to a period and a capital letter.

     Barbara decided to run for public office. However, she knew the odds were against her winning.

   • Link the sentences with a coordinating conjunction (for, and, nor, but, or, yet, so)

     Barbara decided to run for public office, but she knew the odds were against her winning.

   • Turn the second sentence into a dependent clause or phrase.

     Although she knew the odds were against her winning, Barbara decided to run for public office.

7. Rewrite any sentence where "you" is used; eliminate "you" by replacing it with "I," "we," or another noun or pronoun.

   No: You can always identify a person that is wearing a uniform.

   Yes: We can always identify a person that is wearing a uniform.

   Yes: Everyone can identify a person that is wearing a uniform.

8. Use a dictionary to look up words you are unsure of and make sure you've used them correctly.

9. Use spell check to eliminate misspelled words.

10. Be sure all sentences begin with a capital letter and have the appropriate punctuation mark at the end.

Scoring Rubric

High Pass (A, A–, B+)

This score indicates superior writing skills. An essay receiving a high pass has a sophisticated style marked by variety in sentence structure, effective word usage, and mastery of the conventions of written English. The content of the essay responds directly to the writing topic with a persuasive argument and reasoned examples that address and explore the issue in a focused, organized, and thoroughly developed manner.

Pass (B, B–)

This score indicates strong writing skills. A passing essay characteristically shows some variety of usage in syntax and vocabulary and demonstrates competency in the areas of grammar and mechanics. It presents a response to the writing topic that is thoughtful and appropriate. Its argument is well developed using relevant examples and clear reasoning.

Low Pass (C+, C)

This score indicates satisfactory writing skills, which may be marginal in some areas. It often has some sentence level errors, but these errors do not interfere with comprehension, and, for the most part, there is control of grammar and mechanics. The content provides an appropriate but partial or somewhat abbreviated answer to the writing topic. There is an attempt to focus and organize, but ideas and examples may not be logically sequenced or may be so brief as to lack clarity.

High Fail (C–)

This score indicates a problem in one or more of the following areas. Sentences may lack variety, may use vocabulary in an imprecise manner, or may contain an unacceptable number of grammar and mechanical errors. The content of the essay might not adequately respond to the writing topic due to some misreading of the topic, or it may fail to develop its ideas with logic and/or examples. The essay may lack focus because it offers no thesis or central idea, it digresses, or it provides no discernible pattern of organization.

Fail (D+, D)

This score indicates clearly inadequate writing skills. Sentences tend to be simplistic and structurally repetitive. Errors in grammar, mechanics, and word choice are numerous. The essay's content reveals a misunderstanding of the writing topic itself. There are not sufficient examples or any other details or ideas relevant to the topic. Paragraphs are disconnected and the point, or thesis, of the essay is not clear.

Low Fail (D–, F)

This score indicates a complete lack of familiarity with the conventions of written English. There is no control of grammar, mechanics, or vocabulary, and the sentences produced may be unintelligible. The content of the essay fails to respond to the writing topic in any logical manner, and it ordinarily fixates on a single idea or detail. There is no organizational pattern, and what development there is comes from repetition of a digression stemming from the single idea or detail.

A Method for Writing a Timed Essay

When writing an essay under time constraint, you need a clear and thoughtful strategy. Look over the following suggestions and then write a plan of your own that takes into consideration your particular strengths and weaknesses.

1. **Read the question**. Circle the interrogatives (question words: who, what, where, when, why, and how) in the first part of the writing topic.

2. **Read the essay** and underline the information that specifically answers the question(s). Make margin notes.

3. **Write your summary** in a manner that responds directly to the question(s) asked.

4. **Reread the writing topic**. Determine which point of the author's argument you are being asked to agree/disagree with. Think about what you believe and why you believe the way you do. Write your thesis to express that position clearly.

5. **Write a series of paragraphs** that offer developed reasons and concrete examples that support your thesis. In each paragraph, be sure to show the connection between your reasons, your examples, and your thesis.

6. **Write a conclusion**. It should provide a sense of closure for your essay. It can be a restatement of your thesis or a recalling of certain important information in your summary. It must, however, leave no doubt as to your own position on the topic.

7. **Proofread your complete essay.** Then double-check grammar and spelling by reading from the end of your essay to the beginning. Read your essay again to check that your ideas are fully developed and logically connected.

Budgeting Your Time

Here is one person's time plan for a timed final essay exam. You should arrange your own time plan in a way that works best for your particular skills and the time you have.

Step 1: Reading the question—5 minutes

Step 2: Reading/marking the essay—20 minutes

Step 3: Writing the summary—15 minutes

Step 4: Writing the thesis—10 minutes

Step 5: Supporting the thesis—60 minutes

Step 6: Writing the conclusion—10 minutes

Step 7: Proofreading the essay—45 minutes

Using Your Handbook

Your handbook is a valuable tool and resource. Many students own a handbook but fail to use it. Others, however, keep their handbook next to them when they are writing and consult it when they have questions or when they need some prewriting activities to help develop their ideas. Here is an exercise to help familiarize you with some of the resources available in a handbook.

Writing is like a journey; it has a beginning and an end. To reach your final destination, it is best to have a map. Even with a good map, wrong turns and detours are to be expected, but without a map, the trip can be prolonged and frustrating. A handbook provides a useful map for any kind of writing.

Handbooks help at every stage of the writing process. There are sections that show you how to get started by defining your purpose and your audience. Your handbook has chapters that can aid you as you make a plan for your writing and chapters that can lead you through the drafting process. When your rough draft is completed, your handbook will give you ideas and techniques for improving and revising the work you have done. Most importantly, a handbook contains all the information and explanations of the conventions of written English. You will want to consult your handbook extensively as you correct and edit your final draft.

You need to familiarize yourself with two important features of your handbook: the **table of contents** and the **index.** Learning how to use them and training yourself to consult them will save you time and improve your writing.

The Table of Contents

The table of contents appears at the beginning of your handbook. It gives the title (topic) of each chapter and lists the subtopics covered in each of the chapters. A page number follows each listing for easy access to the information.

<u>Example:</u> Your instructor has given a general assignment for your paper. You are to write a research paper on the novel *Beloved*, by Toni Morrison, but you are expected to come up with your own topic. You have no idea where to begin. Checking the table of contents reveals the following listing under Chapter 2, "Planning and Shaping":

"How can I think through a writing topic?" 25
Turning to page 25, you find a discussion and concrete suggestions that lead you through the following steps:
"Selecting a Topic"
"Broadening/Narrowing a Topic"

But you don't yet have a topic. You continue reading, however, and find sections that tell you exactly what to do to help yourself come up with ideas for your paper:

freewriting
brainstorming

mapping
questioning

You try them all, but the final technique, using the question words, produces the following:

Who? Sethe
What? escaped
When? pre-Civil War
Where? Sweet Home Plantation to a free state
Why? slavery
How? Underground Railroad

The final question, "How?" produces a relevant and researchable topic, *the Underground Railroad*. You can research that topic. Once you have gathered information, you are able to return to the section in the handbook on narrowing your topic and begin to refine your topic. Then you can formulate a thesis.

Index

The index appears at the very end of your handbook. It contains an alphabetical listing of every topic, concept, and problem addressed within the handbook's pages. A page number or a sequence of page numbers follows each listing. These numbers indicate pages where information on a particular listing can be found.

Example: You are writing about your family and you want to discuss the origins of the family name. You have written the following sentence:

My family, the Taylors, got their name from an ancestor's occupation.

You are unsure about your pronoun choice. Should it be "their" or "its"? You know that "family" is a collective (group) noun. You look up collective nouns and find the following listing:

"Collective nouns"
    "pronoun agreement with"
    "verb agreement with"

You might first want to refresh your memory about collective nouns in general, but, if you feel confident about their definition, you could go directly to the index listing for pronoun agreement. There you will discover that collective nouns like "family" can take both the singular and plural pronoun, depending on the contents and meanings of the sentence. If the group (collective noun) functions as a whole, or one, the singular pronoun is correct. If the members of the group act individually, the plural pronoun is needed. In your sentence, the family is acting as a unit. Which pronoun would be correct?

Diagnostic Test 1

In exercises 1–10, circle the correct word in each set of parentheses.

Regular/Irregular Verbs

1. Clive Staples Lewis is best known as C. S. Lewis, the man who (brang/brung/brought) us the Narnia books.
2. His legal name was Clive, but his friends and family (knew/knowed/known) him as Jack.
3. Millions of children and adults love the Narnia books and are familiar with their illustrations (drew/drawed/drawn) by Pauline Baynes.
4. Lewis, who had already (wrote/writed/written) a science fiction trilogy, (begun/began/begin) the first Narnia volume in the 1940s.
5. *The Lion, the Witch and the Wardrobe* first (come/came) out in 1950.

Subject–Verb Agreement

6. *The Lion, the Witch and the Wardrobe* (begin/begins) in 1940, when the four Pevensie children go to stay with an elderly and eccentric professor.
7. The group of children (have/has) been sent to the country because of Nazi air raids on London.
8. One of the children (hide/hides) in an old wardrobe during a game of hide and seek; pushing her way to the back, Lucy finds herself next to a lamppost in the middle of a forest.
9. She meets a faun named Mr. Tumnus. He and she (sips/sip) tea in his comfortable cave.
10. Neither she nor the faun (seem/seems) surprised that they both speak the same language.

For exercises 11–17, write a C next to any passage that is clear and correct. Write an X next to any incorrect passage, and underline any pronouns with disagreement or reference problems.

Pronoun Reference/Agreement

11. Lucy is intrigued by the faun and enjoys their stories, but then, Mr. Tumnus begins to cry.
12. Mr. Tumnus admits that he is employed by an evil queen, the White Witch. She keeps Narnia in perpetual winter and has told him to capture any humans he finds, but he is kind-hearted and allows her to go back through the wardrobe to England.
13. Peter, Susan, and Edmund do not believe that Narnia exists, and he begins to tease Lucy.

14. Lucy has no evidence because, instead of opening up onto a forest, the wardrobe has become an ordinary piece of furniture with a solid back panel; this is how Lucy originally got into Narnia.
15. Next, Edmund hides in the wardrobe, meets the White Witch, and eats her enchanted food. As a result, he falls under her spell.
16. After Edmund returns, he refuses to admit that Lucy was right. If anyone has read this far, you will realize that Edmund is a sulky and spiteful boy.
17. Sometimes, children in a large family will adopt negative behaviors so he or she will receive more attention.

In 18–21, write a C next to any correct passage. Write an X next to any incorrect passage, and underline any dangling or misplaced modifiers.

Dangling/Misplaced Modifiers

18. Peter and Susan, the two oldest children, approach the professor with worries that Lucy is mentally unstable. But the professor says that Lucy might be telling the truth.
19. A historical landmark, the professor allows sightseers to tour his house.
20. Trying to avoid a group of tourists, the wardrobe once again becomes a passageway to Narnia.
21. Excited to be in Narnia together, the four children decide to visit Mr. Tumnus.

In 22–40, write a C next to any correct passage and an X next to any incorrect passage.

Run-On Sentences

22. A terrible surprise awaits them Mr. Tumnus has been arrested by the White Witch.
23. Lucy is sad because she knows that Mr. Tumnus was arrested for not betraying her.
24. The children decide to help Mr. Tumnus if they can. Soon a friendly beaver approaches them.
25. Mr. Beaver introduces the children to Mrs. Beaver they all have a fine meal and begin to plan.
26. Mr. Beaver tells the children that the White Witch may have turned Mr. Tumnus into a statue the beaver also informs them that they cannot save the faun by themselves.

Comma Splices

27. The children learn about Aslan, a great lion who is the King of Narnia.

28. Mr. Beaver says the children must have help, they must meet Aslan at the Stone Table.
29. Mr. Beaver recites an old rhyme, according to the prophesy, humans, also known as Sons of Adam and Daughters of Eve, will sit on the throne at Cair Paravel and overcome the evil in Narnia.
30. The White Witch knows that the four children can put an end to her wicked reign, so she wants to make sure that the prophecy is never fulfilled.
31. Edmund quietly leaves, Mr. Beaver knows that the boy has gone to the White Witch.

Fragments

32. Because Edmund has eaten enchanted food provided by the White Witch, he plans to betray his family to her.
33. Which frightens everyone.
34. Assembling food for the journey and making up a pack for each of them by Mrs. Beaver.
35. When the children and beavers are partway through the journey and are given presents by Father Christmas, whom Americans know as Santa Claus.

Parallelism

36. Father Christmas gives Lucy a dagger and a vial of healing potion, Peter a sword and shield, and Susan receives a bow and arrows, as well as an ivory horn.
37. In true English fashion, Father Christmas also provides a pot of tea, a bowl of sugar, and some cream.
38. Meanwhile, Edmund is having a terrible time. The Queen has interrogated him, he is put into a cell, and gets only bread and water.
39. Edmund is not only hungry but also fears the White Witch.
40. She takes Edmund on a long sleigh journey, and he wishes he were warm, well-fed, and having a bad dream.

In 41–55, circle the correct word in each set of parentheses.

Adjectives/Adverbs

41. Spring is finally coming to Narnia, so the sleigh must be abandoned. This necessity makes the White Witch very (angry/angrily).

42. The other three children and the beavers arrive at the Stone Table, where the (patient/patiently) Aslan waits.
43. The White Witch prepares to kill Edmund. Clearly, she does not feel (badly/bad) for him.
44. She thinks that she can thwart the prophecy if she kills a Son of Adam, but she does not realize that Aslan has a (more deeply/deeper) knowledge of magic.
45. Aslan (willing/willingly) offers his own life instead. The White Witch agrees to his bargain.

Apostrophes

46. That night, Lucy and Susan cannot sleep. They probably (should'nt/shouldn't) leave their tent and wander around, but they do anyway.
47. Aslan (let's/lets/lets') the girls walk with him before he surrenders to the White Witch.
48. After she kills Aslan, the Witch thinks that victory is (hers/hers'/her's).
49. But (Aslans' / Aslan's) magic is stronger than the (Witch'es/Witch's/Witches'), so he comes back to life.
50. While the White Witch is in the field, preparing for battle, Aslan heads to her castle. His breath turns the statues into flesh again. He also breathes on Mr. (Tumnus/Tumnus's/Tumnuses') statue.

Capital Letters

51. Before rejoining Peter and Edmund in their battle against the White Witch, Aslan liberates many creatures that do not exist in the (english/English) countryside.
52. Speaking of Edmund, Peter says, ("We'd/"we'd) have been beaten if it hadn't been for him."
53. Using her potion on Edmund, Lucy heals his wounds, but Aslan reminds her that others are waiting. "Yes, I know," (replies/Replies) Lucy, and she moves on to someone else.
54. Now that the White Witch is defeated, the children live long and eventful lives as kings and queens in Narnia. As adults, they encounter a familiar lamppost in the woods. In a later book, this location is a well-known geographical landmark called (Lantern Waste/lantern waste).
55. The four siblings keep walking and emerge from the wardrobe into the house of their old friend, the eccentric professor. No time has passed, and they are children again. Here the story ends. But fortunately, there are six more books in the (series/Series).

Sentence Skills Assessment for Diagnostic Test 1

Problem	Needs Review	Needs Study	Completed
Regular/ Irregular Verbs			
Subject-Verb Agreement			
Pronoun Agreement			
Pronoun Reference			
Dangling/ Misplaced Modifiers			
Run-On Sentences			
Comma Splices			
Fragments			
Parallelism			
Adjectives/ Adverbs			
Capital Letters			
Apostrophes			

Diagnostic Test 2

Write X in the answer space if you think a mistake appears in the sentence. Write C in the answer space if you think the sentence is correct.

Fragments

_____ 1. *The Lord of the Rings*, a work by J. R. R. Tolkien that is made up of three parts: *The Fellowship of the Ring*, *The Two Towers*, and *The Return of the King*.

_____ 2. In the first part of the trilogy, *The Fellowship of the Ring*, a young hobbit, Frodo Baggins, inherits from his uncle Bilbo a ring of great importance.

_____ 3. The ring, an instrument of absolute power, was lost by the evil Sauron.

_____ 4. When Gandalf, a wizard, warns Frodo that he should leave the Shire and keep the ring out of Sauron's hands.

_____ 5. While Frodo and his fellow travelers must carry the ring across Middle-earth to the Cracks of Doom, in the kingdom of Mordor, where they can destroy it forever.

Run-On Sentences and Comma Splices

_____ 6. They must cross Sauron's kingdom, where Sauron, the dark Lord of Mordor, is amassing an army of orcs he hopes to take the ring and control the world.

_____ 7. The ring's ability to endow its possessor with absolute power exerts a corrupting influence on those who come in contact with it.

_____ 8. Frodo takes the responsibility of carrying the ring to Mordor, he must have the strength and ability to resist the constant temptation of its power.

_____ 9. In addition to his strength of character, Frodo relies on the help of three hobbit friends, Sam, Pippin, and Meriadoc, who join him on his journey, and their loyalty and bravery are put to the ultimate test as they try to fulfill their quest.

_____ 10. Sam is decent, simple, and honest, Pippin is homespun and optimistic, Meriadoc is clever, fun-loving, and brave.

Standard Verbs

_____ 11. Hobbits are gentle, and they enjoy the simple things in life, such as smoking pipes, eating, and storytelling.

_____ 12. Hobbits reach an average height of three and a half feet and lives to be about 100 years old.

_____ 13. The humans Aragorn and Boromir, both valiant and skilled at fighting, officially joins the Fellowship at the Council of Elrond.

_____ 14. An elf named Legolas and a dwarf named Gimli also join the Fellowship and accompanies Frodo for a part of his journey to Mordor.

_____ 15. Legolas is the son of an elf king, and, in the many dangerous confrontations the Fellowship faces, he will prove his skill as a superior archer.

Irregular Verbs

_____ 16. Gimli represents the dwarfs of Middle-earth and fighted with an axe, and Legolas and Gimli grow to respect each other's differences and rely on each other in battle.

_____ 17. The evil Saruman, once the head of the Council of the Wise, has gave in to the dark temptations of the ring and is willing to use his grotesque, savage Uruk-hai army to get the ring from Frodo and seize control of the world.

_____ 18. When Frodo is wounded, Aragorn (called Strider) leads the group safely to the country of the elves, where Elrond heals Frodo's wound, and everyone gets needed rest.

_____ 19. The group leaves elf country and heads south, but it be December when they depart, and a heavy snow begins to fall.

_____ 20. The snow becomed overwhelming as they cross Mount Caradhras, so they dig their way out and turn back.

Subject–Verb Agreement

_____ 21. Gandalf decide to pass through the mountains by traveling below them through the caves of Moria, but the caves are dangerous and the group resist.

_____ 22. Gandalf is the only one who knows his way through the caves, and he lead them along safely for two nights.

_____ 23. Then the group are attacked by orcs, and, as they run for the bridge leading out of the caves, the evil Balrog confronts them with a sword of fire.

_____ 24. Gandalf destroys the bridge and sends the Balrog to his death, but in the battle Gandalf loses his footing and falls to the bottomless depths below.

_____ 25. The remaining members of the Fellowship escapes to safety on the other side, but with Gandalf gone, they are thrown into despair and turn to Aragorn for leadership.

Parallelism

_____ 26. They spend ten days walking along the Anduin River, eating lightly, and to watch for orcs and the Dark Riders.

_____ 27. Sam spots Gollum, who has followed them since they left the caves of Moria, and he feels worried, protective of Frodo, and suspicion.

_____ 28. The conclusion of *The Fellowship of the Ring* recounts Frodo's decision about which path to take to Mordor and Boromir's attempt to take the ring from him.

_____ 29. Frodo finally decides to go to Mordor alone; he does not want his friends to suffer, he knows that they will try to protect him from the danger of Mordor, and the ring must be destroyed.

_____ 30. As the first book of the trilogy ends, Frodo steals away from the group with Sam, who refuses to leave his side, and the two hobbits set out alone looking for a path to Mordor.

Illogical Shifts

_____ 31. *The Fellowship of the Ring* portrays a variety of cultures that will make up Middle-earth, such as hobbits, elves, dwarfs, humans, wizards, orcs, Dark Riders, and Uruk-hai.

_____ 32. Each culture has its own way of life, customs, myths, ways of dress, and even style of fighting that the story develops for you.

_____ 33. *The Fellowship of the Ring* teaches readers that, in spite of our personal and cultural differences, you can be stronger by working together.

_____ 34. The first book of the trilogy keeps readers in suspense and looking forward to the second book to find out if evil Sauron, the Dark Lord, can reclaim the ring and reestablish his power over Middle-earth.

Sentence Skills Assessment for Diagnostic Test 2

Problem	Needs Review	Needs Study	Completed
Fragments			
Run-On Sentences			
Standard Verbs			
Irregular Verbs			
Subject-Verb Agreement			
Parallelism			
Illogical Shifts			

Writing Assignments

Composition studies have identified four basic stages of the writing process—prewriting, drafting, revising, and editing. Research has taught us that writers use these stages either explicitly or implicitly whenever they write. These stages, however, do not necessarily progress one after the other, step by step, from first to last in a linear fashion. Instead, they are recursive, meaning that you will turn back to each stage again and again as you need it over the course of a writing project. Becoming skilled in using the writing process demands time and effort. But *Write It* will support that effort by giving you clear strategies for writing, strategies that you can use each time you are asked to complete an argument essay. You will find that the more deliberate you become at making use of the recursiveness of the process, the stronger your writing will become in both form and content. Giving you practice with this aspect of writing is one of the goals of this book.

A note on the organization of Part 2: For each essay assignment, additional reading material is provided in the "Extended Activities" section. These supplemental readings are meant to fill in a context for the argument in the main reading selection and help you explore the subject of that selection in greater depth. You will be encouraged to think about these supplemental readings as you develop your own ideas, formulate your thesis statement, and support it with discussion and evidence. We encourage you to continue using all of the prewriting activities provided. They will ensure that you develop your thoughts and organize them within an effective essay format.

Assignment 1

"In Praise of Margins"

This assignment focuses on the subject of free time and its place in our lives. You will want to think about your definition of free time and the place it has—at least ideally—in our lives. The lead essay that you will respond to is written by Ian Frazier and is called "In Praise of Margins." Read his essay carefully to determine how he defines free time in terms of "marginal" time and the position he takes regarding the value of marginal time and activities.

After reading Frazier's essay, look carefully at the writing topic that follows it. You will write an essay that responds to this writing topic. Be sure to make good use of the pages that follow Frazier's essay. They will help you to understand Frazier's ideas and develop your own argument in response to the writing topic.

We hope you will come to see the value in doing extensive prewriting as you work to build a draft of your essay. The prewriting exercises in this chapter will take you through the writing process and help you analyze Frazier's argument and formulate one of your own. For this first assignment, you should complete all of the pages, carefully following the directions and guidelines. As you move through subsequent writing assignments in *Write It*, you will become familiar with these prewriting strategies, and you will be able to customize them to suit your own thinking and writing style.

In Praise of Margins

Essay

IAN FRAZIER

Ian Frazier is an American writer and humorist. He was born in 1951 and grew up in Hudson, Ohio. He attended Western Reserve Academy, and later Harvard University, where he was on the staff of The Harvard Lampoon. *After graduating, he worked as a magazine writer in Chicago, and then later moved to New York City, where he wrote for* The New Yorker *magazine. He has written several books, including* Family *(1994) and* Gone to New York: Adventures in the City *(2005).*

As kids, my friends and I spent a lot of time out in the woods. "The woods" was our part-time address, destination, purpose, and excuse. If I went to a friend's house and found him not at home, his mother might say, "Oh, he's out in the woods," with a tone of airy acceptance. It's similar to the tone people sometimes use nowadays to tell me that someone I'm looking for is on the golf course or at the hairdresser's or at the gym, or even "away from his desk." The combination of vagueness and specificity in the answer gives a sense of somewhere romantically incommunicado. I once attended an awards dinner at which Frank Sinatra was supposed to appear, and when he didn't, the master of ceremonies explained that Frank had called to say he was "filming on location." Ten-year-olds suffer from a scarcity of fancy-sounding excuses to do whatever they feel like for a while. For us, saying we were "out in the woods" worked just fine.

We sometimes told ourselves that what we were doing in the woods was exploring. Exploring was a more prominent idea back then than it is today. History, for example, seemed to be mostly about explorers, and the semi rural part of Ohio where we lived still had a faint recollection of being part of the frontier. Our explorations, though, seemed to have less system than the historic kind: something usually came up along the way. Say we began to cross one of the little creeks plentiful in the second-growth forests we frequented and found that all the creek's moisture had somehow become a shell of milk-white ice about eight inches above the now-dry bed. No other kind of ice is as satisfying to break. The search for the true meridian would be postponed while we spent the afternoon breaking the ice, stomping it underfoot by the furlong.

Stuff like that—throwing rocks at a fresh mudflat to make craters, shooting frogs with slingshots, making forts, picking blackberries, digging in what we were briefly persuaded was an Indian burial mound—occupied much of our time in the woods. Our purpose there was a higher sort of un-purpose, a free-form aimlessness that would be beyond me now. The woods were ideal for those trains of thought that involved tedium and brooding. Often when I went by myself I would climb a tree and just sit. I could list a hundred pointless things we did in the woods. Climbing trees, though, was a common one. There were four or five trees that we visited regularly—tall beeches, easy to climb and comfortable to sit in. We spent hours at a time in trees, afflicting the best perches with so many carved-in names, hearts, arrows, and funny sayings from the comic strips.

It was in a tree, too, that our days of fooling around in the woods came to an end. By then some of us had reached seventh grade and had begun the bumpy ride of adolescence. In March, the month when we usually took to the woods again after winter, two friends and I set out to go exploring. Right away, we climbed a tree, and soon were indulging in the spurious nostalgia of kids who have only short pasts to look back upon. The "remember whens" faltered, finally, and I think it occurred to all three of us at the same time that we really were rather big to be up in a tree. Some of us had started wearing unwoodsy outfits like short-sleeved madras shirts and penny loafers, even after school. Soon there would be the spring dances on Friday evenings in the high school cafeteria. We looked at the bare branches around us receding into obscurity, and suddenly there was nothing up there for us. Like Adam and Eve, we saw our own nakedness, and that terrible grown-up question "What are you doing?" made us ashamed.

We went back to the woods eventually—and when I say "we," I'm speaking demographically, not just of my friends and me. Millions of us went back, once the sexual and social business of early adulthood had been more or less sorted out. But significantly, we brought that same question with us. Now we had to be seriously doing—racing, strengthening, slimming, traversing, collecting, achieving.

"What are you doing?" The question pursues me still. When I go fishing and catch no fish, the idea that it"s fun simply to be out on the river consoles me for not one second. I must catch fish; and if I do, I must then catch more and bigger fish. On a Sunday afternoon last summer I took my two young children fishing with me on a famous trout stream near my house. My son was four and my daughter was eight, and I kidded myself that in their company I would be able to fish with my usual single-minded mania. I suited up in my waders and gear and led my kids from the parking area down toward the water. On the way, however, we had to cross a narrow, shallow irrigation ditch dating from when this part of the valley had farms. Well, the kids saw that little ditch and immediately took off their shoes and waded in and splashed and floated pine cones. I didn't have the heart to drag the kids away, and as I was sitting in all my fishing gear beside that unlikely trickle, a fly fisherman about my age and just as geared-up came along. He took me in at a glance, noticed my equipment and my idleness, and gave a small but unmistakable snort of derision. I was offended, but I understood how he felt as he and his purpose hurried on by.

Here, I'd like to consider a word whose meaning has begun to drift like a caterpillar on a stream. That word is margin. Originally its meaning—the blank space around a body of type or the border of a piece of ground—had neutral connotations. But its adjective form, *marginal*, now has a negative tinge. Marginal people or places or activities are ones that don't quite work out, don't sufficiently account for themselves in the economic world. But especially as the world gets more jammed up, we need margins. A book without margins is impossible to read. And marginal behavior can be the most important kind. Every purpose-filled activity we pursue in the woods began as just fooling around. The first person to ride his bicycle down a mountain trail was doing a decidedly marginal thing. The margin is where you can try out odd ideas that you might be afraid to admit to with people looking on. Scientists have a term for research carried on with no immediate prospects of economic gain: "blue-sky research." Marginal places are the blue-sky research zones of the outdoors.

Writing Topic

According to Frazier, why are "marginal" places and activities valuable? What do you think of his views? To develop your position, be sure to discuss specific examples. Those examples can be drawn from anything you've read—including, if you choose, "In Praise of Margins" itself—as well as from your own observations and experiences.

Vocabulary Check

Good writers choose their words carefully so that their ideas will be clear. In order for you, the reader, to understand an essay, it is important to think about its key vocabulary terms and the way they are used by the author. Words can have a variety of meanings, or they can have specialized meanings in certain contexts. Look up the definitions of the following words or phrases from the essay. Choose the meaning that you think Frazier intended when he selected that particular word or phrase for use in this essay. Then explain the way the meaning or concept behind the definition is key to understanding his argument.

frontier

   definition: _____

   _____

   explanation: _____

   _____

   _____

aimlessness

   definition: _____

   _____

   explanation: _____

   _____

   _____

nostalgia

   definition: _____

   _____

   explanation: _____

   _____

   _____

marginal

definition: _____

_____

explanation: _____

_____

_____

Questions to Guide Your Reading

Answer the following questions so you can gain a thorough understanding of "In Praise of Margins."

Paragraph 1

What roles, according to Ian Frazier, did "the woods" play in his childhood? Explain the way "the woods" managed to function as each of them. Did you, as a child, have somewhere that filled some of these roles for you? Where, and which roles?

Paragraph 2

What did Frazier and his friends like to think they were doing in the woods? Why? What were they actually doing? How do you explain the discrepancy?

Paragraph 3

What does Frazier now see to be the purpose of the time spent in the woods? By what kind of actions was that purpose manifested?

Paragraph 4

Why did the visits to the woods come to an end? Do you think the visits necessarily needed to end at this time? What could have helped them to continue?

Paragraph 5

When and why did Frazier and his peers return to the woods? How did the time he spent in the woods as an adult differ from the time he spent there as a boy?

Paragraph 6

What happened when Frazier took his children to the woods? How did that visit clarify his change in consciousness for him?

Paragraph 7

How does Frazier say that the adjective form of "margins"—"marginal"—differs from the noun? Is he comfortable with this difference? Why or why not?

Prewriting for a Directed Summary

Now that you have used the questions above to understand "In Praise of Margins" as a whole, use the following questions as a guide to focus your attention on a particular perspective in the essay. This perspective will be important when you are working on your own essay in response to the writing topic for this assignment. Be sure to use the answers you give below when it is time to write a clear and coherent directed summary in response to the writing topic's first question:

> writing topic's first question: *According to Frazier, why are "marginal" places and activities valuable?*

Although this question asks you to explain Frazier's views, it doesn't ask you to summarize the entire essay. Be sure to keep the question in mind as you present his ideas.

Hint

Don't forget to review Part 1's "Guidelines for Writing a Directed Summary."

Focus Questions

1. What does Frazier mean when he uses the word "marginal"?

   Places or activities that have no value in the "economic world."

2. What are some examples of places and activities in his own life that he now thinks of as being "marginal"?

   - watching his kids play in the ditch
   - the woods   - fishing on the river.

3. When did being in "marginal" places and engaging in "marginal" activities become embarrassing for Frazier and his friends? Why?

   Adolescence. They grew up and associated the woods with childhood; thus believing it was childish.

4. Why does Frazier now believe that margins are important?

   the "jammed up" world = too much happening, not enough time to enjoy the simple pleasures of life.

Opinion and Working Thesis Statement

The second question in the writing topic for "In Praise of Margins" asks you to take a position of your own. Your response to this part of the writing topic will become the thesis statement of your essay, so it is important to spend some time ensuring that it is fully developed and an accurate reflection of the position you want to take on the importance of margins. Use the framework below to help you develop your working thesis, but keep an open mind as you complete the prewriting pages that follow this one and read the positions other writers take in the essays in the "Extended Activities" section of this chapter. You may find that, after giving more thought to the idea of margins, you want to modify your position.

writing topic's second question: *What do you think of his views?*

Do you agree with Frazier that marginal places and activities can be the most important? As you think about the position you want to take in your working thesis statement, keep in mind Frazier's definition of "marginal activities and places" that you analyzed in "Questions to Guide Your Reading."

1. Use the following **thesis frame** to identify the basic elements of your working thesis statement:

   a. What is the main subject of "In Praise of Margins" that the writing topic's first question asks you to consider?

   The value of marginal places and activities.

   b. What is Frazier's opinion about that subject?

   These places hold value in our lives like the woods

   c. What is your opinion about the subject, and will you agree or disagree with Frazier's opinion?

   I will agree that marginal places hold value in our lives. I feel that everyone needs a detour from the structured path.

2. Now use the elements you isolated in 1a, b, and c to write a thesis statement. You may have to revise it several times until it captures your idea clearly.

   _____

   _____

Prewriting to Find Support for Your Thesis Statement

The last part of the writing topic asks you to support the position you put forward in your thesis statement. Well-developed ideas are crucial when you are making an argument because you will have to be clear, logical, and thorough if you are to be convincing. As you work through the exercises below, you will generate much of the 4Cs material you will need when you draft your essay's body paragraphs.

> writing topic's last question: *To develop your position, be sure to discuss specific examples. Those examples can be drawn from anything you've read—including, if you choose, "In Praise of Margins" itself—as well as from your observations and experiences.*

Complete each section of this prewriting activity; your responses will become the material you will use in the next stage—planning and writing the essay.

1. As you begin to develop your own examples, consider the idea of marginality, as Frazier understands it, in relation to your own life. In the space below, list or freewrite about personal experiences that involved you, your friends, or your family in which you encountered "marginal people or places or activities," in the sense that Frazier understands them. Feel free to include any experience, however minor or incidental.

   Once you've written your ideas, look them over carefully. Try to group your ideas into categories. Then give each category a label. In other words, cluster ideas that seem to have something in common and, for each cluster, identify that shared quality by giving it a title.

2. Now broaden your focus; list or freewrite about examples from your studies, your readings, and your knowledge of current events. Whom do you know that might be called "marginal"? What places or activities are you familiar with that Frazier would identify as marginal?

Feel free to include specific examples from Frazier's essay, as the writing topic allows you to draw examples from it.

Once you've written your ideas, look them over carefully. Try to group your ideas into categories. Then give each category a label. In other words, cluster ideas that seem to have something in common and, for each cluster, identify that shared quality by giving it a title.

3. Once you've created topics by clustering your ideas into categories, go through them and pick two or three specific ones to develop in your essay. Make sure that they are relevant to your thesis and that they have enough substance to be compelling to your reader. Then, in the space below, briefly summarize each item.

Hint

Once you've decided which categories and items you will use in your essay, take some time to explain below how each category and its items connect to your thesis statement. You will use these details for the next stage.

Revising Your Thesis Statement

Now that you have spent some time working out your ideas more systematically and developing some supporting evidence for the position you want to take, look again at the working thesis statement you crafted earlier to see if it is still accurate. As your first step, look again at the writing topic's second question and then write your original working thesis on the lines that follow it:

writing topic's second question: *What do you think of his views?*

Working Thesis Statement:

_____

_____

_____

Take some time now to see if you want to revise your thesis statement. Often after extensive prewriting and focused thought, the working thesis statement is no longer an accurate reflection of what you plan to say in your essay. Sometimes, only a word or phrase must be added or deleted; other times, the thesis statement must be significantly rewritten, as either or both the subject and the claim portions are inaccurate.

After examining your working thesis statement and completing any necessary revisions, check it one more time by asking yourself the following questions:

a. Does the thesis directly identify Frazier's argument regarding the importance of margins?

b. Do you make clear your opinion about the value of the marginal activities or spaces as Frazier defines them?

If you answered "no" to either of these questions, revise your thesis statement once more to add the missing elements.

_____

_____

Planning and Drafting Your Essay

Getting started on the draft is often the hardest part of the writing process because this is where you move from exploring and planning to getting your ideas down in a unified, coherent shape. Creating an outline will give you a basic structure for incorporating all the ideas you have developed in the preceding pages. An outline will also give you a bird's-eye view of your essay and help you spot problems in development or logic.

Hint

This outline doesn't have to contain polished writing. You may only want to fill in the basic ideas in phrases or terms.

Creating an Outline for Your Draft

I. Introductory Paragraph

    A. An opening sentence that gives the reading selection's title and author and begins to answer the first part of the writing topic:

    _____

    B. Main points to include in the directed summary:

       1.

       2.

       3.

       4.

    C. Write out your thesis statement. (Look back to "Opinion and Working Thesis Statement," where you sketched your working thesis statement.) It should clearly agree or disagree with "In Praise of Margins" and state a clear position using your own words.

    _____

II. Body Paragraphs

    A. Subject of the paragraph: _____

        1. **C**ontrolling idea sentence:

                 _____

        2. **C**orroborating details:

                 _____

                 _____

                 _____

        3. **C**areful description of the details' relevance:

                 _____

                 _____

                 _____

                 _____

                 _____

        4. **C**onnection to the thesis statement:

                 _____

    B. Subject of the paragraph: _____

        1. **C**ontrolling idea sentence:

                 _____

                 _____

        2. **C**orroborating details:

                 _____

                 _____

                 _____

3. Careful description of the details' relevance:

    _____

    _____

    _____

    _____

    _____

4. Connection to the thesis statement:

    _____

C. Subject of the paragraph: _____

1. Controlling idea sentence:

    _____

2. Corroborating details:

    _____

    _____

    _____

3. Careful description of the details' relevance:

    _____

    _____

    _____

    _____

    _____

4. Connection to the thesis statement:

    _____

   D. Subject of the paragraph: _____

      1. **C**ontrolling idea sentence:

          _____

      2. **C**orroborating details:

          _____

          _____

          _____

      3. **C**areful description of the details' relevance:

          _____

          _____

          _____

          _____

      4. **C**onnection to the thesis statement:

          _____

III. Conclusion

   A. Type of conclusion to be used:

       _____

   B. Key words or phrases to include:

       _____

Doing a Peer Draft Review

Use the following guidelines to give a classmate feedback on his or her draft. Read the draft through first and then answer each of the items below as specifically as you can.

Name of draft's author: _____

Name of draft's reader: _____

Introduction

1. Within the opening sentences,

   a. the author is correctly identified by first and last name   yes   no

   b. the writing selection's title is included and placed within quotation marks   yes   no

2. The opening contains a summary that

   a. explains what Frazier means by "marginal" activities and places   yes   no

   b. explains why he thinks they are important   yes   no

3. The opening provides a thesis that

   a. makes Frazier's conclusions clear   yes   no

   b. gives the draft writer's opinion about those conclusions   yes   no

If the answers to 3 above are yes, state the thesis below as it is written. If the answer to one or both of these questions is no, explain to the writer what information is needed to make the thesis complete.

Body

1. How many paragraphs comprise the body of this essay? _____

2. To support the thesis, this number is   sufficient   not enough

3. Do paragraphs contain the 4Cs?

    Paragraph 1   Controlling idea sentence   yes   no
                   Corroborating details   yes   no
                   Careful description of the details' relevance   yes   no
                   Connection to the thesis statement   yes   no

    Paragraph 2   Controlling idea sentence   yes   no
                   Corroborating details   yes   no
                   Careful description of the details' relevance   yes   no
                   Connection to the thesis statement   yes   no

    Paragraph 3   Controlling idea sentence   yes   no
                   Corroborating details   yes   no
                   Careful description of the details' relevance   yes   no
                   Connection to the thesis statement   yes   no

    Paragraph 4   Controlling idea sentence   yes   no
                   Corroborating details   yes   no
                   Careful description of the details' relevance   yes   no
                   Connection to the thesis statement   yes   no

    Paragraph 5   Controlling idea sentence   yes   no
                   Corroborating details   yes   no
                   Careful description of the details' relevance   yes   no
                   Connection to the thesis statement   yes   no

    (Continue as needed)

4. Identify any of the above paragraphs that are not fully developed (too short).

5. Identify any of the above paragraphs that fail to support the thesis. _____

6. Identify any of the above paragraphs that are redundant or repetitive. _____

7. Suggest any ideas for additional paragraphs that might improve this essay.

Conclusion

1. Does the final paragraph contain any material that should have been developed in the body of the essay?

   a. examples   yes   no

   b. new ideas   yes   no

2. Does the conclusion provide closure (let readers know that the end of the essay has been reached)?   yes   no

3. Does the conclusion leave readers with an understanding of the significance of the argument?   yes   no

   State in your own words what the draft writer considers to be important about his or her argument.

   _____

   _____

4. Identify the type of conclusion used (see the guidelines for conclusions in Part 1).

Revision

1. During revision, the writer should pay attention to the following problems in mechanics:

   comma splices

   comma placement

   fragments

   run-on sentences

   apostrophe use

   quotation mark use

   capital letter use

   spelling

2. During revision, the writer should pay attention to the following areas of grammar:

   verb tense
   subject-verb agreement
   pronoun type
   pronoun reference
   pronoun agreement
   irregular verbs
   noun plurals
   dangling modifiers
   prepositions
   misplaced modifiers

Final Draft Check List

Content:

- My essay has an appropriate title.
- I provide an accurate summary of Frazier's position on the topic presented in "In Praise of Margins."
- My thesis states a clear position that can be supported by evidence.
- I have a sufficient number of paragraphs and concrete examples to support my thesis.
- Each body paragraph is relevant to my thesis.
- Each body paragraphs contains the 4Cs.
- I use transitions whenever necessary to connect paragraphs and ideas to each other.
- The final paragraph of my essay (the conclusion) provides readers with a sense of closure.

Grammar and Mechanics:

- I use the present tense to discuss Frazier's argument and examples.
- All of my verb tense shifts are correctly used to show the chronology of events.
- I have verb tense consistency throughout my sentences.
- My sentences are correctly marked and punctuated.
- If I present items in a series (nouns, verbs, prepositional phrases), they are parallel in form.
- If I include material spoken or written by someone other than myself, I have correctly punctuated it with quotation marks, using the MLA style guide's rules for citation.
- I have checked for subject-verb agreement in all of my sentences.

Extended Activities

Readings

"The Shallows" by Nicholas Carr

"Hitting Pay Dirt" by Annie Dillard

"The Dance within My Heart" by Pat Mora

"Blue-Sky Research" by Sir John Vane

"Everyday Playtime for Adults" by Dulce Zamora

Class Discussion

Using Comparisons

Homework

"The Importance of Free Time" by Bhagwad Jal Park (a blog)

Reviewing Your Graded Essay

The Shallows

Essay

NICHOLAS CARR

Nicholas Carr has published books and articles on business, technology, and culture. He has been a critic of technological utopianism, expressing his views in books such as The Big Switch and Does IT Matter? *(2004). He has written for* The New York Times, Atlantic, New Republic, *and* Wired. *He was educated at Dartmouth College and Harvard University. In January 2008, Carr became a member of the Editorial Board of Advisors of* Encyclopædia Brittanica. *The following is an excerpt from his recent book* The Shallows: What the Internet Is Doing to Our Brains *(2010).*

What exactly was going on in Nathaniel Hawthorne's head as he sat in the green seclusion of Sleepy Hollow and lost himself in contemplation? And how was it different from what was going through the minds of the city dwellers going about their daily business? A series of psychological studies over the past twenty years has revealed that after spending time in a quiet rural setting, close to nature, people exhibit greater attentiveness, stronger memory, and generally improved cognition. Their brains become both calmer and sharper. The reason, according to attention restoration theory, or ART, is that when people aren't being bombarded by external stimuli, their brains can, in effect, relax. They no longer have to tax their working memories by processing a stream of bottom-up distractions. The resulting state of contemplativeness strengthens their ability to control their mind.

The results of the most recent such study were published in *Psychological Science* at the end of 2008. A team of University of Michigan researchers, led by psychologist Marc Berman, recruited some three dozen people and subjected them to a rigorous, and mentally fatiguing, series of tests designed to measure the capacity of their working memory and their ability to exert top-down control over their attention. The subjects were then divided into two groups. Half of them spent about an hour walking through a secluded woodland park, and the other half spent an equal amount of time walking along busy downtown streets. Both groups then took the tests a second time. Spending time in the park, the researchers found, "significantly improved" people's performance on the cognitive tests, indicating a substantial increase in attentiveness. Walking in the city, by contrast, led to no improvement in test results.

The researchers then conducted a similar experiment with another set of people. Rather than taking walks between the rounds of testing, these subjects simply looked at photographs of either calm rural scenes or busy urban ones. The results were the same. The people who looked at pictures of nature scenes were able to exert substantially stronger control over their attention, while those who looked at city scenes showed no improvement in their attentiveness. "In sum," concluded the researchers, "simple and brief interactions with nature can produce marked increases in cognitive control." Spending time in the natural world seems to be of "vital importance" to "effective cognitive functioning."[1]

There is no Sleepy Hollow on the Internet, no peaceful spot where contemplativeness can work its restorative magic. There is only the endless, mesmerizing buzz of the urban street. The stimulations of the Net, like those of the city, can be invigorating and inspiring. We wouldn't want to give them up. But they are, as well, exhausting and distracting. They can easily, as Hawthorne understood, overwhelm all quieter modes of thought. One of the greatest dangers we face as we automate the work of our minds, as we cede control over the flow of our thoughts and memories to a powerful electronic system, is a slow erosion of our humanness and our humanity.

It's not only deep thinking that requires a calm, attentive mind. It's also empathy and compassion. Psychologists have long studied how people experience fear and react to physical threats, but it's only recently that they've begun researching the sources of our nobler instincts. What they're finding is that, as Antonio Damasio, the director of USC's Brain and Creativity Institute, explains, the higher emotions emerge from neural processes that "are inherently slow."[2] In one recent experiment, Damasio and his colleagues had subjects listen to stories describing people experiencing physical or psychological pain. The subjects were then put into a magnetic resonance imaging

---

[1]Marc G. Berman, John Jonides, and Stephen Kaplan, "The Cognitive Benefits of Interacting with Nature," *Psychological Science*, 19, no. 12 (December 2008): 1207-12.
[2]Carl Marziali, "Nobler Instincts Take Time," USC Web site, April 14, 2009, http://college.usc.edu/news/stories/547/nobler-instincts-take-time.

machine and their brains were scanned as they were asked to remember the stories. The experiment revealed that while the human brain reacts very quickly to demonstrations of physical pain—when you see someone injured, the primitive pain centers in your own brain activate almost instantaneously—the more sophisticated mental process of empathizing with psychological suffering unfolds much more slowly. It takes time, the researchers discovered, for the brain "to transcend immediate involvement of the body" and begin to understand and to feel "the psychological and moral dimensions of a situation."

The experiment, say the scholars, indicates that the more distracted we become, the less able we are to experience the subtlest, most distinctively human forms of empathy, compassion, and other emotions. "For some kinds of thoughts, especially moral decision-making about other people's social and psychological situations, we need to allow for adequate time and reflection," cautions Mary Helen Immordino-Yang, a member of the research team. "If things are happening too fast, you may not ever fully experience emotions about other people's psychological states."[4] It would be rash to jump to the conclusion that the Internet is undermining our moral sense. It would not be rash to suggest that as the Net reroutes our vital paths and diminishes our capacity for contemplation, it is altering the depth of our emotions as well as our thoughts.

There are those who are heartened by the ease with which our minds are adapting to the Web's intellectual ethic. "Technological progress does not reverse," writes a *Wall Street Journal* columnist, "so the trend toward multitasking and consuming many different types of information will only continue." We need not worry, though, because our "human software" will in time "catch up to the machine technology that made the information abundance possible." We'll "evolve" to become more agile consumers of data.[5] The writer of a cover story in *New York* magazine says that as we become used to "the 21st-century task" of "flitting" among bits of online information, "the wiring of the brain will inevitably change to deal more efficiently with more information." We may lose our capacity "to

---

[3]Mary Helen Immordino-Yang, Andrea McColl, Hanna Damasio, and Antonio Damasio, "Neural Correlates of Admiration and Compassion," *Proceedings of the National Academy of Sciences,* 106, no. 19 (May 12, 2009): 8021-26.
[4]Marziali, "Nobler Instincts."
[5]L. Gordon Crovitz, "Information Overload? Relax," *Wall Street Journal,* July 6, 2009.

concentrate on a complex task from beginning to end," but in recompense we'll gain new skills, such as the ability to "conduct 34 conversations simultaneously across six different media."[6] A prominent economist writes, cheerily, that "the web allows us to borrow cognitive strengths from autism and to be better infovores."[7] An *Atlantic* author suggests that our "technology-induced ADD" may be "a short-term problem," stemming from our reliance on "cognitive habits evolved and perfected in an era of limited information flow." Developing new cognitive habits is "the only viable approach to navigating the age of constant connectivity."[8]

These writers are certainly correct in arguing that we're being molded by our new information environment. Our mental adaptability, built into the deepest workings of our brains, is a keynote of intellectual history. But if there's comfort in their reassurances, it's of a very cold sort. Adaptation leaves us better suited to our circumstances, but qualitatively it's a neutral process. What matters in the end is not our becoming but what we become. In the 1950s, Martin Heidegger observed that the looming "tide of technological revolution" could "so captivate, bewitch, dazzle, and beguile man that calculative thinking may someday come to be accepted and practiced *as the only* way of thinking." Our ability to engage in "meditative thinking," which he saw as the very essence of our humanity, might become a victim of headlong progress.[9] The tumultuous advance of technology could [...] drown out the refined perceptions, thoughts, and emotions that arise only through contemplation and reflection. The "frenziedness of technology," Heidegger wrote, threatens to "entrench itself everywhere."[10]

It may be that we are now entering the final stage of that entrenchment. We are welcoming the frenziedness into our souls.

Discussion Questions

1. In what ways and to what extent, according to psychological studies, does time spent outside affect people's performance? Discuss how the results of this research apply to your own life.

---

[6]Sam Anderson, "In Defense of Distraction," *New York*, May 25, 2009.
[7]Tyler Cowen, *Create Your Own Economy* (New York: Dutton, 2009), 10.
[8]Jamais Cascio, "Get Smarter," *Atlantic*, July/August 2009.
[9]Martin Heidegger, *Discourse on Thinking* (New York: Harper & Row, 1966), 56.
[10]Martin Heidegger, *The Question Concerning Technology and Other Essays* (New York: Harper & Row, 1977), 35.

2. Explain the relationship psychologists see between deep thinking and emotions. As the technological orientation of our own society increases, what specific social manifestations do you expect to see?

3. Why do you agree or disagree with the prominent economist that Carr quotes who believes the web will make us "better infovores"? Do you yourself want or not want to be one?

4. How would you respond to Carr's conclusion that we "are welcoming the frenziedness into our souls"?

Hitting Pay Dirt

ANNIE DILLARD

Annie Dillard is known primarily as an essayist, especially for works such as Pilgrim at Tinker Creek *(1974), which won a Pulitzer Prize,* Teaching a Stone to Talk *(1982), and* For the Time Being *(2000), but she is also well respected for her poetry and novels. The essay below is taken from her autobiography* An American Childhood *(1987).*

After I read *The Field Book of Ponds and Streams* several times, I longed for a microscope. Everybody needed a microscope. Detectives used microscopes, both for the FBI and at Scotland Yard. Although usually I had to save my tiny allowance for things I wanted, that year for Christmas my parents gave me a microscope kit.

In a dark basement corner, on a white enamel table, I set up the microscope kit. I supplied a chair, a lamp, a batch of jars, a candle, and a pile of library books. The microscope kit supplied a blunt black three-speed microscope, a booklet, a scalpel, a dropper, an ingenious device for cutting thin segments of fragile tissue, a pile of clean slides and cover slips, and a dandy array of corked test tubes.

One of the test tubes contained "hay infusion." Hay infusion was a wee brown chip of grass blade. You added water to it, and after a week it became a jungle in a drop, full of one-celled animals. This did not work for me. All I saw in the microscope after a week was a wet chip of dried grass, much enlarged.

Another test tube contained "diatomaceous earth." This was, I believed, an actual pinch of the white cliffs of Dover. On my palm it was an airy, friable chalk. The booklet said it was composed of the silicaceous bodies of diatoms—one-celled creatures that lived in, as it were, small glass jewelry boxes with fitted lids. Diatoms, I read, come in a variety of transparent geometrical shapes. Broken and dead and dug out of geological deposits, they made chalk and a fine abrasive used in silver polish and toothpaste. What I saw in the microscope must have been the fine abrasive—grit enlarged. It was years before I saw a recognizable, whole diatom. The kit's diatomaceous earth was a bust.

All that winter I played with the microscope. I prepared slides from things at hand, as the books suggested. I looked at the transparent membrane inside an onion's skin and saw the cells. I looked at a section of cork and saw the cells, and at scrapings from the inside of my cheek, ditto. I looked at my blood and saw not much; I looked at my urine and saw long iridescent crystals, for the drop had dried.

All this was very well, but I wanted to see the wildlife I had read about. I wanted especially to see the famous amoeba, who had eluded me. He was supposed to live in the hay infusion, but I hadn't found him there. He lived outside in warm ponds and streams, too, but I lived in Pittsburgh, and it had been a cold winter.

Finally late that spring I saw an amoeba. The week before, I had gathered puddle water from Frick Park; it had been festering in a jar in the basement. This June night after dinner I figured I had waited long enough. In the basement at my microscope table I spread a scummy drop of Frick Park puddle water on a slide, peeked in, and lo, there was the famous amoeba. He was as blobby and grainy as his picture; I would have known him anywhere.

Before I had watched him at all, I ran upstairs. My parents were still at the table, drinking coffee. They, too, could see the famous amoeba. I told them, bursting, that he was all set up, that they should hurry before his water dried. It was the chance of a lifetime.

Father had stretched out his long legs and was tilting back in his chair. Mother sat with her knees crossed, in blue slacks, smoking a Chesterfield. The dessert dishes were still on the table. My sisters were nowhere in evidence. It was a warm evening; the big dining-room windows gave onto blooming rhododendrons.

Mother regarded me warmly. She gave me to understand that she was glad I had found what I had been looking for, but that she and Father were happy to sit with their coffee, and would not be coming down.

She did not say, but I understood at once, that they had their pursuits (coffee?) and I had mine. She did not say, but I began to understand then, that you do what you do out of your private passion for the thing itself.

I had essentially been handed my own life. In subsequent years my parents would praise my drawings and poems, and supply me with books, art supplies, and sports equipment, and listen to my troubles and enthusiasms, and supervise my hours, and discuss and inform, but they would not get involved with my detective work, nor hear about my reading, nor inquire about my homework or term papers or exams, nor visit the salamanders I caught, nor listen to me play the piano, nor attend my field hockey games, nor fuss over my insect collection with me, or my poetry collection or stamp collection or rock collection. My days and nights were my own to plan and fill.

When I left the dining room that evening and started down the dark basement stairs, I had a life. I sat down to my wonderful amoeba, and there he was, rolling his grains more slowly now, extending an arc of his edge for a foot and drawing himself along by that foot, and absorbing it again and rolling on. I gave him some more pond water.

I had hit pay dirt. For all I knew, there were paramecia, too, in that pond water, or daphniae, or stentors, or any of the many other creatures I had read about and never seen: volvox, the spherical algal colony; euglena with its one red eye; the elusive, glassy diatom; hydra, rotifers, water bears, worms. Anything was possible. The sky was the limit.

Discussion Questions

1. When Annie Dillard claims that a microscope is something that everyone wants and needs, is she expressing something she believes as an adult or an idea she had as a child? How do you know?

2. Although her activities with the microscope could be considered educational, she calls them play. Why?

3. Considering the time Dillard spent in her basement that winter, in what ways might this time qualify for Frazier as time spent on the margins?

4. Consider the last two sentences of Dillard's essay. Discuss the way that kind of belief and passion can be the product of marginal activities. Do you think these are thoughts that are unique to childhood, or can they be a part of an adult's life as well? Explain the reasons and give examples to support your answer.

The Dance within My Heart

Essay

PAT MORA

Pat Mora is a poet, essayist, and children's book author. After receiving degrees from Texas Western College and the University of Texas at El Paso (UTEP), she served as Director of the University Museum at UTEP. She has published books of poetry, a collection of essays, a children's story, and a family memoir titled House of Houses *(1997).*

For a Southwesterner, early spring in the Midwest is a time for jubilation. Another winter survived. Why, then, on a soft spring Saturday would I choose to leave the dogwoods and daffodils and spend my day inside museums? Certainly, I didn't spend my youth enduring trips through solemn rooms, being introduced to "culture." There was only one small art museum in my hometown, and I'm not sure how comfortable my parents would have felt there. My father worked evenings and weekends to support the four of us and to give us what he and my mother hadn't had, a youth without financial worries. And my mother not only helped him in his optical business but was our willing chauffeur in addition to assisting the grandmother and aunt who lived with us, our extended Mexican American family.

But as an adult I began to visit those echoing buildings. A fellowship allowed trips to modest and grand museums in New York, Paris, Washington, Mexico, Hawaii, and the Dominican Republic. And much to my surprise, I even found myself directing a small university museum for a time, having the opportunity to convince people of all ages and backgrounds that indeed the museum was theirs. I was hooked for life.

For me, museums are pleasure havens. When I enter, my breathing changes just as it does when I visit aquariums, zoos, botanical gardens. These latter sites offer a startling array of living species. Unless we have become totally desensitized to nature's grandeur, to its infinite variations, arboretums and nature centers inspire us to treat our planet with more care, to be more attentive to the life around us, no matter how minute. I stand entranced by the sprightliness of glass shrimp, the plushness of the jaguar, the haughtiness of birds of paradise in bloom. Parrots make me laugh, fins spin my blood, ferns hush my doubts. I leave refreshed.

When they were younger, my children could far more easily understand my desire to visit displays of living creatures than they could my penchant for natural history and art museums, for gazing at baskets and pottery, at sculpture and flashing neon. It sounded like work walking through room after room, up and down stairs, being relatively quiet, not eating, reading small cards of text, staring at "weird" objects. This is fun?

But museums remind me of the strength and inventiveness of the human imagination through time. They remind me that offering beauty to a community is a human habit, a needed reminder in a society with little time for observing, listening, appreciating. I gaze at African masks crusted with cowrie shells, at drums and carvings of old, wrinkled wood, at the serenity of Buddha. I watch my fellow visitors, drawn to cases both by the beauty and craft but also as a kind of testimony to humans who once sat under our sun and moon and with rough hands graced our world.

I walk on to see the sturdy pre-Columbian female figures from Nayarit, Mexico, women of broad dimensions who occupy space rather than shrink as we sometimes do. I see pan pipes and bone flutes from Peru, 180 B.C., back then, high in the Andes, hear a man transforming his breath into music.

Room after room I watch light and shadow play on sandstone, silver, wood, bronze, earthenware, copper, ivory, hemp, oil, acrylic, watercolor, straw, gold. I study toenails on a headless marble statue, watch light stroke the soft curves, wish I could touch her outstretched Roman hand. The next room, or turning a corner, can yield surprise, the halls and rooms a pleasure maze. I stand in Chagall's blue light, see his glass bird poised to fly from room to room.

I ignore the careful museum maps, enjoying the unexpected, the independence of viewing at will, the private pleasure of letting myself abandon order and logic room to room. Purposeless wandering? Not really, for I now know I come not only for the intellectual and sensory stimulation but for comfort. I come to be with humans I admire, with those who produced these drums and breathing dancers, who through the ages added beauty to this world. Their work gives me hope, reminds me that art is not a luxury: it nourishes our parched spirits. It is essential.

I think again of how privileged I am to be in these quiet rooms, not having to wait for a free day, having time to spend wandering these galleries rather than having to care for someone else's children while mine are alone, or having to iron clothes that I will never wear. And certainly free days and increased public programming—the democratization of museums—are an improvement from past eras, an acknowledgment, although sometimes grudging, that not only the "washed and worthy" deserve entrance. Museums are slowly changing, realizing that artifacts and art belong to all people, not some people. Museums are even becoming a bit embarrassed about how they acquired what they own, about why they arrogantly ushered certain groups past their polished doors. The faces viewing with me have been more varied in recent years.

I walk on. I, who can barely sew a button, study an array of quilts, glad that such women's art is now displayed, think of the careful fingers—stitch, stitch, stitch—and probably careful voices that produced these works. The text of a bronze of Shiva says that her dance takes place within her heart. I study her and think of that dance, of the private nature of that spring of emotion. I watch a group of teenage girls walk by and wonder if they can hear or feel their private dance in a world that equates noise and brutality with entertainment.

The contemporary art halls most baffled my children when they were young. "Why, I could do that!" they would scoff staring at a Jackson Pollock. I smile secretly when my youngest, now taller than I am, asks, "Where are our favorite rooms?" meaning, yes, those rooms with massive canvases, with paint everywhere, the rooms that loosen me up inside, that provide escape from the confines of the predictable.

I walk outside glad to breathe in sky and wind but also brimming with all I saw and felt, hearing the dance within my heart.

Discussion Questions

1. How does the location of Mora's marginal childhood activity differ from those that Frazier discusses in his article? What commonality exists in Frazier's and Dillard's activity that is only present some of the time for Mora? How do these changes expand your own understanding of margins?

2. Discuss the success or lack of success that Frazier and Mora had with introducing their children to their own childhood marginal activity. How do you explain the difference?

3. Think of a marginal activity that you enjoyed as a child. Do you still make time for that activity in your life today? If you do, explain what rewards you receive from participating in it. If you don't, explain why it no longer appeals to you.

Blue-Sky Research

Essay

Excerpts from a Talk by Sir John Vane
(Nobel Laureate, Physiology/Medicine – 1982)

Sir John Vane, FFS, was awarded the Nobel Prize in Physiology/Medicine in 1982. He is the Director of Research and Development at the Wellcome Foundation. He is the Founder, Chairman, and Director General of The William Harvey Research Foundation (London), and a Fellow of the Royal Society. He was knighted in 1984.

Academic, basic, or "blue-sky" research, holds great promise for the community and for the health of mankind. But today's urgency to show a return on investment is leading pharmaceutical companies to demand that research be project- and market-oriented, so much so that "blue-sky" research is threatened. This industry threat is very real and is spreading to governmental funding of academia because of the same short-sighted philosophy.

I will give some examples from my own experience that illustrate the way in which "blue-sky" research can lead to totally unexpected benefits for the health of mankind. The first is aspirin.

Just under 100 years ago in the German drug company Bayer, a chemist named Felix Hoffmann was asked by his father, who was taking salicylate for his rheumatism, whether anything could be done to improve its bitter taste. Felix Hoffmann then invented aspirin by adding a simple side-arm to the salicylate molecule. This was the beginning of Bayer aspirin and nowadays hundreds of thousands of tons of aspirin are used around the world for the treatment of headaches, rheumatism, fevers and so on. But nobody knew how it worked until some 25 years ago.

My laboratory was working on a group of chemical messengers formed in many parts of the body called prostaglandins. At the time, it was becoming clear that certain prostaglandins were involved in causing inflammation and fever. I was writing a review over the weekend at home when suddenly it occurred to me that maybe aspirin and similar drugs were working by preventing the body from making these prostaglandins. In the laboratory on Monday morning, I said to my colleagues, "I think I know how aspirin works!" I am not a biochemist and so I had never made enzyme preparations before. I went to the literature and found out something about the enzyme that makes prostaglandins in the body. I prepared it in a test-tube and then added different doses of aspirin and other similar substances, including morphine, as control. I found that aspirin, or an aspirin-like drug, reduced the production of prostaglandins by this enzyme according to dose.

First of all they started out with large doses, the sort of dose (6 tablets a day) that was used in rheumatoid arthritis. However, over the years, clinical trials in the thousands and thousands of people have shown that only a small dose is needed and that even baby aspirin (75 mg or 1/4 of a normal tablet) taken once a day is sufficient to prevent the platelets from sticking together. This is such a small dose that in lectures I jokingly say that we should keep an aspirin tablet in the bathroom cupboard and lick it every morning! Indeed, clinical trials worldwide have shown that taking an aspirin every day reduces the risks of heart attack or stroke by up to 50%. So there are many thousands or even millions of people alive today because they take a daily aspirin for the prevention of heart attacks and strokes. These people would not otherwise have been with us had I not done that crucial experiment on a Monday morning. That is directly a result of our "blue-sky" research.

My second example comes from the same family of prostaglandins. Anatomists over the generations have known that blood stays fluid in healthy arteries but clots in dead ones. This was never understood but we also knew that the very same platelets that I have been talking about do not normally stick to the inner healthy walls of arteries. In 1976, we found that this was because the inner walls of the arteries make a prostaglandin, which prevents the platelets from sticking to them. We called it prostacyclin and this work opened up an enormous field of research. We now think that platelets stick to arteries when compounds such as prostacyclin failed to be formed. However, the therapeutic importance of this finding is that prostacyclin-like substances are now being marketed for use in obstructive vascular diseases such as those that normally lead to foot or leg amputations.

My third example shows how a new important kind of drug can come through serendipity, international collaboration, and of course, "blue-sky" research. In the mid-1960s when I was working at the Royal College of Surgeons in England, I had an application for a post-doc position from a Brazilian scientist named Sergio Ferreira. For his PhD, he had worked on the venom of a particularly nasty Brazilian snake called *Bothrops jararaca*. He had shown that extracts of this venom contained small peptides that potentiated the action of a pain-producing substance in the venom called bradykinin, probably by enzyme inhibition.

He came to my laboratory carrying some of his venom extracts in his pocket. I suggested to Sergio that we should study his snake venom extract on the renin-angiotensin system, so called because an enzyme known as renin is released from the kidney into the bloodstream and thus leading to the formation of a very strong pressure substance called angiotensin. However, he had other plans. He wanted to continue his work on bradykinin, and being a forceful personality, he convinced me to let him do that. We worked together on bradykinin for two years, and only at the end of that period did I persuade another colleague, Mick Bakhle, to test the snake venom on the renin-angiotensin system. It turned out to be a potent inhibitor of a key enzyme—angiotensin converting enzyme (ACE) in that system.

At the time I was consulting with Squibb in New Jersey. Nobody knew whether angiotensin was important in high blood pressure even though it was suspected. I suggested to Squibb that this inhibition of ACE by the snake venom peptide would test the concept as to whether angiotensin was involved in high blood-pressure or not. Scientists at Squibb were enthusiastic and started a programme to isolate the active venom peptide. The marketing people were unenthusiastic because they could not see a market for an anti-hypertensive compound that had to be injected, as a peptide would. I visited Squibb three times a year and each time found that I had to re-infuse enthusiasm into the programme. It was almost dropped because of marketing pressure. Eventually, they made a kilogram of the peptide from the snake venom, which was shown in New York by John Laragh to reduce high blood pressure. Thus, the concept had been proven. Now if only a similar compound absorbed by mouth could be found, there would be great therapeutic potential.

Having introduced the programme to Squibb and kept it alive for several years, I then joined Burroughs Wellcome, a competing pharmaceutical company, as the R & D Director, thus allowing me to no longer consult with Squibb. Nevertheless, a few years later their own scientists had discovered an orally-active ACE inhibitor, which they took to the market calling it Captopril or Capoten. Merck also found an ACE inhibitor around two or three years later, which they called Enalopril or Innovace. I have a paternal pride in the fact that these two compounds alone now have $20 billion worth of sales per annum around the world. That would not have happened without the "blue-sky" research on the snake venom that started in Brazil and then went on in my laboratories in London. There were so many extraordinary coincidences that were needed in order for that process to fructify, including Ferreira's choice to visit my laboratory rather than Oxford.

With these examples, I hope that I have begun to convince you that breakthroughs in medical science must come from "blue-sky" research. Without it, and without public support for it, society would be poorer as would our health. And taken in perspective, "blue-sky" research is not all that costly compared with the development process following it. Of course, the whole process of drug discovery takes many years and the work of many hundreds of people—a whole sort of inverted pyramid of costs balancing on the much less costly, but inescapable, "blue-sky" research. Without this fundamental research, important drugs such as antibiotics, the beta blockers, the H2 antagonists, and the calcium channel blockers would not now exist.

An especially fertile area for basic or "blue-sky" research is, of course, the brain. This has been left last by scientists because of the enormous technical difficulties of studying the brain. The kind of exploration of how nerves work and how brain cells communicate with each other is being studied by Dr. Bazan's Neuroscience Center and is vital for our future understanding of how the brain works. Without it, we shall not find effective cures for strokes and neurological diseases, such as Alzheimer's, as well as problems, such as schizophrenia, epilepsy, and depression that are so empirically treated by present-day drugs.

Over the last 40 years or so, I have visited many laboratories around the world. Here in New Orleans, you have excellent universities and the LSU Neuroscience Center, which is led by the enthusiasm and energy of Nicolas Bazan. It is a real centre of excellence and is recognized as such around the world.

Discussion Questions

1. Define "blue-sky" research. Why is the continuation of such research threatened? What does Sir John Vane believe to be the promise of "blue-sky" research? Do you think, for the most part, "blue-sky" research keeps this promise?

2. What type of support does Vane offer for his argument? What do you think of the nature and variety of his support?

3. How does Vane counter the argument that "blue-sky" research is not financially advantageous for pharmaceutical companies? If you were in chart of a company like Squibb or Merck, which employed Vane, would you be inclined/not be inclined to fund any non-goal-oriented project that Vane proposed?

4. How does Ian Frazier, author of "In Praise of Margins," connect "blue-sky" research to playing in the woods as a child? Why do you think the two activities are the same or different?

Everyday Playtime for Adults

Be a Kid Again

BY DULCE ZAMORA

WebMD Feature

REVIEWED BY CHARLOTTE E. GRAYSON MATHIS, MD

Remember making mud pies as a kid? Think of how squishy the wet soil felt between your hands, and how you loved to shape the patties. Or how about the time when you rode your bike for hours around the neighborhood, stopping only when you got tired? The days of pure fun, when you could run around without a care in the world, may seem far away with today's endless list of things to do, but it may be possible to recapture some of the enjoyment of childhood and incorporate it into a busy adult life.

How? First of all, before figuring out how to integrate playtime into the juggernaut, it may help to know exactly what we're trying to fit in. In order for something to be enjoyable, experts agree that freedom of choice and the perception of control are critical factors. For example, a person who loves gourmet cooking might not necessarily find pleasure in preparing a dinner that he or she feels roped into doing. Likewise, people who think they ought to schedule leisure time into their lives may be defeating the purpose.

It's another *should* in the day, explains Gina Dingwell, RN, coordinator of the Mind-Body Program at the Tzu Chi Institute for Complementary and Alternative Medicine in Vancouver. Dingwell says people tend to go on overdrive and pack even their off-work time with too many activities they think they should be doing, such as sports or social events. Instead of stacking up the shoulds, she recommends finding ways to ease up, and having compassion for ourselves.

too much purpose

"It's about checking in," says Dingwell, noting that the following questions might help determine whether an activity is the right thing to do at the moment: Is this going to energize me? Is it going to be putting me in a place where I'm going to feel better? Or am I just going to feel more like this is a duty?

[margin note: duty vs enjoyment.]

The answer to some of these queries entails knowing yourself, whether you are a social person, or someone who prefers more intimate settings. It will involve knowing whether you like playing softball, figuring out crossword puzzles, or watching the opera. The crucial element is that you are doing something that is inherently delightful to you, and not partaking in it because of other incentives such as guilt, pay, or social status. Take the little child who is making mud patties. He is doing it because he is enjoying himself and for no other reason. Howard E. A. Tinsley, PhD, professor emeritus of psychology at Southern Illinois University, says the proper level of stimulation is also key to enjoyment. For instance, if a person who likes to work crossword puzzles finds the clues too easy, he or she may be bored with it. On the other hand, a puzzle that requires knowing a technical vocabulary may be so difficult that there is no opportunity to feel good about filling in the spaces.

The concept of fitting in leisure time in a hectic schedule may seem impractical for some people who think they lack the hours, money, or other resources. Experts say, however, that failing to let loose may mean the difference between sickness and health. "You don't have time to make yourself sick," says Blair Justice, PhD, professor of psychology at the University of Texas School of Public Health and author of *Who Gets Sick: How Beliefs, Moods, and Thoughts Affect Your Health.* Justice says people who are stressed get into a "state of dis-ease," in which harmful chemicals such as cortisol and norepinephrine can wreak havoc on the immune system, often causing edginess and hostility. He points to studies that show a link between high levels of such chemicals in the arteries and plaque buildup leading to heart disease. In addition, in his work with patients at the University of Texas MD Anderson Cancer Center, Justice says women with breast cancer often tell him that they were under a lot of pressure prior to being diagnosed with the ailment. Stress may not have caused their illness, but it is reportedly an important factor among many (including genetics and the environment) that determine what happens inside the body.

On a brighter note, the benefits of leisure time seem bountiful. Besides the fact that it's enjoyable, it apparently elevates levels of dopamine and serotonin—nerve transmitters that are known to have pleasurable and calming properties. Depending on the chosen activity, leisure time provides a chance to connect with people, look inward, enhance skills, or get fit. It can also renew, relax, and work off steam. Among the ill, it is known to promote recovery and a sense of well-being despite disease. "You feel happier, healthier, and more fulfilled when you can do things that provide the kind of satisfaction you're looking for," says Tinsley. "Over the long term, the ability to do these kinds of things leads to a greater level of physical and mental health, and to a higher quality of life." But many of us don't need much convincing about the rewards of play. The challenge is usually how to build it into the hustle and bustle of our lives.

The scientific literature has suggested that people tend to find things such as nature, water, pets, poetry, hobbies, and the company of other humans enjoyable. "People take drugs like heroin and cocaine to raise serotonin and dopamine, but the healthy way to do it is to pet your dog, or hug your spouse, watch sunsets, or get around something beautiful in nature," says Justice, who recently hiked the Colorado Rockies with his wife and two dogs.

A full-fledged vacation is not necessary, though, to get the benefits of playtime. In fact, health advocates say it might be better to interject leisure into the scheme of the day. The best things to do depend on the person, but some suggestions include taking a walk, listening to music, window shopping, browsing through a magazine, talking to a good friend, or looking up jokes on the Internet. For the really busy folks, it might help to periodically stop what you're doing and just *breathe*. There may not be anything that can be done about the stress of the moment, but it's crucial to allow ourselves permission for downtime, and to recognize when our lives are so packed that we don't have time to reorganize or pause for perspective. "We may not completely restore and rejuvenate," says Dingwell, "but you're still a minute ahead of where you were before."

It is even possible for people to have fun while working. Those who find their jobs interesting can lose sight of the fact that they are working for a paycheck, and try to perform the appropriate tasks because they find joy in doing them. There are formal tests available to determine the careers that best suit individuals. Such exams can be found in vocational counseling centers, universities, employment agencies, and psychologists' offices.

Sources: Gina Dingwell, RN, coordinator of the Mind-Body Program at the Tzu Chi Institute for Complementary and Alternative Medicine, Vancouver. Howard E.A. Tinsley, PhD, professor emeritus of psychology, Southern Illinois University. Blair Justice, PhD, professor of psychology, University of Texas School of Public Health; author, *Who Gets Sick: How Beliefs, Moods, and Thoughts Affect Your Health.* © 2002 WebMD, Inc. All rights reserved.

Discussion Questions

1. What do experts say are the necessary factors for an activity to be enjoyable? Do you think it is possible for these factors to be present in something that is not fun? Give some reasons or examples to support your answer.

2. What are some of the things this article suggests can provide opportunities for adult play? Would each of them function that way for everyone? Explain your answer.

3. What conditions are necessary to make work fun? Do you think Frazier would be able to see a connection between work and marginal activities? Could Dillard ever define work as play? Explain your conclusions.

4. Do you think Zamora would encourage adults to participate in none, some, or all of the marginal activities discussed by Frazier, Dillard, and Mora? Why?

Class Discussion
Using Comparisons

At times, when trying to describe or explain something, it is helpful to consider that thing in relation to other familiar things. Writers often examine similarities and differences to help develop their point or achieve their purpose. This technique is referred to as comparing and contrasting. Comparisons show the ways two things are alike, and contrasts show the way two things are different. To signal the reader that what follows is a comparison, writers often use conjunctive adverbs such as *similarly* or *likewise*. To show the reader that differences are being pointed out, writers use other conjunctive adverbs such as *conversely*, *instead*, or *otherwise*.

Make two lists. For the first list, write down as many games and activities as you can think of that would be considered by Dillard and Frazier to be examples of traditional childhood play. On the other list, write down the games and activities you participated in when you were between six and twelve years of age. Compare and contrast your two lists. Using conjunctive adverbs to indicate similarities and differences in your two lists, be ready to explain to the class why you believe Frazier and Dillard would or would not approve of your childhood activities.

Homework

Here is a blog from a recent Internet site.
Write a response to his ideas.
How would you respond if you were his boss? his family? his friend?

The Importance of Free Time

Essay

BHAGWAD JAL PARK

Yesterday was Saturday and I was asked to come to work on Sunday, which is today, for three hours, though experience shows that it's usually longer than what they say. I refused to come. They say it's important. It implies that my free time and my home life are not.

I know the importance of the meeting. I know that people have flown down from other cities, and even though it wasn't planned until the last minute, the meeting will decide some critical issues. The point is, I find my home life, and what I do on Sunday, even more important.

I won't say that I have some commitment, or that I write some book, or some other occupation like that. I just waste my time. And it's very important for me to waste my time, more important than anything else. Wasting time is all for me. I wish I could waste decades of my time, but I'm forced to work. It turns out that, when I waste time for long periods, I paradoxically become more productive. My last two years which were wasted were the most productive of my life. I learned the guitar, played chess, wrote poetry and articles, picked up a bit of Japanese, and learned a good deal of psychology, among other things.

But that's hardly the point. Even if I didn't do anything productive, I still have the right to make wasting time a priority. I choose to do so.

Reviewing Your Graded Essay

After your essay has been graded by your instructor, you may have the opportunity to revise your paper and raise your grade. Even if you are not submitting a revised version of this essay to your instructor, it is important that you review your work carefully in order to understand its strengths and weaknesses. This sheet will guide you through the evaluation process.

You will want to continue to use the techniques that worked well for you and to find strategies to overcome the problems that you identify in this sample of your writing. In order to help yourself recognize areas that might have been problematic for you, look back at the scoring rubric in this book. Match the numerical/verbal/letter grade received on your essay to the appropriate category. Study the explanation given on the rubric for your grade.

Write a few sentences below in which you identify your problems in each of the following areas. Then, suggest specific changes you could make that would improve your paper. Don't forget to use your handbook as a resource.

1. Grammar/mechanics

My problem:

My strategy for change:

2. Thesis/response to assignment

My problem:

My strategy for change:

3. Organization

My problem:

My strategy for change:

4. Paragraph development/examples/reasoning

My problem:

My strategy for change:

5. Assessment

In the space below, assign a grade to your paper using a rubric other than the one used by your instructor. In other words, if your instructor assigned your essay a grade of *High Fail*, you might give it the letter grade you now feel the paper warrants. If your instructor used the traditional letter grade to evaluate the essay, choose a category from the rubric in this book, or any other grading scale that you are familiar with, to show your evaluation of your work. Then write a short narrative explaining your evaluation of the essay and the reasons it received the grade you gave it.

Grade:_____

Narrative:_____

_____

_____

_____

_____

Assignment 2

"Buried Alive: Our Children and the Avalanche of Crud"

This unit focuses on popular culture and its effect on our lives. In order to write a successful essay, you will have to understand what is meant by "popular culture" and present a compelling argument about its influence on all of us, particularly young people. David Denby writes the lead essay that you will respond to in an essay of your own. Read his essay carefully to determine the position he takes on the way popular culture affects young people today, and then study the writing topic that follows it. Just as you did in Assignment 1, be sure to make good use of the sections that follow Denby's essay. Fill these pages in thoroughly and carefully because they will help you to understand Denby's ideas and develop your own argument in response to the writing topic.

We hope you realize, now that you have completed Assignment 1, the value in doing extensive prewriting as you work on an essay. Be sure to make good use of the prewriting and drafting exercises in Assignment 2. Instructors have told us that they can always tell which students are using these pages because their essays are consistently more successful than the essays of those students who skip these helpful exercises. That said, feel free to use these supporting exercises in ways that suit your own thinking and writing style.

Buried Alive: Our Children and the Avalanche of Crud

Essay

DAVID DENBY

David Denby is an American journalist and a film critic for The New Yorker. *He has a B.A. and a master's in journalism from Columbia University. His book* Great Books: My Adventures with Homer, Rousseau, Woolf, and Other Indestructible Writers of the Western World *(1996) is an important study of canonical literature at American universities and was a* New York Times *bestseller. His memoir* American Sucker *(2004) details his investment misadventures in the dot-com stock market bubble, and his latest book,* Snark, *is a polemical dissection of public speech. The following essay is adapted from an essay published in* The New Yorker *(1996).*

To my surprise, I find myself welcoming, or at least not opposing, the advent of the V-chip—the little device that is to be installed in new television sets sold from 1998 on and that will allow parents to block out programs they don't want their children to see. Many parents I know have similar feelings, and quite a few are surprised by the depths of their ambivalence about the way pop culture in all its forms has invaded their homes, and the habits, manners, and souls of their children. My friends are drawn from a small circle of well-educated New Yorkers; we are a fairly compact and no doubt privileged group. Yet our anguish about bringing up children is, I believe, widely shared by parents of all kinds. *Married...with Children* and the computer game *Doom* are the same in Montana and in Manhattan.

Even parents who enjoy their share of pop are feeling wary and sore, as if someone has made fools of them. And a few parents I know have given themselves over to bitter rage and are locked in an unwinnable struggle to shut out pop culture and the life of the streets—the two are now indistinguishable—from their children's experience.

Someone is bound to say, "It was ever thus," meaning that, as far as their elders are concerned, every generation of children is immersed in something that's no good for them. New York kids in the eighteen-sixties grew up in a rough city with gangs, street violence,

1860s

and prostitutes, and most of them were no doubt familiar with such raucous and unenlightening entertainments as cockfighting and bare-knuckle boxing. It was ever thus. Someone is bound to say, "After all, many of us watched a good bit of TV as children, yet we wound up O.K., didn't we? What has changed?"

It was not ever thus. Our reality has changed. The media have become three-dimensional, inescapable, omnivorous, and self-referring—a closed system that seems, for many of the kids, to answer all their questions. The older children teach the younger ones the games and movie references, so they have something to talk about when they're alone. I've just run into a three-year-old girl who knew the names of the characters in *The Hunchback of Notre Dame* before the movie opened. Disney has already claimed her. Pop has also absorbed the edgy, in-your-face tone that teenagers adopt as the sound of independence. That jeering tone has spread like a rash through the whole culture. "It's awesome." "It sucks."

Some sort of commercialized aggression is always putting parents on the defensive—Jim Carrey with ketchup coming out of his ears in movie after movie, or Sylvester Stallone machine-gunning the population of Cleveland, or video arcades with so many shooting games that the noise level exceeds that of the Battle of the Somme. *Beavis and Butthead* is a clever show—it mocks the cruddy teen culture even as it sells it to teens. The show brilliantly sends itself up. Still, it's hard to take. Hip parents may appreciate the wryness of B. & B.'s self-extinction, but it's dismaying that everything on teen TV—even irony—is a commodity.

The kids in the dating-game programs treat each other as commodities, the girls swinging their shoulders and smiling as they show themselves off, the audience whooping as the boys pull off their shirts and reveal their pecs and tattoos. Hardly the end of Western civilization, I admit, but the way the shows force teens to stereotype one another is awful. Children don't understand vulgarity as a concept, and the makers of commercial culture would be happy if they never understood it. Parents have to teach them what vulgarity is somehow. When I have the energy, I argue, I satirize, I get the boys to agree that the shows are stupid. Yet I don't turn off the set, because doing that would only cause them to turn it back on when I'm not there. I want *them* to turn it off.

Whether the sets are off or on, the cruddy tone is in the air and on the streets. The kids pick it up and repeat it, and every week there are moments when I feel a spasm of fury that surges back and forth

how kids are harmed

between resentment and self-contempt. In those moments, I don't like the way my boys talk—I don't like the way they think. The crude, bottom-line attitudes they've picked up, the nutty obsessive profanity, the echo chamber of voices and attitudes, set my teeth on edge. What American parent hasn't felt that spasm? Your kid is rude and surly, sees everything in terms of winning or losing or popularity, becomes insanely interested in clothes, and seems far, far from courage and selfhood.

Aided by armies of psychologists and market researchers, the culture industries reach my children at every stage of their desires and their inevitable discontent. What's lost is the old dream that parents and teachers will nurture the organic development of the child's own interests, the child's own nature. That dream is largely dead. In this country, people possessed solely by the desire to sell have become far more powerful than parents tortuously working out the contradictions of authority, freedom, education, and soul-making.

Writing Topic

What does Denby think is distinctive and damaging about the way popular culture influences children in the United States today? Do you agree with his view? Be sure to discuss specific examples to support your position; these examples may be taken from your own experiences or observations, or from any of your reading, including the course material we have read and discussed in class.

Vocabulary Check

Good writers choose their words carefully so that their ideas will be clear. In order for you, the reader, to understand an essay, it is important to think about its key vocabulary terms and the way they are used by the author. Words can have a variety of meanings, or they can have specialized meanings in certain contexts. Look up the definitions of the following words or phrases from the essay. Choose the meaning that you think Denby intended when he selected that particular word or phrase for use in this essay. Then explain the way the meaning or concept behind the definition is key to understanding the author's argument.

self-referential

   definition: _____

   _____

   _____

   _____

   explanation: _____

   _____

   _____

   _____

   _____

commodity

   definition: _____

   _____

   _____

   _____

   explanation: _____

_____

_____

_____

_____

_____

vulgarity

   definition: _____

_____

_____

_____

   explanation: _____

_____

_____

_____

_____

_____

Questions to Guide Your Reading

Answer the following questions to ensure that you have a sound comprehension of "Buried Alive: Our Children and the Avalanche of Crud."

Paragraph 1

What kinds of feelings do the parents in Denby's social group have about the V-chip?

Paragraph 2

Why do you think the author says many parents are engaged in an "unwinnable struggle"?

Paragraph 3

What does he think people commonly say in response to the concerns of these parents?

Paragraph 4

Why does Denby say that "reality has changed"?

Paragraphs 5–6

Explain why Denby thinks that the content of material presented to teenagers on television is a "commodity."

Paragraph 7

How, according to Denby, have the attitudes conveyed in television shows manifested in the behaviors and values of American children?

Paragraph 8

How, according to Denby, has television managed to appropriate the parental role?

Prewriting for a Directed Summary

Just as you did in Assignment 1, take time now to answer the questions below. Your answers will help you to focus on *a particular idea* in Denby's essay, and this greater understanding will enable you to respond effectively to the first question in the writing topic:

> first part of the writing topic: *What does Denby think is distinctive and damaging about the way popular culture influences children in the United States today?*

It is important to keep in mind the exact wording of the writing topic. If you write an introductory paragraph that summarizes Denby's *entire* essay, your opening will suggest that you did not pay careful enough attention to the writing topic or that you did not fully understand Denby's ideas. Be sure to notice two of the key terms in the question, "distinctive" and "damaging." When you begin drafting your essay, your introduction will have to summarize the *important characteristics of popular culture* that Denby is talking about as well as the *damaging effects* these characteristics have on young people. The answers to the questions below will help you to do that effectively.

Hint

Don't forget to review Part 1's "Guidelines for Writing a Directed Summary."

Focus Questions

1. How, according to Denby, does the cultural reality imposed on children by the media make the world of childhood different from the way it always was in the past?

2. What category of behaviors portrayed in the media puts parents in a defensive position, according to Denby?

3. How do television shows such as dating-game programs teach children to treat each other, according to Denby?

4. In Denby's argument, how do children act and think because of their media experiences?

5. What does Denby believe is lost from the process of childhood development because of our media culture?

Opinion and Working Thesis Statement

The second question in the writing topic that follows "Buried Alive: Our Children and the Avalanche of Crud" asks you to take a position of your own. Your response will become the thesis statement of your essay, so it is important to spend some time ensuring that it is fully developed and that it accurately reflects the position you want to take on the topic. Use the framework below to help you develop your thesis. But as you move through the remaining pages in this assignment, keep an open mind. You may want to modify, or even reverse, your position once you have read the background essays in the "Extended Activities" section, and have thought more carefully and systematically about the subject.

second part of the writing topic: *Do you agree with his view?*

Do you think that Denby's portrayal, both of popular culture and its effects, is valid? At this stage of the writing process, simply put down the view you have now and think of it as your "working thesis" rather than your final one.

Hint

Even if you are prepared to write a working thesis now, be sure to keep an open mind because, as you think more carefully about the subject and develop some strong supporting topics, you may want to revise it to reflect your more thoughtful viewpoint.

1. Use the following **thesis frame** to identify the basic elements of your working thesis statement:

   a. What is the main subject of "Buried Alive: Our Children and the Avalanche of Crud" that the writing topic questions ask you to consider?

   _____

   b. What is Denby's opinion about that subject?

   _____

   c. What is your opinion about the subject, and will you agree or disagree with Denby's opinion?

   _____

   _____

   _____

2. Now use the elements you isolated in the thesis frame to write a working thesis statement. You may have to revise it several times until it captures your idea clearly.

   _____

   _____

3. When you've finished, check to see that you've made clear your position on popular culture and its effects on young people and that you've stated your position in relation to Denby's.

Hint

Turn back to Part 1's "A Suggested Structure for an Essay" and look at the elements that are included in the introduction. Note that, when you use this particular structure, the thesis statement commonly comes at the end of the introductory paragraph. Later, as you begin drafting your essay, remember to include the thesis statement you work out on this page and in the "Revising Your Thesis Statement" page.

Prewriting to Find Support for Your Thesis Statement

The third part of the writing topic asks you to support the argument you put forward in your thesis statement:

> third part of the writing topic: *Be sure to discuss specific examples to support your position; these examples may be taken from your own experiences or observations, or from any of your reading, including the course material we have read and discussed in class.*

Your response to this part of the writing topic will form the basis for the majority of your essay. Hence, it is important that you work carefully and at length with the below directives. The more time you spend working with them, the more ideas you will form and, in turn, the more interesting and compelling your final essay will be. As you work with these directives, feel free to make lists, look up key words in a dictionary and thesaurus, freewrite, draw flowcharts or diagrams, or use any other means you can think of to broaden and deepen your thinking. Your responses will become the material you will use in the next stage—planning and writing the essay.

Although you will naturally begin looking for evidence and examples that support the working thesis statement you developed on the previous page, try not to limit your thinking. Allow alternative viewpoints to develop, if that is where your exploration leads you. You can always modify your thesis statement, if necessary.

Some Questions and Directives to Help You Develop Your Ideas

1. What television shows do you watch on a regular basis? What television shows are popular among your friends? List them and then next to each add some of the details that you think make the show popular.

After you complete your list, look back at Denby's essay and list the characteristics he associates with television's representations of popular culture. Do you find these characteristics in any of the shows you listed, even if your interpretation of their portrayal of popular culture differs from Denby's? Go back to your list and after each show you have named, write down the ways in which popular culture is depicted. For example, if the show has young people in it, how do they dress, talk, and act? What do they do for fun? How do they interact with the adults in the show? How do they act with each other? How would you describe the overall representation of popular culture in the majority of these shows? Are there exceptions? If so, explain.

2. Other than television, can you think of any other media that contain forms of popular culture, such as the Internet, music videos, magazines, or advertisements you and your friends are exposed to frequently? List all the examples you can think of. Again, look back at the characteristics Denby associates with television's representations of popular culture. Do you find these characteristics in any of the other media forms you listed, even if your interpretation of these characteristics differs from Denby's? Go back to your list and, after each example you have named, write down the ways in which popular culture is depicted.

Once you've written your lists and ideas, look them over carefully. Try to group ideas into categories and give each category a label. In other words, cluster ideas that seem to have something in common and, for each cluster, identify that shared quality by giving it a name. These categories may become the supporting foundation for your argument.

3. Now broaden your focus; list or freewrite about examples from your studies, your readings, and your knowledge of current events. Where do you see patterns of popular culture in this larger sphere? Do Denby's observations of pop culture and its influence seem true? What examples might you use to demonstrate the dominant patterns you see between media representations of pop culture and the representation of pop culture you see in society as a whole?

    Once you've written your ideas, look them over carefully. Try to group your ideas into categories. Then give each category a label. In other words, cluster ideas that seem to have something in common and, for each cluster, identify that shared quality by giving it a name. Again, some or all of these categories may offer the supporting topics for your thesis statement.

4. Once you've created topics by clustering your ideas into categories, go through them and pick two or three specific ones to develop in your essay. Make sure they are relevant to your thesis and that they have enough substance to be compelling to your reader. Then, in the space below, briefly summarize each item.

    Once you've decided which items and categories on your lists you will use in your essay, take some time to explain below how each category and its items connect to your thesis statement. You will use these details for the next stage.

Revising Your Thesis Statement

Now that you have spent some time working out your ideas more systematically and developing some supporting evidence for the position you want to take, look again at the working thesis statement you crafted earlier to see if it is still accurate. As your first step, look again at the writing topic and then write your original working thesis on the lines that follow it:

second part of the writing topic: *Do you agree with his view?*

Working Thesis Statement:

_____

_____

_____

Take some time now to see if you want to revise your thesis statement. Often, after extensive prewriting and focused thought, you realize that the working thesis statement is no longer an accurate reflection of what you plan to say in your essay. Sometimes, only a word or phrase must be added or deleted; other times, the thesis statement must be significantly rewritten.

After examining your working thesis statement and completing any necessary revisions, check it one more time by asking yourself the following questions:

a. Does the thesis directly identify Denby's argument that popular culture is degrading young people today?

b. Do you clearly state your argument regarding popular culture and its effects on youth?

If you answered "no" to either of these questions, revise your thesis statement once more to add the missing elements.

_____

_____

Planning and Drafting Your Essay

Now that you have examined Denby's argument and have thought at length about your own views, you are ready to draft an essay that responds to all parts of the writing topic. Do not neglect to use the material you developed in the earlier pages of this assignment to compose your draft: the "Prewriting for a Directed Summary" pages will give you the language and information necessary to draft your essay's introduction; the "Opinion and Working Thesis Statement" page and the "Revising Your Thesis Statement" page will help you answer the second part of the writing topic and will ensure that your essay has a clear argument to make; and the "Prewriting to Find Support for Your Thesis Statement" pages will give you the supporting elements (the 4Cs) for your thesis statement.

Getting started on the draft is often the hardest part of the writing process because this is where you move from exploring and planning to getting your ideas down in a unified, coherent shape. Creating an outline will give you a basic structure for incorporating all the ideas you have developed in the preceding pages. An outline will also give you a bird's-eye view of your essay and help you spot problems in development or logic.

Hint

This outline doesn't have to contain polished writing. You may only want to fill in the basic ideas in phrases or terms.

Creating an Outline for Your Draft

I. **Introductory Paragraph**

   A. An opening sentence that gives the reading selection's title and author and begins to answer the first part of the writing topic:

   _____

   B. Main points to include in the directed summary:

   1.

   2.

   3.

   4.

C. Look again at the thesis statement you wrote in "Revising Your Thesis Statement" and make any changes you think necessary. Then copy your thesis statement below. It should clearly agree or disagree with the argument put forward in "Buried Alive: Our Children and the Avalanche of Crud," and it should clearly state your position using your own words.

_____

II. Body Paragraphs

A. Subject of the paragraph: _Miley Cyrus SelenaGomez & Influence._

   1. **C**ontrolling idea sentence:

_____

   2. **C**orroborating details:

_____

_____

_____

   3. **C**areful description of the details' relevance:

_____

_____

_____

_____

_____

   4. **C**onnection to the thesis statement:

_____

B. Subject of the paragraph: _Steinheimer's Truth about culture_

   1. **C**ontrolling idea sentence:

     Popculture is not the sole culprit, It has assistants

     Pop culture turns kids into whatever is

        ^sponge

    advertised.

2. <u>C</u>orroborating details:

_____

_____

_____

3. <u>C</u>areful description of the details' relevance:

_____

_____

_____

_____

_____

4. <u>C</u>onnection to the thesis statement:

_____

C. Subject of the paragraph: <u>Personal Experience'</u>

1. <u>C</u>ontrolling idea sentence:

_____

2. <u>C</u>orroborating details:

_____

_____

3. <u>C</u>areful description of the details' relevance:

_____

_____

_____

_____

_____

4. **C**onnection to the thesis statement:

   _____

D. Subject of the paragraph: _____
   1. **C**ontrolling idea sentence:

      _____

   2. **C**orroborating details:

      _____

      _____

      _____

   3. **C**areful description of the details' relevance:

      _____

      _____

      _____

      _____

      _____

   4. **C**onnection to the thesis statement:

      _____

III. Conclusion

A. Type of conclusion to be used:

   _____

B. Key words or phrases to include:

   _____

Doing a Peer Draft Review

It is difficult to find weaknesses in our own writing, especially writing that we have recently completed. Hence, getting a classmate to read and respond to your draft can be a great opportunity to find weak spots in your essay that you had not noticed. After completing the rough draft of your essay, have a classmate read it and use the form below to give you some constructive feedback on the draft's strengths and weaknesses. Use the feedback you receive as a guide to revising your essay once more to ensure that it best represents your argument.

   If you are asked to use the form below to respond to a classmate's draft, be sure to offer as much constructive feedback as possible. Spend time reading the draft and examining its parts carefully to identify problems and recognize successes. Give as much feedback as you can in writing so that the essay's writer can take your feedback home and use it to do one more revision.

1. Discuss this introduction's success in accomplishing each of the tasks of an essay's opening paragraph. (See "An Introduction in an Argument Essay" in Part 1 for discussion of the goals of an introductory paragraph.)

2. Look at the directed summary of Denby's argument presented in this paper. Point out any inaccuracies or irrelevant material and identify any important but missing points of the argument. (See "Guidelines for Writing a Directed Summary" in Part 1 for a review of summary requirements.)

3. Consider the overall argument presented in this essay: in what ways does the body of the paper adequately support the thesis of the paper; which specific paragraphs need further development; where are the connections unclear between the thesis and the body paragraphs? (See "Writing Paragraphs that Support Your Thesis" in Part 1 for a reminder of the parts necessary for fully developed paragraphs and essays.)

4. Read the conclusion of this essay. What makes it effective and/or ineffective in providing closure to the essay?

5. Give the writer your overall impression of this draft. What, in your opinion, does this essay do particularly well, and what parts of the essay should the writer focus his or her attention on during the revision process?

Final Draft Check List

This checklist will help you do your own final check to ensure that your essay is complete and correct. If you find you cannot put a check mark next to one of the items below, go back to Part 1 and review the requirements for the aspect of your essay that still needs some work. For grammar and mechanical problems, use the table of contents and the index in your handbook to help you correct any errors.

Content:

- My essay has an appropriate title.
- I provide an accurate summary of the position on the topic set out by David Denby in "Buried Alive: Our Children and the Avalanche of Crud."
- My thesis statement takes a position that can be defended.
- I have a sufficient number of body paragraphs to support my thesis.
- Each body paragraph is relevant to my thesis.
- Each body paragraph contains the 4Cs.
- I use transitions whenever necessary to connect paragraphs and ideas to each other.
- The final paragraph of my essay (the conclusion) provides readers with a sense of closure.

Grammar and Mechanics:

- I use the present tense to discuss Denby's argument and supporting examples.
- All of my verb tense shifts make sense in terms of chronology.
- I use verb tense consistently throughout my sentences and paragraphs.
- My sentences begin and end with the correct punctuation.
- If I present items in a series (nouns, verbs, prepositional phrases), they are parallel in form.
- If I include material spoken or written by someone other than myself, I have correctly punctuated it with quotation marks and other necessary punctuation.
- I have checked for subject-verb agreement in all of my sentences.

Extended Activities

Readings

"The Parable of the Ring Around the Collar" by Neil Postman

"How Well Does Television Handle Social Issues?" by Elizabeth Thoman

"As the World Watches: Media Events Are Modern 'Holy Days'" by Rosalind Silver

"Storytellers Shape Spiritual Values" by Michael Warren

"Addicted to Violence: Has the American Dream Become a Nightmare?" by Charles M. Johnston

"Altered States: How Television Changes Childhood," an excerpt of an interview with Joshua Meyrowitz by Barbara Osborn

"The Truth about Pop Culture's Influence on Children" by Karen Sternheimer

Homework

"Ways today's youth sound like completely uneducated apes (oh and please stop)"—A Blog from July 2008

Reviewing Your Graded Essay

The Parable of the Ring Around the Collar

Essay

NEIL POSTMAN

Neil Postman was an American critic and educator. Postman received his B.S. from the State University of New York and his M.A. and Ed.D. from Columbia University. He was the Paulette Goddard Chair of Media Ecology at New York University and Chair of the Department of Culture and Communication. His pedagogical and scholarly interests included media and education, as can be seen in many of his seventeen books, including Amusing Ourselves to Death *(1985).*

Television commercials are a form of religious literature. To comment on them in a serious vein is to practice hermeneutics, the branch of theology concerned with interpreting and explaining the Scriptures. This is what I propose to do here. The heathens, heretics, and unbelievers may move on to something else.

I do not claim, for a start, that every television commercial has religious content. Just as in church the pastor will sometimes call the congregation's attention to non-ecclesiastical matters, so there are television commercials that are entirely secular. Someone has something to sell; you are told what it is, where it can be obtained, and what it costs. Though these may be shrill and offensive, no doctrine is advanced and no theology invoked.

But the majority of important television commercials take the form of religious parables organized around a coherent theology. Like all religious parables, they put forward a concept of sin, intimations of the way to redemption, and a vision of Heaven. They also suggest what are the roots of evil and what are the obligations of the holy. Consider, for example, the Parable of the Ring Around the Collar. This is to television scripture what the Parable of the Prodigal Son is to the Bible, which is to say it is an archetype containing most of the elements of form and content that recur in its genre. To begin with, the Parable of the Ring Around the Collar is short, occupying only about thirty seconds of one's time and attention. There are three reasons for this, all obvious. First, it is expensive to preach on television; second, the attention span of the congregation is not long and is highly vulnerable to distraction; and third, a parable does not need to be long—tradition dictating that its narrative structure be tight, its symbols unambiguous, its explication terse.

The narrative structure of the Parable of the Ring Around the Collar is, indeed, comfortably traditional. The story has a beginning, a middle, and an end. A married couple is depicted in some relaxed setting—a restaurant, say—in which they are enjoying each other's company and generally having a wonderful time. But then a waitress approaches their table, notices that the man has a dirty collar, stares at it boldly, sneers with cold contempt, and announces to all within hearing the nature of his transgression. The man is humiliated and glares at his wife with scorn, for she is the source of his shame. She, in turn, assumes an expression of self-loathing mixed with a touch of self-pity. This is the parable's beginning: the presentation of the problem. The parable continues by showing the wife at home using a detergent that never fails to eliminate dirt around the collars of men's shirts. She proudly shows her husband what she is doing, and he forgives her with an adoring smile. This is the parable's middle: the solution of the problem. Finally, we are shown the couple in a restaurant once again, but this time they are free of the waitress's probing eyes and bitter social chastisement. This is the parable's end: the moral, the explication, the exegesis. From this, we should draw the proper conclusion.

As in all parables, behind the apparent simplicity there are some profound ideas to ponder. Among the most subtle and important is the notion of where and how problems originate. Embedded in every belief system there is an assumption about the root cause of evil from which the varieties of sinning take form. In science, for example, evil is represented in superstition. In psychoanalysis, we find it in early, neurotic transactions with our parents. In Christianity, it is located in the concept of Original Sin. In television-commercial parables, the root cause of evil is Technological Innocence, a failure to know the particulars of the beneficent accomplishments of industrial progress. This is the primary source of unhappiness, humiliation, and discord in life. And, as forcefully depicted in the Parable of the Ring, the consequences of technological innocence may strike at any time, without warning, and with the full force of their disintegrating action.

The sudden striking power of technological innocence is a particularly important feature of television-commercial theology, for it is a constant reminder of the congregation's vulnerability. One must never be complacent or, worse, self-congratulatory. To attempt to live without technological sophistication is at all times dangerous, since the evidence of one's *naiveté* will always be painfully visible to the vigilant. The vigilant may be a waitress, a friend, a neighbor, or even a spectral figure—a holy ghost, as it were—who materializes in your kitchen, from nowhere, to give witness to your sluggardly ignorance.

Technological innocence refers not only to ignorance of detergents, drugs, sanitary napkins, cars, salves, and foodstuffs, but also to ignorance of technical machinery such as savings banks and transportation systems. One may, for example, come upon one's neighbors while on vacation (in television-commercial parables, this is always a sign of danger) and discover that they have invested their money in a certain bank of whose special interest rates you have been unaware. This is, of course, a moral disaster, and both you and your vacation are doomed.

As demonstrated in the Ring Parable, there is a path to redemption, but it can be entered only on two conditions. The first requires that you be open to advice or social criticism from those who are more enlightened. In the Ring Parable, the waitress serves the function of counselor, although she is, to be sure, exacting and very close to unforgiving. In some parables, the adviser is rather more sarcastic than severe. But in most parables, as for example in all sanitary napkin, mouthwash, shampoo, and aspirin commercials, the advisers are amiable and sympathetic, perhaps all too aware of their own vulnerability on other matters.

The Innocent are required to accept instruction in the spirit in which it is offered. This cannot be stressed enough, for it instructs the congregation in two lessons simultaneously: one must be eager to accept advice, and just as eager to give it. Giving advice is, so to speak, the principal obligation of the holy. In fact, the ideal religious community may be depicted in images of dozens of people, each in his or her turn giving and taking advice on technological advances.

The second condition involves one's willingness to act on the advice given. As in traditional Christian theology, it is not sufficient to hear the gospel or even preach it. One's understanding must be expressed in good works. In the Ring Parable, the once-pitiable wife acts almost immediately, and the parable concludes by showing the congregation the effects of her action. In the Parable of the Person with Rotten Breath, of which there are several versions, we are shown a woman who, ignorant of the technological solution to her problem, is enlightened by a supportive roommate. The woman takes the advice without delay, with results we are shown in the last five seconds: a honeymoon in Hawaii. In the Parable of the Stupid Investor, we are shown a man who knows not how to make his money make money. Upon enlightenment, he acts swiftly and, at the parable's end, he is rewarded with a car, or a trip to Hawaii, or something approximating peace of mind.

Because of the compactness of commercial parables, the ending—that is, the last five seconds—must serve a dual purpose. It is, of course, the moral of the story: if one will act in such a way, this will be the reward. But in being shown the result, we are also shown an image of Heaven. Occasionally, as in the Parable of the Lost Traveler's Checks, we are given a glimpse of Hell: Technological Innocents lost and condemned to eternal wandering far from their native land. But mostly we are given images of a Heaven both accessible and delicious: that is, a Heaven that is here, now, on earth, in America, and quite often in Hawaii.

But Hawaii is only a convenient recurring symbol. Heaven can, in fact, materialize and envelop you anywhere. In the Parable of the Man Who Runs Through Airports, Heaven is found at a car-rental counter to which the confounded Runner is shepherded by an angelic messenger. The expression of ecstasy on the Runner's face tells clearly that this moment is as close to transcendence as he can ever hope for.

Ecstasy is the key idea here, for commercial parables depict the varieties of ecstasy in as much detail as you will find in any body of religious literature. At the conclusion of the Parable of the Spotted Glassware, a husband and wife assume such ecstatic countenances as can only be described by the word "beatification." Even in the Ring Parable, which at first glance would not seem to pose as serious a moral crisis as spotted glassware, we are shown ecstasy, pure and serene. And where ecstasy is, so is Heaven. Heaven, in brief, is any place where someone has joined his or her soul with the Deity—the Deity, of course, being Technology.

Just when, as a religious people, we replaced our faith in traditional ideas of God with a belief in the ennobling force of Technology is not easy to say. Television commercials played no role in bringing about this transformation, but they reflect the change, document it, and amplify it. They constitute the most abundant literature we possess of our new spiritual commitment. That is why we have a solemn obligation to keep television commercials under the continuous scrutiny of hermeneutics.

Discussion Questions

1. Discuss the analogy Postman draws between television commercials and religious parables. How do television advertisements function, according to him? Does Postman's explanation change the way you will view these commercials in the future? Do you feel offended/enlightened/something else by Postman's analogy?

2. Discuss television commercials in terms of narrative structure. In your experience, have the majority of commercials followed this structure? Give examples to illustrate your answer.

3. How do television commercials define both sin and redemption? In your opinion, are today's television-viewing children sophisticated or unsophisticated enough to accept such a message from these advertisements?

How Well Does Television Handle Social Issues?

ELIZABETH THOMAN

Elizabeth Thoman, a pioneering leader in the U.S. media literacy field, founded Media&Values *magazine in 1977 and the Center for Media Literacy in 1989. She is a graduate of the Annenberg School for Communication at the University of Southern California and continues her leadership through consulting, speaking, and serving as a founding board member of the Alliance for a Media Literate America (AMLA).*

Ever since Newton Minow, then chairman of the Federal Communications Commission, accused television of being a "vast wasteland," media analysts have debated whether television indeed has any redeeming social value. Television has changed considerably since Minow's statement, and many formerly taboo subjects are now treated openly, even on prime-time. Compared to the insipid content of the early days of television, today's programming is often bold and provocative, with society the better for millions of viewers having experienced the anguish of marriage to a man who is violently abusive (*The Burning Bed*), the tragic consequences of incest (*Something About Amelia*), or the potential devastation of nuclear war (*The Day After*). Nevertheless, Minow's assessment still haunts us.

Norman Lear is generally credited with having stimulated the shift to "socially relevant" television programming. His lovable bigot Archie Bunker paved the way in the early seventies not only to a new kind of television comedy, but to programming that could cover controversial issues of personal and social significance: Maude's abortion, Edith's rape, Meathead's anti-war activism. With the advent of "ensemble shows" like *Hill Street Blues* and *St. Elsewhere*, continuing dramatic series began to incorporate more gritty realism into plots and characters. Now not only do physicians treat disease in others, on *St. Elsewhere* they become patients themselves. Cops not only confront crime in the streets, but Mary Beth Lacey has her house robbed and her colleague Izbecki buys illegal drugs to ease the lingering death of his much-loved mother. On such programs viewers see the intricacy of human suffering and the complexity of values decisions, as well as the complications of relationships among characters whose values and backgrounds differ—sometimes even clash.

However, it is in the long-form features—the made-for-television movies and mini-series—where social issues have been handled most effectively. Although many laugh at the "disease of the week" syndrome, still, done with passion and compassion, a two-hour (or more) drama has the time and the talent (along with the budget) to create a dramatic experience that can be both profound and challenging for the viewer.

I believe, in fact, that many extraordinary television productions have served at least to set the national agenda regarding many confusing social issues. No one can know or understand all the causes of teenage suicide or the mysterious progress of Alzheimer's disease. Yet both can touch lives suddenly and tragically. For many adult Americans, prime-time television is the only "continuing education" available to learn to cope with contemporary crises. Entertainment programs may or may not be profound. But they are socially useful for many millions of people. I am, however, drawn to a deeper question—and a deeper reflection. It has to do with what kinds of issues are handled, even the ones that are handled "well." I do not have to be a sociologist to see that there are basically two kinds of problems confronting us or any society:

- Personal-social problems are primarily person-centered, that is, they consist of extraordinary circumstances that affect individuals or individual units of society—usually, crises in relationships or health. Every year the list gets longer but includes rape, spouse abuse, missing children, teen suicide, anorexia, cancer, AIDS, drug and alcohol addiction, mental illness, etc.

- Such problems—although personal in nature—become problems for society as a whole when the sheer quantity of persons affected challenges our ability to provide both understanding and assistance to those involved.

- Social-political issues include those more global concerns which can, indeed, affect individuals, but which individuals—by themselves—cannot begin to handle: the arms race, the impact of the world debt, racism and sexism, the effects of colonialism in developing nations, homelessness, and so on.

- To confront these kinds of issues requires commitment by individuals, institutions and governments; they also generally call into question the established social, political, cultural and economic structures of society.

Now a survey of television of the 80s indicates that the social issues that television generally handles are primarily the ones that fall under the personal-social category. This is easily rationalized since the very nature of these issues makes them coverable as somebody's story. Defenders of television are quick to remind one that this is so and will always be so, because television is a business and its task is not to create a social conscience in the viewing public, but to deliver an audience to its advertisers. To maximize this potential, television needs entertainment, and entertainment, if it is to hold the attention of the audience, requires a story about people caught up in conflict, adventure or romance that moves in clear dramatic progress from beginning to middle to end. Stories, it is true, are the very stuff of television.

And it is also true that millions and millions of people form their vision of social reality primarily by the kinds of stories they see day after day on television. Despite protestations that television "just entertains," even the public knows it does more than that. In the past months, media leaders have acknowledged responsibility for media's role in a major social problem: drug use. Film and television representatives have voluntarily agreed to monitor more carefully the images they present of drug use and abuse. In doing so, the industry admitted that it knows it has power to do more than create laughs and sell automobiles. Television is one of the mirrors by which Americans view themselves and their society. By watching and listening over months and years, one learns to act—with a conscience or without.

Not that we haven't occasionally seen entertaining stories that incorporated a larger worldview. There was, after all, *The Day After*. *M*A*S*H* offered profound episodes on the futility of war and, most recently, *Cagney and Lacey* confronted the dilemma of apartheid when the team was assigned to protect a South African marathon runner. But it is not enough. It is not enough because by experiencing only a world of personal-social problems, TV viewers are left with a false sense of the relative importance of the issues facing our society and each of us as members of that society, and as inhabitants of the planet. It is not enough because focusing primarily on individuals overcoming personal obstacles distorts the truth of the real world where there are forces beyond the living room—or bedroom—that are conspiring toward massive economic and political exploitation, and even global annihilation.

Some will argue that, given the entertainment role of prime-time television, serious global issues are best left to PBS documentaries, the news, history books or perhaps as the subject of critically acclaimed theatrical films—*Testament*, for example, or *Missing*, or *Platoon*. The fact that serious films often find their way to prime-time television a few years later serves to underscore the real reason behind this argument—television is, by its very nature, timid.

Gary David Goldberg relates how he once pitched an idea for a network series about a group of press people stationed in Vietnam. It would have had the usual motley crew of characters and poignant but pointed drama, perhaps not unlike the highly popular *M*A*S*H*. But he proposed the series in the late 1970s, and the network turned it down flat. The reality of Vietnam was still too near, he was told. *M*A*S*H* is clearly the most exceptional series on the issues of war and peace. Still, the setting was the Korean War—long before most current U.S. TV watchers were born. In the worldview of commercial television in the 1970s it was acceptable to do a series set in Korea, but not in Vietnam. In Korea, remember, we didn't suffer the same losses. Because television—as a business more than an art form—is integrally intertwined with the capitalist economy, to challenge the economic and political system that glues capitalism together is potentially to bite the very hand that feeds it. It is not only easier then, but politically safer, to commission a two-hour movie on AIDS or even incest than one on the destruction of indigenous cultures in the Third World resulting from the aggressive marketing of consumer products to countries that can barely build and sustain a subsistence economy.

As members of the human family, we must not be lulled into complacency by easy public service issues—whether on television or in everyday life. Frankly, I believe that the most significant values question facing us today is not one of personal sexuality but rather economic justice: What kind of world do we create when the rich just get richer while the poor don't count? Unless television can make clear the economic, cultural and political meanings behind social conditions, then all of its docudramas and socially relevant sitcoms will be "like sounding brass and tinkling cymbals."

Of course, the reply from the creative community will be that this is "not anybody's story." But I just cannot believe that somewhere in Hollywood there is not a drama waiting to be written—or that possibly already has been written but is sitting on the shelf—about the questions someone is feeling about their part in contributing to the economic exploitation of, for instance, women factory workers in the Orient by the same multinational corporations that are the biggest advertisers on U.S. network television.

I doubt, however, that it will ever get on prime-time. And until it does, I don't think we can really talk about how "well" television handles the social issues of our day.

Discussion Questions

1. Why does the author believe that television today is less the "vast wasteland" it was when Newton Minow coined the term? In what ways do you think television programming has changed for the better and for the worse? In what ways do your answers change when discussing children's television?

2. Do you think television has a responsibility to its viewers and society as a whole to educate the audience about both kinds of problems that Thoman says confront us as a society? Why or why not?

3. Think of a plot for a television show that is centered on an issue of economic justice.

Essay

As the World Watches: Media Events Are Modern "Holy Days"

ROSALIND SILVER*

Rosalind Silver, who started as a volunteer writer for Media&Values *magazine in 1983, was named editor in 1989 and continued on staff until the magazine ceased publication in 1993. She is now a copy editor on the* Press-Telegram, *Long Beach, California. Silver holds an M.A. in Journalism from the University of Southern California.*

That bright morning in 1961 should have been a normal commuting day. But police monitoring the early morning traffic in California became more and more puzzled by a break in the pattern. Instead of proceeding to work, an ever-growing number of commuters slowed down, pulled off the road, and parked. They were listening to the radio. Since the patrolling officers did not have AM radio, it took them a while to realize the cause of this phenomenon. The bemused drivers were merely joining the workers, housewives, and students who were already gathered around television sets in homes, offices, and classrooms all over the country. The first American astronaut was going into space. Ordinary activities were irrelevant. The whole world was watching. The absorbed witnesses to the happenings of that day have been joined since then by the multitudes of mourners at Kennedy's funeral, the half-a-world-away celebrants who got up in the middle of the night to attend Charles and Diana's wedding, and the countrywide citizen-judges of the Watergate hearings. Journalist Tom Wolfe, who described the astronaut launching in his book *The Right Stuff*, likened the astronauts to medieval knights who were doing single combat for their society** [(41)]. Since their role appealed to the nation's need for a

---

*All references to outside sources are not cited by Silver in the original article. These sources—both in-line citations and Works Cited information—have been provided by Benedict Jones. He also provides the following notes:

** Wolfe is actually commenting on a quotation by Colonel Harrison R. Thyng, who writes: "Like olden knights the F-86 pilots ride up over North Korea to the Yalu River, the sun glinting off silver aircraft, contrails streaming behind, as they challenge the numerically superior enemy to come on up and fight" (qtd. in Wolfe 41).

way to fight the Cold War, their actions and fate assumed an overarching importance that transcended the events themselves.

In fact, this centrality of importance in which television provides a ritual outlet for the whole society is the crucial characteristic of what are often called "media events," or what communications researcher Elihu Katz calls "the high holidays of television."*** Katz, Director of the Communications Institute at the Hebrew University, Jerusalem, and Professor at the Annenberg School of Communications at the University of Southern California, is involved in a systematic study of this phenomenon. He proposes that "media events" are a specifically delimited kind of happening that may be easily distinguished from ordinary news and entertainment by the application of proper criteria [(85)]. Their study sheds light on the events, ceremonies, and values that depend on television to help make life meaningful in our society.

To begin with, true media events are broadcast live, taking full advantage of the excitement inherent in being present when something important occurs. Although they must be preplanned in some sense, they are not set up by the networks and they exist for a higher purpose than hype. That is, they are not publicity-created "pseudo-events." In some ways "media events" share a number of the characteristics of news. They are tied to specific events that have a beginning and an end. They depend on a combination of visual transmission and factual commentary. They usually take place in public and are acknowledged as possessing common interest for the society as a whole. And they are extremely dependent on television's often-noted capacity for making the grandiose and complex, intimate and personal (Katz 84-5).

But unlike the news of the day, media events reach far beyond the day-to-day round of misfortune and circumstance to create a compelling sense of occasion that transfixes viewers. Watching them often becomes a communal outlet transformed into a participatory requirement—a kind of sacred obligation (holy day of obligation?) for complete society membership. As Katz points out, special television happenings are one of the few types of programming that transform TV watching into an occasion instead of a casual everyday experience. People get dressed up and visit each other's homes to celebrate the Super Bowl; the whole world watched the moon landings [(Katz 84)].

*** This exact quotation does not appear in any of the sources I have found. Katz, Dayan, and Motyl's "In Defense of Media Events" uses the phrase "the high holidays of mass communication" (Katz, Dayan, and Motyl 43). Katz's article "Media Events: The Sense of Occasion" contains the following passage: "the `high holidays' of the media" (Katz 84).

But most important and typical about these "media high holidays"—and which goes a long way towards explaining their sacred character—is the sense of heroic participation, conflict, and resolution they represent. Like classical tragedy, folk and fairy tales, a real media event nearly always features a heroic man, woman, or group whose struggle to bring something of meaning to the society is witnessed directly on the TV screen by the breathless, watching multitudes who are being given the gift. This reverence is often heightened by the news commentator who drops from the usual attitude of cheerful cynicism into the hushed dramatic tones of a high priest [(Katz 85)]. Frequently even the chatter of the commercials is absent, as viewers settle back to ponder the important questions: Will things work out as planned? Will something untoward occur to interrupt the resolution provided by the unfolding ceremony? Will our side win? And it's generally very clear from the commentary which side is "ours" as the battle between the forces of light and darkness unfolds before our very eyes. What could be more important? In a sense, every viewer shares in Galahad's quest for the Holy Grail and David's contest with Goliath.

In fact, media holidays celebrate modern quests—the *contests* (presidential debates, the Super Bowl, the World Series), *conquests* (the Pope in Poland, Watergate, landing on the moon), *coronations* (the royal wedding, presidential inaugurations) and *rites of passage* (the Kennedy funeral) that move us as they did our ancestors [(Katz, Dayan, and Motyl 48)]. Other examples could be: Nixon's trip to China (a hero defying national law); Sadat in Jerusalem (his decision to go was news; his arrival was a media event); the Olympics. The first, a heroic mission, provides the most classical example of mythical conflict. The second is a heroic state occasion and the third is a more familiar contest, but "one subject to shared and enforceable rules, and with a sense of what there is in common," writes Katz [(86)]. ****

Watergate, a continuing national preoccupation for over three years, can serve as another good example, since it had aspects that fell into all of these categories and in effect served as a modern ritual of purification, with the whole nation finally serving as citizen-judges. The original break-in was news. The *Washington Post* series featured heroic figures (Woodward and Bernstein) who revealed the

---

**** Katz actually writes: "Traditional rivalries are enacted before audiences of hundreds of millions, but these rivalries are subject to shared and enforceable rules, and the sense of what there is in common typically outweighs the partisanship" (Katz 86).

hidden truth to a watching world. The hearings provided an opportunity for leaders like Sam Ervin and other legislators to testify to patriotism and religious values, and Nixon's mea culpa and Ford's inauguration reaffirmed cultural agreement and identity. Seldom recognized in evaluations of "the long national nightmare" is its provision of a mediagenic opportunity for affirmation of societal values—an agreement that had been totally lacking in the turbulent decade of the 1960s.

Because media holidays have been viewed formerly as "journalism writ large," their effects as shaping rituals and potential societal myths have not been systematically evaluated before. But as Katz and other commentators have cautioned, society can't afford the indiscriminate formation of rituals. Has the spontaneous development of media holidays served us well? Does it reflect, enhance or distort our views and values?

The effect, possibly pernicious, of cameras and microphones on the events themselves has been dealt with by many critics, most notably by Daniel Boorstin in *The Image*. Writing in the early 60s, he warned against the dangers of "pseudo-events" [(9)]. As elaborations of spontaneous happenings, true media events fortunately resist public relations piggybacking. Worth considering, however, are the layers of additional meanings that are typically added by visuals and commentary. The home viewer gains comfort and an Olympian perspective, with analysis, color, and camera angles chosen by others. Viewers have no means of knowing exactly what has been added or left out. On the other hand, the crowd on the spot sees only a small piece of the action, but has the freedom to draw its own conclusions.

As a corollary to this process, consider TV's other shaping role—as a co-planner of the events themselves. For example, in negotiations for the royal wedding, television executives were consulted along with officials of church and state, and camera angles determined some parts of the ceremony. "A lot of people try to persuade television that their event is of historic importance," Katz says. "And television decides which events it thinks will capture the imagination of the people. In effect, the event as it actually happens is less important than the event as represented by television. The broadcast is what the mass audience reacts to—not what actually takes place. The actions of the actual participants in the event are also shaped by how that event is presented on television."*****

***** The source for this quotation has not yet been located.

Do the events and heroes who star in media rituals make history? Or will they merely be floating pebbles as the flood of impersonal and complex forces carves out the bend in the channel? With its preference for the individual and personal, journalism—especially broadcasting—may be the last refuge of the "great man" theory of history, turning societal forces into modern Thucydidean dramas. Historians may object that history is not event but process, but the average viewer joins the journalist in an instinctive feeling that somebody should be visible and accountable.

In supporting the integrative vision behind media holidays, Katz points out that a sense of participation and reconciliation of conflicts are deep and continuing needs. And as he says, audience response itself can be used to test an event's authenticity. "When Sadat arrived in Jerusalem, there were very few cynics left who doubted the genuineness of his peace initiative...Sadat and Israel confronted each other as much on television as on the streets" [(Katz, Dayan, and Motyl 55)]. To summarize, media events induce participation and a sense of resolution, change attitudes, and provide a feeling for process and the way things work.

All these factors combine to make them a crucial and perhaps irreplaceable avenue of meaning and values transmission in modern society, "events which testify that the deeds of human beings, especially great ones, still make a difference and are worth hearing about" [(Katz, Dayan, and Motyl 53)].****** A striking example of this need for meaning occurs when the closed society responds with the purity of denial to an unexpected view of what the rest of the world takes for granted. The Pope's first visit to Poland is a good example. Katz quotes an interviewer offering this assessment of his homilies as seen and heard on the air: "...words began to fit the reality...of the people who heard them....as if their real semantic value was given back to them.... People were realizing that after all they are not powerless, that what will happen... depends somewhat on them, that something of the future is in their hands" [(qtd. in Katz, Dayan, and Motyl 57)]. This feeling of power and control, the sense that there is some meaning to human history beyond a ceaseless procession into the dark, is what the best kind of media holiday event is all about.

****** The exact quotation reads: "Media events testify that *voluntarism* is still alive, that the deeds of human beings—especially great ones—still make a difference and are worth recording" (Katz, Dayan, and Motyl 53; original italics).

Works Cited

Boorstin, Daniel J. *The Image; or, What Happened to the American Dream*. New York: Atheneum, 1962. Print.

Katz, Elihu. "Media Events: The Sense of Occasion." *Studies in Visual Communication* 6.3 (1980): 84-89. Print.

Katz, Elihu, Daniel Dayan, and Pierre Motyl. "In Defense of Media Events." *Communications in the Twenty-First Century*. Ed. Robert W. Haigh, George Gerbner, and Richard B. Byrne. New York: Wiley, 1981. 43-59. Print.

Wolfe, Tom. *The Right Stuff*. New York: Farrar, 1979. Print.

Discussion Questions

1. How does Elihu Katz define "media events" and how is his definition central to Rosalind Silver's argument? Tell about a media event that you remember watching on television. Do you think that your perception of the event was influenced by the media's presentation?

2. According to Silver, what characteristics do media events share with the daily news? What differentiates a media event from a common news story? What news show do you most commonly watch? Can you think of a television show, perhaps an episode in a series you often watch, that blurs the distinction between a media event and a news story? Explain.

3. Discuss the possible dangers that exist in the reporting of both "pseudo-events" and real media events. What steps will you as a viewer take to guard against these dangers?

4. What advice do you think David Denby, the author of Assignment Two's reading selection "Buried Alive: Our Children and the Avalanche of Crud," would give to parents whose children are watching a media event on television?

Storytellers Shape Spiritual Values

MICHAEL WARREN

Michael Warren is a professor of theology and religious education at St. John's University in New York. His book Communication and Cultural Analysis: A Religious View *was published in 1992.*

The question, "Who tells the stories?" is one of special significance to those working in the church or synagogue in today's media age. Who imagines the world for us and what are the procedures by which they do so? What story do they tell? George Gerbner pinpoints the importance of the question when he notes: "Children used to grow up in a home where parents told most of the stories. Today television tells most of the stories to most of the people most of the time" (16).

When parents cease being the primary story-tellers, offering their children their own versions of the world, a significant shift has taken place, especially when the power of describing the world has passed into the hands of those who do not know the child personally and may have at heart interests other than the enrichment of that child's inner life. Who has the child's ear? Who has the child's eye?

In my own view, the importance of who is telling the stories cannot be overstated; it can only be understated, or worse, overlooked. Stories are told with certain interests in mind. The agenda of the nonparental, electronic storytellers and of their new stories are obvious to anyone who watches television at the times children are expected to be watching. The basic interests are commercial, that is, toward selling. To name and judge these interests is not to condemn them but rather to recognize the right to take "an interest" in such commercial goals and to be able to evaluate them.

Particular persons with particular interests are imaging the world for us, and these persons are faceless, unnamed and even ignored. Whose imagination of reality am I being exposed to? Is it an imagination that I can accept? In whose interests is an acceptance of this world? Can I accept this kind of behavior for myself? In others? These are the questions that demand our attention and our critique. The bulk of electronically-communicated signification is imaginative, entertainment oriented and plot centered. In dealing with such material, realizing that the world is being imagined for us is an important step toward applying critical thinking to these communications.

In a world with the possibility of producing and communicating electronically at low cost vivid imaginations of what human existence is all about, it may be helpful to make a distinction between two types of culture: the culture of people and the culture produced for the consumption of people. The culture of the people is the network of messages and images and their music, dance, and ritual that express the life of a particular people. In contrast, the process by which the world is imagined for us deserves careful study. We are confronted with the imagined self everywhere. It meets us at every turn. Unfortunately, it is not our own image of our own selves coming from our center but rather a concocted imagined self, pasted together by others and then presented to us for our consumption. They are all commercial images, because all are put together not out of a quest for truth but out of a quest for consumption, and profit, as if to say, "Here, participate in my image of your life, what life is, what it could be." What we are offered is akin to a frozen dinner, easy and filling but of questionable nourishment. The less we are aware of what is being offered us—a way of imaging ourselves—the greater the tendency to embrace it and make it our own.

Todd Gitlin, media analyst, offers this interpretation of the world presented by television: "Television's world is relentlessly upbeat, clean, and materialistic. . . . [W]ith few exceptions, prime time gives us people preoccupied with personal ambition. If not utterly consumed by ambition and the fear of ending up as losers, these characters take both the ambition and the fear for granted. If not surrounded by middle-class arrays of consumer goods, they themselves are glamorous incarnations of desire. The happiness they long for is private, not public; they make few demands on society as a whole, and even when troubled they seem content with the existing institutional order. Personal ambition and consumerism are the driving forces in their lives. The sumptuous and brightly lit settings of most series amount to advertisements for a consumption-centered version of the good life . . ." (268-69). In today's image culture, the crisis of the human spirit is the crisis of knowing what things to pay attention to. In the United States alone, there are thousands of well-paid persons whose constant preoccupation is to orchestrate the attention of the populace. In clever and subtle ways, these voices can be heard whispering, "Pay attention to this"; "No! Look over here." In the face of such pressure for attention, religious persons are especially challenged, because religion itself is a way of paying attention to matters not fully perceptible; which is to say the religious attention is a specially heightened, focused attention. The ultimate attention, from a religious standpoint, is to the presence of God. Religious people recognize, perhaps instinctively, that what we pay attention to and how we pay attention is what shapes our hearts.

I would like to propose a way of thinking and acting in our media world that may help us reclaim the power of the story, the power that gives meaning to our lives. I call it "cultural agency." In contrast to "cultural passivity," it connotes the continuing possibility of making judgments and then decisions about what we will or will not listen to or see. Cultural agency is about a level of awareness and intention, a matter of knowing or working to know which aspects of the meaning system one will accept and which ones one will resist. Cultural agency happens when a person decides to exercise judgment and control over the kinds of cultural materials she or he will accept and reject. Thus some people decide they will not purchase or look at pornography or will not allow TV vulgarity into their homes. Many parents exercise cultural agency when they try to offer children a humanizing imagination of the world, consciously selecting toys that stimulate creative activity or games that provide noncompetitive participation.

As cultural agents, parents consciously shape the tastes of children, a task involving years of painstaking attention. At the opposite pole of such agency is the unspoken policy of "leaving it to McDonald's" to shape children's tastes. There is sure to be pressure from other families whose tastes have been shaped by McDonald's. This is a particularly sticky problem. The only way of countering those pressures is to insist on the cultural specificity of a family's own ways—to have your own ways. "This is how we do it here." "We have these values and these commitments."

It would help if we could identify other parents and families with values and judgments similar to our own. This is where the church and temple are essential and why religious institutions must address issues of media and culture in their educational and counseling programs, community life, even worship. The family is a necessary cultural agent but an insufficient one. It must be complemented by a chorus of others who help us realize we are not nuts.

---

*Warren's references to outside sources are not cited by Warren in the original article. The Works Cited information has been provided by Benedict Jones.

Works Cited*

Gerbner, George. "Liberal Information in the Digital Age." *Current Issues in Higher Education* 39.1 (1983-1984): 14-18. Print.

Gitlin, Todd. *Inside Prime Time*. New York: Pantheon, 1983. Print.

Discussion Questions

1. In the past, who commonly told children stories? What is the main source of stories for today's children? In what ways do you think the supplier of the story changes the message of the story?

2. Explain the distinction Warren is drawing between the "culture of people" and the "culture produced for the consumption of people." How does this distinction explain Warren's problem with television's influence on children?

3. What way of thinking and acting does Warren propose to "reclaim the power of the story"? What specific actions do you recommend that parents take to avoid becoming "culturally passive" about television?

Addicted to Violence: Has the American Dream Become a Nightmare?

Essay

CHARLES M. JOHNSTON

Charles M. Johnston, M.D., is a psychiatrist and director of the Institute for Creative Development, a think tank and center for leadership training in Seattle, Washington. He is the author of The Creative Imperative *(1986) and* Necessary Wisdom: Meeting the Challenge of a New Cultural Maturity *(1991).*

At a psychological level, the drama and titillation of violent scenarios serve to create a sense of excitement, potency and significance that is missing from most people's daily lives. When we consider media violence, we think first of television's increasingly violent content. We fear that a populace incessantly bombarded with the images, sounds and emotions of shootings, bombings and rapes will become desensitized to such violent acts; or worse, learn to think of them as valid responses to life's growing stresses. The evidence suggests these fears are valid. But media violence also affects us at a deeper and ultimately more problematic level. To make these connections, we must look beyond the literal content on the screen to the subliminal dynamics that animate them, as well as the social context that gives them their power.

An analogy can help. As a futurist, I am frequently asked to address the background and expected developments of various problems plaguing today's world. In talking about the drug crisis, for example, I might comment that while it is most frequently framed as a moral crisis—a problem created by the bad actions of people who should be doing good—I see it more as a crisis of cultural purpose. We find ourselves in times when significant opinions of the population are ingesting substances that mimic real meaning—real excitement, real power, real passion, real spirituality—rather than taking the life risks required to provide meaning as authentic experience.

The dynamics of media violence work in a similar way. At a psychological level, the drama and titillation of these violent scenarios and our identification with their heroes and heroines serve to create a sense of excitement, potency and significance that is missing from most people's daily lives. Beneath these secondary influences lie effects more directly neurological in nature. Here, it is less violence per se—behavior driven by anger or aggression—that hooks us to violent programming than the generalized rush of adrenalin we feel in response to violent situations presented to us. As good action/adventure directors know, a car chase or a plane crash, or even just an explosion, can be as effective as a premeditated shooting in keeping our attention glued to the screen. The addictive power of this generalized stimulation is illustrated all too vividly by a classic experiment with rats. Wires are inserted directly into excitement centers in the rat's brain, then attached to a depressible pedal in its cage. After discovering the connection between the pedal and the pleasure it brings, the rat depresses the pedal with growing frequency. Gradually the animal neglects other activities. In time it even forgets to eat—and starves to death.

Programmers learned long ago that, as with the rat, regular jolts of empty stimulation are the easiest and cheapest means of keeping viewers glued to the screen. Thus, "jolts per minute" programming has come to pervade not only the action/adventure genre, but nearly every aspect of media. Soap operas and afternoon talk shows prosper through their ability to whip up polarized emotions. And the evening news, sold as television's time for serious analysis, has increasingly become an ever more predictable litany of each day's killings and disasters. Serious information is secondary at best.

While media violence can thus be directly addictive, we must go beyond this awareness to fully understand its deeper dynamics. Addiction on a broad scale requires more than an addictive substance; it requires as well social circumstances that support the addictive response. As we watch our children—and often ourselves—hypnotized by violence on the screen, we have to ask: "Why don't we all cry out in protest? Why don't we just say no?" The question returns us to the notion of a cultural crisis of purpose.

Addiction in individuals occurs when a person stops seeing a reason to risk the vulnerability required for real fulfillment. A drug may be so powerful that it simply replaces the struggle to build a satisfying life. Or sometimes a person's life circumstances make fulfillment of normal dreams and desires unlikely. But usually there is something more fundamental, more at the level of meaning. The person's life story has become inadequate to inspire him or her to live life fully. Statistics such as the doubling of teen suicide over the last 10 years suggest all too graphically that, for many, our cultural story has become inadequate to inspire full participation in life.

We find ourselves in the awkward position of telling youth to "just say no" while we ourselves are often unable to articulate a vision of the future that deeply and compellingly says "yes." The role of cultural purpose in the dynamics of violence—and particularly in the increasingly disturbing phenomena of random violence—came home strongly for me when I prepared for a number of speeches I made following the April 1992 civil disturbances in south Central Los Angeles. While reviewing the events of those days, I realized that the driving force behind the rioting changed over time. In its early hours, it seemed to be driven mostly by anger and frustration—ultimately the anger and frustration of people who felt they had little chance of winning at the American Dream. But as the violence became more and more chaotic and random in its targets, it seemed driven less by doubts about participants' chances for success in gaining the American Dream than by knowing at some level that even winning would mean little, that the dream itself had become empty. This ultimate despair became a force for destruction.

The addicting power of violence—both real and in the media—increases exponentially during times of transition, those times when a familiar story has ceased to provide inspiration and a new one has yet to take its place. At these times, people are particularly vulnerable to using both violence itself and the witnessing of violent actions to inject themselves with excitement, engagement, and influence—feelings lacking in their own lives. And random violence—violence as undifferentiated stimulation—becomes particularly addictive in a new way. Its power to give voice to the feelings of fear and chaos so central to these times while hiding them from us through its empty intensity has a peculiar attraction.

The cure for our addiction to media violence lies in two related tasks. We must first teach the basics of media literacy to help people distinguish between genuine feelings of excitement born from true fulfillment and the seductive pseudo-excitement of empty consumable stimulation. Successful media literacy education counters people's susceptibility to manipulation by violence's hypnotic effects. It provides both insight into how these effects work and an emotional climate that supports people's natural desire to be in charge of their lives, to escape harm and to avoid manipulation.

The second part of the solution defines the fundamental challenge of our time—to work together to write the much-needed next chapter in our cultural story. Like the drug epidemic, most of the critical crises of our time are really crises of purpose demanding not just revised policies, but new defining metaphors, new ways of talking about what matters. They challenge us to a unique and critical kind of conversation at all levels—in our schools, in community meetings, in government at all levels, in boardrooms, between friends and family members. Ultimately, those at risk will be able to say no to the seductions of violent pseudo-excitement and pseudo-meaning only to the degree they experience real excitement and real meaning as possible and worth the risk. The deadening attraction of media violence will diminish to the exact degree its potency is countered by a newly mature and compelling collective cultural vision.

Discussion Questions

1. What medium, according to Charles Johnston, is the focus of most people's concerns on the topic of media violence? Discuss the first ideas and examples that come to your mind when you consider this topic.

2. Explain Johnston's thesis about the more problematic effects of media violence. How do you see his idea as contradicting or supplementing your own?

3. Identify and explain the analogy Johnston uses to show the powerful effect of media violence. In what way does this analogy help convince or dissuade you from accepting his position?

4. What two solutions to the problem of addiction to media violence does the author offer? Construct a plan for implementing one or both of them in your community.

Altered States: How Television Changes Childhood: an excerpt of an interview with Joshua Meyrowitz

Essay

BARBARA OSBORN

Josh Meyrowitz is a professor in the Communications department at the University of New Hampshire. He has published works regarding the effects of mass media, including No Sense of Place: The Impact of Electronic Media on Social Behavior, *an analysis of the effects that have been caused by television and other media technologies.*

Barbara Osborn is a former media literacy teacher and a freelance journalist in Los Angeles. She is currently pursuing her doctoral degree in sociology.

Osborn: In your award-winning book *No Sense of Place: The Impact of Electronic Media on Social Behavior*, you deal with television's role in blurring traditional distinctions between public and private spheres. In particular, you say that TV and other electronic media have connected the home to the outside world. What impact has this had on the family?

Meyrowitz: The family sphere used to be defined by its isolation from the public realm. There was the public male realm of "rational accomplishment" and brutal competition, and the private female and child-rearing sphere of home, intuition and emotion. The private realm was supposed to be isolated from the nasty realities of adult life. For both better and worse, television and other electronic media tend to break down the difference between those two worlds. The membrane around the family sphere is much more permeable. Children are now exposed to many aspects of adult male life, and even homebound women are no longer fully isolated from the public realm. TV takes public events and transforms them into dramas that are played out in the privacy of our living rooms, kitchens, and bedrooms.

Parents used to be the channel through which children learned about the outside world. They could decide what to tell their children and when to tell it to them. Since children learn to read in stages, books provide a kind of natural screening process, where adults can decide what to tell and not tell children of different reading abilities. Television destroyed the system that segregated adult from child knowledge and separated information into year-by-year slices for children of different ages. Instead, it presents the same information directly to children of all ages, without going through adult filters. TV takes our kids across the globe before parents give them permission to cross the street. Children don't necessarily understand everything that they see on television, but they are exposed to many aspects of the adult world that parents might not have decided to tell them about.

So television presents a real challenge to adults. While a parent can read a newspaper without sharing it with children in the same room, television is accessible to everyone in that space. And unlike books, television doesn't allow us to flip through it and see what's coming up. We may think we're giving our children a lesson in science by having them watch the *Challenger* take off, and then suddenly they learn about death, disaster and adult mistakes. We have no way to protect them from that. Books allow adults to discuss privately what to tell or not tell children. This also allows parents to keep adult material secret from children and keep their secret-keeping secret. Take that same material and put it on *The Today Show* and you have 800,000 children hearing the very things the adults are trying to keep from them. More importantly, kids learn the "secret of secrecy," that adults conspire over what to tell or not tell children. They learn that adults are worried and anxious about being parents.

Osborn: How has this altered parental authority?

Meyrowitz: I think adults feel somewhat exposed now and no longer pretend to know everything in front of their children. This is not to say that adults have absolutely lost their authority. Kids look up to adults and want them to know a lot of answers. But through television, kids come to realize that adults do have many, many problems: adults fight, adults kill each other, adults cry, adults lose control, and so on. And adults now know that kids know these things about them.

Television supports the desire for adult authority but also makes children aware that it's not always there and that kids may even have to help parents gain authority over them. This paradoxical approach to adult authority is seen most dramatically in the public service messages where kids are shown urging an alcoholic parent to become more responsible. TV empowers children to empower their parents.

This doesn't mean that adults should abdicate their authority over children. Adults are more experienced and knowledgeable. Adults should try to control and discuss what their kids watch. They should also try and maintain authority in their relationships with children in face-to-face interaction. But the old support system for unquestioned adult authority has been undermined significantly by television.

Osborn: What's the psychic price of this blurring of adult and child spheres?

Meyrowitz: That's a complex question. I can give you a partial, historical answer. Up until the last 400 years in Western culture, there was no such thing as childhood as we have come to think of it. Even as late as the Middle Ages, children dressed like adults, drank in taverns, gambled, went to war, and those few who attended schools often went armed. The modern notions of childhood and adulthood only developed with the spread of literacy.

We must realize, however, that while TV encourages a kind of blurring of roles, it doesn't provide the social mechanisms for allowing change to happen. In fact, the initial short-term outcome isn't more harmony or equality; if anything, it's more tension and frustration. TV makes us aware of all the places we can't go, all the people we can't be, all the things we can't possess. TV makes us so aware of the larger world that many of us—especially women, children, and minorities—begin to feel unfairly isolated in some corner of it.

By encouraging behaviors not yet supported by societal institutions, television places families under a lot of stress. Children now know more about the adult world, and most mothers have entered what was once the male workplace. Yet some schools continue to follow lesson plans that assume children's degree of awareness of the world still correlates only with age and reading ability. And many businesses continue to function as if each employee—whether male or female—has a wife at home cooking, cleaning, and watching the kids. There have to be adjustments in the expectations of what goes on in schools, offices, and at home. For example, there must be more flexible work schedules and more integration of family life and children in the business world.

Discussion Questions

1. Explain the way in which Meyrowitz believes the media have blurred the distinction between the public and the private realm. Do you think the family sphere still exists in some form or do you think it has disappeared?

2. According to Meyrowitz, what kinds of challenges does television present to parents? What do you think parents should do to meet these challenges?

3. How has television changed children's perception of adult authority? Explain ways in which this change can be a good or a bad thing.

The Truth about Pop Culture's Influence on Children

KAREN STERNHEIMER

Dr. Karen Sternheimer's articles have appeared in the Los Angeles Times, Newsday, *the* San Jose Mercury News, *and other newspapers around the country. In addition, she has provided commentary for CNN, MSNBC, Fox News, The History Channel, 20/20, The O'Reilly Factor, and many local news broadcasts. She has been a guest on numerous radio shows nationally and internationally, including NPR's* Marketplace, Bloomberg Radio, *and* Voice of America. *She teaches in the sociology department at the University of Southern California. The following excerpt is taken from her book* It's Not the Media *(2003). Her most recent book is titled* Connecting Popular Culture and Social Problems: Why the Media Is Not the Answer *(2009).*

Since the Industrial Revolution, our economy has become more complex and adults and children have increasingly spent their days separated. From a time when adults and children worked together on family farms to the development of institutions specifically for children, like age-segregated schools, daycare, and organized after-school activities, daily interaction in American society has become more separated by age. Popular culture is another experience that kids may enjoy beyond adult supervision. [An increase of youth autonomy has created fear within adults, who worry that violence, promiscuity, and other forms of "adult" behavior will emerge from these shifts and that parents will have a declining level of influence on their children. Kids spend more time with friends than with their parents as they get older, and more time with popular culture too.] These changes explain in large part why childhood is experienced differently now than in the past and are not only the result of changes in popular culture.

Perhaps the biggest concern one generation can have for the next is the fear that they will be without values and lack a connection with society. Young people are [routinely described in public discourse] as oversexed, dangerous, self-centered fools, creating a rather convenient

---

[1]Laura Sessions Stepp, "Why Johnny Can't Feel; Poor Relationships With Adults May Explain Youth Alienation," *Washington Post*, April 23, 1999, p. C1.

class of scapegoats for difficult social problems. Articles like *The Washington Post*'s "Why Johnny Can't Feel" reveal a sense that a new problem has emerged amongst the young.[i] According to a story called "It's Hard to See the Line Where Alienation Leads to Violence," being a teenage outcast today is somehow worse than ever before.[ii] "It never seemed to matter as much as it does now," the authors state, and assert that kids today are "more sensitive than ever," which could potentially lead to violence."[iii] Allegedly "the difference between alienated youths and violent youths may be little more than an inadvertent bump or whispered taunt."[iv] The news media would have us believe that kids are ticking time bombs, waiting to blow. The reality is that young people are becoming *less* violent, yet they are continually maligned in public discourse. The "epidemic" of school shootings is used to support the contention that more and more young people are becoming cold-blooded killers in spite of the fact that homicides in schools *decreased* during the 1990s.[v] The facts only get in the way of creating a sensational story about the tragic downfall of the next generation.

Rather than promote an atmosphere in which we discuss the realities of children's and adolescents' lives and reconsider the pressure adults and adult-run institutions place on them by, for instance, cutting education budgets, the conversation has turned towards attempting to further restrict young people. Curfews and harsher sentences for juvenile offenders have grown in popularity despite the dearth of empirical evidence in support of these punitive policies. Calls for further media restrictions are also heard, including a group in the Senate who in spring 2001 introduced the Media Marketing Accountability Act, which would fine producers who advertise "adult-oriented" entertainment to teenagers.

Is there any wonder that many young people feel disconnected from adult authority figures? We call teens stupid and immoral, condemn them for the video games, music, and movies they like, and try to take what freedoms they have away. We wonder why, after hearing politicians blame them for many of our nation's problems, they don't rush to the polls to vote when they turn eighteen. In addition to

---

[ii]Matthew Ebnet and James Rainey, "It's Hard to See the Line Where Alienation Turns to Violence," *Los Angeles Times*, April 22, 1999, Orange County Edition.
[iii]Ebnet and Rainey.
[iv]Ebnet and Rainey.
[v]U.S. Department of Education, *Indicators of School Crime and Safety* (Washington, D.C.: Government Printing Office, 2000).

blaming media for social problems, we all too often blame young people themselves.

So I decided to study popular culture from a safe distance. I began to notice that just as I had mixed feelings about the entertainment industry, on a societal level we have developed a real ambivalence about Hollywood. We celebrate its excesses, make icons of actors, and include box-office tallies in our weekly news, as if we are all somehow shareholders in the business of entertainment. We have magazines like *People*, *Us*, and *Entertainment Weekly* with huge circulations, and celebrity gossip is regularly featured within mainstream news. Yet we are just as obsessed with the notion that popular culture is a major destructive force, that generations of children may be turned bad by Hollywood's misguided influence. I have to admit, when I think back to some of the jerks I met years ago, I'd like to believe all the complaints about media effects. But focusing so much energy on popular culture as the root of American social problems is like fixing a patient's x-ray and disregarding the actual tumor. All too often we choose to focus on media and ignore the major issues that are really behind today's challenges. We blame media rather than look at social changes that have altered American social life and the experience of childhood.

To adults, children often represent vulnerability and innocence, which is why we respond so viscerally when we are given information on how we may best "protect" them. As representatives of the future, children remind us that the world ahead is yet unknowable, and perhaps more unnerving, uncontrollable. The media remind us of and represent this uncontrolled, unknown future. We often fear media's influence on children because kids serve as both powerful symbols of the future and of change, and we are anxious about both.

So while our fears are very real, quite often the actual threat is not. The media may always be visible, often unavoidable, and sometimes downright annoying, but the real things we should be concerned about are less visible and thus easier to overlook, such as the widespread impact of child poverty—children comprise a majority of the nation's poor, and poverty is closely linked with many of the problems that we usually blame the media for, like violence, alienation, and teen pregnancy. Both youth and youth culture are symbolic of change, of a loss of adult centrality and control. Popular culture is often the bastion of the young and in many ways reflects the contemporary experience of youth, which could seem frightening to adults. We often prefer to deny both the aggression and sexual curiosity young people feel, so when we encounter these themes in popular culture we often blame media for their existence.

That said, there are ways that we can cope with an increasingly media-driven society. There is much that journalists, policymakers, educators, parents, and everyone else can do, such as starting book drives for poorly funded schools, donating to food banks and homeless shelters, volunteering time at local public schools or daycare centers, and creating a grassroots organization to support children's issues. While changing media culture may truly concern us at times, we need to be sure to keep our real challenges in sight. It would be a mistake only to focus on the negative in these changing times and overlook the positive aspects of both media culture and the next generation.

Discussion Questions

1. What changes, according to Karen Sternheimer, help explain the differences between the way childhood was experienced in the past and the way it is being experienced today?

2. What image of today's youth is presented in the media? Discuss the portrayal of today's youth in a television show or a movie that you have seen recently. Do you think that the creators of this media experience considered any of the facts that Sternheimer presents? Why or why not?

3. Who does the author feel, other than the media, deserves the blame for changes in the experience of childhood? What or who do you think is largely responsible for these changes? Explain.

4. How do you imagine that Denby, author of "Buried Alive: Our Children and the Avalanche of Crud," would respond to Sternheimer's point about the difference between the media's portrayal of children and what children actually are like?

Homework

Write a response to the blog posted by a college student in July 2008 at the following link:

http://otakurevolution.com/content/ways-todays-youth-sounds-like-completely-uneducated-apes-oh-and-please-stop

Reviewing Your Graded Essay

After your essay has been graded by your instructor, you may have the opportunity to revise your paper and raise your grade. Even if you are not submitting a revised version of this essay to your instructor, it is important that you review your work carefully in order to understand its strengths and weaknesses. This sheet will guide you through the evaluation process.

You will want to continue to use the techniques that worked well for you and to find strategies to overcome the problems that you identify in this sample of your writing. In order to help yourself recognize areas that might have been problematic for you, look back at the scoring rubric in Part 1 of this book. Match the numerical/verbal/letter grade received on your essay to the appropriate category. Study the explanation given on the rubric for your grade.

Write a few sentences below in which you identify your problems in each of the following areas. Then suggest specific changes you could make that would improve your paper. Don't forget to use your handbook as a resource.

1. Grammar/mechanics

My problem:

My strategy for change:

2. Thesis/response to assignment

My problem:

My strategy for change:

3. Organization

My problem:

My strategy for change:

4. Paragraph development/examples/reasoning

My problem:

My strategy for change:

5. Assessment

In the space below, assign a grade to your paper using a rubric other than the one used by your instructor. In other words, if your instructor assigned your essay a grade of *High Fail*, you might give it the letter grade you now feel the paper warrants. If your instructor used the traditional letter grade to evaluate the essay, choose a category from the rubric in this book, or any other grading scale that you are familiar with, to show your evaluation of your work. Then write a short narrative explaining your evaluation of the essay and the reasons it received the grade you gave it.

Grade:_____

Narrative:_____

_____

_____

_____

_____

Assignment 3

Bruno Bettelheim's "The Uses of Enchantment"

The following essay, Bruno Bettelheim's "The Uses of Enchantment," presents and supports a thesis statement about fairy tales and ends with a writing topic that you will use as the basis for an essay. In order to respond successfully to that writing topic, you will have to present, develop, and support your own thesis statement about fairy tales.

To help prepare you to respond in a thoughtful and insightful way, the Extended Activities section includes some background readings: a couple of fairy tales that will give you an opportunity to test Bettelheim's ideas, and a group of thesis-centered essays that develop their own arguments about fairy tales. Read these background readings carefully and respond as fully as possible to their discussion questions. Then use the pages that follow "The Uses of Enchantment" to begin forming your response to Bettelheim's argument. These pages will help you to formulate your essay's thesis statement and develop your ideas so that your essay is insightful, persuasive, and coherent.

The Uses of Enchantment

Essay

BRUNO BETTELHEIM

Bruno Bettelheim was an American developmental psychologist born in Austria. He received his doctoral degree in 1938 from the University of Vienna. He was imprisoned in the Dachau and Buchenwald concentration camps during the Nazi occupation of Austria. He emigrated to the United States in 1939 and taught psychology at the University of Chicago from 1944–1973. He wrote a number of influential works on childhood development, including The Informed Heart *(1960),* The Empty Fortress *(1967), and* The Uses of Enchantment *(1976), which contains the following excerpt.*

The message that fairy tales get across to the child in manifold form is that a struggle against severe difficulties in life is unavoidable, is an intrinsic part of human existence—but that if one does not shy away, but steadfastly meets unexpected and often unjust hardships, one masters all obstacles and at the end emerges victorious.

The child needs most particularly to be given suggestions in symbolic form about how he may deal with these issues and grow safely into maturity. Many modern stories written for young children mention neither death nor aging, the limits to our existence, nor the wish for eternal life. The fairy tale, by contrast, confronts the child squarely with the basic human predicaments.

For example, many fairy stories begin with the death of a mother or father; in these tales the death of the parent creates the most agonizing problems, as it (or the fear of it) does in real life. Other stories tell about an aging parent who decides that the time has come to let the new generation take over. But before this can happen, the successor has to prove himself capable and worthy. The Brothers Grimm's story "The Three Feathers" begins: "There was once upon a time a king who had three sons. . . . When the king had become old and weak, and was thinking of his end, he did not know which of his sons should inherit the kingdom after him." In order to decide, the king sets all his sons a difficult task; the son who meets it best "shall be king after my death."

The fairy tale takes children's existential anxieties and dilemmas very seriously and addresses itself directly to them: the need to be loved and the fear that one is thought worthless; the love of life, and the fear of death. Further, the fairy tale offers solutions in ways that the child can grasp on his level of understanding. For example, fairy tales pose the dilemma of wishing to live eternally by occasionally concluding: "If they have not died, they are still alive." The other ending—"And they lived happily ever after"—does not for a moment fool the child that eternal life is possible. But it does indicate that which alone can take the sting out of the narrow limits of our time on this earth, forming a truly satisfying bond to another. The tales teach that when one has done this, one has reached the ultimate in emotional security; and this alone can dissipate the fear of death. If one has found true adult love, the fairy story also tells, one doesn't need to wish for eternal life. This is suggested by another ending found in fairy tales: "They lived for a long time afterward, happy and in pleasure."

It is characteristic of fairy tales to state an existential dilemma briefly and pointedly. This permits the child to come to grips with the problem in its most essential form, where a more complex plot would confuse matters for him. The fairy tale simplifies all situations. Its figures are clearly drawn, and details, unless very important, are eliminated. Contrary to what takes place in many modern children's stories, in fairy tales evil is as omnipresent as virtue. It is this duality of evil and virtue that poses a moral problem, and requires the struggle to solve it.

Evil is not without its attractions—symbolized by the mighty giant or dragon, the power of the witch, the cunning queen in "Snow White"—and often it is temporarily in the ascendancy. In many fairy tales a usurper succeeds for a time in seizing the place which rightfully belongs to the hero—as the wicked sisters do in "Cinderella." It is not that the evildoer is punished at the story's end which makes immersing oneself in fairy stories an experience in moral education, although this is part of it. In fairy tales, as in life, punishment or fear of it is only a limited deterrent to crime, and that is why in fairy tales the bad person always loses out. It is not the fact that virtue wins out at the end that promotes morality, but that the hero is more attractive to the child, who identifies with the hero in all his struggles. Because of this identification the child imagines that he suffers with the hero his trials and tribulations, and triumphs with him as virtue is victorious. The child makes such identifications all on his own, and the inner and outer struggles of the hero imprint morality on him.

The figures in fairy tales are not ambivalent—not good and bad at the same time, as we all are in reality. A person in a fairy tale is either good or bad, nothing in between. One brother is stupid, the other is clever. One sister is virtuous and industrious, the others are vile and lazy. One is beautiful, the others are ugly. One parent is all good, the other evil. Presenting the polarities of character permits the child to comprehend easily the difference between the two, which he could not do as readily were the figures drawn more true to life, with all the complexities that characterize real people.

Only by going out into the world can the fairy-tale hero and the child who identifies with him find themselves there; and as they do, they will also find the other with whom they will be able to live happily ever after. The fairy tale is future-oriented and guides the child—in terms he can understand—to achieve a more satisfying independent existence.

Writing Topic

According to Bettelheim, how do fairy tales, by presenting life's problems in their "most essential form," guide children's development? Do you find the evidence convincing? To develop your answer, be sure to include specific examples; those examples can be drawn from anything you have read, as well as from your own observations and experiences.

Fairy tales in their "most essential form" guide the child to learn virtue, perserverance, and ~~happiness~~ future happiness

Vocabulary Check

Good writers choose their words carefully so that their ideas will be clear. In order for you, the reader, to understand an essay, it is important to think about its key vocabulary terms and the way they are used by the author. Words can have a variety of meanings, or they can have specialized meanings in certain contexts. Look up the definitions of the following words or phrases from the essay. Choose the meaning that you think Bettelheim intended when he selected that particular word or phrase for use in this essay. Then explain the way the meaning or concept behind the definition is key to understanding the author's argument.

existential

definition:

_____

_____

_____

explanation:

_____

_____

_____

tribulations

definition:

_____

_____

_____

explanation:

_____

_____

_____

usurper

definition:

_____

_____

_____

explanation:

_____

_____

_____

ambivalent

definition:

_____

_____

_____

explanation:

_____

_____

_____

Questions to Guide Your Reading

Before you begin to answer these questions, review "Steps for a Thoughtful Reading of an Essay" in Part 1 and, using it as a guide, spend some time on "The Uses of Enchantment" to be sure that you understand its ideas.

Paragraph 1

What do fairy tales teach children about problems in life?

Paragraph 2

How do fairy tales, according to Bettelheim, differ from most modern children's stories? Is what he claims true for your childhood reading experience? Give some examples of stories you remember reading when you were young.

Paragraph 3

What human predicament does Bettelheim illustrate in the story "The Three Feathers"? What other story or stories can you remember that begin with the same or a similar parental dilemma?

Paragraph 4

What are the three common fairy tale endings? Which of these endings is most realistic? Which one do you prefer? Why?

Paragraph 5

Bettelheim says that fairy tales present a complex problem in a simple form. How do they accomplish this task?

Paragraph 6

How do the struggles of the hero or heroine of a fairy tale teach children about moral values?

Paragraph 7

How do characters in fairy tales differ from real people? Why is this difference important?

Paragraph 8

Bettelheim believes that fairy tales help children discover how they can live "happily ever after" because they guide children to find an "independent existence." What does he mean by this? Do you think he is right? Explain.

Prewriting for a Directed Summary

You will find that providing thorough answers to these questions will help you write a clear and accurate summary. Remember that you will want to write a *directed* summary, meaning one that responds to the following part of the writing topic:

> *first part of the writing topic*: According to Bettelheim, how do fairy tales, by presenting life's problems in their "most essential form," guide children's development?

Hint

Notice that this question asks you to explain one of Bettelheim's main assertions—it does not ask you to summarize the entire essay. Hence, be sure to focus your summary so that you answer this question specifically. It asks you to tell how fairy tales represent life to children and how this presentation guides their maturation. To help plan your response, answer the following questions. Remember to turn back to "Guidelines for Writing a Directed Summary" in Part 1 for guidance.

1. What childhood anxieties and dilemmas do fairy tales address, according to Bettelheim?

2. How do modern children's stories address these issues, or "basic human predicaments"?

3. Explain some of the ways Bettelheim shows fairy tales confronting these predicaments. What specific examples does he use to support his argument? How does the simplicity of fairy tales offer children strategies for dealing with struggle and hardship?

4. How do these lessons guide them in their development toward adulthood?

Opinion and Working Thesis Statement

The second question in the writing topic that follows "The Uses of Enchantment" asks you to take a position of your own. Your response will become the thesis statement of your essay, so it is important to spend some time ensuring that it is fully developed and an accurate reflection of the position you want to take on the topic. Use the framework below to help you develop your thesis. But as you move through the remaining pages in this chapter, keep an open mind. You may want to modify, or even reverse, your position once you've read the background essays in the "Extended Activities" section of this chapter, and you've thought more carefully and systematically about the subject. In a later page of this chapter, you will be asked to review and perhaps revise the working thesis statement you develop below.

second part of the writing topic: Do you find the evidence convincing?

Do you think that Bettelheim's viewpoint on the role of fairy tales in children's lives is a valid one? At this stage of the writing process, simply put down the view you have now and think of it as your "working thesis" rather than your final one.

Hint

Even if you are prepared to write a working thesis now, be sure to keep an open mind because, as you think more carefully about the subject and develop some strong supporting topics, you may want to revise it to reflect your more thoughtful viewpoint.

1. Use the following **thesis frame** to identify the basic elements of your working thesis statement:

   a. What is the main subject of "The Uses of Enchantment" that the writing topic questions ask you to consider?

   _____

   b. What is Bettelheim's opinion about that subject?

   _____

   c. What is your opinion about the subject, and will you agree or disagree with Bettelheim's opinion?

   _____

   _____

   _____

   _____

2. Now, use the elements you isolated in parts a, b, and c of the thesis frame to write a working thesis statement. You may have to revise it several times until it captures your idea clearly.

   _____

   _____

3. When you've finished, check to see that you've made clear your position on the role of fairy tales in children's lives and that you've stated your position in relation to Bettelheim's.

Hint

Turn back to Part 1's "A Suggested Structure for an Essay" and look at the elements that are included in the introduction. Note that, in this particular structure, the thesis statement commonly comes at the end of the introductory paragraph. Later, as you begin drafting your essay, remember to include the thesis statement. It will present the unifying point of your essay.

Prewriting to Find Support for Your Thesis Statement

The third part of the writing topic asks you to support your thesis statement:

> *third part of the writing topic*: To develop your answer, be sure to include specific examples; those examples can be drawn from anything you have read as well as from your own observations and experiences.

Respond as fully as possible to the guidelines on this page because the information you provide will give you the material you need to develop and support your argument. After completing this prewriting activity, you will be ready to use your responses to build an outline and draft your essay

Hint

The subject of Bettelheim's essay—fairy tales—should be familiar to you. The supplemental readings provided in this section, however, will help you explore this subject more fully. The four fairy tales will give you the opportunity to take another look at fairy tales—this time from an analytical perspective—something you may not have done before. And the supplemental essays will give you some perspectives other than Bettelheim's and will help you work out your ideas more insightfully. These readings will also provide you with material you may want to include in your own essay as you develop and support your thesis statement. If you do use another author's ideas, be sure in your essay to attribute them to the author.

1. As you begin to develop your own examples, consider the subject's relation to your own life: your own childhood fears and anxieties, your own memories of fairy tales, your observation of how children you know react to or are influenced by fairy tales. In the space below, freewrite about or list all the connections you can think of, even those about which you are hesitant.

   Once you've written your ideas, look them over carefully. Try to group your ideas into categories and give each category a label. In other words, cluster ideas on your list or in your freewriting that seem to have something in common and, for each cluster, identify that shared quality by giving it a name.

2. Next, consider the subject in relation to the supplemental readings. How does "Briar Rose" affect children? How do the fairy tale analyses by Midori Snyder, G. K. Chesterton, and Louise Bernikow differ from Bettelheim's? According to these writers, how do fairy tales influence children? Will any of their ideas or examples help you support your own thesis? List all the connections you can think of, even those about which you are hesitant.

Once you've written your ideas down, look them over carefully. Try to group your ideas into categories. Then give each category a label. In other words, cluster ideas that seem to have something in common and, for each cluster, identify that shared quality by giving it a name.

3. Once you've clustered and labeled your ideas, go through them and pick two or three specific clusters to develop as supporting topics in your essay. Make sure they are relevant to your thesis and that they have enough substance to be compelling to your reader. Then, in the space below, briefly summarize each item and explain its connection to your thesis statement.

Hint

Be sure to look back to "Writing a Paragraph That Supports Your Thesis Statement" to review how to use these examples in your draft.

Revising Your Thesis Statement

Now that you have spent some time reading and thinking about fairy tales and their influence, you should have a good idea of the position you want to take in your essay and the supporting evidence you want to use to support your claim. Now is a good time to review the working thesis statement you crafted earlier to see if it is still accurate. As your first step, look again at the writing topic question and then write your original working thesis on the lines that follow it:

> *second part of the writing topic*: Do you find his evidence convincing?

Working thesis statement:

_____

_____

_____

Take some time now to see if you want to revise your thesis statement. Often after extensive prewriting and focused thought, the working thesis statement is no longer an accurate reflection of what you plan to say in your essay. Sometimes, only a word or phrase must be added or deleted; other times, the thesis statement must be significantly rewritten, as either or both the subject and the claim portions are inaccurate.

After examining your working thesis statement and completing any necessary revisions, check it one more time by asking yourself the following questions:

a. Does the thesis directly identify Bettelheim's argument that fairy tales present children with life strategies and help them to become emotionally and morally sound adults?

b. Do you clearly state your argument regarding the role of fairy tales in the lives of children?

If you answered "no" to either of these questions, revise your thesis statement once more to add the missing elements.

_____

_____

_____

Planning and Drafting Your Essay

Now that you have examined Bettelheim's argument and thought at length about your own views, draft an essay that responds to all parts of the writing topic question. Use the material you developed in this section to compose your draft, and then exchange drafts with a classmate and use the peer review form that follows to help revise your draft. Don't forget to go back to Part 1, especially "A Suggested Structure for an Essay That Responds to Another Writer's Work," for further guidance on the essay's conventional structure.

Use the following form to create an outline or writing plan before you begin your draft. It doesn't have to be detailed. For some parts, you may only want to list brief sentences, phrases, or even words to capture the essence of what you plan to develop in each section.

Don't forget to turn back to the thesis development page and the thesis support page and incorporate the thesis statement and supporting topics you developed there. Creating an outline will give you an overview of your essay and a basic structure for incorporating all of the ideas you have developed in the preceding pages.

_____

Creating an Outline for Your Draft

I. Introductory Paragraph

A. An opening sentence that gives the reading selection's title and author and begins to answer the first part of the writing topic:

_____

B. Main points to include in the directed summary:

1.

2.

3.

4.

C. Look again at the thesis statement you wrote in "Revising Your Thesis Statement" and make any changes you think necessary. Then copy your thesis statement below. It should clearly agree or disagree with the argument in "The Uses of Enchantment" and state a clear position using your own words.

_____

II. Body Paragraphs

A. Subject of the paragraph: _Briar Rose_

   1. **C**ontrolling idea sentence:

    Fairy tales illustrate that one can be victorious if one perserveres through the obstacles,

   2 **C**orroborating details:

    The prince pushes through the rose bush to reach Briar Rose.

_____

   3. **C**areful description of the details' relevance:

    The collective effort of the princes to push through the thorns is the physical barrier and struggle that stands in the way.

_____

   4 . **C**onnection to the thesis statement:

_____

B. Subject of the paragraph: _Chesterton_

   1. **C**ontrolling idea sentence:

_____

_____

   2. **C**orroborating details:

_____

_____

_____

3. **C**areful description of the details' relevance:

_____

_____

_____

_____

_____

4. **C**onnection to the thesis statement:

_____

C. Subject of the paragraph: _____

1. **C**ontrolling idea sentence:

_____

2. **C**orroborating details:

_____

_____

_____

3. **C**areful description of the details' relevance:

_____

_____

_____

_____

_____

4. **C**onnection to the thesis statement:

_____

D. Subject of the paragraph: _____

1. **C**ontrolling idea sentence:

_____

2. **C**orroborating details:

_____

_____

_____

3. **C**areful description of the details' relevance:

_____

_____

_____

_____

_____

4. **C**onnection to the thesis statement:

_____

III. Conclusion

A. Type of conclusion to be used:

_____

B. Key words or phrases to include:

_____

Peer Draft Review Sheet

Use the following guidelines to give a classmate feedback on his or her draft. Read the draft through first and then answer each of the items below as specifically as you can.

Name of draft's author: _____

Name of draft's reader: _____

Introduction

1. Within the opening sentences,

   a. the author is correctly identified by first and last name.   yes   no
   b. the reading selection's title is included and placed within quotation marks.   yes   no

2. The opening contains a summary that

   a. explains Bettelheim's idea about the differences between fairy tales and modern children's stories.   yes   no
   b. explains his understanding of the way fairy tales present children with life's unavoidable struggles and offer them strategies for dealing with these struggles.   yes   no

3. The opening provides a thesis that

   a. tells the draft writer's opinion of Bettelheim's thesis.   yes   no
   b. responds to both issues: that fairy tales present life's problems in their "most elemental form" and guide children's development.   yes   no

If the answers to #3 above are yes, state the thesis below as it is written. If the answer to one or both of these questions is no, explain to the writer what information is needed to make the thesis complete.

Body

1. How many paragraphs are in the body of this essay? _____

2. To support the thesis, this number is   sufficient   not enough

3. Do paragraphs contain the 4Cs?

Paragraph 1	Controlling idea sentence	yes	no
	Corroborating details	yes	no
	Careful description of the details' relevance	yes	no
	Connection to the thesis statement	yes	no
Paragraph 2	Controlling idea sentence	yes	no
	Corroborating details	yes	no
	Careful description of the details' relevance	yes	no
	Connection to the thesis statement	yes	no
Paragraph 3	Controlling idea sentence	yes	no
	Corroborating details	yes	no
	Careful description of the details' relevance	yes	no
	Connection to the thesis statement	yes	no
Paragraph 4	Controlling idea sentence	yes	no
	Corroborating details	yes	no
	Careful description of the details' relevance	yes	no
	Connection to the thesis statement	yes	no
Paragraph 5	Controlling idea sentence	yes	no
	Corroborating details	yes	no
	Careful description of the details' relevance	yes	no
	Connection to the thesis statement	yes	no

(Continue as needed)

4. Identify any of the above paragraphs that are not fully developed (too short).

5. Identify any of the above paragraphs that fail to support the thesis. _____

6. Identify any of the above paragraphs that are redundant or repetitive. _____

7. Suggest any ideas for additional paragraphs that might improve this essay.

Conclusion

1. Does the final paragraph contain any material that should have been developed in the body of the essay?

a. examples	yes	no
b. new ideas	yes	no

2. Does the conclusion provide closure (let the readers know that the end of the essay has been reached)? yes no

3. Does the conclusion leave readers with an understanding of the significance of the argument?   yes   no

   State in your own words what the writer considers to be important about his or her argument.

   _____

   _____

4. Identify the type of conclusion used (see the guidelines for conclusions in Part 1).

Revision

1. During revision, the writer should pay attention to the following problems in mechanics:

   comma splices
   comma placement
   fragments
   run-on sentences
   apostrophe use
   quotation mark use
   capital letter use
   spelling

2. During revision, the writer should pay attention to the following areas of grammar:

   verb tense
   subject-verb agreement
   pronoun type
   pronoun reference
   pronoun agreement
   irregular verbs
   noun plurals
   dangling modifiers
   prepositions
   misplaced modifiers

Final Draft Check List

Content:

- My essay has an appropriate title.
- I provide an accurate summary of Bettelheim's position presented in "The Uses of Enchantment."
- My thesis takes a position that can be supported with evidence.
- I have a sufficient number of paragraphs and arguments to support my thesis.
- Each body paragraph is relevant to my thesis.
- Each body paragraphs contains the 4Cs.
- I use transitions whenever necessary to connect paragraphs and ideas to each other.
- The final paragraph of my essay (the conclusion) provides the readers with a sense of closure.

Grammar and Mechanics:

- I use the present tense to discuss Bettelheim's argument and examples.
- All of my verb tense shifts can be accounted for by the time sequence of events.
- I have used verb tense consistently and appropriately throughout my sentences and paragraphs.
- My sentences are punctuated clearly and correctly.
- If I present items in a series (nouns, verbs, prepositional phrases), they are parallel in form.
- If I include material spoken or written by someone other than myself, I have correctly punctuated it with quotation marks and cited it appropriately according to the MLA style guide.
- I have checked for subject-verb agreement in all of my sentences.

Extended Activities

Readings

"Briar Rose" by the Grimm Brothers

"Hansel and Gretel" by the Grimm Brothers

"The Goose-Girl" by the Grimm Brothers

"The Monkey Girl" by Midori Snyder

"Change and Sexuality: Ursula and Ariel as Markers of Metamorphosis in *The Little Mermaid*" by Paul Beehler

"Construction of the Female Self" by Jill Birnie Henke, Diane Zimmerman Umble, Nancy J. Smith

"Cinderella: Saturday Afternoon at the Movies" by Louise Bernikow

"Fairy Tales Are Good for Children" by G. K. Chesterton

"The Criminological Significance of the Grimms' Fairy Tales" by Gerhard O. W. Mueller

Class Discussion

Review of the Four Basic Sentence Shapes

Homework

Locating Information in a Handbook

Reviewing Your Graded Essay

Briar Rose

THE GRIMM BROTHERS

Jacob Ludwig Carl Grimm and his brother Wilhelm Carl Grimm were born in Hanau, Germany, in the late 1700s. Both brothers studied law at the University of Marburg, but it was their scholarly work on linguistics, folklore, and medieval studies that resulted in their most famous work, a two-volume collection of German legends titled Kinder- und Haus-märchen (Children's and Household Tales). *The collection went through six editions during the Grimm Brothers' lifetime.*

A king and queen once upon a time reigned in a country a great way off, where there were in those days fairies. Now this king and queen had plenty of money, and plenty of fine clothes to wear, and plenty of good things to eat and drink, and a coach to ride out in every day: but though they had been married many years they had no children, and this grieved them very much indeed. But one day as the queen was walking by the side of the river, at the bottom of the garden, she saw a poor little fish, that had thrown itself out of the water, and lay gasping and nearly dead on the bank. Then the queen took pity on the little fish, and threw it back again into the river; and before it swam away it lifted its head out of the water and said, "I know what your wish is, and it shall be fulfilled, in return for your kindness to me—you will soon have a daughter." What the little fish had foretold soon came to pass; and the queen had a little girl, so very beautiful that the king could not cease looking on it for joy, and said he would hold a great feast and make merry, and show the child to all the land. So he asked his kinsmen, and nobles, and friends, and neighbours. But the queen said, "I will have the fairies also, that they might be kind and good to our little daughter." Now there were thirteen fairies in the kingdom; but as the king and queen had only twelve golden dishes for them to eat out of, they were forced to leave one of the fairies without asking her. So twelve fairies came, each with a high red cap on her head, and red shoes with high heels on her feet, and a long white wand in her hand; and after the feast was over, they gathered round in a ring and gave all their best gifts to the little princess. One gave her goodness, another beauty, another riches, and so on till she had all that was good in the world.

Just as eleven of them had done blessing her, a great noise was heard in the courtyard, and word was brought that the thirteenth fairy was come, with a black cap on her head, and black shoes on her feet, and a broomstick in her hand: and presently up she came into the dining-hall. Now, as she had not been asked to the feast she was very angry, and scolded the king and queen very much, and set to work to take her revenge. So she cried out, "The king's daughter shall, in her fifteenth year, be wounded by a spindle, and fall down dead." Then the twelfth of the friendly fairies, who had not yet given her gift, came forward, and said that the evil wish must be fulfilled, but that she could soften its mischief; so her gift was, that the king's daughter, when the spindle wounded her, should not really die, but should only fall asleep for a hundred years.

However, the king hoped still to save his dear child altogether from the threatened evil; so he ordered that all the spindles in the kingdom should be bought up and burnt. But all the gifts of the first eleven fairies were in the meantime fulfilled; for the princess was so beautiful, and well behaved, and good, and wise, that everyone who knew her loved her.

It happened that, on the very day she was fifteen years old, the king and queen were not at home, and she was left alone in the palace. So she roved about by herself, and looked at all the rooms and chambers, till at last she came to an old tower, to which there was a narrow staircase ending with a little door. In the door there was a golden key, and when she turned it the door sprang open, and there sat an old lady spinning away very busily. "Why, how now, good mother," said the princess; "what are you doing there?" "Spinning," said the old lady, and nodded her head, humming a tune, while buzz! went the wheel. "How prettily that little thing turns round!" said the princess, and took the spindle and began to try and spin. But scarcely had she touched it, before the fairy's prophecy was fulfilled; the spindle wounded her, and she fell down lifeless on the ground.

However, she was not dead, but had only fallen into a deep sleep; and the king and the queen, who had just come home, and all their court, fell asleep too; and the horses slept in the stables, and the dogs in the court, the pigeons on the house-top, and the very flies slept upon the walls. Even the fire on the hearth left off blazing, and went to sleep; the jack stopped, and the spit that was turning about with a goose upon it for the king's dinner stood still; and the cook, who was at that moment pulling the kitchen-boy by the hair to give him a box on the ear for something he had done amiss, let him go, and both fell asleep; the butler, who was slyly tasting the ale, fell asleep with the jug at his lips: and thus everything stood still, and slept soundly.

A large hedge of thorns soon grew round the palace, and every year it became higher and thicker; till at last the old palace was surrounded and hidden, so that not even the roof or the chimneys could be seen. But there went a report through all the land of the beautiful sleeping Briar Rose (for so the king's daughter was called): so that, from time to time, several kings' sons came, and tried to break through the thicket into the palace. This, however, none of them could ever do; for the thorns and bushes laid hold of them, as it were with hands; and there they stuck fast, and died wretchedly.

After many, many years there came a king's son into that land: and an old man told him the story of the thicket of thorns; and how a beautiful palace stood behind it, and how a wonderful princess, called Briar Rose, lay in it asleep, with all her court. He told, too, how he had heard from his grandfather that many, many princes had come, and had tried to break through the thicket, but that they had all stuck fast in it, and died. Then the young prince said, "All this shall not frighten me; I will go and see this Briar Rose." The old man tried to hinder him, but he was bent upon going.

Now that very day the hundred years were ended; and as the prince came to the thicket he saw nothing but beautiful flowering shrubs, through which he went with ease, and they shut in after him as thick as ever. Then he came at last to the palace, and there in the court lay the dogs asleep; and the horses were standing in the stables; and on the roof sat the pigeons fast asleep, with their heads under their wings. And when he came into the palace, the flies were sleeping on the walls; the spit was standing still; the butler had the jug of ale at his lips, going to drink a draught; the maid sat with a fowl in her lap ready to be plucked; and the cook in the kitchen was still holding up her hand, as if she was going to beat the boy.

Then he went on still farther, and all was so still that he could hear every breath he drew; till at last he came to the old tower, and opened the door of the little room in which Briar Rose was; and there she lay, fast asleep on a couch by the window. She looked so beautiful that he could not take his eyes off her, so he stooped down and gave her a kiss. But the moment he kissed her she opened her eyes and awoke, and smiled upon him; and they went out together; and soon the king and queen also awoke, and all the court, and gazed on each other with great wonder. And the horses shook themselves, and the dogs jumped up and barked; the pigeons took their heads from under their wings, and looked about and flew into the fields; the flies on the walls buzzed again; the fire in the kitchen blazed up; round went the jack, and round went the spit, with the goose for the king's dinner upon it; the butler finished his draught of ale; the maid went on plucking the fowl; and the cook gave the boy the box on his ear.

And then the prince and Briar Rose were married, and the wedding feast was given; and they lived happily together all their lives long.

Discussion Questions

1. Discuss the ways that magic plays a part in the life of Briar Rose from her conception to her marriage.

2. Bettelheim claims in his essay "The Uses of Enchantment" that fairy tale characters are never ambivalent; they are either good or evil. Discuss the behavior of the thirteenth fairy. Do you think there are mitigating circumstances related to her behavior? Is she the only one responsible for Briar Rose's fate? Explain your opinion on this matter.

3. Discuss the coincidence of the prince's arriving on the very day the hundred years are ended and kissing Briar Rose as she awakens from her trance. Do you think this event in the fairy tale reinforces a harmful myth about romantic love, or does it merely present a satisfying ending? Explain your position.

Hansel and Gretel

Essay

THE GRIMM BROTHERS

Jacob Ludwig Carl Grimm and his brother Wilhelm Carl Grimm were born in Hanau, Germany in the late 1700s. Both brothers studied law at the University of Marburg, but it was their scholarly work on linguistics, folklore, and medieval studies that resulted in their most famous work, a two-volume collection of German legends titled Kinder- und Haus- märchen (Children's and Household Tales). *The collection went through six editions during the Grimm brothers' lifetime.*

Hard by a great forest dwelt a poor wood-cutter with his wife and his two children. The boy was called Hansel and the girl Gretel. He had little to bite and to break, and once when great dearth fell on the land, he could no longer procure even daily bread. Now when he thought over this by night in his bed, and tossed about in his anxiety, he groaned and said to his wife: "What is to become of us? How are we to feed our poor children, when we no longer have anything even for ourselves?" "I'll tell you what, husband," answered the woman, "early to-morrow morning we will take the children out into the forest to where it is the thickest; there we will light a fire for them, and give each of them one more piece of bread, and then we will go to our work and leave them alone. They will not find the way home again, and we shall be rid of them." "No, wife," said the man, "I will not do that; how can I bear to leave my children alone in the forest— the wild animals would soon come and tear them to pieces." "O, you fool!" said she, "then we must all four die of hunger, you may as well plane the planks for our coffins," and she left him no peace until he consented. "But I feel very sorry for the poor children, all the same," said the man.

The two children had also not been able to sleep for hunger, and had heard what their step-mother had said to their father. Gretel wept bitter tears, and said to Hansel: "Now all is over with us." "Be quiet, Gretel," said Hansel, "do not distress yourself, I will soon find a way to help us." And when the old folks had fallen asleep, he got up, put on his little coat, opened the door below, and crept outside. The moon shone brightly, and the white pebbles which lay in front of the house glittered like real silver pennies. Hansel stooped and stuffed the little pocket of his coat with as many as he could get in.

Then he went back and said to Gretel: "Be comforted, dear little sister, and sleep in peace, God will not forsake us," and he lay down again in his bed. When day dawned, but before the sun had risen, the woman came and awoke the two children, saying: "Get up, you sluggards! We are going into the forest to fetch wood." She gave each a little piece of bread, and said: "There is something for your dinner, but do not eat it up before then, for you will get nothing else." Gretel took the bread under her apron, as Hansel had the pebbles in his pocket. Then they all set out together on the way to the forest. When they had walked a short time, Hansel stood still and peeped back at the house, and did so again and again. His father said: "Hansel, what are you looking at there and staying behind for? Pay attention, and do not forget how to use your legs." "Ah, father," said Hansel, "I am looking at my little white cat, which is sitting up on the roof, and wants to say good-bye to me." The wife said: "Fool, that is not your little cat, that is the morning sun which is shining on the chimneys." Hansel, however, had not been looking back at the cat, but had been constantly throwing one of the white pebble-stones out of his pocket on the road.

When they had reached the middle of the forest, the father said: "Now, children, pile up some wood, and I will light a fire that you may not be cold." Hansel and Gretel gathered brushwood together, as high as a little hill. The brushwood was lighted, and when the flames were burning very high, the woman said: "Now, children, lay yourselves down by the fire and rest, we will go into the forest and cut some wood. When we have done, we will come back and fetch you away."

Hansel and Gretel sat by the fire, and when noon came, each ate a little piece of bread, and as they heard the strokes of the wood-axe they believed that their father was near. It was not the axe, however, but a branch which he had fastened to a withered tree which the wind was blowing backwards and forwards. And as they had been sitting such a long time, their eyes closed with fatigue, and they fell fast asleep. When at last they awoke, it was already dark night. Gretel began to cry and said: "How are we to get out of the forest now?" But Hansel comforted her and said: "Just wait a little, until the moon has risen, and then we will soon find the way." And when the full moon had risen, Hansel took his little sister by the hand, and followed the pebbles which shone like newly-coined silver pieces, and showed them the way.

They walked the whole night long, and by break of day came once more to their father's house. They knocked at the door, and when the woman opened it and saw that it was Hansel and Gretel, she said: "You naughty children, why have you slept so long in the forest—we thought you were never coming back at all!" The father, however, rejoiced, for it had cut him to the heart to leave them behind alone.

Not long afterwards, there was once more great dearth throughout the land, and the children heard their mother saying at night to their father: "Everything is eaten again, we have one half loaf left, and that is the end. The children must go, we will take them farther into the wood, so that they will not find their way out again; there is no other means of saving ourselves!" The man's heart was heavy, and he thought: "It would be better for you to share the last mouthful with your children." The woman, however, would listen to nothing that he had to say, but scolded and reproached him. He who says A must say B, likewise, and as he had yielded the first time, he had to do so a second time also.

The children, however, were still awake and had heard the conversation. When the old folks were asleep, Hansel again got up, and wanted to go out and pick up pebbles as he had done before, but the woman had locked the door, and Hansel could not get out. Nevertheless he comforted his little sister, and said: "Do not cry, Gretel, go to sleep quietly, the good God will help us."

Early in the morning came the woman, and took the children out of their beds. Their piece of bread was given to them, but it was still smaller than the time before. On the way into the forest Hansel crumbled his in his pocket, and often stood still and threw a morsel on the ground. "Hansel, why do you stop and look round" said the father, "go on." "I am looking back at my little pigeon which is sitting on the roof, and wants to say good-bye to me," answered Hansel. "Fool!" said the woman, "that is not your little pigeon, that is the morning sun that is shining on the chimney." Hansel, however, little by little, threw all the crumbs on the path.

The woman led the children still deeper into the forest, where they had never in their lives been before. Then a great fire was again made, and the mother said: "Just sit there, you children, and when you are tired you may sleep a little; we are going into the forest to cut wood, and in the evening when we are done, we will come and fetch you away." When it was noon, Gretel shared her piece of bread with Hansel, who had scattered his by the way. Then they fell asleep and evening passed, but no one came to the poor children. They did not awake until it was dark night, and Hansel comforted his little sister and said: "Just wait, Gretel, until the moon rises, and then we shall see the crumbs of bread which I have strewn about, they will show us our way home again." When the moon came they set out, but they found no crumbs, for the many thousands of birds which fly about in the woods and fields had picked them all up.

Hansel said to Gretel: "We shall soon find the way," but they did not find it. They walked the whole night and all the next day too from morning till evening, but they did not get out of the forest, and were very hungry, for they had nothing to eat but two or three berries, which grew on the ground. And as they were so weary that their legs would carry them no longer, they lay down beneath a tree and fell asleep.

It was now three mornings since they had left their father's house. They began to walk again, but they always came deeper into the forest, and if help did not come soon, they must die of hunger and weariness. When it was mid-day, they saw a beautiful snow-white bird sitting on a bough, which sang so delightfully that they stood still and listened to it. And when its song was over, it spread its wings and flew away before them, and they followed it until they reached a little house, on the roof of which it alighted; and when they approached the little house they saw that it was built of bread and covered with cakes, but that the windows were of clear sugar. "We will set to work on that," said Hansel, "and have a good meal. I will eat a bit of the roof, and you Gretel, can eat some of the window, it will taste sweet." Hansel reached up above, and broke off a little of the roof to try how it tasted, and Gretel leant against the window and nibbled at the panes. Then a soft voice cried from the parlor:

> "Nibble, nibble, gnaw,
> Who is nibbling at my little house?"

The children answered:

> "The wind, the wind,
> The heaven-born wind,"

and went on eating without disturbing themselves. Hansel, who liked the taste of the roof, tore down a great piece of it, and Gretel pushed out the whole of one round window-pane, sat down, and enjoyed herself with it. Suddenly the door opened, and a woman as old as the hills, who supported herself on crutches, came creeping out. Hansel and Gretel were so terribly frightened that they let fall what they had in their hands. The old woman, however, nodded her head, and said: "Oh, you dear children, who has brought you here. Do come in, and stay with me. No harm shall happen to you." She took them both by the hand, and led them into her little house. Then good food was set before them, milk and pancakes, with sugar, apples, and nuts. Afterwards two pretty little beds were covered with clean white linen, and Hansel and Gretel lay down in them, and thought they were in heaven.

The old woman had only pretended to be so kind; she was in reality a wicked witch, who lay in wait for children, and had only built the little house of bread in order to entice them there. When a child fell into her power, she killed it, cooked and ate it, and that was a feast day with her. Witches have red eyes, and cannot see far, but they have a keen scent like the beasts, and are aware when human beings draw near. When Hansel and Gretel came into her neighborhood, she laughed with malice, and said mockingly: "I have them, they shall not escape me again!" Early in the morning before the children were awake, she was already up, and when she saw both of them sleeping and looking so pretty, with their plump and rosy cheeks, she muttered to herself: "That will be a dainty mouthfull." Then she seized Hansel with her shriveled hand, carried him into a little stable, and locked him in behind a grated door. Scream as he might, it would not help him. Then she went to Gretel, shook her till she awoke, and cried: "Get up, lazy thing, fetch some water, and cook something good for your brother, he is in the stable outside, and is to be made fat. When he is fat, I will eat him." Gretel began to weep bitterly, but it was all in vain, for she was forced to do what the wicked witch commanded.

And now the best food was cooked for poor Hansel, but Gretel got nothing but crab-shells. Every morning the woman crept to the little stable, and cried: "Hansel, stretch out your finger that I may feel if you will soon be fat." Hansel, however, stretched out a little bone to her, and the old woman, who had dim eyes, could not see it, and thought it was Hansel's finger, and was astonished that there was no way of fattening him. When four weeks had gone by, and Hansel still remained thin, she was seized with impatience and would not wait any longer. "Now, then, Gretel," she cried to the girl, "stir yourself, and bring some water. Let Hansel be fat or lean, to-morrow I will kill him, and cook him." Ah, how the poor little sister did lament when she had to fetch the water, and how her tears did flow down her cheeks! "Dear

God, do help us," she cried. "If the wild beasts in the forest had but devoured us, we should at any rate have died together." "Just keep your noise to yourself," said the old woman, "it won't help you at all."

Early in the morning, Gretel had to go out and hang up the cauldron with the water, and light the fire. "We will bake first," said the old woman, "I have already heated the oven, and kneaded the dough." She pushed poor Gretel out to the oven, from which flames of fire were already darting. "Creep in," said the witch, "and see if it is properly heated, so that we can put the bread in." And once Gretel was inside, she intended to shut the oven and let her bake in it, and then she would eat her, too. But Gretel saw what she had in mind, and said: "I do not know how I am to do it; how do I get in?" "Silly goose," said the old woman. "The door is big enough; just look, I can get in myself!" and she crept up and thrust her head into the oven. Then Gretel gave her a push that drove her far into it, and shut the iron door, and fastened the bolt. Oh then she began to howl quite horribly, but Gretel ran away, and the godless witch was miserably burnt to death.

Gretel, however, ran like lightning to Hansel, opened his little stable, and cried: "Hansel, we are saved! The old witch is dead!" Then Hansel sprang like a bird from its cage when the door is opened. How they did rejoice and embrace each other, and dance about and kiss each other! And as they had no longer any need to fear her, they went into the witch's house, and in every corner there stood chests full of pearls and jewels. "These are far better than pebbles!" said Hansel, and thrust into his pockets whatever could be got in, and Gretel said: "I, too, will take something home with me," and filled her pinafore full. "But now we must be off," said Hansel, "that we may get out of the witch's forest."

When they had walked for two hours, they came to a great stretch of water. "We cannot cross," said Hansel, "I see no foot-plank, and no bridge." "And there is also no ferry," answered Gretel, "but a white duck is swimming there; if I ask her, she will help us over." Then she cried:

> "Little duck, little duck, dost thou see,
> Hansel and Gretel are waiting for thee?
> There's never a plank, or bridge in sight,
> Take us across on thy back so white."

The duck came to them, and Hansel seated himself on its back, and told his sister to sit by him. "No," replied Gretel, "that will be too heavy for the little duck; she shall take us across, one after the other." The good little duck did so, and when they were once safely across and had walked for a short time, the forest seemed to be more and more familiar to them, and at length they saw from afar their father's house. Then they began to run, rushed into the parlor, and threw themselves round their father's neck. The man had not known one happy hour since he had left the children in the forest; the woman, however, was dead. Gretel emptied her pinafore until pearls and precious stones ran about the room, and Hansel threw one handful after another out of his pocket to add to them. Then all anxiety was at an end, and they lived together in perfect happiness.

Discussion Questions

1. Why do their mother and father leave Hansel and Gretel in the woods alone? How would Bettelheim use this event to show the way fairy tales address common childhood anxieties?

2. Bettelheim states that people in fairy tales are never ambiguous; they are either all good or all bad. Examine the main characters in "Hansel and Gretel"—Hansel, Gretel, the mother, the father, and the witch. Which ones would you categorize as good? Which ones would you categorize as evil? Are there any characters you have difficulty categorizing? Do your decisions about these characters confirm Bettelheim's claim? Why or why not?

3. Fairy tales have happy or satisfying endings. What elements of the conclusion of this story make it happy or satisfying? Through what means are each of these elements achieved? What positive psychological benefits do you think Bettelheim might say children gain from this ending? Do you think he would be right? Why or why not?

The Goose-Girl

THE GRIMM BROTHERS

There once lived an old queen whose husband had been dead for many years, and she had a beautiful daughter. When the princess grew up she was promised in marriage to a prince who lived far away. When the time came for her to be married, and she had to depart for the distant kingdom, the old queen packed up for her many costly vessels and utensils of silver and gold, and trinkets also of gold and silver, and cups and jewels, in short, everything that belonged to a royal dowry, for she loved her child with all her heart.

She likewise assigned to her a chambermaid, who was to ride with her, and deliver her into the hands of the bridegroom. Each received a horse for the journey. The princess's horse was called Falada, and could speak. When the hour of departure had come, the old mother went into her bedroom, took a small knife and cut her fingers with it until they bled. Then she held out a small white cloth and let three drops of blood fall into it. She gave them to her daughter, saying, "Take good care of these. They will be of service to you on your way."

Thus they sorrowfully took leave of one another. The princess put the cloth into her bosom, mounted her horse, and set forth for her bridegroom. After they had ridden for a while she felt a burning thirst, and said to her chambermaid, "Dismount, and take my cup which you have brought with you for me, and get me some water from the brook, for I would like a drink."

"If you are thirsty," said the chambermaid, "get off your horse yourself, and lie down near the water and drink. I won't be your servant."

So in her great thirst the princess dismounted, bent down over the water in the brook and drank; and she was not allowed to drink out of the golden cup. Then she said, "Oh, Lord," and the three drops of blood answered, "If your mother knew this, her heart would break in two." But the king's daughter was humble. She said nothing and mounted her horse again. They rode some miles further. The day was warm, the sun beat down, and she again grew thirsty. When they came to a stream of water, she again called to her chambermaid, "Dismount, and give me some water in my golden cup," for she had long ago forgotten the girl's evil words.

But the chambermaid said still more haughtily, "If you want a drink, get it yourself. I won't be your servant."

Then in her great thirst the king's daughter dismounted, bent over the flowing water, wept, and said, "Oh, Lord," and the drops of blood again replied, "If your mother knew this, her heart would break in two."

As she was thus drinking, leaning over the stream, the cloth with the three drops of blood fell from her bosom and floated away with the water, without her taking notice of it, so great were her concerns. However, the chambermaid saw what happened, and she rejoiced to think that she now had power over the bride, for by losing the drops of blood, the princess had become weak and powerless.

When she wanted to mount her horse again, the one that was called Falada, the chambermaid said, "I belong on Falada. You belong on my nag," and the princess had to accept it.

Then with many harsh words the chambermaid ordered the princess to take off her own royal clothing and put on the chambermaid's shabby clothes. And in the end the princess had to swear under the open heaven that she would not say one word of this to anyone at the royal court. If she had not taken this oath, she would have been killed on the spot. Falada saw everything, and remembered it well.

The chambermaid now climbed onto Falada, and the true bride onto the bad horse, and thus they traveled onwards, until finally they arrived at the royal palace. There was great rejoicing over their arrival, and the prince ran ahead to meet them, then lifted the chambermaid from her horse, thinking she was his bride.

She was led upstairs, while the real princess was left standing below. Then the old king looked out of the window and saw her waiting in the courtyard, and noticed how fine and delicate and beautiful she was, so at once he went to the royal apartment, and asked the bride about the girl she had with her who was standing down below in the courtyard, and who she was.

"I picked her up on my way for a companion. Give the girl some work to do, so she won't stand idly by."

However, the old king had no work for her, and knew of nothing else to say but, "I have a little boy who tends the geese. She can help him." The boy was called Kürdchen (Little Conrad), and the true bride had to help him tend geese.

Soon afterwards the false bride said to the young king, "Dearest husband, I beg you to do me a favor." He answered, "I will do so gladly."

"Then send for the knacker, and have the head of the horse which I rode here cut off, for it angered me on the way." In truth, she was afraid that the horse might tell how she had behaved toward the king's daughter.

Thus it happened that faithful Falada had to die. The real princess heard about this, and she secretly promised to pay the knacker a piece of gold if he would perform a small service for her. In the town there was a large dark gateway, through which she had to pass with the geese each morning and evening. Would he be so good as to nail Falada's head beneath the gateway, so that she might see him again and again?

The knacker's helper promised to do that, and cut off the head, and nailed it securely beneath the dark gateway. Early in the morning, when she and Conrad drove out their flock beneath this gateway, she said in passing, "Alas, Falada, hanging there!"

Then the head answered:

> Alas, young queen, passing by,
> If this your mother knew,
> Her heart would break in two.

Then they went still further out of the town, driving their geese into the country. And when they came to the meadow, she sat down and unbound her hair which was of pure gold. Conrad saw it, was delighted how it glistened, and wanted to pluck out a few hairs. Then she said:

> Blow, wind, blow,
> Take Conrad's hat,
> And make him chase it,
> Until I have braided my hair,
> And tied it up again.

Then such a strong wind came up that it blew Conrad's hat across the fields, and he had to run after it. When he came back, she was already finished combing and putting up her hair, so he could not get even one strand. So Conrad became angry, and would not speak to her, and thus they tended the geese until evening, and then they went home.

The next morning when they were driving the geese out through the dark gateway, the maiden said, "Alas, Falada, hanging there!"

Falada answered:

> Alas, young queen, passing by,
> If this your mother knew,
> Her heart would break in two.

She sat down again in the field and began combing out her hair. When Conrad ran up and tried to take hold of some, she quickly said:

> Blow, wind, blow,
> Take Conrad's hat,
> And make him chase it,
> Until I have braided my hair,
> And tied it up again.

Then the wind blew, taking the hat off his head and far away. Conrad had to run after it, and when he came back, she had already put up her hair, and he could not get a single strand.

Then they tended the geese until evening.

That evening, after they had returned home, Conrad went to the old king and said, "I won't tend geese with that girl any longer."

"Why not?" asked the old king.

"Oh, because she angers me all day long."

Then the old king ordered him to tell what it was that she did to him. Conrad said, "In the morning when we pass beneath the dark gateway with the flock, there is a horse's head on the wall, and she says to it, 'Alas, Falada, hanging there!' And the head replies:

> Alas, young queen, passing by,
> If this your mother knew,
> Her heart would break in two."

Then Conrad went on to tell what happened at the goose pasture, and how he had to chase his hat.

The old king ordered him to drive his flock out again the next day. As soon as morning came, he himself sat down behind the dark gateway, and heard how the girl spoke with Falada's head. Then he followed her out into the country and hid himself in a thicket in the meadow. There he soon saw with his own eyes the goose-girl and the goose-boy bringing their flock, and how after a while she sat down and took down her hair, which glistened brightly. Soon she said:

> Blow, wind, blow,
> Take Conrad's hat,
> And make him chase it,
> Until I have braided my hair,
> And tied it up again.

Then came a blast of wind and carried off Conrad's hat, so that he had to run far away, while the maiden quietly went on combing and braiding her hair, all of which the king observed. Then, quite unseen, he went away, and when the goose-girl came home in the evening, he called her aside, and asked why she did all these things.

"I am not allowed to tell you, nor can I reveal my sorrows to any human being, for I have sworn under the open heaven not to do so, and if I had not so sworn, I would have been killed."

He urged her and left her no peace, but he could get nothing from her. Finally he said, "If you will not tell me anything, then tell your sorrows to the iron stove there," and he went away. So she crept into the iron stove, and began to cry sorrowfully, pouring out her whole heart. She said, "Here I sit, abandoned by the whole world, although I am the daughter of a king. A false chambermaid forced me to take off my royal clothes, and she has taken my place with my bridegroom. Now I have to do common work as a goose-girl. If my mother knew this, her heart would break in two."

The old king was standing outside listening by the stovepipe, and he heard what she said. Then he came back inside, and asked her to come out of the stove. Then they dressed her in royal clothes, and it was marvelous how beautiful she was.

The old king summoned his son and revealed to him that he had a false bride who was only a chambermaid, but that the true one was standing there, the one who had been a goose-girl. The young king rejoiced with all his heart when he saw her beauty and virtue. A great feast was made ready to which all the people and all good friends were invited.

At the head of the table sat the bridegroom with the king's daughter on one side of him, and the chambermaid on the other. However, the chambermaid was deceived, for she did not recognize the princess in her dazzling attire. After they had eaten and drunk, and were in a good mood, the old king asked the chambermaid as a riddle, what punishment a person deserved who had deceived her master in such and such a manner, then told the whole story, asking finally, "What sentence does such a person deserve?"

The false bride said, "She deserves no better fate than to be stripped stark naked, and put in a barrel that is studded inside with sharp nails. Two white horses should be hitched to it, and they should drag her along through one street after another, until she is dead."

"You are the one," said the old king, "and you have pronounced your own sentence. Thus shall it be done to you."

After the sentence had been carried out, the young king married his true bride, and both of them ruled over their kingdom in peace and happiness.

Discussion Questions

1. How is nature portrayed in "The Goose-Girl"? Compare it to the portrayal of nature in "Hansel and Gretel."

2. What advice does the goose-girl's mother give her when she leaves home? What results from her failure to heed her mother's advice?

3. What specific actions by the goose-girl lead to the tale's happy ending? How is justice defined by this ending?

The Monkey Girl

MIDORI SNYDER

Midori Snyder received her M.A. degree in English Literature from the University of Wisconsin. She has published six acclaimed novels for adults, as well as children's fiction and short stories. Her first novel, Soulstring, *is an adult fairy tale, and was published in 1987. Snyder has devoted much of her studies to the myths, folk customs, and cultures of people around the world.*

When I was a girl reading fairy tales, I appreciated those courageous maidens tromping off in iron shoes or flying on the back of the west wind to find their future husbands where they, imprisoned by trolls or cannibal mothers, waited to be rescued. I admired those young women and their single-minded purpose. They were bold, resourceful, and spirited. And they were certainly a far cry from the "waiting-to-be-awakened" girls or the girls expecting to be fitted with a shoe, a Prince, and a future all at the same time.

Yet even in their plucky natures and heroic tales, there was still something about them that troubled me. Perhaps it was the assumption of happily-ever-after, or at least the seeming surrender of all that reckless adventure. Their rites of passage completed, the journey to find a husband over, there was an expectation that life for these young women would settle once again into neatly defined roles and an untroubled routine. This assumption didn't sit well with me at all. I knew from my own family that such happily-ever-afters were not true. I had parents who had met and married in a passion, and then just as passionately argued, accused, betrayed, and divorced each other. The photographs of their early years depict the blissful expressions worn by most newly married couples, but the later years proved ugly, full of dark misadventures and contentious battles over money. Though I left home at seventeen, inspired I think by the example of those stalwart maidens, I roamed the world in iron shoes forged by my parents' issues and no other goal in my mind except to escape their battles. Eventually, my money dissolved, the shoes became as thin as paper, and I returned home.

What a surprise then to discover a scant year later that home had all but disappeared. A Central Asian scholar, my mother had boarded a bus in Istanbul and traveled for two weeks across Afghanistan, following the Silk Road up to India, where she was now living, indefinitely it seemed. My father and his new wife returned from Africa and moved to another state. My older brother and I temporarily inherited the house along with its mortgage and one of my mother's dysfunctional, melancholic friends as a roommate. I received phone calls from my mother at odd hours of the night, from Delhi, Calcutta, and Bombay, mostly asking me to wire money. During the days I worked at a movie theater, selling popcorn and watching *Dirty Harry* play to a nearly empty house. It didn't seem right. She was out there reinventing herself and I was here, stuck. I wanted to be angry with her, but the truth was I admired her. She was difficult, unpredictable, but also interesting and indomitable. I concluded that she had needed that difficult spirit to survive the dismal destruction of her happily-ever-after.

At the end of my eighteenth year I enrolled in college and met my husband. It happened with the unreal grace of a fairy tale—a single sentence really. There was an introduction, a smile, a night, and almost immediately we were attached at the hip. As pleased with each other as we were, it was disconcerting to find our joy not shared by our friends. According to his family and certainly his suburban friends from high school, I was an unlikely choice, a disaster, and an aberration. It was the seventies; I was too political for them, too opinionated; I wore flannel shirts and glasses and said "fuck" earnestly and often. His friends whispered that he had been snared by a girl who wasn't playing by the usual rules. I was neither compliant, nor pretty in the way one expects of an accessory, and I was known to have claws, verbal comebacks that stung. His parents were convinced that I was the reason he strayed from the church. I was a fornicator, from the wrong class, a pathetic child of a broken home who could only spell disaster for their errant son.

Yet on the other side of the field my women friends from the university shook their heads in equal disapproval. Self-proclaimed radical feminists, these "Red Sisters" argued that marriage was bourgeois, that women in such bonds were no more than property, and they determined that the only way to avoid the trap was to sleep with one another's husbands and boyfriends, swapping them like shoes or sweaters. I refused such invitations—I had already seen where that road led and I wasn't anxious to retrace my parents' footsteps. Monogamy and true love may have been reactionary, but I found them challenging, full of creative possibilities, and, among my girl-friends, mostly untried.

Still, it was difficult and lonely to be on the margins of two worlds, so I remember the thrill I felt recognizing a kindred spirit the first time I encountered "The Monkey Girl," a tale from the Kordofan people of the Sudan. The youngest son of an Emir is asked to choose a bride from the eligible maidens of his village. The Prince rides his horse up and down, spear in hand, ready to cast it at the door of the chosen girl. But he seems unable to decide and, in a moment of frustration, casts the spear far out into the desert. For two days he journeys after it only to discover the spear embedded in the trunk of a lone tree, and in whose leafless branches sits a monkey. As the Prince approaches, the monkey inclines her head and in a gentle voice accepts the proposal of marriage. And the Prince? Well, he is the hero, a man of integrity, true to his word, so he pulls the monkey up behind him on the horse and together they return to the village to be married.

As one might imagine, it's difficult for the Prince. The Emir is appalled; the Prince's brothers, married to wealthy brides, pity him. Hearing the Prince's heavy sighs, the monkey makes him an offer. "Return me to the desert and I promise there will be another woman, more beautiful than you can imagine, waiting for you on your return." "And you?" the Prince inquires. "What will happen to you?" "I will die," she answers simply. The Prince is a decent and compassionate sort, and though it would improve his situation immensely, he refuses to sacrifice the monkey's life. Yet when the Emir decides to dine in each one of his sons' homes, the young Prince is overwhelmed with dismay, for their house is a dark hovel, their meals poor fare. The monkey repeats her offer, but once again the Prince refuses. The monkey tells the Prince to invite his father for the evening meal and that all will be ready for his arrival. When father and son enter the house, the Prince is astonished to discover a miraculous transformation. Beneath the golden gleam of a hundred oil lamps the once-barren rooms are now sumptuously decorated. There are plush carpets patterned with flowers, embroidered silk pillows on which to recline, and low tables spread with silver and copper platters of rich, steaming food. The men are amazed, and for the first time, the Prince begins to wonder about his bride.

What follows is a delicious, slow striptease as the monkey unveils her secrets to the Prince one pale limb at a time over a number of nights. Three times the curious Prince spies on the monkey and manages to catch sight of her sitting before a mirror and deftly peeling back a portion of her furry hide. By moonlight he can see a slender wrist, the curve of her ivory breast, a naked shoulder. Each time he moves toward her, she twirls her finger and a sandstorm fills the little room, blinding him. Only when she is at last ready to emerge as a lovely young woman is the Prince able to steal the skin and burn it. As she stands before him in all her splendor, the Prince is appropriately humbled and awed by his fantastic bride. United at last as a couple, their marriage is now on a sure and heroic footing.

That should have been enough of a happy ending. But it isn't and with good reason.

How can a woman of power, of fantastic substance from that world beyond the boundaries of the human world, be tamed, slotted into the narrow role of a wife? What indeed would be the point of reducing her to the ordinary? The Prince and the Monkey Girl are happily married, but the happily-ever-after is threatened when the Emir begins to lust after the young woman. He imposes impossible tasks on his son, proclaiming death if the Prince fails to complete them. Of course, it is his fantastic bride who rescues him. Effortlessly drawing on her power, she makes the gardens bear fruit overnight and just as easily consumes a storehouse of food during the second night. In the final task she tricks the Emir into agreeing to his own death should the Prince succeed in making a newborn infant learn to walk and talk in a single day. The following morning the child walks into the hall announcing the Emir's death sentence and the ascension of the young Prince to the throne. Not just a pretty face, this Monkey Girl, but wise and adept at managing agriculture, politics, law, and dangerous men.

What fascinated me the most in this story was not the obvious ugly monkey to beautiful woman transformation. It was the idea that the Monkey Girl controlled not only the destiny of her own rite of passage, but also that of the Prince. Through the agency of the spear—a wonderful manipulation of the phallic sign—she brings the Prince out into the fantastic realm to her to begin his journey. Similarly, cloaked in the animal skin, she embarks on her own rite of passage, journeying back to the human world while the storyteller in her recounts in figurative language the scenario of her death as an adolescent girl and her resurrection as an adult woman ready for marriage. She uses her disguise not only to complete her rite of passage, but also to test her husband's worthiness, his integrity, his compassion, and the strength of their bond. Little by little, she reveals herself to him, gradually making him aware of the considerable hidden power she possesses. Can he handle it? Will he be frightened? Or worse, will he try to control and possess her like the Emir?

It is the task of the hero to wrestle with the ambiguous power of the fantastic world and return with its fully creative potential in hand. The young Prince proves his loyalty and compassion and from the monkey's bestial skin there emerges a beautiful bride. This bride is unlike her mortal counterparts, no matter how brave and courageous they may appear in the other tales, for she represents a union, a partnership between the human hero and the creative forces of the fantastic world. In their marriage, hero and fantastic bride work together as equals to enrich each other's lives and strengthen their community.

But this is one bride who must never be underestimated or taken for granted in the happily-ever-after. The beastly bride, while she may shed her skin or commit herself as a sensual partner, never surrenders her power and therefore always remains a little dangerous, a little unpredictable. There are beastly brides who hide their scales, their fur, and don the bodies of women in order to marry men for their own reasons and have children. Perhaps these brides should come with warning labels—disrespect us at your own peril! Husbands transgressing by peering into keyholes to learn the hidden truth about their wives run the risk of losing all the privileges such fantastic women provide them. And while the tales of beastly brides may be regarded as the cautionary warnings of a patriarchal society convinced that the difficult woman hides a furry tail, scaled thighs, or a demon's appetite, I, for one, rejoice in them. They force the essential questions of marriage: Can you respect the power I hold, the secrets that are mine, the space that is reserved for me alone, and still be loving? Can marriage be a union of two forces, each with their own gifts to be offered freely, mutually acknowledged, respected, and supported? And if the answer is no and the marriage hits a bump, a snag in the happily-ever-after, these women pack their bags and leave for the forests, the deserts, the deep oceans, or India, angry but undaunted. Years after their divorce, my father confessed to me that he had often told my mother in their bitter fights that it seemed she couldn't decide whether to be a mother or an academic. It was with regret that he had recognized too late that had he supported her, she could have been both. A beastly bride, my mother was too difficult and too rich in resources for my father to appreciate and love until she was gone.

The tale of the Monkey Girl gave me what I needed most at a critical time in my life: the image of the creative and complex woman, unique to herself but willing to share those considerable gifts with a man capable of intuiting the wealth of her worth hidden beneath the skin. But more than that, the Monkey Girl also suggested that I need not be afraid of the fragile happily-ever-after, that I had resources of my own, and that I would not have to contort myself into a restrictive social role for fear of losing that fairytale ending. There was always travel. I gained courage resisting the tyranny of those opposing sides: the one that argued I was too radical and sharp, and the other that insisted I was a deluded, romantic traditionalist caught in the jaws of a bourgeois trap. Thirty years later, still happily married to the same man, I feel a debt of gratitude to the powerful example of the fantastic bride.

When I began to write novels I experienced again the presence of the Monkey Girl at my shoulder, pushing me, encouraging me. What better teacher could I have had? For out of the mysteries, the imagination, the realm of all things fantastic, she creates and transforms life: gardens out of the desert sands, wealth out of a hovel, feasts out of dry bread, precocious children out of newborns, and a husband out of a promising but confused young hero. She has a flair for drama, disguise, and illusion. From the moment the Prince releases his spear in her direction, she controls the story, manipulating the narrative, repetition fueling a smoldering sexual anticipation that climaxes when she at last reveals herself quite nude and available.

But behind the Monkey Girl is another woman, the one who tells this tale, the one who repeats it over and over again so that we may always remain respectfully awed by the provocative and resplendent power of the fantastic bride. Who could resist admiring the skill of such a potent storyteller? Certainly not me, and so it is in my own work that I follow this well-worn path and take pleasure in writing the tales of difficult women, ambiguous and fantastic women, women whose fairytale-like stories I never grow tired of imagining.

Discussion Questions

1. In what ways does the author, Midori Snyder, find the typical fairy tale heroine to be disappointing and unrealistic?

2. In what ways that appeal to the author does the story of the Monkey Girl differ from other, more traditional and familiar, fairy tales?

3. The author calls the Monkey Girl her teacher. How has this character fulfilled this role in the author's own life? Do you think "The Monkey Girl" provides the same kind of guidance Bettelheim claims for the more traditional fairy tales? Why or why not?

Change and Sexuality: Ursula and Ariel as Markers of Metamorphosis in *The Little Mermaid*

PAUL BEEHLER

Paul Beehler, Ph.D. is a faculty member in the University Writing Program at the University of California, Riverside. He has published articles on Shakespeare and composition pedagogy, and he is currently working on material involving religion and Shakespeare. The following essay is an excerpt from a longer piece that will soon appear in Collision of Realities – Establishing Research on the Fantastic in Europe *(2011) with Peter Lang Publishers, Hamburg. Beehler has also presented a number of papers at various national and international conferences. A version of this paper was presented at the Universitat Hamburg at a conference entitled* Gesellschaft fur Fantastikforschung.

Even after some twenty years, Disney's *The Little Mermaid* (1989) is perceived as one of the "new classics" and many copies of the DVD can be found in libraries throughout the world.[1] Indeed, Disney, in August of 2008, saw fit to produce and release the third sequel to *The Little Mermaid, The Little Mermaid: Ariel's Beginning*, in an attempt to capitalize upon the renewed interest around the characters and concept. Even more recent is the debut of Disney's *World of Color*, a production Disney released in their California Adventure theme park on June 11, 2010. Offering a keenly prominent position specifically for Ariel, Disney's *World of Color* is the culmination of a highly technical show that relies extensively on animation, lights, lasers, and water cannons. With the span of time comes a greater appreciation (and in

---

[1]Indeed, according to www.the-numbers.com/movies/1989/LMERM-DVD.php, three releases of *The Little Mermaid* have taken place: November 15, 1989; November 14, 1997; and December 7, 1999. During the last period that the DVD was released from the vault, sales were epic: 6,290,363 copies were sold for a total of $95,266,221 between October 8 of 2006 and December 3 of 2006. What is more astounding is that these sales numbers only apply to the DVD and not Blu-ray nor VHS (which reported over four million copies sold in the first week alone of the re-release). The recent release (late August of 2008) of the third sequel that showcases Ariel, *The Little Mermaid: Ariel's Beginning* (2008), is certain to ignite sales and reinvigorate interest once again in *The Little Mermaid* and all its accompanying lore.

[2]Recently, I polled my students to get an anecdotal sense of how pervasive *The Little Mermaid* is with an audience that is removed from the film in time by a full generation. To my surprise, all of the women in my class demonstrated an impressive familiarity with the film, even to the point that some spontaneously broke out into song. The men seemed aware, but much less so of the film.

this case greater verve for the work) as well as a certain perspective that can be applied through criticism.[2] That Ariel, the protagonist of *The Little Mermaid*, undergoes a profound metamorphosis in both Disney's and H. C. Andersen's versions of the fairy tale is undisputed. Laura Sells, in a chapter entitled "Where Do the Mermaids Stand," is perhaps one of the more vocal critics of the film, and she directly identifies the theme of change as she positions the film, and specifically Ariel, in a feminist discourse. After considering Barbara Bush's use of mermaid imagery when speaking to a group of Wellesley students, Sells asserts that, "*The Little Mermaid* reflects some of the tensions in American feminism between reformist demands for access, which leave in place the fixed and complementary definitions of masculine and feminine gender identities, and radical refigurings of gender that assert symbolic change as preliminary to social change" (177). Change in the film is seemingly desirable, inevitable, and essential, but what Sells only tangentially mentions (and this is an argument generally found wanting in the field) is the intense scrutiny regarding the agent of that change, Ursula—a self-proclaimed "witch." A study of the actual change and its political/feminist ramifications is most certainly a productive conversation, but a complete exegesis of *The Little Mermaid* must move beyond the transformation into a broader argument regarding the catalyst for such change. This odyssey, an investigation that has thus far eluded critics, is essential to any plenary appreciation of the work, so the character Ursula requires close scrutiny if one is to appreciate Ariel and her role fully.

Historically, the experienced and prurient widow was a seminal component of the Early Modern witch, but the other common image of the sixteenth and seventeenth century English witch is equally important: that of the young unmarried temptress. Ostracized and banned from society, witches who were in part identified as unattached women scratched out a living in the outskirts of villages by offering counsel and herbs to other women as a form of *uenificium*. Those women who tended to women, especially in matters of reproduction and birth, routinely faced the hazards of witch hunts. Their powers could be officially indicted under *maleficium*. The formal profession of midwife offered an especially tempting target for those zealots interested in prosecuting witches through forces like King James and the *Malleus Maleficarum*. Here were a group of women who offered assistance with birth, abortion, and contraception—these women were frequently present in the lives of other women during crucial periods of feminine transition; for their efforts, they were occasionally rewarded with fines, imprisonment, scorn, and even execution. Like these historical witches, Ursula serves as a midwife to assist Ariel during her process of transformation, and Ariel stands before a crossroads: will she be fashioned in the image of Ursula, or will she assume the role of young temptress/witch? Essentially, Ariel finds herself poised between the two primary roles of witch: on one hand, Ariel faces the possibility of assuming the position of a seductively threatening woman while on the other hand the heroine may, under the tutelage of Ursula, refashion her identity into the witch who has knowledge of sex and can manipulate society through this position of power. Neither form of the feminine nightmare is suitable, especially for an ascending princess of Ariel's magnitude. Indeed, Ariel must simultaneously divorce herself from her current form while avoiding the undue influence and auspices of Ursula. Bruno Bettelheim sums up the situation of Disney's heroine best when he argues that with every fairy tale's

> end the hero has mastered all trials and despite them remained true to himself, or in successfully undergoing them has achieved his true selfhood. He has become an autocrat in the best sense of the word—a self-ruler, a truly autonomous person, not a person who rules over others. (127)

Ariel requires Ursula's guidance to achieve, ultimately, a new form that serves as a delicately tempered hybrid of the sexual witch and the experienced matron/witch; however, Ariel extricates herself in the final moments of the film to claim, at least in relation to Ursula, the ostensible role of Bettelheim's autocrat. Would that such a role enjoyed some traction; unfortunately in Ariel's case, the heroine's liberty is perhaps more ephemeral than even that of a common mayfly because she quickly delivers herself to the much anticipated wedding nuptials.

Ariel's role as seductress or matron has yet to be determined when The *Little Mermaid* opens. Her breasts are those of a budding adolescent, and this image benefits from a certain intensity with Ariel's line, "I'm sixteen years old. I'm not a child." Ariel's line is delivered in one of the opening scenes, and she openly declares that she is not a child; indeed, the audience does not know what she is just yet, and this is where the female threat is poised. Ariel's physical body—that of mermaid or human—is as ambiguous as her role in the film. Is she a girl or a woman? Does she reside in the water or on land? Is she the maternal or the seductress? The movie can essentially be read as a journey for the protagonist, a journey that results in the birth of her identity and then a renunciation of identity, an act that yields to a solidification of her position in society. This birth is appropriately mired in the image of water and forcefully moves upwards towards the concretely defined surface of land. Of greatest consequence is that this process can only be negotiated with the aid of Ursula, the mid-wife witch, and Ursula harbors her own agenda. Chris Richards, in his essay "Room to Dance: Girls' Play and *The Little Mermaid*," addresses the dramatic binaries that stand before Ariel at the moment she considers the flotsam of the human world:

> Ariel's song sets out a series of binary oppositions and it is through these that her yearning is constructed. Her desire is animated by the distance between the treasured, but lifeless, objects in her cavern and the vibrant mobility of life on two legs shared by the people on land. The wish to be part of that world above, from which her physical form appears irrevocably to exclude her, is expressed in terms which divide her fishy attributes from those which might be associated with maturity and sexuality. (144)

The transformation of forms and the binaries present in the film are also powerfully communicated through the image of the breast. Ariel's scanty clothing reveals, upon her introduction, shapely and youthful breasts. Like the other mermaids, she has a single tail with no vaginal opening. She is, at one and the same time, oddly seductive and disturbingly asexual: Richards' binary is potently communicated through such an image. The camera is trained on Ariel throughout her opening sequences, and she becomes the object of "the gaze" because the young mermaid with her scantily clad breasts and "V" shaped scales around her navel is an unapproachable seductress who, without some form of physical transformation, is incapable of assuming the role of mother. Ariel faces a dilemma of the greatest magnitude: will she maintain her current form, thereby becoming a nexus of frustrating and threatening actions to society and the larger audience as a whole, or will the worlds below and above conspire against her by consigning her to the acceptable and controlled role of matron? In other words, the audience confronts a question of identity regarding the little mermaid: will Ariel frustrate society by retaining social power through the traits of sexual seduction, or will society find a comedic resolution by robbing Ariel of any social force by extricating the seductive and replacing such characteristics with the role of wife and, eventually, mother? Disney's heroine actively struggles with this role of identity, and Ariel must decide whether she will subvert or reinforce the power structure before her. Ariel becomes a malleable object hidden deep beneath the waters of the subconscious, and she serves as a frustration which must ultimately be resolved in the course of the film.

When Disney's film concludes, Ariel is poised to assume the role of queen by kissing Prince Eric in a wedding ceremony; her ascension to the role of queen requires, in part, that she, to use Bettelheim's terminology, have "gained mature adulthood" (128), and this act is steeped in the mystique of "what sex consists of; that is the secret of adults which {s}he wishes to discover" (128). Through Ursula's intimate guidance, Ariel has mastered the secret power of sex: she now physically signals the profound transformation through her covered breast, a breast that neither intimidates nor threatens society. Ariel is no longer the seductress/witch, nor has she overshot her mark to become the sexually knowledgeable witch; instead, Ariel enjoys but a brief existence in the role of autocrat only to accept her position as society and Prince Eric define it—that is, as a function of deference. When the film concludes, Ariel's existence as an independent force is tragically best characterized as momentary in nature.

Ariel's nudity and the unfettered breast, upon the conclusion of Disney's film, are deftly exchanged for a series of dresses and clothing that fully efface any seductive trace of Ariel's breast. With the single exception of a brief retransformation of Ariel into a mermaid (which, interestingly enough, enables Prince Eric to again express his amorous desires), the images of Ariel's breast become increasingly stifled and controlled until Disney offers its final image of the heroine: Ariel in a wedding dress. Even when King Triton, in the final moments of the film, extends his trident to transfigure his daughter one last time from mermaid to human, Ariel emerges from the ocean not as an unclothed woman, but as an enchanting female donning a luminescent gown. This emergence is significantly different from the earlier resurrection of Ariel that revealed a nude heroine. No chance is afforded for the emergence of the autocrat as Ariel runs into the arms and subsequent protection of Prince Eric. Ariel's sleeveless gown is then, in a single moment, replaced with the image of Ariel in her wedding dress, a piece of clothing that almost entirely eclipses Ariel's body—even white gloves hide Ariel's hands. The movie, as well as Ariel's transfiguration, comes to an irrefutable conclusion, and Ariel assumes her contained position in society—a position that comes at the cost of her independence and sexual expressiveness. In Andersen's conclusion, Ariel meets a less tragic ending in that she is released upon the sea as bubbles and so meets a physical demise, but her identity and determinism remain intact. Acts of violence and social transgressions, while not resolved in a comfortable manner, are at least recognized, and a clear sense of loss is conveyed. Disney's more comic ending, at least in the sense of a Shakespearean comedy, is in many ways much more disturbing because Ariel is physically passed from her father, King Triton, to her husband, Prince Eric. The final minutes of the film suggest that Ariel's window to fulfill the role of autocrat may indeed have been very brief if, alas, it ever existed in this world of illusion.

Works Cited

Andersen, Hans Christian. *The Little Mermaid and Other Stories*. Trans. R. Nisbet Bain. Lawrence and Bullen: London, 1893. Print.

Bettelheim, Bruno. *The Uses of Enchantment: The Meaning and Importance of Fairy Tales*. New York: Vantage Books, 1989. Print.

Bynum, Caroline Walker. *Jesus as Mother: Studies in the Spirituality of the High and Middle Ages*. Berkeley: University of California Press, 1982. Print.

Byrne, Eleanor, and Martin McQuillan. *Deconstructing Disney*. London: Pluto Press, 1999. Print.

Campbell, Joseph. *The Hero with a Thousand Faces*. New York: Pantheon Books, 1949. Print.

Finkelstein, Richard. "Disney's *Tempest*: Colonizing Desire in *The Little Mermaid*." *The Emperor's Old Groove: Decolonizing Disney's Magic Kingdom*. Ed. Brenda Ayres. New York: Peter Lang, 2003. 131-149. Print.

Holmes, Ronald. *Witchcraft in British History*. London: Frederick Muller Ltd., 1974. Print.

The Little Mermaid. Dir. Ron Clements and John Musker. Perf.

Samuel E. Wright, Jodi Benson, Pat Carroll, and Kenneth Mars. Disney Feature Animation, 1989. DVD.

The Little Mermaid: Ariel's Beginning. Dir. Peggy Holmes. Perf. Jodi Benson, Sally Field, Jim Cummings, and Samuel E. Wright. Disney Toon Studios, 2008. DVD.

Nash Information Services, LLC. 3 September 2008. The Numbers: Box Office Data, Movie Stars, Idle Speculation. Web. 3 September 2008. http://www.thenumbers.com/movies/1989/LMERM-DVD.php.

Richards, Chris. "Room to Dance: Girls' Play and *The Little Mermaid*." *In Front of the Children*. Ed. Cary Bazalgette and David Buckingham. London: British Film Institute, 1995. 141-50.

Sells, Laura. "Where Do the Mermaids Stand?: Voice and Body in *The Little Mermaid*." *From Mouse to Mermaid: The Politics of Film, Gender, and Culture*. Ed. Elizabeth Bell, Lynda Haas, and Laura Sells. Bloomington: Indiana University Press, 1995. 175-192. Print.

Willis, Deborah. *Malevolent Nurture: Witch-Hunting and Maternal Power in Early Modern England*. Ithaca: Cornell UP, 1995. Print.

Discussion Questions

1. What role, according to Paul Beehler, does Ursula play in Ariel's transformation from mermaid to human? What is the historical context in which he places this role? Why does Ariel need to be guided by and to divorce herself from Ursula? Explain your reasons for accepting or rejecting Beehler's exploration of Ursula's role.

2. According to Paul Beehler, what relationship exists between Ariel's identity, her transformation, and society? Why do you think the same basic argument applies to all/some/no modern brides?

3. Discuss the necessity and implications of the physical changes Ariel undergoes.

4. How does Beehler use Bettelheim to explain the role of a hero in fairy tales? Why do you think Ariel could or could not be said to fulfill this role as defined by Bettelheim?

Construction of the Female Self: Feminist Readings of the Disney Heroine

Jill Birnie Henke, Diane Zimmerman Umble, Nancy J. Smith

THIS ESSAY EXAMINES THE WAY in which the female self is constructed in five Disney films: *Cinderella, Sleeping Beauty, The Little Mermaid, Beauty and the Beast,* and *Pocahontas.* Standpoint feminist theory and feminist scholarship on the psychological development of the perfect girl are used to form questions about selfhood, relationships, power, and voice. Although heroines have expressed voice and selfhood in some of the later films, Disney's interpretations of children's literature and history remain those of a white, middle-class, patriarchal society.

Americans swim in a sea of Disney images and merchandise. Children can watch Disney videos before they brush their teeth with Disney character toothbrushes, go to sleep in *Beauty and the Beast* pajamas, rest their heads on *The Little Mermaid* pillow cases, check the time on *Pocahontas* watches, and drift off to sleep listening to Cinderella sing, "No matter how your heart is grieving, if you keep on believing, the dream that you wish will come true" on their tape recorders. American children and their families watch Disney stories over and over again courtesy of their home video recorders. The Disney corporation produces myriad texts that form part of the cultural experience of American children and adults. Not only does Disney create a "wonderful world" of images, but the corporation also makes money in the process.

Disney re-releases its animated features to theaters on a seven-year rotation as a marketing strategy to attract a following in each new generation (Landis, "Hibernation," p. 5D). Following theatrical showings, video cassettes are sold for a limited time. *Aladdin* earned $200 million in theaters in 1993, while its predecessor *Beauty and the Beast* grossed $20 million from the sale of videotapes alone (Landis, "Princely," p. 1D). This home video library provides families with opportunities for repeated viewing of such Disney films as *The Little Mermaid, Sleeping Beauty, Cinderella,* and *Pocahontas.*

This essay focuses on five animated features that span over fifty years of Disney story-telling and that portray a heroine as central to the story line: *Cinderella* (1950), *Sleeping Beauty* (1959), *The Little Mermaid* (1989), *Beauty and the Beast* (1991), and *Pocahontas* (1995).[1] In light of the ubiquity of Disney's images, sounds, and stories, we examine the kind of world the Disney corporation constructs through its animated feature films, specifically what it means to be young and female.

This project grew out of our own experiences as media consumers, teachers, scholars, and mothers of daughters. We began with the assumption that mass media articulates cultural values about gender by portraying women, men, and their relationships in particular ways. In addition, Julia Wood (1994) argues that the media also reproduces cultural definitions of gender by defining what is to be taken for granted. Disney stories, then, have become part of a cultural repertoire of ongoing performances and reproductions of gender roles by children and adults; moreover, these stories present powerful and sustained messages about gender and social relations. Because our analysis is shaped by conversations with our daughters and our students as they began to adopt a critical stance toward Disney texts, the analytical framework we apply to these films is based on a synthesis of two streams of feminist thought: the psychological development of females, and standpoint feminist theory. Together, the perspectives illuminate the meaning and implications of Disney's filmic portrayal of girls.

The Oxymoron of Power and the Perfect Girl

Research by Carol Gilligan and her colleagues chronicles the psychological development of women's conceptualizations of the self. Gilligan (1982) argues that women learn to value connections with others and at least in part define themselves through their relationships with others. Orenstein (1994), who examines the related concern of how gender is constructed in the classroom, describes the hidden curriculum that teaches girls to view silence and compliance as virtues.

---

[1]When we first began our study of the Disney animated heroines, *Snow White* had not been released on video nor re-released in the theaters, so it was not included among the films we analyzed. However, the themes introduced in the two earliest films, *Cinderella* and *Sleeping Beauty*, were also present in *Snow White*. We did not include *Aladdin* because the story really centers around the boy, Aladdin, whereas Princess Jasmine is cast in a secondary role and commands little screen time. Princess Jasmine is important, however, in that she is Disney's first non-Caucasian princess.

Those values present a dilemma for bright girls who must simultane-ously be "selfless and selfish, silent and outspoken, cooperative and competitive" (pp. 36–37). After studying white middle-class girls at all-girls schools, Brown and Gilligan (1992) suggest that the solution to this dilemma rests with females' invention of a self: the "perfect girl." The perfect girl, in white middle-class America, is "the girl who has no bad thoughts or feelings, the kind of person everyone wants to be with, the girl who, in her perfection, is worthy of praise and attention, worthy of inclusion and love.... [She is the] girl who speaks quietly, calmly, who is always nice and kind, never mean or bossy" (p. 59). Yet, these same girls know from their own experiences that people do get angry, wish to speak, and want to be heard. The consequence of these contradictory gender/social messages is that a girl is "caught between speaking what she knows from experience about relationships and increased pressure to negate this knowledge for an idealized and frau-dulent view of herself and her relationships" (p. 61). Hence, Brown and Gilligan (1992) conclude that on the way to womanhood a girl experi-ences a loss of voice and loss of a sense of self as she silences herself.

During the process of this intellectual and emotional silencing, girls also are developing physically in new ways. According to Brown and Gilligan (1992), changes in girls' bodies "visually disconnect them from the world of childhood and identify them in the eyes of others with women" (p. 164). Girls conflate standards of beauty and standards of goodness by learning to pay attention to their "looks" and by listening to what others say about them. They learn to see themselves through the gaze of others, hear about themselves in ways that suggest they can be perfect, and believe that relationships can be free of conflict. These girls "struggle between knowing what they know through experience and what others want them to know, to feel and think" (p. 64). As a result, girls learn that speaking up can be dis-ruptive and dangerous because it might put relationships at risk. The cruel irony is that by withholding their voices, girls also risk losing relationships that are genuine and authentic. In effect, girls struggle daily with the "seduction of the unattainable, to be all things to all people, to be perfect girls and model women" (p. 180).

Julia Wood's (1992) critique of Gilligan's line of research expands our application of Gilligan's work on the construction of the female self to Disney films. Wood explores the tension between Gilligan's apparently essentializing stance and a post-structural stance which emphasizes the structural effects of cultural life on individuals. The result is what Wood calls "standpoint epistemology."

"Standpoint theory prompts study of conditions that shape lives and the ways individuals construct those conditions and their experiences within them" (Wood, 1992, p. 15). For women, this theory helps explain how a female's position within a culture shapes her experiences. Because cultures define people by gender, race, and class, they often impose limits on women's experiences and women's ability to appreciate the experiences of others. Standpoint feminism argues that women have been and still are treated as "others" and "outsiders" in patriarchal societies. Although women's experiences are diverse to be sure, Wood (1992) argues that scholars should look for conditions among women that unify them. Oppression, for example, is one condition that seems universal among women: "Survival for those with subordinate status often depends quite literally on being able to read others, respond in ways that please others, and assume responsibility for others' comfort" (p. 16).

Yet, differences among women, as individuals and as members of identifiable categories within broadly shared social conditions, should not be overlooked. Our analysis of Disney characters responds to this call by articulating their similarities and their differences. Indeed, our analysis suggests that one value of standpoint feminist epistemology lies in unveiling which differences are conspicuously absent. For example, the heterosexist assumption underlying all five Disney films is not only the dominant social construct influencing relationships, it is the only social construct. None of the female figures questions that assumption. Standpoint theory, then, provides the means to understand how women's voices are muted and how women can regain their voices and become empowered (Wood, 1991).

Mary Parker Follett, an American intellectual whose ideas were touted by the business community in the 1940s, wrote about the construction and use of power in society in *Creative Experience* (1924). "Coercive power," Parker Follett wrote, "is the curse of the universe; coactive power, the enrichment of every human soul" (p. xii). In later works she defined two types of power—"power-over" and "power-with": "It seems to me that whereas power usually means power-over, the power of some person or group over some other person or group, it is possible to develop the conception of power-with, a jointly developed power, a co-active, not a coercive power" (1944, p. 101). While Parker Follett did not explicitly use the expression "power from within," this understanding is embedded in her discussion of the need for social constructs which preserve the integrity of the individual. She argues that a society can only progress if individuals' internal needs are met in the processes adopted by the group.

Parker Follett's conceptualization of power, in conjunction with the principles contained in standpoint feminist theory and Gilligan's perspective on the psychological development of girls, forms the foundation for a series of questions that the following analysis of Disney's animated films hopes to answer: How do the worlds of Disney films construct the heroine's sense of self? To what degree is her self-knowledge related to or in response to her relationships with others? Do Disney heroines model the "perfect girl"? On the way to womanhood, what does the Disney heroine give up? What are the ways in which the female characters experience their lives as "others" and themselves as strangers in their relationship to self and others? And what are the power dynamics of those relationships?

Until the recent publication of *From Mouse to Mermaid: The Politics of Film, Gender, and Culture* (Bell, Haas, & Sells, 1995), few scholarly analyses addressed the foregoing questions about gender constructions in the worlds of Disney animated films.[2] However, with the Bell, Haas, and Sells' edition, critical analyses of Disney discourses entered a new phase. This edited collection maps "the ideological contours of economics, politics, and pedagogy by drawing Disney films as vehicles of cultural production" (p. 7). Within this ideological map, the cultural reproduction of gender is examined by several authors.

For example, Jack Zipes (1995) argues that characterizations of Disney heroines remain one-dimensional and stereotypical, "arranged according to a credo of domestication of the imagination" (p. 40). The values imparted in Disney fairy tales are not those of original folk tellers, nor of the original writers such as Perrault or Andersen; instead, they are the values of Disney's male writers. Thus, even when the fairy tale is supposed to focus on the heroine (Snow White, Cinderella, Sleeping Beauty, Beauty, or the Little Mermaid), "these figures

---

[2]Brody (1976) describes the success of Disney fairy tales from a psychoanalytic perspective. Trites (1991) contrasts Disney's version of *The Little Mermaid* with the original Hans Christian Andersen tale from a Freudian perspective. Other analysts (May, 1981; Stone, 1975) critique the way in which Disney selectively appropriates classics of children's literature. Sex role stereotyping is the focus of work by Levinson (1975) and Holmlund (1979). They extend concerns about stereotyping using a Marxist feminist approach to the sexual politics of Disney films. Some work has celebrated the Disney tradition for its connections with the oral tradition (Allan, 1988) and its artistic accomplishments (Morrow, 1978).

are pale and pathetic compared to the more active and demonic characters in the film" (p. 37). These alleged heroines are "helpless ornaments in need of protection, and when it comes to the action of the film, they are omitted" (p. 37). In contrast, while Laura Sells' (1995) Marxist feminist analysis of *The Little Mermaid* sees the story's resolution as a "dangerous message about appropriation" (p. 185), Sells remains hopeful nevertheless because "Ariel enters the white male system with her voice—a stolen, flying voice that erupted amidst patriarchal language, a voice no longer innocent because it resided for a time in the dark continent that is the Medusa's home" (p. 185).

Our analysis elaborates upon the two themes that Zipes and Sells introduce: the relative power or powerlessness of the Disney heroine, and the discovery or loss of that heroine's voice. Thus, our exploration of the construction of the female self and the interaction of that self with other film characters corroborates and extends the work of Bell, Haas, and Sells. We utilize standpoint feminist theory, Follett's theories of power, and Gilligan and Brown's theories of female psychological development to chronicle the nature and evolution of Disney's construction of the female self.

Construction of the Female Self

Disney's early heroines, Cinderella and Aurora, are portrayed as helpless, passive victims who need protection. Indeed, Cinderella is the quintessential "perfect girl," always gentle, kind, and lovely. Their weaknesses are contrasted with the awesome and awful power of the evil women with whom they struggle. However, later Disney films shift from simple stories of passive, young virgins in conflict with evil, mature women to more complex narratives about rebellion, exploration, and danger. Heroines Ariel, Belle, and Pocahontas display an increasingly stronger sense of self, of choice, and of voice.

This growing empowerment of Disney heroines is reflected in shifting depictions of their intimate relationships. While early heroines fall in love at first sight and easily marry to live happily ever after, love relationships for the later heroines come at a cost. Ariel temporarily gives up her voice and ultimately relinquishes her cultural identity. Belle discovers love only through trials, sacrifice, and learning to look beneath the surface. Ultimately, though, her love releases the Beast from the bonds of his own selfishness so they, too, are "empowered" to live happily ever after together.

Of all of Disney's characters, Pocahontas seems to break new ground. The narrative begins with her as a young woman in possession of a strong, well-developed sense of self, and a conviction that her destiny only remains to be discovered. Unlike other Disney heroines, she resists losing her identity to another for the sake of a marriage relationship. Her position and value in her community, her relationships with other females, and her understanding of her interdependence with the earth provide the most holistic picture yet of a co-actively empowered character in Disney animated films.

In her classic essay, "The Solitude of Self," Elizabeth Cady Stanton (1892) advanced a feminist vision in which women experience the sovereignty of the self, and women and girls are empowered from within. Stanton indicted patriarchy for systematically denying women the skills and rights to exist as sovereign selves. Over a century later, feminists still envision a diversity of female figures acting on the world from knowledge of their own worth and dreams. Are traces of these visions contained in Disney's filmic heroines?

The five films we examine situate the central female character—who is portrayed as gentle, kind, beautiful, and virginal—in an oppressive social milieu where mothers or other sources of female guidance and wisdom are largely absent. Until *Pocahontas*, in fact, these young heroines faced the challenges of their lives without the benefit of other women's support, nurturance, or guidance.

Cinderella, Aurora, Ariel, Belle, and Pocahontas also share another quality: they all have dreams. Each differs, however, in her power to make that dream come true. The conventional Disney tale introduces the heroine near the film's beginning through a song in which she expresses these dreams. For example, viewers first meet Cinderella when she awakens from a dream and sings, "No matter how your heart is grieving, if you keep on believing, the dream that you wish will come true." Minutes later, viewers discover that her daily reality is anything but dreamy. Supported by an army of mice and barnyard animals who come to her aid, Cinderella is continuously reminded by humans in the household that she is unworthy of their "refined" company. Cinderella's stepmother and stepsisters control Cinderella, keeping her locked away from both society and opportunity. Cinderella is portrayed as powerless to act on her own behalf. Hence, she can only dream.

Perhaps Cinderella best illustrates the Disney pattern of subjugating and stifling heroines' voices and selfhood. Her gentleness and goodness are defined by her lack of resistance to abuse by her step-family in the film's world. She never disobeys an order, never defends her rights, and never challenges their authority over her. She rarely eats, seldom sleeps, and receives not even the simplest of courtesies, except from her animal friends. Her father's fortune is squandered for the benefit of her stepsisters. She is powerless to control her own fate in her own home. Unable to control her own time, she also is unable to control her own destiny. Cinderella does not act, she only reacts to those around her, a sure sign of both external and internalized oppression. In the face of all this abuse, she somehow remains gentle, kind and beautiful—the perfect girl.

Similarly, *Sleeping Beauty*'s Aurora is a playful teenager whose friends are forest animals, and whose dream is expressed in the song "Some day my prince will come." Aurora is on the verge of celebrating her sixteenth birthday—the day her identity will be revealed to her. At this point she has no knowledge that she really is a princess who was betrothed at birth. Her parents' choices for her define Aurora's destiny and she has no voice in shaping that destiny.

Like Cinderella, Aurora is obedient, beautiful, acquiescent to authority, and essentially powerless in matters regarding her own fate. Furthermore, there is no one Aurora can trust. Although the fairies "protect" her from the truth about her identity and the curse on her future "for her own good," Aurora can take no action on her own behalf. Passively, she is brought back to the castle where she falls under the spell of Maleficent, touches the spinning wheel, and sleeps through most of the film while others battle to decide her future. When she awakens, she finds her "dream come true," a tall, handsome prince who rescues her from an evil female's curse.

Beginning with *The Little Mermaid*, however, the female protagonist shows signs of selfhood. Near the beginning of the film, Ariel sings of her dream to explore and her feelings of being misunderstood. She also expresses frustration and resistance: "Betcha on land they understand. Bet they don't reprimand their daughters. Bright young women, sick of swimmin', ready to stand." She asks, "When's it my turn?"

In contrast to the two previous demure female protagonists, Ariel is characterized as willful and disobedient. She follows her dreams even though she knows her actions run counter to the wishes of her father, King Triton. As a result, Triton charges the crab, Sebastian, with chaperoning his daughter "to protect her from herself." One might also read his actions as patriarchy's efforts to prevent her from achieving an independent identity. However, despite Triton's efforts to control Ariel, she explores, she asks questions, she makes choices, and she acts. For example, she rescues the human, Prince Eric, from the sea. She strikes a bargain with the sea witch, Ursula, to trade her voice for legs. Additionally, she prevents Eric's marriage to Ursula and protects him from Ursula's attack in the film's final battle. Nevertheless, it is Eric who finally kills the sea witch and it is Triton whose power enables Ariel to return to the human world by transforming her permanently into a human. Thus, while Ariel chooses to leave her own people for a life with Eric, it is still not her power but her father's power which enables her dreams to come to fruition.

Articulating one's own dreams and wishes—possessing an autonomous voice—is a strong indicator of the development of selfhood. Little wonder, then, that alarms sound for feminists concerned with the psychological development of girls and women's sense of self when Ariel literally sacrifices her voice and mermaid body to win Eric's love. What is gained by females who silence themselves in a masculinist society? What are the costs to their psychic selves for not doing so? Scholars in feminist psychological development describe the seductiveness of external rewards by denying one's selfhood (Brown & Gilligan, 1992). Having a voice, a sense of selfhood, is risky because it is inconsistent with images of the "perfect girl" or the true woman. When one's loyalty is not to the "masculinist system," one can end up on the margins at best and at worst socially "dead." Ultimately, Ariel's voice is silenced and she sacrifices her curiosity to gain the love of a man.

Reality for Belle in *Beauty and the Beast* means being female and wanting to experience adventure in the "great wide somewhere." Like the earlier Disney heroines, Belle dreams of having "so much more than they've got planned." Belle is the first of the Disney heroines to read, but her reading also alienates her from others in the community. She experiences herself as an "other." Townspeople call her peculiar and say that "she doesn't quite fit in." While Belle is aware of their opinions of her, and understands that she is supposed to marry a villager, raise a family, and conform, she also knows that she *is* different and *wants* something different—something "grand." Although Belle is unsure about how to attain her dreams, she does refuse to marry Gaston, the community "hunk" and its most eligible bachelor. She reads rather than socialize with the villagers, and she accepts that she can be nothing other than different from them. Belle likes herself and trusts her own judgment. Nevertheless, Belle is marginalized by the community for her uniqueness, for her sense of self.

Unlike her counterparts in *Cinderella* and *Sleeping Beauty*, Belle is no damsel in distress. Neither is she a helpless witness to the film's action nor removed from it. Belle occupies double the screen time of any other character in the film (Thomas, 1991), and Belle acts for herself. She dreams of more than a "provincial life"; she wants adventure and, as she sings, "for once it might be grand, to have someone understand, I want so much more than they've got planned." The line might have continued, "for a girl!"

Gaston, the village brute, is attracted to Belle because of her appearance not her brain. He sings that she's "the most beautiful, so that makes her the best." He offers her a place in the community with his marriage proposal. While other women swoon for his attention, Belle rejects him: "His little wife. No, sir. Not me!" Belle's sense of self is strong enough that she refuses to settle for less than a relationship which acknowledges and values her mind, in essence, her self. However, when her father is captured by the Beast, Belle comes to his rescue and offers herself in his place. By trading her life for her father's, she seems to have relinquished her selfhood. Once a prisoner in the Beast's castle, she laments to Mrs. Potts, a kind teapot, that she has lost her father, her dreams, "everything." However, this lament suggests that she still has dreams of her own and a sense of identity apart from that of a dutiful daughter.

Belle's dilemma occurs in part because she has a caring, co-active power relationship with her father (Parker Follett, 1944). Decision making undertaken by women who attempt to maintain selfhood but also exist in a power-with relation to others becomes much more complex, as Gilligan (1977) notes. This complexity is further illustrated by the choices that Belle subsequently makes in her relationship with the Beast. Belle negotiates the conflict she feels between freedom from the Beast and her growing affection for him. She decides not to leave him in the woods after he rescues her from wolves. Although she could escape, she chooses to help him instead. Later in the film, she again chooses to return to the Beast's castle to warn him of the impending mob, even though the Beast has released her from her promise to stay in his castle.

Like Ariel, Belle has freedom to make choices and to act on her own behalf as well as on the behalf of others; and she exercises that freedom. However, whereas Ariel at least initially seems to act out of a sense of rebellion, Belle's motivation appears to come from a craving for intellectual engagement. A simple masculinist interpretation might be that Belle acts out of a sense of personal honor or duty (to sacrifice her freedom first to help her father and later to keep the Beast). A more feminist interpretation based on Gilligan's psychoanalytic developmental work and standpoint theory might be that Belle acts as a result of the tension from seeking selfhood and relationships with others simultaneously. Thus, Belle's actions can be read as a series of complex decisions about when to act, and when to care for someone, how to administer comfort, when to take matters into her own hands, when to risk her personal safety. She is concerned not only with others but with herself as well, and her actions speak to both needs.

No victim, Belle sets the terms for the bargains she makes. In this sense, she exercises more power on her own behalf than previous Disney heroines. For Cinderella, Aurora, and Ariel, someone in power established the conditions within which their dreams could be realized. For example, Cinderella's fairy godmother gave her only until midnight to make her dream come true. At Aurora's christening, the good fairy Merryweather saved Aurora from Maleficent's death curse by decreeing that Aurora would sleep until awakened by a prince's kiss. And when Ariel gave her voice to Ursula in return for the sea witch's magical ability to transform Ariel into a human, Ursula placed a three day time limit on Ariel's pursuit to win Eric's love. Unlike Belle, these females have limited and tenuous opportunities to achieve their dreams. In contrast, Belle exercises substantial control over setting the terms of her own fate. She preserves her own options—by refusing Gaston's overtures and brushing off the villagers' criticisms, and she gives others options—by freeing her father from the Beast's prison, becoming a prisoner herself, and saving the Beast from the wolves. *She* holds *their* futures in her hands. Yet, ironically, one reading of the narrative conclusion is that Belle's liberation of the Beast from his spell ends with her becoming yet another "perfect girl" who marries the prince and lives happily ever after.

Another theme introduced in *Beauty and the Beast*—heroine as teacher—is expanded in *Pocahontas*. Just as Belle teaches the Beast how to be civil, gentle, and caring, Pocahontas teaches John Smith, her tribe, and the Englishmen about nature, power, and peace. Like Belle, Pocahontas exercises power over her future. Viewers first are introduced to

Pocahontas going where the wind (the spirit of her mother) leads her; as the chief's daughter, however, she knows that she must take "her place" among her people. Her father tells her, "Even the wild mountain stream must someday join the big river." She sings, "We must all pay a price. To be safe, we lose our chance of ever knowing what's around the river bend.... Why do all my dreams stand just around the river bend.... Is all my dreaming at an end?"

Like Ariel, Pocahontas defies her father in exploring her world. Like Belle, she is an active doer, not a passive victim. She also has a savage to tame in the form of an Englishman. Pocahontas introduces John Smith to the colors of the wind and to the mysteries of the world of nature. She takes political stances such as advocating alternatives to violence, and she makes choices about her life. For example, Pocahontas' decision to reject both her father's wish that she marry Kocoum, the Powhatan warrior, and John Smith's plea to go with him back to England signify that the power to control her actions is in her hands. Pocahontas' choices reflect a sense of selfhood that is a bold stroke for a Disney heroine. A feminist psychological reading might see in her decision to embrace her cultural roots an alternative to Disney's typical heterosexual narratives in which the "perfect girl's" destiny is a monogamous relationship with a (white) man. Indeed, far more than Belle, Pocahontas finds power within to express a self which is separate from that defined through relationships to a father or love interest.

Our reading of Pocahontas implies that she is clearly the most elaborate and complex character in this group of heroines. Her dreams direct her choices. She weighs the risks of choosing a smooth course versus seeking the unknown course to see what awaits her just around the river bend. With counsel from female mentors, Grandmother Willow and the spirit of the wind that symbolizes her mother, Pocahontas finds the strength to listen to her own inner voice, and to choose the less safe, uncharted course of autonomous womanhood. When confronted with the option of leaving her community in order to accompany her love interest, John Smith, she rejects his offer and instead takes her place as an unattached female leader of her people.

Pocahontas brings to the forefront the absence of diversity among Disney's previous female characters. From Cinderella through Belle, Disney's female protagonists easily could be the same characters with only slight variations in hair color. Pocahontas, too, varies only slightly in skin color, but she is the first non-Anglo heroine who is the subject of a Disney animated film. Furthermore, although some of the women may not have difficult family circumstances (e.g., Cinderella), as Caucasians, they all belong to the privileged class in their societies, as daughters of kings, Indian chiefs, and educated inventors.

As this examination of Cinderella, Aurora, Ariel, Belle, and Pocahontas demonstrates, over time Disney's female protagonists have begun to look beyond home, to practice resistance to coercion, and to find their own unique female voices. Indeed, in Pocahontas Disney offers an adventurous female who develops a sense of self in a culture other than the dominant Anglo culture, and who chooses a destiny other than that of heterosexual romantic fulfillment.

References

Allen, R. (1988). Fifty years of Snow White. *Journal of Popular Film and Television, 15*, 156–163.

Bell, E., Haas, L., & Sells, L. (Eds.). (1995). *From mouse to mermaid: The politics of film, gender, and culture*. Bloomington, IN: Indiana University Press.

Discussion Questions

1. Explain the authors' thesis about the relationship between Disney's interpretation of fairy tales and middle-class white male society. What effect do you think exposure to this relationship via Disney movies has on little girls in our society?

2. According to the study by Brown and Gilligan, what is society's definition of the "perfect girl"? Other than in Disney movies, where do you see other characters who fit this definition in present-day media?

3. What does Zipes claim is different about the heroine in Disney versions and original versions of the fairy tales? How do you think Bettelheim would feel about these changes? Why?

4. Explain the specific ways in which the examples of Cinderella, Aurora, Ariel, Belle, and Pocahontas show a change over time in the role of the heroine in Disney movies.

Cinderella: Saturday Afternoon at the Movies

Essay

LOUISE BERNIKOW

I begin with a memory of movies and mother, a dark theatre and a Saturday afternoon. In a miasma of Walt Disney images, Bambi burning and Snow White asleep, the most memorable is "Cinderella." I carry her story with me for the rest of my life. It is a story about women alone together and they are each other's enemies. This is more powerful as a lesson than the ball, the Prince, or the glass slipper. The echoes of "Cinderella" in other fairy tales, in myth and literature, are about how awful women are to each other. The girl onscreen, as I squirm in my seat, needs to be saved. A man will come and save her. Some day my Prince will come. Women will not save her; they will thwart her. There is a magical fairy godmother who does help her, but this, for me, has no relation to life, for the fairy is not real, and the bad women are. The magical good fairy is a saccharine fluff.

There are two worlds in the Cinderella cartoon, one of women, one of men. The women are close by and hostile, the men distant and glittering. Stepsisters and stepmother are three in one, a female battalion allied against Cinderella. The daughters are just like their mother. All women are alike. Lines of connection, energy fields, attach sisters to mother, leaving Cinderella in exile from the female community at home.

Father is far off. On film, neither he nor the Prince has much character. Father is her only tie, her actual blood tie, but the connection does her no good. Daddy is King in this world; I cannot keep Daddy and King apart in my memory. My own father was as far off, as full of authority, as surrounded by heraldry, the trumpets of fantasy, to me, to my mother. King Daddy.

The Prince is rich and handsome. Rich matters more than handsome. The girl among the cinders, dressed in rags, will escape—I am on her side, I want her to escape, get away from the cinders and the awful women—because the Prince will lift her out. The world of the Prince is the world of the ball, music, fine clothes, and good feeling. Were everything to be right at home, were the women to be good to one another and have fun together, it would not be sufficient. The object is the ball, the Prince, the big house, the servants. Class mobility is at stake. Aspiration is being titillated.

To win the Prince, to be saved, requires being pretty. All the women care about this. Being pretty is the ticket, and because Cinderella is pretty, the stepmother and stepsisters want to keep her out of the running. There is no other enterprise. Cinderella does not turn up her nose and hide in a corner reading a book. Being pretty, getting to the ball, winning the Prince is the common ground among the women. What we have in common is what keeps us apart.

Cinderella must be lonely. Why, I wonder, doesn't she have a friend? Why doesn't she go to school? Why doesn't her father tell the awful women to stop? A hurt and lonely girl, with only a prince to provide another kind of feeling. Why doesn't she run away? Why can't the situation be changed? It is as though the house they live in is the only world; there is no other landscape. Women are always in the house, being awful to each other.

Magic. Cinderella has a fairy godmother who likes her and wants her to be happy. She gives the girl beautiful clothes. She doesn't have to instruct Cinderella or give her advice about how to waltz or how to lift her skirt, or even give her directions to the palace. Only the clothes and the accoutrements—and a prohibition about coming home at midnight. A powerful woman who wants Cinderella to be pretty and successful in the social world. I know, at whatever age it is that I watch this story unfold, that the mother beside me is not the woman on the screen. Her feelings on such matters are, at best, mixed up. She is not so powerful.

I am stirred and confused by the contrast between bad and good women and the way it all seems to revolve around the issue of being pretty. Some women are hostile and thwarting, others enabling and powerful. The stepmother hates Cinderella's prettiness; the fairy godmother adorns it. I look sideways at my mother, trying to decide which kind of woman she is, where she stands on the business of pretty. Often, she braids my hair and settles me into polka dot, parades me before my beaming father. It is good to be pretty. Yet, onscreen, it is bad to be pretty—Cinderella is punished for it. In the enterprise of pretty, other women are your allies and your enemies. They are not disinterested. The heat around the issue of pretty, the urgency and the intensity of it, is located among the women, not the men, at whom it is supposedly aimed. Luckily, we move on to the ball and the lost slipper.

This is one of the oldest and most often-told stories, varying significantly from one version to another, one country to another, one period to another. What appears on movie theatre screens or television on

Saturday afternoons comes from as far away as China, as long ago as four hundred years. Each teller, each culture along the way, retained some archetypal patterns and transformed others, emphasized some parts of the story, eradicated others. Disney took his version of Cinderella from one written down by a Frenchman named Perrault in the seventeenth century. Perrault's is a "civilized" version, cleaned up, dressed up, and given several pointed "lessons" on top of the original material.

Many of the details about fashionability that we now associate with the story come from Perrault. His has the atmosphere of Coco Chanel's dressing rooms, is modern and glamorous. He concocted a froufrou, aimed at an aristocratic audience and airily decorated with things French. He named one of the sisters Charlotte and set the action in a world of full-length looking glasses and inlaid floors. He invented a couturière called Mademoiselle de Poche to create costumes for the ball, linens and ruffles, velvet suits and headdresses. Disney dropped the French touches.

Perrault's story is set in a world of women with their eyes on men. Even before the King's ball is announced, the stepmother and stepsisters are preoccupied with how they look. They are obsessed with their mirrors, straining to see what men would see. Once the ball is on the horizon, they starve themselves for days so that their shapes shall be, when laced into Mademoiselle de Poche's creations, as extremely slender as those in our own fashion magazines. The ball—and the prospects it implies—intensifies the hostility toward Cinderella. They have been envious. Now, they must keep the pretty girl out of competition. Most of the action of Perrault's story is taken up with the business of the ball.

Cinderella is a sniveling, self-pitying girl. Forbidden to go to the ball, she does not object but, instead, dutifully helps her stepsisters adorn themselves. She has no will, initiates no action. Then, magically, the fairy godmother appears. She comes from nowhere, summoned, we suppose, by Cinderella's wishes. Unlike the fairy godmother in other versions of the story, Perrault's and Disney's character has no connection to anything real, has no meaning, except to enable Cinderella to overcome the opposition of the women in her home, wear beautiful clothes, and get to the ball. Cinderella stammers, unable to say what she wants—for she is passive, suffering, and good, which comes across as relatively unconscious. The fairy divines Cinderella's desire and equips her with pumpkin/coach, mice/horses, rats/coachmen, lizards/footmen, clothes, and dancing shoes. She adds the famous prohibition that Cinderella return by midnight or everything will be undone.

These details of the fairy godmother's magic—the pumpkin, image of All Hallows' Eve; midnight, the witching hour; mice, rats, and lizards—originated with Perrault. They are specific reminders of an actual and ancient female magic, witchcraft. Since Perrault wrote his story in the seventeenth century, it is not surprising to find echoes of this magic, which was enormously real to Perrault's audience.

Thousands had been burned at the stake for practicing witchcraft, most of them women. A witch was a woman with enormous power, a woman who might change the natural world. She was "uncivilized" and in opposition to the world of the King, the court, polite society. She had to be controlled. Perrault's story attempts to control the elements of witchcraft just as various kings' governments had, in the not too recent past, controlled what they believed to be an epidemic of witchcraft. Perrault controls female power by trivializing it. The witchcraft in this story is innocent, ridiculous, silly, and playful. It is meant to entertain children.

The prohibition that Cinderella return by midnight is also related to witchcraft. She must avoid the witching hour, with its overtones of sexual abandon. The fairy godmother acts in this capacity in a way that is familiar to mothers and daughters—she controls the girl, warns her against darkness, uses her authority to enforce restraint, prevent excess, particularly excess associated with the ball, the world of men, sexuality.

Cinderella's dancing shoes are glass slippers. Perrault mistranslated the fur slipper in the version that came to him, substituting *verre* for *vire* and coming up glass. No pedant came along to correct the mistake, for the glass slipper is immensely appropriate to the story in its modern form and the values it embodies. Call it dainty or fragile, the slipper is quintessentially the stereotype of femininity. I wonder how Cinderella danced in it.

The rags-to-riches moment holds people's imagination long after the details of the story have disappeared. It appeals to everyone's desire for magic, for change that comes without effort, for speedy escape from a bad place—bad feelings. We all want to go to the ball, want life to be full of good feeling and feeling good. But Cinderella's transformation points to a particular and limited kind of good feeling—from ugly to beautiful, raggedy to glamorous. The object of her transformation is not actually pleasure (she does not then walk around her house feeling better) but transportation to the ball with all the right equipment for captivating the Prince.

Transformed, Cinderella goes to the ball, which is the larger world, the kingdom ruled by kings and fathers. The stepmother has no power in that world and does not even appear. This part of the story focuses on men, who are good to Cinderella as forcefully as women have been bad to her. Perrault embellishes Cinderella's appearance in a way that would have been congenial to the French court. In fact, she seems to have gone to the French court. The story is suffused with perfume and "fashionability." The Prince is taken with Cinderella and gives her some candy—"citrons and oranges," according to the text. How French. She, forever good, shares the candy with her stepsisters, who do not, of course, know who she is.

Cinderella has a wonderful time. As readers, hearers, watchers, we have a wonderful time along with her. More than the music and the dancing, the aura of sensual pleasure, everyone's good time comes from the idea that Cinderella is a "knockout." This is exciting. Perrault's word for what happens is that the people are *étonnés*, which means stunned. Cinderella is a showstopper, so "dazzling" that "the King himself, old as he was, could not help watching her." He remarks on this to his Queen, whose reactions we are not told. Being "stunning" is being powerful. This is the way women have impact, the story tells us. This is female power in the world outside the home, in contrast to her former power-lessness, which was within the home, which was another country. This tells me why women spend so much time trying to turn themselves into knockouts—because, in Cinderella and in other stories, it *works*.

Presumably, Cinderella's giddiness over her own triumph at the ball makes her forget her godmother's command and almost miss her midnight deadline. Lest we lose the idea that all men adore Cinderella, Perrault adds a courtier at the end of the story, as the search for the missing Cinderella is carried out, and has him too, say how attractive Cinderella is. She fulfills, then, the masculine idea of what is beautiful in a woman. She is the woman men want women to be.

Cinderella flees at midnight and loses her shoe. Perrault plays this part down, but Disney has a visual festival with the glinting glass slipper on the staircase and the trumpet-accompanied quest to find its owner. Perrault's Prince sends a messenger to find the shoe's owner, which puts the action at some distance, but Disney gives us a prince in all his splendor.

Cinderella is a heroine and in the world of fairy tales what the heroine wins is marriage to the Prince. Like any classic romance, wafted by perfume and fancy clothes, the young girl is lifted from a lowly powerless situation (from loneliness and depression, too) by a powerful man. He has no character, not even a handsome face, but simply represents the things that princes represent, the power of the kingdom.

Opposition to achieving this triumph comes from the women in the house; help comes from daydream and fantasy. The only proper activity for women to engage in is primping. What is expected of them is that they wait "in the right way" to be discovered. Cinderella obeys the rules. Her reward is to be claimed by the Prince. The lesson of Cinderella in these versions is that a girl who knows and keeps her place will be rewarded with male favor.

Like a saint, she shows neither anger nor resentment toward the women who treated her so badly. In fact, she takes her stepsisters along to the castle, where she marries each off to a nobleman. Now everyone will be happy. Now there will be no conflict, no envy, no degradation. If each woman has a prince or nobleman, she will be content and the soft humming of satisfaction will fill the air. Women otherwise cannot be alone together.

This is the sort of story that poisoned Madame Bovary's imagination. In Flaubert's novel, a woman married to a country doctor, with aspirations for a larger life, goes to a ball where a princely character pays her some attention. The ball and the Prince, seen by Emma Bovary as possibilities for changing everyday life, haunted her uneasy sleep. The ball was over. Wait as she might for its return, for a second invitation, all she got was a false prince—a lover who did not lift her from the ordinariness of her life—and then despair.

The romance depends on aspiration. The Prince must be able to give the heroine something she cannot get for herself or from other women. He must represent a valuable and scarce commodity, for the women must believe there is only one, not enough to go around, and must set themselves to keeping other women from getting it. In "Cinderella," like other fairy tales and other romances, the world of the Prince represents both actual and psychological riches.

Perrault's Cinderella is the daughter of a gentleman, turned into a peasant within the household. She has been declassed by female interlopers, reduced to the status of servant, for she belongs to her father's class only precariously. One of the ways women exercise their power, the story tells us, is by degrading other women. Cinderella will be saved from her female-inflicted degradation first by another female, the fairy godmother, who puts her on the road to her ultimate salvation. At the end of the story, she is restored to her class position, or, better, raised to an even higher position by the Prince.

Her fall from class is represented not only by her tattered clothes, but by the work she is forced to do. She is the household "drudge" and housework is the image of her degradation. Her work has no value in the story; it is the invisible, repetitious labor that keeps things going and makes it possible for the sisters and stepmother to devote themselves to *their* work, which is indolence on the one hand and trying to be beautiful for men on the other. Historically, indolence has been revered as the mark of a lady. What is "feminine" and "ladylike" is far removed from the world of work. Or the world of self-satisfying work. A man prides himself on having a wife who does not work; it increases his value in the eyes of other men; it means he provides well; it enforces conventional bourgeois "masculinity." A lady has long fingernails, neither the typewriter nor the kitchen floor has cracked them. She has porcelain skin; neither the rough outdoors nor perspiration has cracked that. Out of the same set of values comes the famous glass slipper.

The stepmother's class position is as precarious as Cinderella's is. The story does not tell, but we can imagine that whether she was married before to a poorer man or one equally a gentleman, her status and security are now tied to the man she has married and the ones she can arrange for her daughters. History, experience, and literature are full of landless, propertyless women trying to secure marriage to stand as a bulwark against poverty, displacement, and exile, both actual and psychological. The actual situation bears emphasis. The economic reality behind the fairy tale and the competition among the women for the favor of the Prince is a world in which women have no financial lives of their own. They cannot own businesses or inherit property. The kingdom is not theirs. In order to survive, a woman must have a husband. It is in the interest of her daughters' future—and her own—that the stepmother works to prevent competition from Cinderella. She is not evil. Within the confines of her world and the value systems of that world, she is quite nice to her own daughters, only cruel to Cinderella.

Still, the stepmother is an archetypal figure in fairy tales, always a thwarter, often a destroyer of children. Psychologists, and Bruno Bettelheim in particular, have a psychological explanation for this. The "bad" stepmother, Bettelheim points out, usually coexists with the "good" mother, representing two aspects of a real mother as experienced by a child. The stepmother is shaped by the child's unacceptable anger against her own mother. But there are real facts of life at work in these stepmother stories, too, especially as they describe what can happen among women at home. To a man's second wife, the daughter of the first marriage is a constant reminder of the first wife. The second wife is continually confronted with that memory and with the understanding that wives are replaceable, as they frequently and actually *were* in a world where women died young in childbirth, and men remarried, moved on.

A woman marries a man who has a daughter and comes to his household, where the daughter's strongest connection is to her father; the stepmother's strongest connection is to the husband. The Eternal Triangle appears, husband/father at the center, mediating the relationship, stepmother and daughter as antagonists, competing for the husband/father's attention and whatever he may represent. Anxious, each in her own way and equally displaced, they face each other with enmity. The masculine imagination takes prideful pleasure in the story, placing, as it does, husband/father at center stage, making him King, arbiter of a world of women.

I am writing an essay about Cinderella, spending mornings at the typewriter, afternoons in libraries, interpreting information on index cards of various colors and sheets of yellow paper. I discover something bizarre woven in the story as we now know it: that the story took root in ancient China. The remnants of that culture, especially of the ancient practice of foot-binding, are in the story, in the value of the small foot, in the use of the shoe to represent the potential bride. I see, then, the historical truth behind the terrible moment at the end of "Cinderella."

The Prince brings the slipper to the house of Cinderella's father. First one stepsister, then the other attempts to slip her foot into it, but each foot is too large. The first stepsister's toe is too large. The stepmother hands her daughter a knife and says "Cut off the toe. When you are Queen you won't have to walk anymore." The second stepsister's heel is too large and her mother repeats the gesture and the advice.

Mutilation. Blood in the shoe, blood on the knife, blood on the floor and unbearable pain, borne, covered, masked by the smile. It is too familiar, frightening in its familiarity. The mother tells the daughter to mutilate herself in the interests of winning the Prince. She will not have to walk. Again, indolence enshrined. As mothers, in fact, did in China until the twentieth century—among the upper classes as unquestioned custom and among peasants as great sacrifice and gamble.

It began when the girl was between five and seven years old. The bandages were so tight, the girl might scream. Her mother pulled them tighter and might have tried to soothe her. Tighter. At night, in agony, the girl loosens them. She is punished, her hands tied to a post to prevent unlacing. The bones crack. The pain is constant. Tighter. She cannot walk. Tighter. By her adolescence, the girl has learned to bind her feet herself and the pain has lessened. She has, as a reward, special shoes, embroidered and decorated for her tiny feet.

I translate the actual foot-binding, the ritual interaction of mother and daughter, to metaphor. A black mother straightens her daughter's hair with a hot iron, singeing the scalp, pulling and tugging. The daughter screams. My mother buys me a girdle when I am fifteen years old because she doesn't like the jiggle. She slaps my face when I begin to menstruate, telling me later that it is an ancient Russian custom and she does not know its origin. I sleep with buttons taped to my cheeks to make dimples and with hard metallic curlers in my hair. Tighter. I hold myself tighter, as my mother has taught me to do.

Is the impulse to cripple a girl peculiar to China between the eleventh and twentieth centuries? The lotus foot was the size of a doll's and the woman could not walk without support. Her foot was four inches long and two inches wide. A doll. A girl-child. Crippled, indolent, and bound. This is what it meant to be beautiful. And desired. This women did and do to each other.

Pain in the foot is pain in every part of the body. A mother is about to bind her daughter's feet. She knows the pain in her own memory. She says: "A daughter's pretty legs are achieved through the shedding of tears."

Discussion Questions

1. According to Louise Bernikow, how do myths, literature, and particularly fairy tales influence the nature of relationships among women? Give examples from your own readings that support or contradict her assessment.

2. What in fairy tales is the ultimate goal for women, and what must they do to achieve it? Do you think today's audience for books and movies based on classic fairy tales accept this as the goal for all women? Support your answer with some examples from your own experience or observations.

3. If Bettelheim finds positive guidance for children in fairy tales, how do you think he would respond to Bernikow's assertion of gender stereotyping in most fairy tales?

4. What happens when you analyze "The Monkey Girl" in the terms that Bernikow applies to "Cinderella"?

Fairy Tales Are Good for Children

Essay

G. K. CHESTERTON

G. K. Chesterton (1874–1936), born in England, was a highly respected author of many novels, poems, and essays.

I find that there really are human beings who think fairy tales bad for children. I do not speak of the man in the green tie, for him I can never count truly human. But a lady has written me an earnest letter saying that fairy tales ought not to be taught to children even if they are true. She says that it is cruel to tell children fairy tales, because it frightens them. You might just as well say that it is cruel to give girls sentimental novels because it makes them cry. All this kind of talk is based on that complete forgetting of what a child is like that has been the firm foundation of so many educational schemes. If you kept bogeys and goblins away from children they would make them up for themselves. One small child in the dark can invent more hells than Swedenborg [a Swedish scientist and mystic]. One small child can imagine monsters too big and black to get into any picture, and give them names too unearthly and cacophonous to have occurred in the cries of any lunatic. The child, to begin with, commonly likes horrors, and he continues to indulge in them even when he does not like them. There is just as much difficulty in saying exactly where pure pain begins in his case, as there is in ours when we walk of our own free will into the torture-chamber of a great tragedy. The fear does not come from fairy tales; the fear comes from the universe of the soul.

The timidity of the child or the savage is entirely reasonable; they are alarmed at this world because this world is a very alarming place. They dislike being alone because it is verily and indeed an awful idea to be alone. Barbarians fear the unknown for the same reason that Agnostics worship it—because it is a fact. Fairy tales, then, are not responsible for producing in children fear, or any of the shapes of fear; fairy tales do not give the child the idea of the evil or the ugly; that is in the child already, because it is in the world already. Fairy tales do not give a child his first idea of bogey. What fairy tales give the child is his first clear idea of the possible defeat of bogey. The baby has known the dragon intimately ever since he had an imagination. What the fairy tale provides for him is a St. George to kill the dragon.

Discussion Questions

1. What reason does Chesterton say that a well-meaning woman gave to him in a letter for banning the teaching of fairy tales? What other reasons that neither she, nor Chesterton, nor Bettelheim mentions have you heard about or thought of for keeping these stories away from children?

2. Why does Chesterton believe it is impossible to protect children from scary things? If you were a parent, would you try to keep your child from ever being afraid? What things would you do to make him or her feel safe?

3. Why does Chesterton think that childhood fears are reasonable? What things were you afraid of as a child? Was your fear realistic? How do you think Chesterton would judge the reasonableness of your fear?

4. What do fairy tales themselves give to children to help them deal with their fears? Compare Chesterton's assessment of the use of fairy tales to Bettelheim's. Are they saying the same thing? Explain.

The Criminological Significance of the Grimms' Fairy Tales

GERHARD O. W. MUELLER

Gerhard Mueller was a pioneer in the discipline of criminal justice. In addition to teaching at Rutgers, he published numerous textbooks and hundreds of scholarly articles. He also served as Chief of the United Nations Crime Prevention and Criminal Justice Branch from 1974–1982.

In September 1983, leading newspapers reported the surfacing of another fairy tale from the Grimm Brothers' collection—either fairy tale number 201, or, more likely, legend number 11. It was front-page news for the *New York Times*. People young and old, and scholars in particular, were delighted. Apparently of relatively recent origin, the tale refers to a war that lasted thirty years, probably the Thirty Years War of 1618 to 1648. That war raged particularly in the central German area in which the Grimm Brothers collected most of their tales. In this latest story, mother takes her "dear child" into the forest to protect her from the ravages of the impending war. Of course there is a happy ending. No punishment for child abandonment befalls the mother. After all, had she not acted with good motives and for justifiable ends? How juridical a moral! Juridical indeed, and that is the crux of the matter! Virtually every tale in the Grimm collection contains a message of law—not necessarily criminal law—of justice, of punishment, or of pardon.

The fairy tales caught the immediate attention of German scholars of law, and the legal historians in particular, who found therein the mirror reflection of positive law. The law itself was that which was contained in the (Latin language) codes, the *Leges Barbarorum*, of the early Middle Ages, that is, of the time before lawyers emerged as a class or profession in northern Europe. During the late Middle Ages, after lawyers had established themselves as a dominant caste, positive laws could be found in imperial decrees, city codes, and the judgments of city courts and high tribunals. But living law, especially as applied at the local level, was not the (Latin) lawyers' law; it was, instead, the law as transmitted from generation to generation among

Ruth Bottigheimer, Ed, Fairy Tales & Society, 1987, pp 217–226, "Reprinted with permission of the University of Pennsylvania Press".

nonlawyers (law-receivers, rather than law-givers), in the German tongue. In this sense, the fairy tales were not just a reflection of positive law; they were indeed positive law.

One cannot view the fairy tales collected by the Brothers Grimm as a homogeneous mass, or as a set of rigid legal propositions. The fairy tales vary in age and they metamorphosed with changing social and political conditions. In other words, just as precedents of law do change and must change over time to properly serve the ends of temporal justice as understood at a given time, the fairy tales had to change. Thus, they were indeed precedents.

Jens Christian Jessen, in a decades-long research undertaking, demonstrated this point clearly. He found many bridges between the law in the Grimms' fairy tales and the law of official documentation. Legal references to the fairy tales can indeed be dated to anywhere from the seventeenth century back to the seventh century, with fragments of fairy tales from even earlier dates.

The *external* consistency of the Grimms' fairy tales with officially documented law is, thus, fairly well established. Their *internal* consistency has been established more recently. Internal consistency means that the messages of the fairy tales as a body of largely self-sufficient propositions do not grossly conflict with one another but instead form a harmonious whole. Applying "balance theory," Carol Auster demonstrated that 94% of fairy tales ended with completely balanced, positive relations, leaving the reader or listener with an overall harmonious body of precepts and propositions.

It is astounding that so few criminologists have seen the value of Grimms' fairy tales as a source of criminological information. One of these few was Hans von Hentig, surely the greatest of German–American criminological scholars. His observations on the revelations of the fairy tales, about the nature, form, and severity of punishments, are a major contribution to the history and psychology of crime and punishment.

In these tales of precedent, which the Grimms preserved for us, every category of crime appears along with the punishments to be imposed upon those found guilty. The exact definition and scope of these crimes need not concern us here. But one crime, cannibalism, requires special mention. It is the only crime to appear in the fairy tales—and frequently at that—that does not have a counterpart in the positive law of the Middle Ages. It seems that the problem of cannibalism had been solved by society. Legal prohibitions were no longer needed, yet, in the minds of the people, cannibalism lived on, if only as a nightmare. Two of the fairy tales refer to cannibalism as having occurred long ago, "perhaps two thousand years ago," which means as much as a very long time.

Tales appertaining to witchcraft represent one of the most heinous crimes. This crime frequently, though not necessarily, includes cannibalism or attempted cannibalism, as in "Hansel and Gretel." In that tale the witch dies by fire, incinerated in her own stove. The principal punishment for witchcraft is burning. Indeed, Merowingian law (AD. 481–751) provides for precisely that punishment and as late as 1310 Prussian law proclaimed that punishment for witchcraft.

The Brothers Grimm recorded the remnants of long-dead law transformed into lore.

Discussion Questions

1. What is the basic plot of the newly discovered fairy tale? What similarities and differences do you see between it and other fairy tales you have heard or read?

2. Why are fairy tales, usually considered children's stories, of interest to legal scholars and legal historians?

3. What crime is common in fairy tales but has no counterpart in the law of the middle ages? What explanation does the author give for this oversight?

Class Discussion

Review the four basic sentence shapes:

A simple sentence is a single independent clause that contains a subject and verb.

A compound sentence has at least two independent clauses but no dependent clauses.

A complex sentence has an independent clause and at least one dependent clause.

A compound-complex sentence has at least two independent clauses and at least one dependent clause.

Combine the following to form the type of sentence indicated:

Many fairy stories begin with the death of a mother or father.
The parent's death creates problems for the child.

    a compound sentence _____

_____

_____

Fairy tales help children come to grips with problems in their most essential form.
Fairy tales simplify all situations.

    a complex sentence _____

_____

_____

Fairy tales acknowledge evil.
Snow White has an evil stepmother.
Cinderella has an evil stepmother.
Hansel and Gretel have an evil stepmother.
Evil is punished.
It is punished in the end.
Virtue triumphs.

    a compound-complex sentence _____

_____

_____

Homework Exercises

Locating Information in a Handbook

You will need your handbook to complete the following exercises on punctuation. For each word, locate its meaning using the index in your handbook, give a brief explanation of how it is used, and write a sentence (yours—not one from the handbook) that uses it.

1. **colon**

   Give a brief explanation of how and when it is used:_____

   _____

   On what page(s) in your handbook did you find the explanation? _____

   Write a sentence that contains a colon.

   _____

   _____

2. **semicolon**

   Give a brief explanation of how and when it is used: _____

   _____

   On what page(s) in your handbook did you find the explanation? _____

   Write a sentence that contains a semicolon.

   _____

   _____

3. **hyphen**

   Give a brief explanation of how and when it is used: _____

   _____

   _____

   On what page(s) in your handbook did you find the explanation? _____

Write a sentence that contains a hyphen.

_____

_____

4. **dash**

Give a brief explanation of how and when it is used:_____

_____

On what page(s) in your handbook did you find the explanation? _____

Write a sentence that contains a dash.

_____

5. **possessive apostrophe**

Give a brief explanation of how and when it is used:_____

_____

On what page(s) in your handbook did you find the explanation? _____

Write a sentence that contains a possessive apostrophe.

_____

_____

6. **quotation marks**

Give a brief explanation of how and when they are used:_____

_____

On what page(s) in your handbook did you find the explanation? _____

Write a sentence that contains quotation marks.

_____

_____

7. **italics**

   Give a brief explanation of how and when they are used: _____

   _____

   On what page(s) in your handbook did you find the explanation? _____

   Write a sentence that contains italics.

   _____

   _____

8. Using the correct form (italics or quotation marks), give an example (real or imaginary) of

   the title of a movie:

   the title of a television series:

   the title of one episode in a television series:

   the title of a song:

   the title of a chapter in a book:

   the title of a work of art:

   the name of a ship:

9. Explain one use of the **comma** (not "city, state" or "month, day"). Then write a sentence that uses the comma in the way you have explained.

_____

_____

_____

_____

10. Explain a second use of the **comma** (not "city, state" or "month, day"). Then write a sentence that uses the comma in the way you have explained.

_____

_____

_____

_____

Reviewing Your Graded Essay

After your essay has been graded by your instructor, you may have the opportunity to revise your paper and raise your grade. Even if you are not submitting a revised version of this essay to your instructor, it is important that you review your work carefully in order to understand its strengths and weaknesses. This sheet will guide you through the evaluation process.

You will want to continue to use the techniques that worked well for you and to find strategies to overcome the problems that you identify in this sample of your writing. In order to help yourself recognize areas that might have been problematic for you, look back at the scoring rubric in this book. Match the numerical/verbal/letter grade received on your essay to the appropriate category. Study the explanation given on the rubric for your grade.

Write a few sentences below in which you identify your problems in each of the following areas. Then suggest specific changes you could make that would improve your paper. Don't forget to use your handbook as a resource.

1. Grammar/mechanics

My problem:

My strategy for change:

2. Thesis/response to assignment

My problem:

My strategy for change:

3. Organization

My problem:

My strategy for change:

4. Paragraph development/examples/reasoning

My problem:

My strategy for change:

5. Assessment

In the space below, assign a grade to your paper using a rubric other than the one used by your instructor. In other words, if your instructor assigned your essay a grade of *High Fail*, you might give it the letter grade you now feel the paper warrants. If your instructor used the traditional letter grade to evaluate the essay, choose a category from the rubric in this book, or any other grading scale that you are familiar with, to show your evaluation of your work. Then write a short narrative explaining your evaluation of the essay and the reasons it received the grade you gave it.

Grade: _____

Narrative: _____

_____

_____

_____

_____

Assignment 4

Erich Fromm's "Work in an Industrial Society"

Read Fromm's essay and study the writing topic that follows it. Then use the sections that follow to examine Fromm's ideas and develop your own argument in response to the questions in the writing topic.

We hope you have come to see the value in doing extensive prewriting as you work to build a draft of your essay. The prewriting exercises in this chapter will take you through the writing process and help you analyze Fromm's argument and formulate one of your own. By now, you should be familiar with the prewriting strategies in *Write It*. For this assignment, decide which are most beneficial to your writing and critical thinking style and see if customizing these strategies will help you to maximize their benefits.

Work in an Industrial Society

ERICH FROMM

Erich Fromm was born in Germany and trained as a psychoanalyst in Berlin. He taught at Yale and Columbia and became a well-known psycho-analyst and writer. The following essay is adapted from his book The Sane Society *(1955).*

Craftsmanship, especially as it developed in the thirteenth and four-teenth centuries, constitutes one of the peaks in the evolution of creative work in Western history. During the Middle Ages, the Renaissance, and the eighteenth century, work was not only a useful activity, but one which carried with it a profound satisfaction. The main features of craftsmanship as it existed before the Industrial Revolution have been very lucidly expressed by C. W. Mills:

> There is no ulterior motive in work other than the product being made and the processes of its creation. The details of daily work are meaningful because they are not detached in the worker's mind from the product of the work. The worker is free to control his own working action. The craftsman is thus able to learn from his work; and to use and develop his capacities and skills in its prosecution. There is no split of work and play, or work and culture. The craftsman's way of livelihood determines and infuses his entire mode of living.

By contrast, what happens to the industrial worker today, in 1955? He spends his best energy for seven or eight hours a day in producing "something." He needs his work in order to make a living, but his role is essentially a passive one. He fulfills a small, isolated function in a complicated and highly organized process of produc-tion, and is never confronted with "his" product as a whole—at least not as a producer, but only as a consumer, provided he has the money to buy "his" product in a store. He is concerned neither with the whole product in its physical aspects nor with its wider economic and social aspects. He is put in a certain place, has to carry out a certain task, but does not participate in the organization or management of

Essay

the work. He is not interested in, nor does he know, why he produces this commodity instead of another one—what relation it has to the needs of society as a whole. The shoes, the cars, the electric bulbs, are produced by "the enterprise," using the machines. He is part of the machine, rather than its master as an active agent.

For today's industrial worker, work is a means of getting money, not in itself a meaningful human activity. P. Drucker, observing workers in the automobile industry, expresses this idea very succinctly:

> For the great majority of automobile workers, the only meaning of the job is in the pay check, not in anything connected with the work or the product. Work appears as something unnatural, a disagreeable, meaningless, and stultifying condition of getting the pay check, devoid of dignity as well as of importance. No wonder that this puts a premium on slovenly work, on slowdowns, and on other tricks to get the same pay check with less work. No wonder that this results in an unhappy and discontented worker—because a pay check is not enough to base one's self-respect on.

The alienated and profoundly unsatisfactory character of modern industrial work results in two reactions: one, the ideal of complete laziness; the other, a deep-seated, though often unconscious, hostility toward work and everything and everybody connected with it.

It is not difficult to recognize the widespread longing for the state of complete laziness and passivity. Our advertising appeals to it even more than to sex. There are, of course, many useful and labor-saving gadgets. But this usefulness often serves only as a rationalization for their appeal to complete passivity and receptivity. A package of breakfast cereal is advertised as "new—easier to eat." An electronic toaster is advertised with these words: "...the most distinctly different toaster in the world! Everything is done for you with this new toaster. You need not even bother to lower the bread. Power-action, through a unique electric motor, gently takes the bread right out of your fingers!" Everybody knows the picture of the elderly couple in an advertisement of a life-insurance company, who have retired at the age of sixty, and spend their life in the complete bliss of having nothing to do except just travel.

But there is a far more serious and deep-seated reaction to the meaninglessness and boredom of work. It is hostility toward work that is much less conscious than our craving for laziness and inactivity. Many a businessman feels himself the prisoner of his business and the commodities he sells; he has a feeling of fraudulency about his product and a secret contempt for it. He hates his customers, who force him to put up a show in order to sell. He hates his competitors because they are a threat; he hates his employees as well as his superiors because he is in a constant competitive fight with them. Most important of all, he hates himself because he sees his life passing by without making any sense beyond the momentary intoxication of success. Of course, this hate and this contempt—for others and for oneself, and for the very things one produces—are mainly unconscious. Only occasionally do these feelings come up to awareness in a fleeting thought that is sufficiently disturbing to be set aside as quickly as possible.

Writing Topic

According to Fromm, how did the Industrial Revolution change the way people felt about their work? Do you think his analysis of the work attitudes of post-Industrial-Revolution workers applies to workers in the twenty-first century? Be sure to support the position you take by discussing specific examples; these examples can be drawn from your experience, the readings from this unit, or your knowledge of contemporary American society.

Vocabulary Check

Good writers choose their words carefully so that their ideas will be clear. In order for you, the reader, to understand an essay, it is important to think about its key vocabulary terms and the way they are used by the author. Words can have a variety of meanings, or they can have specialized meanings in certain contexts. Look up the definitions of the following words or phrases from the essay. Choose the meaning that you think Fromm intended when he selected that particular word or phrase for use in this essay. Then explain the way the meaning or concept behind the definition is key to understanding the author's argument.

craftsmanship

definition: _____

_____

explanation: _____

_____

_____

Industrial Revolution

definition: _____

_____

explanation: _____

_____

_____

alienation

definition: _____

_____

explanation: _____

_____

_____

Questions to Guide Your Reading

Before you begin to answer these questions, review "Steps for a Thoughtful Reading of an Essay" in Part 1. Use its strategies to analyze "Work in an Industrial Society" in preparation for answering the questions here.

Paragraph 1

Explain the main features of craftsmanship as it is defined by C. W. Mills.

Paragraph 2

According to Fromm, how does the job of the industrial workers in 1955 differ from the work of craftsmen in the past?

Paragraph 3

What is the only meaning, according to P. Drucker, that jobs hold for the workers in the automobile industry? How does this meaning affect the workers' attitudes toward themselves and their work?

Paragraphs 4–6

Identify and discuss the two reactions that Fromm claims result from work in an industrial society.

Prewriting for a Directed Summary

You will use the answers you fill in here when you write a directed summary in response to the first part of the writing topic for this assignment:

> *first part of the writing topic*: According to Fromm, how did the Industrial Revolution change the way people felt about their work?

Although this question asks you to explain one of Fromm's main assertions, it doesn't ask you to summarize the entire essay. Be sure to keep the question in mind as you present Fromm's ideas.

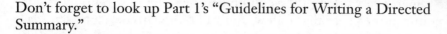

Hint

Don't forget to look up Part 1's "Guidelines for Writing a Directed Summary."

1. According to Fromm, what are the characteristics necessary to change work into craftsmanship? What emotion does a craftsman experience upon completing his work?

2. How does Fromm think the work of an industrial worker in 1955 differs from that of a craftsman?

3. What, according to Fromm, is the industrial worker's reason for doing his work?

4. How does the industrial worker feel about the work he does, according to Fromm?

5. How does the work make the industrial worker feel about himself?

Opinion and Working Thesis Statement

To fully answer the writing topic that follows "Work in an Industrial Society," you will have to take a position of your own on the issue Fromm addresses.

> *second part of the writing topic*: Do you think his analysis of the work attitudes of post-Industrial-Revolution workers applies to workers in the twenty-first century?

Do you think his ideas about work apply to people today? In order to make your position clear to readers, state it clearly early in your essay, preferably at the end of your introductory paragraph. A clear thesis statement, one that takes a position on the relation of today's worker to the work she or he does, will unify your essay and allow it to communicate effectively with readers.

It is likely that you aren't yet sure what position you want to take in your essay. Use this page to generate a working thesis statement, one that best represents your position at this point. In the pages that follow, you will be able to develop your ideas through specific evidence drawn from your experience. Then you will be given an opportunity to refine your working thesis statement based on the discoveries you made when you explored your ideas more systematically.

Hint

Do your best to write a working thesis now, but be sure to come back to it once you have thought more systematically about the subject. You may have to revise it to reflect your ideas after you've worked them out more extensively.

1. Use the following **thesis frame** to identify the basic elements of your thesis statement:

   a. What time period is Fromm criticizing?

   _____

   b. What does he argue about workers during the time period he is talking about?

   _____

   c. Will your position be that Fromm's claim about workers after the Industrial Revolution applies, or doesn't apply, to people working today?

   _____

   _____

   _____

2. Now use the elements you isolated in parts 1a, b, and c of the thesis frame to write a thesis statement. You may have to revise it several times until it captures your idea clearly.

_____

_____

_____

_____

Prewriting to Find Support for Your Thesis Statement

The last question in the writing topic asks you to support the argument you put forward in your thesis statement:

> *last part of the writing topic*: Be sure to support the position you take by discussing specific examples; these examples can be drawn from your experience, the readings from this unit, or your knowledge of contemporary American society.

Use the following questions to help develop examples you might use to support your thesis statement.

Hint

Complete each section of this prewriting activity; your responses will become the material you will use in the next stage—planning and writing the essay.

1. As you begin to develop your own examples, consider the subject's relation to your own life. In the space below, list or freewrite about personal experiences (either concerning you, your friends, or your family) with work, noting the tasks that had to be accomplished and the attitude of you and others toward the work required. Feel free to include any experience, however minor or incidental.

   Once you've written your ideas, look them over carefully. Try to group your ideas into categories. Then give each category a label. In other words, cluster ideas that seem to have something in common and, for each cluster, identify that shared quality by giving it a name.

2. Now, broaden your focus; list or freewrite about examples from your studies, your readings, and your knowledge of current events. If you have read the background readings in this chapter, you may include their ideas in your exploration; you may even decide to include an example or two from these readings in your own essay (don't forget to acknowledge your source, if necessary).

Once you've written your ideas, look them over carefully. Try to group your ideas into categories. Then give each category a label. In other words, cluster ideas that seem to have something in common and, for each cluster, identify that shared quality by giving it a name.

3. Once you've created topics by clustering your ideas into categories, go through them and pick two or three specific ones to develop in your essay. Make sure that they are relevant to your thesis and that they have enough substance to be compelling to your reader. Then, in the space below, briefly summarize each item.

Once you've decided which items and categories on your lists you will use in your essay, take some time to explain below how each category and its items connect to your thesis statement. You will use these details when you write the rough draft of your essay.

Revising Your Thesis Statement

Now that you have spent some time working out your ideas more systematically and developing some supporting evidence for the position you want to take, look again at the working thesis statement you crafted earlier to see if it is still accurate. As your first step, look again at the writing topic and then write your original working thesis on the lines that follow it:

> *second part of the writing topic*: Do you think his analysis of the work attitudes of post-Industrial-Revolution workers applies to workers in the twenty-first century?

working thesis statement:

_____

_____

_____

Take some time now to see if you want to revise your thesis statement. Often after extensive prewriting and focused thought, the working thesis statement is no longer an accurate reflection of what you plan to say in your essay. Sometimes, only a word or phrase must be added or deleted; other times, the thesis statement must be significantly rewritten, as either or both the subject and the claim portions are inaccurate.

After examining your working thesis statement and completing any necessary revisions, check it one more time by asking yourself the following questions:

a. Does the thesis directly identify Fromm's argument (the plight of the worker in an increasingly industrial society)?
b. Do you make clear your opinion regarding the similarity between workers then and workers now?

If you answered "no" to either of these questions, then rewrite your thesis statement so that it is fully developed.

_____

_____

Planning and Drafting Your Essay

Now that you have examined Fromm's argument and thought at length about your own views, draft an essay that responds to all parts of the writing topic. Use the material you developed in the previous pages of this chapter to compose your draft, and then exchange drafts with a classmate and use the peer review form that follows to help revise your draft. Don't forget to review Part 1, especially "A Suggested Structure for an Essay That Responds to Another Writer's Work," for further guidance on the essay's conventional structure.

Getting started on the draft is often the hardest part of the writing process because this is where you move from exploring and planning to getting your ideas down in a unified, coherent shape. Creating an outline will give you a basic structure for incorporating all the ideas you have developed in the preceding pages. An outline will also give you a bird's-eye view of your essay and help you spot problems in development or logic. The form below is modeled on "A Suggested Structure" in Part 1, and it is meant to help you create an outline or writing plan before you begin drafting your essay.

Hint

This outline doesn't have to contain polished writing. You may only want to fill in the basic ideas in phrases or terms.

Creating an Outline for Your Draft

I. Introductory Paragraph

    A. An opening sentence that gives the reading selection's title and author and begins to answer the first part of the writing topic:

    _____

    B. Main points to include in the directed summary:

        1.

        2.

        3.

        4.

    C. Look again at the thesis statement you wrote in "Revising Your Thesis Statement" and make any changes you think necessary. Then copy your thesis statement below. It should clearly state whether Fromm's position regarding the post-industrial worker applies to today's society.

_____

II. Body Paragraphs

    A. Subject of the paragraph: _____

        1. **C**ontrolling idea sentence:

        _____

        2. **C**orroborating details:

        _____

        _____

        _____

        3. **C**areful description of the details' relevance:

        _____

        _____

        _____

        _____

        _____

        4. **C**onnection to the thesis statement:

        _____

    B. Subject of the paragraph: _____

        1. **C**ontrolling idea sentence:

        _____

        _____

2. **C**orroborating details:

_____

_____

_____

3. **C**areful description of the details' relevance:

_____

_____

_____

_____

4. **C**onnection to the thesis statement:

_____

C. Subject of the paragraph: _____

1. **C**ontrolling idea sentence:

_____

2. **C**orroborating details:

_____

_____

_____

3. **C**areful description of the details' relevance:

_____

_____

_____

_____

_____

    4. **C**onnection to the thesis statement:

_____

D. Subject of the paragraph: _____

    1. **C**ontrolling idea sentence:

_____

    2. **C**orroborating details:

_____

_____

_____

    3. **C**areful description of the details' relevance:

_____

_____

_____

_____

_____

    4. **C**onnection to the thesis statement:

_____

III. Conclusion

    A. Type of conclusion to be used:

_____

    B. Key words or phrases to include:

_____

Peer Draft Review Sheet

Use the following guidelines to give a classmate feedback on his or her draft. Read the draft through first and then answer each of the items below as specifically as you can.

Name of draft's author: _____

Name of draft's reader: _____

Introduction

1. Within the opening sentences,
   a. the author is correctly identified by first and last name.   yes   no
   b. the reading selection's title is included and placed within
      quotation marks.   yes   no

2. The opening contains a summary that
   a. explains the way Fromm believes workers in 1955 feel
      about their jobs.   yes   no
   b. identifies the characteristics of the work being done in 1955.   yes   no
   c. connects the character of the work to workers' attitudes.   yes   no

3. The opening provides a thesis that
   a. makes Fromm's conclusions clear.   yes   no
   b. gives the draft writer's opinion about how Fromm's
      conclusions apply to today's workers.   yes   no

If the answers to 3 above are yes, state the thesis below as it is written. If the answer to one or both of these questions is no, explain to the writer what information is needed to make the thesis complete.

Body

1. How many paragraphs are in the body of this essay? _____

2. To support the thesis, this number is   sufficient   not enough

3. Do paragraphs contain the 4Cs?:

Paragraph 1	Controlling idea sentence	yes	no
	Corroborating details	yes	no
	Careful description of the details' relevance	yes	no
	Connection to the thesis statement	yes	no
Paragraph 2	Controlling idea sentence	yes	no
	Corroborating details	yes	no
	Careful description of the details' relevance	yes	no
	Connection to the thesis statement	yes	no
Paragraph 3	Controlling idea sentence	yes	no
	Corroborating details	yes	no
	Careful description of the details' relevance	yes	no
	Connection to the thesis statement	yes	no
Paragraph 4	Controlling idea sentence	yes	no
	Corroborating details	yes	no
	Careful description of the details' relevance	yes	no
	Connection to the thesis statement	yes	no
Paragraph 5	Controlling idea sentence	yes	no
	Corroborating details	yes	no
	Careful description of the details' relevance	yes	no
	Connection to the thesis statement	yes	no

(Continue as needed.)

4. Identify any of the above paragraphs that are not fully developed (too short).

5. Identify any of the above paragraphs that fail to support the thesis. _____

6. Identify any of the above paragraphs that are redundant or repetitive. _____

7. Suggest any ideas for additional paragraphs that might improve this essay.

Conclusion

1. Does the final paragraph contain any material that should have been developed in the body of the essay?

a. examples	yes	no
b. new ideas	yes	no

2. Does the conclusion provide closure (let the reader know
   that the end of the essay has been reached)?   yes   no

3. Does the conclusion leave the reader with an understanding
   of the significance of the argument?   yes   no

State in your own words what the writer considers to be important about his or her
argument.

_____

_____

4. Identify the type of conclusion used (see the guidelines for conclusions in
   Part 1).

Revision

1. During revision, the writer should pay attention to the following problems in
   mechanics:

   comma splices

   comma placement

   fragments

   run-on sentences

   apostrophe use

   quotation mark use

   capital letter use

   spelling

2. During revision, the writer should pay attention to the following areas of
   grammar:

   verb tense

   subject-verb agreement

   pronoun type

   pronoun reference

   pronoun agreement

   rregular verbs

   noun plurals

   dangling or misplaced modifiers

   prepositions

Final Draft Check List

Content:

- My essay has an appropriate title.
- I provide an accurate summary of the position on the topic set out by Fromm's essay.
- My thesis contains a claim that I can support with evidence.
- I have a sufficient number of paragraphs and arguments to support my thesis.
- Each body paragraph is relevant to my thesis.
- Each body paragraph contains the 4Cs.
- I use transitions whenever necessary to connect paragraphs and ideas to each other.
- The final paragraph of my essay (the conclusion) provides the reader with a sense of closure.

Grammar and Mechanics:

- I use the present tense to discuss Fromm's arguments.
- All of my verb tense shifts are correct to show time order.
- I have verb tense consistency throughout my sentences and paragraphs.
- My sentence are punctuated clearly and correctly.
- If I present items in a series (nouns, verbs, prepositional phrases), they are parallel in form.
- If I include material spoken or written by someone other than myself, I have correctly punctuated it with quotation marks and other necessary punctuation and used MLA rules for citation.
- I have checked for subject-verb agreement in all of my sentences.

Extended Activities

Readings

"Work, Labor, Play" by W. H. Auden

"Men at Work" by Anna Quindlen

"Time Off for the Overworked American" by Courtney E. Martin

"The Importance of Work" by Betty Friedan

"The Men We Carry in Our Minds" by Scott Russell Sanders

"Woe Is the American Worker" by Paul Waldman

"The Protestant Work Ethic: Just Another 'Urban Legend'?" by Jonathan Klemens

Class Discussion

Paraphrasing

Homework

How do you see it?

Reviewing Your Graded Essay

Work, Labor, Play

Essay

W. H. AUDEN

Wystan Hugh Auden (1907–1973) was born in England and moved to the United States in 1939. Although he is primarily regarded as a major poet, he was also a prolific writer of prose essays and reviews on literary, political, psychological, and religious subjects. He also worked at times on documentary films, poetic plays, and other forms of performance. Throughout his career, he was both controversial and influential, and he is regarded by many as one of the most important writers of the twentieth century.

So far as I know, Miss Hannah Arendt[1] was the first person to define the essential difference between work and labor. To be happy, a person must feel, firstly, free and secondly, important. He cannot be really happy if he is compelled by society to do what he does not enjoy doing, or if what he enjoys doing is ignored by society as of no value or importance. In a society where slavery in the strict sense has been abolished, the sign that what a man does is of social value is that he is paid money to do it, but a laborer today can rightly be called a wage slave. A man is a laborer if the job society offers him is of no interest to himself but he is compelled to take it by the necessity of earning a living and supporting his family.

The antithesis to labor is play. When we play a game, we enjoy what we are doing, otherwise we should not play it, but it is a purely private activity; society could not care less whether we play it or not.

Between labor and play stands work. A man is a worker if he is personally interested in the job which society pays him to do; what from the point of view of society is necessary labor is from his own point of view voluntary play. Whether a job is to be classified as labor or work depends, not on the job itself, but on the tastes of the individual who undertakes it. The difference does not, for example, coincide with the difference between a manual and a mental job; a gardener or a cobbler may be a worker, a bank clerk a laborer. Which a man is can be seen from his attitude towards leisure. To a worker, leisure means simply the hours he needs to relax and rest in order to work efficiently.

---

[1] A distinguished political philosopher who published *The Human Condition* in 1958.

He is therefore more likely to take too little leisure than too much; workers die of coronaries and forget their wives' birthdays. To the laborer, on the other hand, leisure means freedom from compulsion, so that it is natural for him to imagine that the fewer hours he has to spend laboring, and the more hours he is free to play, the better.

What percentage of the population in a modern technological society are, like myself, in the fortunate position of being workers? At a guess I would say sixteen percent, and I do not think that figure is likely to get bigger in the future.

Technology and the division of labor have done two things: by eliminating in many fields the need for special strength or skill, they have made a very large number of paid occupations which formerly were enjoyable work into boring labor, and by increasing productivity they have reduced the number of necessary laboring hours. It is already possible to imagine a society in which the majority of the population, that is to say, its laborers, will have almost as much leisure as in earlier times was enjoyed by the aristocracy. When one recalls how aristocracies in the past actually behaved, the prospect is not cheerful. Indeed, the problem of dealing with boredom may be even more difficult for such a future mass society than it was for aristocracies. The latter, for example, ritualized their time; there was a season to shoot grouse, a season to spend in town, etc. The masses are more likely to replace an unchanging ritual by fashion which it will be in the economic interest of certain people to change as often as possible. Again, the masses cannot go in for hunting, for very soon there would be no animals left to hunt. For other aristocratic amusements like gambling, dueling, and warfare, it may be only too easy to find equivalents in dangerous driving, drug-taking, and senseless acts of violence. Workers seldom commit acts of violence because they can put their aggression into their work, be it physical like the work of a smith, or mental like the work of a scientist or an artist. The role of aggression in mental work is aptly expressed by the phrase "getting one's teeth into a problem."

Discussion Questions

1. According to Hannah Arendt, what is the difference between work and labor?

2. How does play stand in relation to work and to labor?

3. Auden believes he is among what percentage of people in modern technological society who are workers? Do you think his estimate is an accurate one? Why or why not?

4. What social problems does Auden imagine will increase as more people in society become laborers rather than workers? Do you think he is correct in attributing such problems to people's jobs? Why or why not?

5. Discuss Fromm's concept of "craftsmanship" in relation to Auden's definitions of work, labor, and play.

6. What relationship do both Fromm and Auden see between work and happiness? Discuss the merit you see in their views.

Men at Work

Essay

ANNA QUINDLEN

Anna Quindlen has worked as a reporter and columnist for The New York Post *and* The New York Times, *and she currently works as a columnist for* Newsweek. *She published a novel,* Object Lessons, *in 1991. Her* New York Times *column received the Pulitzer Prize for Commentary. The following essay is from a collection of her work titled* Thinking Out Loud *(1993).*

The five o'clock dads can be seen on cable television these days, just after that time in the evening the stay-at-home moms call the arsenic hours. They are sixties sitcom reruns, Ward and Steve and Alex, and fifties guys. They eat dinner with their television families and provide counsel afterward in the den. Someday soon, if things keep going the way they are, their likenesses will be enshrined in a diorama in the Museum of Natural History, frozen in their recliner chairs. The sign will say, "Here sit lifelike representations of family men who worked only eight hours a day."

The five o'clock dad has become an endangered species. A corporate culture that believes presence is productivity, in which people of ambition are afraid to be seen leaving the office, has lengthened his workday and shortened his homelife. So has an economy that makes it difficult for families to break even at the end of the month. For the man who is paid by the hour, that means never saying no to overtime. For the man whose loyalty to the organization is measured in time at his desk, it means goodbye to nine to five.

To lots of small children it means a visiting father. The standard joke in one large corporate office is that dads always say their children look like angels when they're sleeping because that's the only way they ever see them. A Gallup survey taken several years ago showed that roughly 12 percent of the men surveyed with children under the age of six worked more than sixty hours a week, and an additional 25 percent worked between fifty and sixty hours. (Less than 8 percent of the working women surveyed who had children of that age worked those hours.)

No matter how you divide it up, those are twelve-hour days. When the talk-show host Jane Wallace adopted a baby recently, she said one reason she was not troubled by becoming a mother without becoming a wife was that many of her married female friends were "functionally single," given the hours their husbands worked. The evening commuter rush is getting longer. The 7:45 to West Backofbeyond is more crowded than ever before. The eight o'clock dad. The nine o'clock dad.

There's a horribly sad irony to this, and it is that the quality of fathering is better than it was when the dads left work at five o'clock and came home to café curtains and tuna casserole. The five o'clock dad was remote, a "Wait till your father gets home" kind of dad with a newspaper for a face. The roles he and his wife had were clear: she did nurture and home, he did discipline and money.

The role fathers have carved out for themselves today is a vast improvement, a muddling of those old boundaries. Those of us obliged to convert behavior into trends have probably been a little heavy-handed on the shared childbirth and egalitarian diaper-changing. But fathers today do seem to be more emotional with their children, more nurturing, more open. Many say, "My father never told me he loved me," and so they tell their own children all the time that they love them—when they're home.

There are people who think that this is changing even as we speak, that there is a kind of perestroika of home and work that we will look back on as beginning at the beginning of the 1990s. A nonprofit organization called the Families and Work Institute advises corporations on how to balance personal and professional obligations and concerns, and Ellen Galinsky, its cofounder, says she has noticed a change in the last year. "When we first started doing this the groups of men and women sounded very different," she said. "If the men complained at all about long hours, they complained about their wives' complaints. Now if the timbre of the voice was disguised I couldn't tell which is which. The men are saying: 'I don't want to live this way anymore. I want to be with my kids.' I think the corporate culture will have to begin to respond to that."

This change can only be to the good, not only for women but especially for men, and for kids, too. The stereotypical five o'clock dad belongs in a diorama, with his "Ask your mother" and his "Don't be a crybaby." The father who believes hugs and kisses are sex-blind and a dirty diaper requires a change, not a woman, is infinitely preferable. What a joy it would be if he were around more.

"This is the man's half of having it all," said Don Conway-Long, who teaches a course at Washington University in St. Louis about men's relationships that drew 135 students this year for thirty-five places. "We're trying to do what women want of us, what children want of us, but we're not willing to transform the workplace." In other words, the hearts and minds of today's fathers are definitely in the right place. If only their bodies could be there, too.

Discussion Questions

1. Why does Quindlen say that the "five o'clock dad" has become an endangered species?

2. What irony does Quindlen see in the relationship these new "visiting" fathers have with their children?

3. Explain the change in the way men express their dissatisfaction with work hours. What do you think accounts for this change?

4. Referring back to Fromm's and Auden's discussions of work and play, do you think the men being considered by Quindlen could best be described as laborers, craftsmen, or workers? Explain the evidence in her article that led you to your conclusion.

Time Off for the Overworked American

Essay

COURTNEY E. MARTIN

Courtney E. Martin is a writer and speaker originally from Colorado Springs, Colorado. She has an M.A. in writing and social change from the Gallatin School at New York University and a B.A. in political science and sociology from Barnard College. Her book Perfect Girls, Starving Daughters: The Frightening New Normalcy of Hating Your Body *was published in April 2007. She writes a column on politics and gender for* The American Prospect Online, *and she speaks about body image and youth at schools across the nation.*

Remember riding hip to hip with your brothers and sisters in the back of the family van, eating the snacks too soon, fighting over the music selection, losing tiny, indispensable pieces of travel games? Or maybe your family was not of the road trip ilk. Perhaps you remember exciting trips on airplanes, a special pin from the stewardess, watching the clouds take shape out of your own oval window, your grandparents waiting feverishly for your arrival in the sprawling Portland or Poughkeepsie or even Paris airport. As much as you may have resented it then, the family vacation is as quintessentially American as homemade apple pie. It is also just about as rare in this age of store-bought desserts and workaholism.

Last year, 25 percent of American workers got no paid vacation at all, while 43 percent didn't even take a solid week off. A third fewer American families take vacations together today than they did in 1970. American workers receive the least vacation time among wealthy industrial nations. And it is no thanks to the U.S. government—127 other countries in the world have a vacation law. We—the crackberry denizens and Protestant ethic superstars—do not.

A growing movement of nonprofits, citizen advocacy groups, and trade associations is trying to change all that. Take Back Your Time, a national organization with over 10,000 members, has declared getting a federal vacation law that guarantees Americans at least three weeks of paid vacation a top priority issue in 2007. They are joined by Joe Robinson, author of the 2003 book *Work to Live* and a work/life balance coach, and the Adventure Travel Trade Association, among others.

This is not just a plea for more beach time. It is a movement that recognizes that Americans' lives are diminished by our work-above-all-else orientation. Dissatisfaction with work/life balance cuts across class boundaries, leaving too many Americans feeling estranged from the things they believe are most important—family, friends, wellbeing, spiritual practice. In what journalist Keith H. Hammonds calls our "postbalance world," most Americans live their lives in unsatisfying feast or famine. Unfortunately, there is more famine when it comes to relaxation, exploration, and rejuvenation these days—no thanks to federal policy. John Schmitt, senior economist and co-author of "No-Vacation Nation," a recent study by the Center for Economic Policy Research, says, "It's a national embarrassment that 28 million Americans don't get any paid vacation or paid holidays."

We don't get much time at home, and at work, we feel significantly unsupported. In the latest Pew Research Center survey on work, a near majority of workers (45 percent) now says benefits are worse than they had been 20 or 30 years ago. This includes a gamut of policies—health care, paternity leave, flextime—all of which America is pathetically behind other industrialized countries in legislating. There has certainly been a growing conversation about these issues, thanks to the mothers' movement led by groups like MomsRising, but legislated vacation time is often last on the list of demands. (Not so surprising when you consider how difficult it is for most mothers to believe they deserve a rest.)

Not only does less vacation time mean we have less time to develop our most critical and lasting relationships with family members and friends, but our physical health is in jeopardy when we refuse to unchain ourselves from the cubicle. Vacations cut down on stress, which any medical expert will tell you is at the center of so many of America's most pernicious health crises. Two researchers at the State University of New York at Oswego showed that an annual vacation can cut the risk of death from heart disease in women by 50 percent and in men by 32 percent. Taking time out, exploring new horizons, getting away from your desk and moving around, reconnecting with close friends and family are all safeguards against burnout and depression. But this kind of rejuvenation takes time—two weeks, most studies indicate. The average vacation in the United States is now only a long weekend, which just isn't long enough.

Cali Williams Yost, author of the 2005 book *Work+Life: Finding the Fit That's Right for You* and a coach on work/life balance, asserts that it is not just taking vacation that is important, but how we operate while on it that makes the big difference. She advises corporate clients on how to "avoid having technology become the Grinch that Stole Your Christmas (or Hanukkah, or Kwanzaa)" by setting personal goals around technology usage: "We all need to be much more conscious when we go on vacation."

But it's not all about self control; it's also about government control. Why does the government need to get involved? Because in this cutthroat economic environment, vacation—like parental leave—goes the way of the wimp. Even if workers are employed by companies that guarantee vacation time, many of them are afraid to take advantage because they might be seen as slackers. A culture of self-sacrifice has cropped up in so many careers, leaving those who take their full two weeks looking uncommitted and ineffective.

In truth, they are probably *better* employees for taking the time off. Three-week vacations have proven to be a boost to productivity and profits at enlightened American firms where the culture truly supports the practice. Especially in the knowledge economy, clear thinking and a fresh perspective are critical to best practice. How can anyone expect to get the newest ideas and most innovative approaches from workers who only get the occasional weekend getaway, cell phones still permanently attached to their ears?

Some companies are already reporting hard-and-fast evidence of the phenomenon, according to Robinson. Jancoa, a Cincinnati-based cleaning services company, extended its vacation benefits for its 468 employees to three weeks at a total cost of seven cents. Productivity and morale increased so much that the company was able to eliminate overtime and cut its retention and recruiting costs. The H Group, a management firm founded in 1990 and based in Salem, Oregon, has seen profits double since owner Ron Kelemen pushed his three-week vacation program.

The movement rallying around this issue hopes to get vacation law into the 2008 presidential conversation as well. They are framing it not only as a quality of life issue, but as an indispensable ingredient of global competition. The fastest growing economy in the world, China, offers three weeks off, which they call "Golden Weeks."

Robinson quips, "President Bush knows the value of vacation time. He enjoys his trips to his ranch. He ought to be the first to step up and say, 'Send me this bill and I'll sign it.'"

Discussion Questions

1. Compare the vacation time of American workers with that of workers in other wealthy nations. In terms of time off, was the percentage of American workers taking time to go on a family vacation what you expected it to be? Why or why not? Tell about the last time your family went on a vacation together.

2. How does the author feel the lack of sufficient "beach time" is harmful to Americans? Do you think the benefits of less time off outweigh the negatives she raises? Explain your answer.

3. Why do you think Americans are so unwilling to take time away from their jobs? Consider the way many Japanese companies arrange group vacations for their workers. What do you think American companies should do to encourage their employees to take a vacation?

4. Do you think workers at all jobs should get the same amount of vacation, or do you think the number of vacation days should be determined by the kind of work the person does? Whichever of these positions you support, justify your answer.

The Importance of Work

Essay

BETTY FRIEDAN

Betty Friedan was one of the founders of the National Organization for Women. She attended Smith College and the University of California. Friedan is a feminist, a public speaker, and a writer, and her essays have appeared in numerous periodicals. Her books include It Changed My Life *(1976),* The Second Stage *(1981). and* The Feminine Mystique *(1965), which many attribute to starting the "second wave" of the feminist movement.*

The question of how a person can most fully realize his own capacities and thus achieve identity has become an important concern of the philosophers and the social and psychological thinkers of our time—and for good reason. Thinkers of other times put forth the idea that people were, to a great extent, defined by the work they did. The work that a man had to do to eat, to stay alive, to meet the physical necessities of his environment, dictated his identity. And in this sense, when work was seen merely as a means of survival, human identity was dictated by biology.

But today the problem of human identity has changed. For the work that defined man's place in society and his sense of himself has also changed man's world. Work, and the advance of knowledge, has lessened man's dependence on his environment; his biology and the work he must do for biological survival are no longer sufficient to define his identity. This can be most clearly seen in our own abundant society; men no longer need to work all day to eat. They have an unprecedented freedom to choose the kind of work they will do; they also have an unprecedented amount of time apart from the hours and days that must actually be spent in making a living. And suddenly one realizes the significance of today's identity crisis—for women, and increasingly, for men. One sees the human significance of work—not merely as the means of biological survival, but as the giver of self and the transcender of self, as the creator of human identity and human evolution.

For "self-realization" or "self-fulfillment" or "identity" does not come from looking into a mirror in rapt contemplation of one's own image. Those who have most fully realized themselves, in a sense that can be recognized by the human mind even though it cannot be clearly defined, have done so in the service of a human purpose larger than themselves. Men from varying disciplines have used different words for this mysterious process from which comes the sense of self. The religious mystics, the philosophers, Marx, Freud—all had different names for it: man finds himself by losing himself; man is defined by his relation to the means of production; the ego, the self, grows through understanding and mastering reality through work and love.

The identity crisis, which has been noted by Erik Erikson and others in recent years in the American man, seems to occur for lack of, and be cured by finding, the work, or cause, or purpose that evokes his own creativity. Some never find it, for it does not come from busy-work or punching a time clock. It does not come from just making a living, working by formula, finding a secure spot as an organization man. The very argument, by Riesman and others, that man no longer finds identity in the work defined as a paycheck job, assumes that identity for man comes through creative work of his own that contributes to the human community: the core of the self becomes aware, becomes real, and grows through work that carries forward human society.

Work, the shopworn staple of the economists, has become the new frontier of psychology. Psychiatrists have long used "occupational therapy" with patients in mental hospitals; they have recently discovered that to be of real psychological value, it must be not just "therapy," but real work, serving a real purpose in the community. And work can now be seen as the key to the problem that has no name. The identity crisis of American women began a century ago, as more and more of the work important to the world, more and more of the work that used their human abilities and through which they were able to find self-realization, was taken from them.

Until, and even into, the last century, strong, capable women were needed to pioneer our new land; with their husbands, they ran the farms and plantations and Western homesteads. These women were respected and self-respecting members of a society whose pioneering purpose centered in the home. Strength and independence, responsibility and self-confidence, self-discipline and courage, freedom and equality were part of the American character for both men and women, in all the first generations. The women who came by steerage from Ireland, Italy, Russia, and Poland worked beside their husbands in the sweatshops and the laundries, learned the new language, and saved to send their sons and daughters to college. Women were never quite as "feminine," or held in as much contempt, in

America as they were in Europe. American women seemed to European travelers, long before our time, less passive, childlike, and feminine than their own wives in France or Germany or England. By an accident of history, American women shared in the work of society longer, and grew with the men. Grade- and high-school education for boys and girls alike was almost always the rule; and in the West, where women shared the pioneering work the longest, even the universities were coeducational from the beginning.

The identity crisis for women did not begin in America until the fire and strength and ability of the pioneer women were no longer needed, no longer used, in the middle-class homes of the Eastern and Midwestern cities, when the pioneering was done and men began to build the new society in industries and professions outside the home. But the daughters of the pioneer women had grown too used to freedom and work to be content with leisure and passive femininity.

It was not an American, but a South African woman, Mrs. Olive Schreiner, who warned at the turn of the century that the quality and quantity of women's functions in the social universe were decreasing as fast as civilization was advancing; that if women did not win back their right to a full share of honored and useful work, woman's mind and muscle would weaken in a parasitic state; her offspring, male and female, would weaken progressively, and civilization itself would deteriorate.

The feminists saw clearly that education and the right to participate in the more advanced work of society were women's greatest needs. They fought for and won the rights to new, fully human identity for women. But how very few of their daughters and granddaughters have chosen to use their education and their abilities for any large creative purpose, for responsible work in society? How many of them have been deceived, or have deceived themselves, into clinging to the outgrown, childlike femininity of "Occupation: housewife"?

It was not a minor matter, their mistaken choice. We now know that the same range of potential ability exists for women as for men. Women, as well as men, can only find their identity in work that uses their full capacities. A woman cannot find her identity through others—her husband, her children. She cannot find it in the dull routine of housework. As thinkers of every age have said, it is only when a human being faces squarely the fact that he can forfeit his own life, that he becomes truly aware of himself, and begins to take his existence seriously. Sometimes this awareness comes only at the moment of death. Sometimes it comes from a more subtle facing of death: the death of self in passive conformity, in meaningless work. The feminine mystique prescribes just such a living death for women. Faced with the slow death of self, the American woman must begin to take her life seriously.

"We measure ourselves by many standards," said the great American psychologist William James, nearly a century ago. "Our strength and our intelligence, our wealth and even our good luck, are things which warm our heart and make us feel ourselves a match for life. But deeper than all such things, and able to suffice unto itself without them, is the sense of the amount of effort which we can put forth."

If women do not put forth, finally, that effort to become all that they have it in them to become, they will forfeit their own humanity. A woman today who has no goal, no purpose, no ambition patterning her days into the future, making her stretch and grow beyond that small score of years in which her body can fill its biological function, is committing a kind of suicide. For that future half a century after the child-bearing years are over is a fact that an American woman cannot deny. Nor can she deny that as a housewife, the world is indeed rushing past her door while she just sits and watches. The terror she feels is real, if she has no place in that world.

The feminine mystique has succeeded in burying millions of American women alive. There is no way for these women to break out of their comfortable concentration camps except by finally putting forth an effort—that human effort which reaches beyond biology, beyond the narrow walls of home, to help shape the future. Only by such a personal commitment to the future can American women break out of the housewife trap and truly find fulfillment as wives and mothers—by fulfilling their own unique possibilities as separate human beings.

Discussion Questions

1. How does Friedan explain the change in the significance of work from the past to the present?

2. Does Friedan find all kinds of work to be equally satisfying? In what ways do you think Arendt and Auden might wish to elaborate on Friedan's understanding of work's satisfaction?

3. How has the relationship between women and work changed in the history of America? How does Friedan feel about this change? Do you think her perspective has validity? Why or why not?

4. Who, according to Friedan, were the early feminists, and what ways did they succeed in reconstructing our ideas about women and work?

The Men We Carry in Our Minds

SCOTT RUSSELL SANDERS

Scott Russell Sanders earned a B.A. from Brown University and a Ph.D. from Cambridge University. He is a professor in the English department at Indiana University, and the author of several books of fiction and nonfiction, spanning areas from science fiction to historical novels and personal essays.

The first men, besides my father, I remember seeing were black convicts and white guards, in the cottonfield across the road from our farm on the outskirts of Memphis. I must have been three or four. The prisoners wore dingy gray-and-black zebra suits, heavy as canvas, sodden with sweat. Hatless, stooped, they chopped weeds in the fierce heat, row after row, breathing the acrid dust of boll-weevil poison. The overseers wore dazzling white shirts and broad shadowy hats. The oiled barrels of their shotguns flashed in the sunlight. Their faces in memory are utterly blank. Of course those men, white and black, have become for me an emblem of racial hatred. But they have also come to stand for the twin poles of my early vision of manhood—the brute toiling animal and the boss.

When I was a boy, the men I knew labored with their bodies. They were marginal farmers, just scraping by, or welders, steel workers, carpenters; they swept floors, dug ditches, mined coal, or drove trucks, their forearms ropy with muscle; they trained horses, stoked furnaces, built tires, stood on assembly lines wrestling parts onto cars and refrigerators. They got up before light, worked all day long whatever the weather, and when they came home at night they looked as though somebody had been whipping them. In the evenings and on weekends they worked on their own places, tilling gardens that were lumpy with clay, fixing broken-down cars, hammering on houses that were always too drafty, too leaky, too small.

The bodies of the men I knew were twisted and maimed in ways visible and invisible. The nails of their hands were black and split, the hands tattooed with scars. Some had lost fingers. Heavy lifting had given many of them finicky backs and guts weak from hernias. Racing against conveyor belts had given them ulcers. Their ankles and knees ached from years of standing on concrete. Anyone who had worked for long around machines was hard of hearing. They squinted, and the skin of their faces was creased like the leather of old work gloves. There were times, studying them, when I dreaded growing up. Most of them coughed, from dust or cigarettes, and most of them drank cheap wine or whiskey, so their eyes looked bloodshot and bruised. The fathers of my friends always seemed older than the mothers. Men wore out sooner. Only women lived into old age.

As a boy I also knew another sort of men, who did not sweat and break down like mules. They were soldiers, and so far as I could tell they scarcely worked at all. During my early school years we lived on a military base, an arsenal in Ohio, and every day I saw GIs in the guard shacks, on the stoops of barracks, at the wheels of olive drab Chevrolets. The chief fact of their lives was boredom. Long after I left the Arsenal I came to recognize the sour smell the soldiers gave off as that of souls in limbo. They were all waiting—for wars, for transfers, for leaves, for promotions, for the end of their hitch—like so many braves waiting for the hunt to begin. Unlike the warriors of older tribes, however, they would have no say about when the battle would start or how it would be waged. Their waiting was broken only when they practiced for war. They fired guns at targets, drove tanks across the churned-up fields of the military reservation, set off bombs in the wrecks of old fighter planes. I knew this was all play. But I also felt certain that when the hour for killing arrived, they would kill. When the real shooting started, many of them would die. This was what soldiers were *for*, just as a hammer was for driving nails.

Warriors and toilers: those seemed, in my boyhood vision, to be the chief destinies for men. They weren't the only destinies, as I learned from having a few male teachers, from reading books, and from watching television. But the men on television—the politicians, the astronauts, the generals, the savvy lawyers, the philosophical doctors, the bosses who gave orders to both soldiers and laborers—seemed as remote and unreal to me as the figures in tapestries. I could no more imagine growing up to become one of these cool, potent creatures than I could imagine becoming a prince.

A nearer and more hopeful example was that of my father, who had escaped from a red-dirt farm to a tire factory, and from the assembly line to the front office. Eventually he dressed in a white shirt and tie. He carried himself as if he had been born to work with his mind. But his body, remembering the earlier years of slogging work, began to give out on him in his fifties, and it quit on him entirely before he turned sixty-five. Even such a partial escape from man's fate as he had accomplished did not seem possible for most of the boys I knew. They joined the Army, stood in line for jobs in the smoky plants, helped build highways. They were bound to work as their fathers had worked, killing themselves or preparing to kill others.

A scholarship enabled me not only to attend college, a rare enough feat in my circle, but even to study in a university meant for the children of the rich. Here I met for the first time young men who had assumed from birth that they would lead lives of comfort and power. And for the first time I met women who told me that men were guilty of having kept all the joys and privileges of the earth for themselves. I was baffled. What privileges? What joys? I thought about the maimed, dismal lives of most of the men back home. What had they stolen from their wives and daughters? The right to go five days a week, twelve months a year, for thirty or forty years to a steel mill or a coal mine? The right to drop bombs and die in war? The right to feel every leak in the roof, every gap in the fence, every cough in the engine, as a wound they must mend? The right to feel, when the layoff comes or the plant shuts down, not only afraid but ashamed?

I was slow to understand the deep grievances of women. This was because, as a boy, I had envied them. Before college, the only people I had ever known who were interested in art or music or literature, the only ones who read books, the only ones who ever seemed to enjoy a sense of ease and grace were the mothers and daughters. Like the menfolk, they fretted about money, they scrimped and made-do. But, when the pay stopped coming in, they were not the ones who had failed. Nor did they have to go to war, and that seemed to me a blessed fact. By comparison with the narrow, ironclad days of fathers, there was an expansiveness, I thought, in the days of mothers. They went to see neighbors, to shop in town, to run errands at school, at the library, at church. No doubt, had I looked harder at their lives, I would have envied them less. It was not my fate to become a woman, so it was easier for me to see the graces. Few of them held jobs outside the home, and those who did filled thankless roles as clerks and waitresses. I didn't see, then, what a prison a house could be, since houses seemed to me brighter, handsomer places than any factory. I did not realize—because such things were never spoken of—how often women suffered from men's bullying. I did learn about the wretchedness of abandoned wives, single mothers, widows; but I also learned about the wretchedness of lone men. Even then I could see how exhausting it was for a mother to cater all day to the needs of young children. But if I had been asked, as a boy, to choose between tending a baby and tending a machine, I think I would have chosen the baby. (Having now tended both, I know I would choose the baby.)

So I was baffled when the women at college accused me and my sex of having cornered the world's pleasures. I think something like my bafflement has been felt by other boys (and by girls as well) who grew up in dirt-poor farm country, in mining country, in black ghettos, in Hispanic barrios, in the shadows of factories, in Third World nations—any place where the fate of men is as grim and bleak as the fate of women. Toilers and warriors. I realize now how ancient these identities are, how deep the tug they exert on men, the undertow of a thousand generations. The miseries I saw, as a boy, in the lives of nearly all men I continue to see in the lives of many—the body-breaking toil, the tedium, the call to be tough, the humiliating powerlessness, the battle for a living and for territory.

When the women I met at college thought about the joys and privileges of men, they did not carry in their minds the sort of men I had known in my childhood. They thought of their fathers, who were bankers, physicians, architects, stockbrokers, the big wheels of the big cities. These fathers rode the train to work or drove cars that cost more than any of my childhood houses. They were attended from morning to night by female helpers, wives and nurses and secretaries. They were never laid off, never short of cash at month's end, never lined up for welfare. These fathers made decisions that mattered. They ran the world.

The daughters of such men wanted to share in this power, this glory. So did I. They yearned for a say over their future, for jobs worthy of their abilities, for the right to live at peace, unmolested, whole. Yes, I thought, yes yes. The difference between me and these daughters was that they saw me, because of my sex, as destined from birth to become like their fathers, and therefore as an enemy to their desires. But I knew better. I wasn't an enemy, in fact or in feeling. I was an ally. If I had known, then, how to tell them so, would they have believed me? Would they now?

Discussion Questions

1. What were the two work options the young Sanders saw open to the men he knew and the man he imagined he would grow up to be? What other kinds of work did he know that men did? Why couldn't he imagine himself in one of those jobs?

2. What were the jobs relegated to women in the world of Sanders's childhood? In his eyes, how did the lives of women compare to those of men? Why?

3. When Sanders went away to college, what surprised him about the way most of the women he met thought about men and work? How can these differences be explained? What other students on his campus shared his views? Do you think Betty Friedan would or would not have understood Sanders's position? Explain your answer.

4. Do you think Sanders's view of the work lives of men and women is applicable to today's world?

Woe Is the American Worker

PAUL WALDMAN

Paul Waldman is a senior fellow at Media Matters for America and a part-ner in R5 Advisors, a communications consulting firm. He is also a senior correspondent with the American Prospect *magazine. He is the author of* Being Right Is Not Enough: What Progressives Must Learn from Conservative Success. *This essay was published in 2007.*

These are not good times for American workers. Real wages are lower today than they were before the recession of 2001, and barely higher than they were thirty-five years ago. Health insurance is more expensive and harder to obtain than ever before. Manufacturing jobs continue to move overseas. The unions whose efforts might arrest these trends continue to struggle under a sustained assault that began when Ronald Reagan fired striking air-traffic controllers in 1981, in effect declaring war on the labor movement.

This is a story with which you are probably familiar. But these are in no small part symptoms of a larger transformation of the relation-ship between employers and employees, in which Americans increas-ingly sign away their humanity when they sign an employment contract.

Let's take just one component of today's work environment that most people have simply come to accept: drug testing. An article pub-lished last year on *Time* magazine's web site titled, "Whatever Hap-pened to Drug Testing?" reported that in the last decade, the proportion of employers testing their employees for drug use has declined to 62 percent, after having exploded to over 80 percent in the 1990s.

That's right—"only" 62 percent of employers make their employ-ees pee into a cup (or fork over a lock of hair, the current state of the art). The recent decline notwithstanding, the fact remains that most Americans work at places where drug testing is standard practice.

But the classic justifications for drug testing—that it will reduce accidents, absenteeism, and overall productivity—turn out to have very little support. When this study was released 10 years ago, it got a certain amount of attention for what the authors referred to as a "surprising" finding. In their survey of high-tech firms, they found that those that performed drug testing on their employees had *lower* productivity than those that didn't test. Forget all the rhetoric about pot-addled employees missing work and stumbling their way around the office.

But I'd bet that most people who work weren't too surprised. Think about the jobs you've had. Where were you the most productive? Was it when you worked for a boss and an organization that treated you with respect, that valued your contributions, where you actually felt that you were part of something useful? Or were you more productive when you worked for a boss and an organization that governed by fear, that treated you with suspicion and contempt? Most adults have worked for the latter kind, while only some have had the good fortune to work for the former. And many if not most of them do just enough work to stay out of trouble and avoid the wrath of their superiors. That's the spirit fostered in a workplace where employees are treated like criminals.

There is an ideology inherent in the way employers treat their workers, one reflected in the relative amounts of attention paid by the news media to labor issues and the ups and downs of the stock market. Wall Street, of course, makes heroes out of executives who cut benefits and sack workers, like the monstrous "Neutron Jack" Welch, formerly of General Electric. A corporate barbarian of the first order, Welch pocketed hundreds of millions of dollars while firing more than 100,000 employees, then went on to write a series of best-selling books gobbled up by junior executives looking for the secret battle plan to slash their way to the top. He's just one among many; another such executive, who laid off 9,000 people when he was CEO of Halliburton, later became vice president of the United States.

If you are one of those left behind, you get called an "associate" instead of a clerk. In the place of paid vacation, you get company-sponsored activities whose absurdity can only make you more depressed. In the place of a union to represent you, you get assurances that the company considers you part of the "family." Your samples will be analyzed, your movements surveilled, your email read, all in the name of enhancing productivity and rooting out the bad apples. And should they decide your time is done, they will send a security guard to march you out the door in a ritual of public humiliation, lest you decide to pilfer a stapler as a memento of your service.

There is no labor section of the newspaper to tell the stories of the families devastated by layoffs and the workers ground down by the daily parade of indignities. But in the morally inverted world of Wall Street, what's bad for workers is good for stocks, and the cable news "money honeys" will bare their gleaming teeth as they report the inevitable upward swing in share prices that accompanies a mass firing or benefit cut.

It would be positively revelatory to hear a presidential candidate truly speak to the conditions Americans find themselves in at work, to say firmly that companies that treat their employees like dirt are undermining our national spirit. They are the ones who have the ability to change our national conversation on topics like these. What if, instead of simply talking about "creating jobs," expanding health care, or increasing the minimum wage—important goals all—they actually attempted to speak to how people feel about their jobs? When candidates say the American dream is getting harder to attain, one often wonders if they understand all the reasons why that is so.

The Republicans certainly know the kind of workplace they admire. It's one in which power—not values, principles, or fairness, but raw power—determines how people are treated. They find deeply troubling anything that constrains employers from exploiting their workers to whatever degree they see fit. They despise unions precisely because they alter that balance of power in the worker's favor, providing some check on the ability of organizations to intimidate and humiliate, underpay and overwork. But so far, Democrats haven't articulated their vision of what a progressive workplace in the twenty-first century is supposed to look like—and what they're willing to do to create it. I'd be eager to hear.

Discussion Questions

1. In what way, according to Paul Waldman, has the relationship between the American workers and employers changed? Give an example of a place where you or someone you know has worked that supports Waldman's view of the employer/employee relationship.

   Give an example that contradicts his view. For which of the two categories did you find that more examples came to mind?

2. What was one result of drug testing that was "surprising"? Explain your reasons for thinking that drug testing by employers should or should not continue.

3. Explain, in your own words, the relationship between Wall Street and the treatment of workers.

4. What attitudes do you think Fromm would expect to result from the kind of treatment of workers that Waldman discusses?

The Protestant Work Ethic: Just Another "Urban Legend"?

JONATHAN KLEMENS

Jonathan Klemens is an accomplished author, essayist, and practicing pharmacist. He is the Director of Pharmacy at the Jefferson Regional Medical Center (Pittsburgh, PA), Adjunct Assistant Professor of Pharmacy Practice at the Lake Erie College of Osteopathic Medicine School of Pharmacy, and Adjunct Instructor at the University of Pittsburgh School of Pharmacy. He has published numerous essays, articles, and fiction in local, national, and international magazines, a college textbook, e-books, and various web sites.

"Hi Ho! Hi Ho! It's off to work we go!" Like the words in the Disney cartoon melody, every day people merrily trek to a job they apparently enjoy. Are these people misguided social dwarfs out of synch with the rest of the workforce? Well, these people are for real—another "Urban Legend" bites the dust! Even though we often give lip-service to the "work ethic," it really does exist and it is stronger than one might expect. Frank Lloyd Wright, the famous 20th Century architect, stated, "I know the price of success: dedication, hard work, and an unremitting devotion to the things you want to see happen."[1]

The "work ethic" is personified by those who have found work that provides both a service to society and personal satisfaction. It is their passion—their life "calling." One's calling can follow any career path—writer, accountant, missionary, teacher, auto mechanic, carpenter, cook, social worker, attorney, or brain surgeon. It takes commitment and hard work, but you enjoy it and it feels like the right fit for you. You may actually become so intensively involved and committed that your "calling" becomes "one" with the company or organization's mission. Encompassing centuries, this commitment and dedication to hard work has been exemplified in such societies as the Amish, Mennonites, Hutterites and the Shakers. The Shaker phrase attributed to Mother Ann Lee, the founder of the Shaker sect: "Put your hands to

---

[1]ThinkExist.com Quotations Online. 1 Jan. 2011. 2 Feb. 2011. http://thinkexist.com/quotes/frank_lloyd_wright/.

work, and your hearts to God" encourages a simple life of hard work and spirituality. We might also identify with Ben Franklin, who espoused his philosophy of avarice and a strong work ethic.

How could this concept of a work ethic develop and endure in a society where the concept of "entitlement" now seems to be so prevalent? The roots begin with Max Weber, one of the leading founders of modern sociology, and his renowned work on modern social science, *The Protestant Ethic and the Spirit of Capitalism.* In the 1930s, after the book was translated into English, the U.S. workforce began its on-going love affair with the work ethic—a social trait that would become the backbone of American enterprise and world leadership. The arduous work of capitalism, according to Weber, is closely associated with intrinsic Protestant religious beliefs and behavior. Only in the West has rationalization in science, law, and culture developed to the extent where political, technical, and economic conditions depend on highly trained government officials. He further states, "However, all the peculiarities of Western capitalism have derived their significance in the last analysis only from their association with the capitalistic organization of labor."[2]

Historically, certain Protestant denominations had a strong influence on the members' development of business acumen and the ethic of hard work. These Protestants developed a sense of economic rationalism that emphasized diligent and dedicated work. Each and every Sunday, Methodist and Presbyterian ministers extolled the virtues of the work ethic to their congregations through lengthy and tedious sermons.

According to Weber, the following traits characterize a strong work ethic:

- FOCUS ON WORK: We know how precious our time is and that it is limited. We must have a passion and strive for excellence in our work. Work time should be used efficiently and wisely with a desire to make money as a fruit of our labor and not spend it irresponsibly.

- UNPRETENTIOUS AND MODEST: We should act and dress appropriately—dress should not be flashy to attract attention or cause distraction to others.

- HONEST AND ETHICAL: One should possess and exhibit strong ethical beliefs, and a moral code of behavior, i.e., The Ten

---

[2]Weber, Max. *The Protestant Ethic and the Spirit of Capitalism.* BN Publishing, 2008, p. 22.

Commandments. We must do the "right thing" when no one is watching.[3]

The power of a free labor force has made capitalism a very powerful force in our society. Riding high on the wave of post WWII patriotism and intense business competition, we became rightfully proud of our fast-growing economy and the image of hard-working Americans. We take pride in who we were and what we produce as a nation, the greatest and most successful nation on earth. Although the original religious aspects eventually faded, the work ethic is firmly entrenched as a powerful and valued American social trait.

Unquestionably, we do not desire a workforce dominated by mindless "robots" even with a good work ethic. We need innovative thinkers and committed leaders that can guide us through the 21st Century and beyond. It is essential that we continue to build a strong labor force committed to an indomitable work ethic—workers that are honest, ethical, and rational.

We also need leaders that will not be afraid to work and who will take the responsibly to guide new projects and develop employee potentials to exceed projected goals. We need people passionate about a mission. A good work ethic is essential to a strong economy, and a strong vibrant society.

Discussion Questions

1. What are the two aspects, according to Jonathan Klemens, of the "work ethic?" Do you think it is essential to human happiness that work provide both?

2. What connection does the author find between work and Western capitalism? How does he believe both work and capitalism are related to religion? If his assertion is correct, what implications does it have for the importing of capitalism into non-Western cultures?

---

[3]Weber 35.

3. What are the traits that Weber identifies as characterizing a strong work ethic? What items would you add to or subtract from his list?

Class Discussion

Paraphrasing is the restatement in your own words of material from another source. This restatement differs from the original in that though it contains all the ideas of the original, it uses your own words to explain them. Paraphrasing isn't the same as summarizing; a summary is briefer because it simply condenses the argument's thesis and main supporting topics.

Paraphrase the following quotations from Fromm's "Work in an Industrial Society." Does each of your paraphrases accurately reflect the meaning of the original? Are there any errors in grammar and mechanics in your version that need to be fixed?

1. "During the Middle Ages, the Renaissance, and the eighteenth century, work was not only a useful activity, but one which carried with it a profound satisfaction."

2. "He [the worker] is part of the machine, rather than its master as an active agent."

3. "The alienated and profoundly unsatisfactory character of modern industrial work results in two reactions: one, the ideal of complete laziness; the other, a deep-seated, though often unconscious, hostility toward work and everything and everybody connected with it."

4. "Many a businessman feels himself the prisoner of his business and the commodities he sells; he has a feeling of fraudulency about his product and a secret contempt for it."

Homework

1. Describe the job you hope to have after you finish your education.

2. How much vacation time can you realistically expect to have when you are employed in this position? After reading the essays by Martin and Quindlen, how much time off do you believe to be necessary for your mental and physical well being? Explain.

3. If you were given the vacation time that you believe you should have, how would you spend the extra time away from work?

4. Knowing that Americans are granted less vacation time and days than people in most other Western countries, what kinds of changes, if any, would you work to promote?

Reviewing Your Graded Essay

After your essay has been graded by your instructor, you may have the opportunity to revise your paper and raise your grade. Even if you are not submitting a revised version of this essay to your instructor, it is important that you review your work carefully in order to understand its strengths and weaknesses. This sheet will guide you through the evaluation process.

You will want to continue to use the techniques that worked well for you and to find strategies to overcome the problems that you identify in this sample of your writing. In order to help yourself recognize areas that might have been problematic for you, look back at the scoring rubric in this book. Match the numerical/verbal/letter grade received on your essay to the appropriate category. Study the explanation given on the rubric for your grade.

Write a few sentences below in which you identify your problems in each of the following areas. Then suggest specific changes you could make that would improve your paper. Don't forget to use your handbook as a resource.

1. **Grammar/mechanics**

    My problem:

    My strategy for change:

2. **Thesis/response to assignment**

    My problem:

    My strategy for change:

3. **Organization**

    My problem:

    My strategy for change:

4. **Paragraph development/examples/reasoning**

    My problem:

    My strategy for change:

5. Assessment

In the space below, assign a grade to your paper using a rubric other than the one used by your instructor. In other words, if your instructor assigned your essay a grade of *High Fail*, you might give it the letter grade you now feel the paper warrants. If your instructor used the traditional letter grade to evaluate the essay, choose a category from the rubric in this book, or any other grading scale that you are familiar with, to show your evaluation of your work. Then write a short narrative explaining your evaluation of the essay and the reasons it received the grade you gave it.

Grade:_____

Narrative:_____

_____

_____

_____

_____

Assignment 5

Dwight MacDonald's "Reading and Thought"

We hope you have come to see the value in doing extensive prewriting as you work to build a draft of your essay. By now, you should be familiar with the prewriting strategies in *Write It*. For this assignment, decide which are most beneficial to your writing and critical thinking style and customize them to maximize their benefits. Just be sure not to omit a thorough examination of MacDonald's ideas and your own before you formulate your thesis statement and offer your supporting evidence.

Reading and Thought

DWIGHT MACDONALD

Dwight MacDonald (1906–82), was a part of the New York intellectuals of his time, and became famous for his attacks on middlebrow culture. He frequently carried on his debate in essays published in magazines such as The Partisan Review, The New Yorker, Esquire, *and the magazine he edited in the 1940s,* Politics.

Henry Luce[1] has built a journalistic empire on our national weakness for being "well informed." *Time* attributes its present two-million circulation to a steady increase, since it first appeared in 1925, in what it calls "functional curiosity." Unlike the old-fashioned idle variety, this is a "kind of searching, hungry interest in what is happening everywhere— born not of an idle desire to be entertained or amused, but of a solid conviction that the news intimately and vitally affects the lives of everyone now. Functional curiosity grows as the number of educated people grows."

The curiosity exists, but it is not functional since it doesn't help the individual function. A very small part of the mass of miscellaneous facts offered in each week's issue of *Time* (or, for that matter, in the depressing quantity of newspapers and magazines visible on any large newsstand) is useful to the reader; they don't help him make more money, take some political or other action to advance his interests, or become a better person. About the only functional gain (though the *New York Times*, in a recent advertising campaign, proclaimed that reading it would help one to "be more interesting") the reader gets out of them is practice in reading. And even this is a doubtful advantage. *Time*'s educated people read too many irrelevant words—irrelevant, that is, to any thoughtful idea of their personal interests, either narrow (practical) or broad (cultural).

Imagine a similar person of, say, the sixteenth century confronted with a copy of *Time* or the *New York Times*. He would take a whole day to master it, perhaps two, because he would be accustomed to take the time to think and even to feel about what he read; and he could take the time because there was time, there being comparatively little to read in that golden age. (The very name of Luce's

---

[1] The publisher of *Time* magazine.

magazine is significant: *Time*, just because we don't have it.) Feeling a duty—or perhaps simply a compulsion—at least to glance over the printed matter that inundates us daily, we have developed of necessity a rapid, purely rational, classifying habit of mind, something like the operations of a Mark IV calculating machine, making a great many small decisions every minute: read or not read? If read, then take in this, skim over that, and let the rest go by. This we do with the surface of our minds, since we "just don't have time" to bring the slow, cumbersome depths into play, to ruminate, speculate, reflect, wonder, *experience* what the eye flits over. This gives a greatly extended coverage to our minds, but also makes them, compared to the kind of minds similar people had in past centuries, coarse, shallow, passive, and unoriginal.

Such reading habits have produced a similar kind of reading matter, since, except for a few stubborn old-fashioned types—the handcraftsmen who produce whatever is written today of quality, whether in poetry, fiction, scholarship, or journalism—our writers produce work that is to be read quickly and then buried under the next day's spate of "news" or the next month's best seller; hastily slapped-together stuff that it would be foolish to waste much time or effort on either writing or reading. For those who, as readers or as writers, would get a little under the surface, the real problem of our day is how to *escape* being "well informed," how to resist the temptation to acquire too much information (never more seductive than when it appears in the chaste garb of duty), and how in general to elude the voracious demands on one's attention enough to think a little.

Writing Topic

According to MacDonald, what is the nature of the "printed matter that inundates us daily," and what connection does this kind of reading have with thought? What do you think about the position he takes here? Be sure to support your argument with specific examples based on your observations and experiences, as well as on your reading, especially the supplemental essays in this unit.

Vocabulary Check

Good writers choose their words carefully so that their ideas will be clear. In order for you, the reader, to understand an essay, it is important to think about its key vocabulary terms and the way they are used by the author. Words can have a variety of meanings, or they can have specialized meanings in certain contexts. Look up the definitions of the following words or phrases from the essay. Choose the meaning that you think MacDonald intended when he selected that particular word or phrase for use in this essay. Then explain the way the meaning or concept behind the definition is key to understanding the author's argument.

curiosity
> definition:

> explanation:

miscellaneous
> definition:

> explanation:

inundate
> definition:

> explanation:

Questions to Guide Your Reading

Before you begin to answer these questions, review "Steps for a Thoughtful Reading of an Essay" in Part 1. Use its strategies to analyze "Reading and Thought" in preparation for answering the questions here.

Paragraph 1

What is "functional curiosity," and how does Luce believe it relates to the circulation of *Time*?

Paragraph 2

Why does MacDonald say that the kind of curiosity Luce is talking about should not be called functional?

Paragraph 3

Explain the difference between the way people today read *Time* and the way a sixteenth century person would read it. Why is there a difference?

Paragraph 4

What is the problem, according to MacDonald, that today's reading habits have produced? Would you call this situation a problem? Why or why not?

Prewriting for a Directed Summary

You will use the answers you fill in here when you write a directed summary in response to the first part of the writing topic for this assignment:

> *first question in the writing topic*: According to MacDonald, what is the nature of the "printed matter that inundates us daily," and what connection does this kind of reading have with thought?

Although this question asks you to explain one of MacDonald's main assertions, it doesn't ask you to summarize the entire essay. Be sure to keep the question in mind as you present MacDonald's ideas.

Hint

Don't forget to review Part 1's "Guidelines for Writing a Directed Summary."

1. What is meant by the term "functional curiosity"?

2. What is the relationship MacDonald finds between functional curiosity and the reading habits of educated people of today?

3. What, according to the author, is the only thing readers gain from reading out of functional curiosity?

4. According to MacDonald, if a sixteenth century person were confronted with an issue of one of today's magazines or newspapers, how much time would he or she likely devote to reading it? Why would it take so long?

5. What difference does MacDonald find between skimming and reading?

6. According to MacDonald, how can being well informed contribute to shallow thinking?

Opinion and Working Thesis Statement

To fully answer the writing topic that follows "Reading and Thought," you will have to take a position of your own on the issue MacDonald addresses.

> *second question in the writing topic*: What do you think about the position he takes here?

Do you think his position on the connection between reading and thought applies to the reading many of us do on a daily basis? In order to make your position clear to readers, state it clearly early in your essay, preferably at the end of your introductory paragraph. A clear thesis statement, one that takes a position on the importance of the kind of reading we do and its influence on our thinking, will unify your essay and allow it to communicate effectively with readers.

It is likely that you aren't yet sure what position you want to take in your essay. If this is the case, you can explore your ideas on a blank page of this book, or go on to the next section and work on developing your ideas through specific evidence drawn from your experience. Then you will be asked to reexamine the working thesis statement you write here to see if you want to revise it based on the discoveries you made when you explored your ideas more systematically.

1. Use the following **thesis frame** to identify the basic elements of your thesis statement:

   a. What is the subject of "Reading and Thought" that the writing topic asks you to consider?

   _____

   b. What is MacDonald's opinion about that subject?

   _____

   c. What is your opinion about the subject, and will you agree or disagree with MacDonald?

   _____

   _____

   _____

2. Now use the elements you isolated in 1a, b, and c of the thesis frame to write a thesis statement. You may have to revise it several times until it captures your idea clearly.

   _____

   _____

Prewriting to Find Support for Your Thesis Statement

The last part of the writing topic asks you to support the argument you put forward in your thesis statement.

last part of the writing topic: Be sure to support your argument with specific examples based on your observations and experiences, as well as on your reading, especially the supplemental essays in this unit.

Use the following questions to help develop examples you might use to support your thesis statement.

Hint

Complete each section of this prewriting activity; your responses will become the material you will use in the next stage—planning and writing the essay.

1. As you begin to develop your own examples, consider the kinds of reading you've done and its effect on your own thinking. Perhaps make a list of the things you have read in recent weeks. Then consider how this reading influenced your thinking.

   Once you've explored your ideas, look them over carefully. Try to group your ideas into categories. Then give each category a label. In other words, cluster ideas that seem to have something in common and, for each cluster, identify that shared quality by giving it a name.

2. Now broaden your focus; list or freewrite about examples of reading material available on a regular basis for large numbers of people, for example newspapers, popular Internet sites, popular magazines, or any other sources with which you are familiar. Do you think these sources influence people's ideas? Explore your thoughts.

Once you've written your ideas, look them over carefully. Try to group your ideas into categories. Then give each category a label. In other words, cluster ideas that seem to have something in common and, for each cluster, identify that shared quality by giving it a name.

3. Once you've created topics by clustering your ideas into categories, go through them and pick two or three specific ones to develop in your essay. Make sure that they are relevant to your thesis and that they have enough substance to be compelling to your reader. Then, in the space below, briefly summarize each item.

   Once you've decided which items and categories on your lists you will use in your essay, take some time to explain below how each category and its items connect to your thesis statement. You will use these details for the next stage.

Revising Your Thesis Statement

Now that you have spent some time working out your ideas more systematically and developing some supporting evidence for the position you want to take, look again at the working thesis statement you crafted earlier to see if it is still accurate. As your first step, look again at the writing topic and then write your original working thesis on the lines that follow it:

> *second question in the writing topic*: What do you think about the position he takes here?

working thesis statement:

_____

_____

_____

Take some time now to see if you want to revise your thesis statement. Often, after extensive prewriting and focused thought, the working thesis statement is no longer an accurate reflection of what you plan to say in your essay. Sometimes, only a word or phrase must be added or deleted; other times, the thesis statement must be significantly rewritten, as either or both the subject and the claim portions are inaccurate.

After examining your working thesis statement and completing any necessary revisions, check it one more time by asking yourself the following questions:

When you've finished, ask yourself the following questions:

a. Does the thesis directly identify MacDonald's argument (the way much of our reading today affects thought)?

b. Do you make clear your opinion regarding this connection?

If you answered "no" to either of these questions, then rewrite your thesis statement so that it is fully developed.

_____

_____

Planning and Drafting Your Essay

Now that you have examined MacDonald's argument and thought at length about your own views, draft an essay that responds to all parts of the writing topic. Use the material you developed in this section to compose your draft, and then exchange drafts with a classmate and use the peer review activity to help revise your draft.

Getting started on the draft is often the hardest part of the writing process because this is where you move from exploring and planning to getting your ideas down in a unified, coherent shape. Creating an outline will give you a basic structure for incorporating all the ideas you have developed in the preceding pages. An outline will also give you a bird's-eye view of your essay and help you spot problems in development or logic.

Creating an Outline for Your Draft

I. Introductory Paragraph

A. An opening sentence that gives the reading selection's title and author and begins to answer the first question in the writing topic:

_____

B. Main points to include in the directed summary:

1.

2.

3.

4.

C. Look again at the thesis statement you wrote in "Revising Your Thesis Statement" and make any changes you think necessary. Then copy your thesis statement below. It should clearly agree or disagree with the argument in "Reading and Thought" and state a clear position using your own words.

_____

II. Body Paragraphs

A. Subject of the paragraph: _____

1. Controlling idea sentence:

_____

2. **C**orroborating details:

_____

_____

_____

3. **C**areful description of the details' relevance:

_____

_____

_____

_____

4. **C**onnection to the thesis statement:

_____

B. Subject of the paragraph: _____

1. **C**ontrolling idea sentence:

_____

_____

2. **C**orroborating details:

_____

_____

_____

3. **C**areful description of the details' relevance:

_____

_____

_____

_____

_____

4. **C**onnection to the thesis statement:

_____

C. Subject of the paragraph: _____

1. **C**ontrolling idea sentence:

_____

2. **C**orroborating details:

_____

_____

_____

3. **C**areful description of the details' relevance:

_____

_____

_____

_____

_____

4. **C**onnection to the thesis statement:

_____

D. Subject of the paragraph: _____

1. **C**ontrolling idea sentence:

_____

2. **C**orroborating details:

_____

_____

_____

3. **C**areful description of the details' relevance:

_____

_____

_____

_____

_____

4. **C**onnection to the thesis statement:

_____

III. Conclusion

A. Type of conclusion to be used:

_____

B. Key words or phrases to include:

_____

Peer Draft Review Sheet

Use the following guidelines to give a classmate feedback on his or her draft. Read the draft through first and then answer each of the items below as specifically as you can.

Name of draft's author: _____

Name of draft's reader: _____

Introduction

1. Within the opening sentences,

   a. the author is correctly identified by first and last name   yes   no

   b. the reading selection's title is included and placed within
      quotation marks   yes   no

2. The opening contains a summary that

   a. explains the connection MacDonald believes exists
      between reading and thought   yes   no

   b. identifies the specific example MacDonald uses to
      illustrate this connection   yes   no

   c. explains the reason MacDonald believes Luce is wrong in
      calling this example one of "functional curiosity"   yes   no

3. The opening provides a thesis that

   a. Makes clear MacDonald's conclusion about the
      connection between reading and thought   yes   no

   b. gives the draft writer's opinion about that conclusions   yes   no

   If the answers to 3 above are yes, state the thesis below as it is written. If the answer to one or both of these questions is no, explain to the draft writer what information is needed to make the thesis complete.

Body

1. How many paragraphs are in the body of this essay? _____

2. To support the thesis, this number is   sufficient   not enough

3. Do paragraphs contain the 4Cs?

Paragraph 1	Controlling idea sentence	yes	no
	Corroborating details	yes	no
	Careful description of the details' relevance	yes	no
	Connection to the thesis statement	yes	no
Paragraph 2	Controlling idea sentence	yes	no
	Corroborating details	yes	no
	Careful description of the details' relevance	yes	no
	Connection to the thesis statement	yes	no
Paragraph 3	Controlling idea sentence	yes	no
	Corroborating details	yes	no
	Careful description of the details' relevance	yes	no
	Connection to the thesis statement	yes	no
Paragraph 4	Controlling idea sentence	yes	no
	Corroborating details	yes	no
	Careful description of the details' relevance	yes	no
	Connection to the thesis statement	yes	no
Paragraph 5	Controlling idea sentence	yes	no
	Corroborating details	yes	no
	Careful description of the details' relevance	yes	no
	Connection to the thesis statement	yes	no

(Continue as needed)

4. Identify any of the above paragraphs that are not fully developed (too short).

5. Identify any of the above paragraphs that fail to support the thesis. _____

6. Identify any of the above paragraphs that are redundant or repetitive. _____

7. Suggest any ideas for additional paragraphs that might improve this essay.

Conclusion

1. Does the conclusion contain any material that should have been developed in the body of the essay?

   a. examples   yes   no

   b. new ideas   yes   no

2. Does the conclusion provide closure (let the reader know that the end of the essay has been reached)?   yes   no

3. Does the conclusion leave the reader with an understanding of the significance of the argument?   yes   no

   State in your own words what the writer considers to be important about his or her argument.

   _____

   _____

4. Identify the type of conclusion used (see the guidelines for conclusions in Part 1).

Revision

1. During revision, the writer should pay attention to the following problems in mechanics:

   comma splices

   comma placement

   fragments

   run-on sentences

   apostrophe use

   quotation mark use

   capital letter use

   spelling

2. During revision, the writer should pay attention to the following areas of grammar:

verb tense
subject-verb agreement
pronoun type
pronoun reference
pronoun agreement
irregular verbs
noun plurals
dangling modifiers
prepositions
misplaced modifiers

Final Draft Check List

Content:

- My essay has an appropriate title.
- I provide an accurate summary of the position on the topic set out by MacDonald's essay.
- My thesis contains a thesis statement that I can support with evidence.
- I have a sufficient number of paragraphs and arguments to support my thesis.
- Each body paragraph is relevant to my thesis.
- Each body paragraphs contains the 4Cs.
- I use transitions to connect paragraphs and ideas to each other.
- The final paragraph of my essay (the conclusion) provides readers with a sense of closure.

Grammar and Mechanics:

- I use the present tense to discuss MacDonald's argument and examples.
- All of my verb tense shifts are appropriate for the chronology of events.
- I have verb tense consistency throughout my sentences and paragraphs.
- My sentence boundaries are marked clearly and correctly.
- If I present items in a series (nouns, verbs, prepositional phrases), they are parallel in form.
- If I include material spoken or written by someone other than myself, I have correctly punctuated it with quotation marks and other necessary punctuation.
- I have checked for subject-verb agreement in all of my sentences.

Extended Activities

Readings

"Is Google Making Us Stupid? What the Internet Is Doing to Our Brains" by Nicholas Carr

"Yes, People Still Read, But Now It's Social" by Steven Johnson

"The Information Age" by Gordon Crovitz

"Why Literature Matters: Good Books Help Make a Civil Society" by Dana Gioia

"Literary Reading in Dramatic Decline" by the National Endowment for the Arts

"Is Reading Really at Risk?" by Joseph Epstein

"The Future of Books" by Kathy Keeton

"The Sad Decline of Literature" by George Will

Class Discussion

Using the Present Tense

Homework

A Blog: "IS American Literature in Decline?"

Reviewing Your Graded Essay

Is Google Making Us Stupid? What the Internet Is Doing to Our Brains

Nicholas Carr

Nicholas Carr holds a B.A. from Dartmouth College and an M.A., in English and American literature and language, from Harvard University. Carr has been a speaker at MIT, Harvard, Wharton, the Kennedy School of Government, and NASA, as well as at many industry, corporate, and professional events throughout the Americas, Europe, and Asia. He writes on the social, economic, and business implications of technology. He is the author of Does IT Matter *(2004),* The Big Switch: Rewiring the Word, from Edison to Google *(2008), and his latest book* The Shallows: What the Internet Is Doing to Our Brains *(2010). The following essay is an excerpt from his most recent book,* The Shallows.

"Dave, stop. Stop, will you? Stop, Dave. Will you stop, Dave?" So the supercomputer HAL pleads with the implacable astronaut Dave Bowman in a famous and weirdly poignant scene toward the end of Stanley Kubrick's *2001: A Space Odyssey*. Bowman, having nearly been sent to a deep-space death by the malfunctioning machine, is calmly, coldly disconnecting the memory circuits that control its artificial "brain." "Dave, my mind is going," HAL says, forlornly. "I can feel it. I can feel it."

I can feel it, too. Over the past few years I've had an uncomfortable sense that someone, or something, has been tinkering with my brain, remapping the neural circuitry, reprogramming the memory. My mind isn't going—so far as I can tell—but it's changing. I'm not thinking the way I used to think. I can feel it most strongly when I'm reading. Immersing myself in a book or a lengthy article used to be easy. My mind would get caught up in the narrative or the turns of the argument, and I'd spend hours strolling through long stretches of prose. That's rarely the case anymore. Now my concentration often starts to drift after two or three pages. I get fidgety, lose the thread, begin looking for something else to do. I feel as if I'm always dragging my wayward brain back to the text. The deep reading that used to come naturally has become a struggle.

I think I know what's going on. For more than a decade now, I've been spending a lot of time online, searching and surfing and sometimes adding to the great databases of the Internet. For me, as for others, the Net is becoming a universal medium, the conduit for most of the information that flows through my eyes and ears and into my mind. The advantages of having immediate access to such an incredibly rich store of information are many, and they've been widely described and duly applauded. "The perfect recall of silicon memory," *Wired*'s Clive Thompson has written, "can be an enormous boon to thinking." But that boon comes at a price. As the media theorist Marshall McLuhan pointed out in the 1960s, media are not just passive channels of information. They supply the stuff of thought, but they also shape the process of thought. And what the Net seems to be doing is chipping away my capacity for concentration and contemplation. My mind now expects to take in information the way the Net distributes it: in a swiftly moving stream of particles. Once I was a scuba diver in the sea of words. Now I zip along the surface like a guy on a Jet Ski.

I'm not the only one. When I mention my troubles with reading to friends and acquaintances—literary types, most of them—many say they're having similar experiences. The more they use the Web, the more they have to fight to stay focused on long pieces of writing. Some of the bloggers I follow have also begun mentioning the phenomenon. Scott Karp, who writes a blog about online media, recently confessed that he has stopped reading books altogether. "I was a lit major in college, and used to be [a]voracious book reader," he wrote. "What happened?" He speculates on the answer: "What if I do all my reading on the web not so much because the way I read has changed, i.e. I'm just seeking convenience, but because the way I THINK has changed?"

Bruce Friedman, who blogs regularly about the use of computers in medicine, also has described how the Internet has altered his mental habits. "I now have almost totally lost the ability to read and absorb a longish article on the web or in print," he wrote earlier this year. A pathologist who has long been on the faculty of the University of Michigan Medical School, Friedman elaborated on his comment in a telephone conversation with me. His thinking, he said, has taken on a "staccato" quality, reflecting the way he quickly scans short passages of text from many sources online. "I can't read *War and Peace* anymore," he admitted. "I've lost the ability to do that. Even a blog post of more than three or four paragraphs is too much to absorb. I skim it."

Anecdotes alone don't prove much. And we still await the long-term neurological and psychological experiments that will provide a definitive picture of how Internet use affects cognition. But a recently published study of online research habits, conducted by scholars from University College London, suggests that we may well be in the midst of a sea change in the way we read and think. As part of the five-year research program, the scholars examined computer logs documenting the behavior of visitors to two popular research sites, one operated by the British Library and one by a U.K. educational consortium, that provide access to journal articles, e-books, and other sources of written information. They found that people using the sites exhibited "a form of skimming activity," hopping from one source to another and rarely returning to any source they'd already visited. They typically read no more than one or two pages of an article or book before they would "bounce" out to another site. Sometimes they'd save a long article, but there's no evidence that they ever went back and actually read it. The authors of the study report:

> It is clear that users are not reading online in the traditional sense; indeed there are signs that new forms of "reading" are emerging as users "power browse" horizontally through titles, contents pages and abstracts going for quick wins. It almost seems that they go online to avoid reading in the traditional sense.

Thanks to the ubiquity of text on the Internet, not to mention the popularity of text-messaging on cell phones, we may well be reading more today than we did in the 1970s or 1980s, when television was our medium of choice. But it's a different kind of reading, and behind it lies a different kind of thinking—perhaps even a new sense of the self. "We are not only *what* we read," says Maryanne Wolf, a developmental psychologist at Tufts University and the author of *Proust and the Squid: The Story and Science of the Reading Brain*. "We are *how* we read." Wolf worries that the style of reading promoted by the Net, a style that puts "efficiency" and "immediacy" above all else, may be weakening our capacity for the kind of deep reading that emerged when an earlier technology, the printing press, made long and complex works of prose commonplace. When we read online, she says, we tend to become "mere decoders of information." Our ability to interpret text, to make the rich mental connections that form when we read deeply and without distraction, remains largely disengaged.

Reading, explains Wolf, is not an instinctive skill for human beings. It's not etched into our genes the way speech is. We have to teach our minds how to translate the symbolic characters we see into the language we understand. And the media or other technologies we use in learning and practicing the craft of reading play an important part in shaping the neural circuits inside our brains. Experiments demonstrate that readers of ideograms, such as the Chinese, develop a mental circuitry for reading that is very different from the circuitry found in those of us whose written language employs an alphabet. The variations extend across many regions of the brain, including those that govern such essential cognitive functions as memory and the interpretation of visual and auditory stimuli. We can expect as well that the circuits woven by our use of the Net will be different from those woven by our reading of books and other printed works. Never has a communications system played so many roles in our lives—or exerted such broad influence over our thoughts—as the Internet does today. Yet, for all that's been written about the Net, there's been little consideration of how, exactly, it's reprogramming us. The Net's intellectual ethic remains obscure.

Google's headquarters, in Mountain View, California—the Googleplex—is the Internet's high church, and the religion practiced inside its walls is Taylorism.* Google, says its chief executive, Eric Schmidt, is "a company that's founded around the science of measurement," and it is striving to "systematize everything" it does. Drawing on the terabytes of behavioral data it collects through its search engine and other sites, it carries out thousands of experiments a day, according to the *Harvard Business Review*, and it uses the results to refine the algorithms that increasingly control how people find information and extract meaning from it. What Taylor did for the work of the hand, Google is doing for the work of the mind.

The company has declared that its mission is "to organize the world's information and make it universally accessible and useful." It seeks to develop "the perfect search engine," which it defines as something that "understands exactly what you mean and gives you back exactly what you want." In Google's view, information is a kind of commodity, a utilitarian resource that can be mined and processed with industrial efficiency. The more pieces of information we can "access" and the faster we can extract their gist, the more productive we become as thinkers.

---

*Perhaps a reference to Bob Taylor, called one of the fathers of the Internet and considered an Internet visionary by many.

Where does it end? Sergey Brin and Larry Page, the gifted young men who founded Google while pursuing doctoral degrees in computer science at Stanford, speak frequently of their desire to turn their search engine into an artificial intelligence, a HAL-like machine that might be connected directly to our brains. "The ultimate search engine is something as smart as people—or smarter," Page said in a speech a few years back. "For us, working on search is a way to work on artificial intelligence." In a 2004 interview with *Newsweek*, Brin said, "Certainly if you had all the world's information directly attached to your brain, or an artificial brain that was smarter than your brain, you'd be better off." Last year, Page told a convention of scientists that Google is "really trying to build artificial intelligence and to do it on a large scale."

Such an ambition is a natural one, even an admirable one, for a pair of math whizzes with vast quantities of cash at their disposal and a small army of computer scientists in their employ. A fundamentally scientific enterprise, Google is motivated by a desire to use technology, in Eric Schmidt's words, "to solve problems that have never been solved before," and artificial intelligence is the hardest problem out there. Why wouldn't Brin and Page want to be the ones to crack it?

Still, their easy assumption that we'd all "be better off" if our brains were supplemented, or even replaced, by an artificial intelligence is unsettling. It suggests a belief that intelligence is the output of a mechanical process, a series of discrete steps that can be isolated, measured, and optimized. In Google's world, the world we enter when we go online, there's little place for the fuzziness of contemplation. Ambiguity is not an opening for insight but a bug to be fixed. The human brain is just an outdated computer that needs a faster processor and a bigger hard drive.

The idea that our minds should operate as high-speed data-processing machines is not only built into the workings of the Internet, it is the network's reigning business model as well. The faster we surf across the Web—the more links we click and pages we view—the more opportunities Google and other companies gain to collect information about us and to feed us advertisements. Most of the proprietors of the commercial Internet have a financial stake in collecting the crumbs of data we leave behind as we flit from link to link—the more crumbs, the better. The last thing these companies want is to encourage leisurely reading or slow, concentrated thought. It's in their economic interest to drive us to distraction.

Maybe I'm just a worrywart. Just as there's a tendency to glorify technological progress, there's a countertendency to expect the worst of every new tool or machine. In Plato's *Phaedrus*, Socrates bemoaned the development of writing. He feared that, as people came to rely on the written word as a substitute for the knowledge they used to carry inside their heads, they would, in the words of one of the dialogue's characters, "cease to exercise their memory and become forgetful." And because they would be able to "receive a quantity of information without proper instruction," they would "be thought very knowledge-able when they are for the most part quite ignorant." They would be "filled with the conceit of wisdom instead of real wisdom." Socrates wasn't wrong—the new technology did often have the effects he feared—but he was shortsighted. He couldn't foresee the many ways that writing and reading would serve to spread information, spur fresh ideas, and expand human knowledge (if not wisdom).

So, yes, you should be skeptical of my skepticism. Perhaps those who dismiss critics of the Internet as Luddites or nostalgists will be proved correct, and from our hyperactive, data-stoked minds will spring a golden age of intellectual discovery and universal wisdom. Then again, the Net isn't the alphabet, and although it may replace the printing press, it produces something altogether different. The kind of deep reading that a sequence of printed pages promotes is valuable not just for the knowledge we acquire from the author's words but for the intellectual vibrations those words set off within our own minds. In the quiet spaces opened up by the sustained, undis-tracted reading of a book, or by any other act of contemplation, for that matter, we make our own associations, draw our own inferences and analogies, foster our own ideas. Deep reading, as Maryanne Wolf argues, is indistinguishable from deep thinking. If we lose those quiet spaces, or fill them up with "content," we will sacrifice something important not only in ourselves but in our culture. In a recent essay titled "The Pancake People," the playwright Richard Foreman elo-quently described what's at stake:

> I come from a tradition of Western culture, in which the ideal (my ideal) was the complex, dense and "cathedral-like" structure of the highly educated and articulate personality—a man or woman who carried inside themselves a personally constructed and unique version of the entire heritage of the West. [But now] I see within us all (myself included) the replacement of complex inner density with a new kind of self—evolving under the pressure of information overload and the technology of the "instantly available."

As we are drained of our "inner repertory of dense cultural inheritance," Foreman concluded, we risk turning into " 'pancake people'—spread wide and thin as we connect with that vast network of information accessed by the mere touch of a button."

I'm haunted by that scene in *2001*. What makes it so poignant, and so weird, is the computer's emotional response to the disassembly of its mind: its despair as one circuit after another goes dark, its childlike pleading with the astronaut—"I can feel it. I can feel it. I'm afraid"—and its final reversion to what can only be called a state of innocence. HAL's outpouring of feeling contrasts with the emotionlessness that characterizes the human figures in the film, who go about their business with an almost robotic efficiency. Their thoughts and actions feel scripted, as if they're following the steps of an algorithm. In the world of *2001*, people have become so machinelike that the most human character turns out to be a machine. That's the essence of Kubrick's dark prophecy: as we come to rely on computers to mediate our understanding of the world, it is our own intelligence that flattens into artificial intelligence.

Discussion Questions

1. Discuss the types of evidence that Nicholas Carr cites to support his contention that the kind of deep reading that used to come naturally has now become difficult. Which type did you find most interesting or convincing? Explain.

2. What abilities does Maryanne Wolf suggest are being lost due to the proliferation of Internet reading and its effect on the brain? Why do you believe these abilities are important or unimportant to retain?

3. How do you feel about the assertion of Sergey Binn and Larry Page, the founders of Google, that we would all "be better off" if our human brains were somehow replaced by artificial intelligence?

4. Explain the reasons you think Carr, MacDonald, and Johnson would each have for agreeing or disagreeing with Richard Foreman's concept of "Pancake People."

Yes, People Still Read, But Now It's Social

Essay

STEVEN JOHNSON

Steven Johnson is a widely read author who writes on urgent cultural issues in ways that offer new perspectives. His books have been critically acclaimed, and two were chosen as New York Times *Notable Books. His newest book is titled* Where Good Ideas Come From: The Natural History of Innovation *(2010).*

"THE point of books is to combat loneliness," David Wallace observes near the beginning of *Although of Course You End Up Becoming Yourself*, David Lipsky's recently published, book-length interview with him. If you happen to be reading the book on Kindle from Amazon, Mr. Wallace's observation has an extra emphasis: a dotted underline running below the phrase. Not because Mr. Wallace or Mr. Lipsky felt that the point was worth stressing, but because a dozen or so other readers have highlighted the passage on their Kindles, making it one of the more "popular" passages in the book. Amazon calls this new feature "popular highlights."

The "popular highlights" feature may sound innocuous enough, but it augurs even bigger changes to come. Though the feature can be disabled by the user, "popular highlights" will no doubt alarm Nicholas Carr, whose new book, *The Shallows*, argues that the compulsive skimming, linking, and multitasking of our screen reading is undermining the deep, immersive focus that has defined book culture for centuries. With "popular highlights," even when we manage to turn off Twitter and the television and sit down to read a good book, there will be a chorus of readers turning the pages along with us, pointing out the good bits. Before long, we'll probably be able to meet those fellow readers, share stories with them. Mr. Carr's argument is that these distractions come with a heavy cost, and his book's publication coincides with articles in various publications—including *The New York Times*—that report on scientific studies showing how multitasking harms our concentration. A study reported on early this month (see "Your Brain on Computers" *New York Times* June 6, 2010) found that heavy multitaskers performed about 10 to 20 percent worse on most tests than light multitaskers.

These studies are undoubtedly onto something—no one honestly believes he is better at focusing when he switches back and forth between multiple activities—but they are meaningless as a cultural indicator without measuring what we gain from multitasking. Thanks to e-mail, Twitter, and the blogosphere, I regularly exchange information with hundreds of people in a single day: scheduling meetings, sharing political gossip, trading edits on a book chapter, planning a family vacation, reading tech punditry. How many of those exchanges could happen were I limited exclusively to the technologies of the phone, the post office, and the face-to-face meeting? I suspect that the number would be a small fraction of my current rate. I have no doubt that I am slightly less focused in these interactions, but, frankly, most of what we do during the day doesn't require our full powers of concentration. Even rocket scientists don't do rocket science all day long.

To his credit, Mr. Carr readily concedes this efficiency argument. His concern is what happens to high-level thinking when the culture migrates from the page to the screen. To the extent that his argument is a reminder to all of us to step away from the screen sometimes, and think in a more sedate environment, it's a valuable contribution. But Mr. Carr's argument is more ambitious than that: the "linear, literary mind" that has been at "the center of art, science and society" threatens to become "yesterday's mind," with dire consequences for our culture. Here, too, I think the concerns are overstated, though for slightly different reasons. Presumably, the first casualties of "shallow" thinking should have appeared on the front lines of the technology world, where the participants have spent the most time in the hyperconnected space of the screen. And yet the sophistication and nuance of media commentary has grown dramatically over the last 15 years. Mr. Carr's original essay, published in *The Atlantic*—along with Clay Shirky's more optimistic account, which led to the book *Cognitive Surplus*—were intensely discussed throughout the Web when they first appeared as articles, and both books appear to be generating the same level of analysis and engagement in long form. The intellectual tools for assessing the media, once the province of academics and professional critics, are now far more accessible to the masses. The number of people who have written a thoughtful response to Mr. Carr's essay—and, even better, published it online—surely dwarfs the number of people who wrote in public about "Understanding Media," by Marshall McLuhan, in 1964. Mr. Carr spends a great deal of his book's opening section convincing us that new forms of media alter the way the brain works, which I suspect most of his readers have long ago accepted as an obvious truth. The question is not whether our brains are being changed. (Of course new experiences change your brain—that's what experience is, on some basic level.) The question is whether the rewards of the change are worth the liabilities.

The problem with Mr. Carr's model is its unquestioned reverence for the slow contemplation of deep reading. For society to advance as it has since Gutenberg, he argues, we need the quiet, solitary space of the book. Yet many great ideas that have advanced culture over the past centuries have emerged from a more connective space, in the collision of different worldviews and sensibilities, different metaphors and fields of expertise. (Gutenberg himself borrowed his printing press from the screw presses of Rhineland vintners, as Mr. Carr notes.) It's no accident that most of the great scientific and technological innovation over the last millennium has taken place in crowded, distracting urban centers. The printed page itself encouraged those manifold connections, by allowing ideas to be stored and shared and circulated more efficiently. One can make the case that the Enlightenment depended more on the exchange of ideas than it did on solitary, deep-focus reading. Quiet contemplation has led to its fair share of important thoughts. But it cannot be denied that good ideas also emerge in networks.

Yes, we are a little less focused, thanks to the electric stimulus of the screen. Yes, we are reading slightly fewer long-form narratives and arguments than we did 50 years ago, though the Kindle and the iPad may well change that. Those are costs, to be sure. But what of the other side of the ledger? We are reading more text, writing far more often, than we were in the heyday of television. And the speed with which we can follow the trail of an idea, or discover new perspectives on a problem, has increased by several orders of magnitude. We are marginally less focused, and exponentially more connected. That's a bargain all of us should be happy to make.

Discussion Questions

1. Why does Steven Johnson feel that Nicholas Carr's complaint about multitasking is "meaningless"? How much time do you spend in a day multitasking? Do you feel that the quality of your

work improves or decreases when you are multitasking? Give some examples to support your evaluation.

2. What evidence does Johnson use to suggest Carr's concerns are overstated? Evaluate the strengths and weaknesses of this evidence.

3. Explain your inclination for siding with either Carr or Johnson on the issue of the importance of slow reading.

4. Why do you think Dwight MacDonald would or would not appreciate the ideas Johnson presents in this essay?

The Information Age

Essay

GORDON CROVITZ

Gordon Crovitz is a columnist for The Wall Street Journal; *a media and information industry adviser and executive, including former publisher of* The Wall Street Journal; *executive vice president of Dow Jones; and president of its Consumer Media Group. He has been active in digital media since the early 1990s, overseeing the growth of* The Wall Street Journal Online *to more than one million paying subscribers.*

Just in time for summer, Crown Imports has brought back a popular television advertisement for its Corona beer that first aired in 1998. The new one shows a man at the beach skipping rocks into the sea. He decides to do the same with his BlackBerry—a beeper in the earlier version—when it interrupts his relaxation by ringing and vibrating. The ad addresses one of the key causes of anxiety in the information age: What does it mean that for the first time, information is no longer scarce? We have fast and easy access to the communications and the facts we need, through email, the Web, Facebook, Twitter, text messages and other tools. So now we have the problem of too much supply. How can we escape useless information, unneeded emails, and unwanted communications?

Our era in the information age is a transition period of learning how to navigate information abundance. Rather than pitch our Black-Berrys and iPhones into the sea, imagine the benefits once we have figured out how to manage the chaos of endless data and routine multitasking, a process that will help refine our judgment about information and refocus our attention on what's truly important.

For now, popular culture is more troubled than excited by information abundance. Actress Gwyneth Paltrow told an interviewer last week that she spends so much time in Spain because "they seem to enjoy life a little bit more. . . . They don't always have their Blackberrys on." In order to get passengers to pay attention to safety announcements, Air New Zealand decided to show a video of stewardesses and pilots dressed in nothing but body paint.

One of the companies that led the charge on information is trying to make a business out of solving the problem. Xerox says,

"We've been navigating the flood of information for 70 years—since the first xerographic print launched the 'sharing era.'" It makes the case that "too much information can make you feel powerless and unproductive," reporting that more than half of people think that less than half the information they get at work is valuable. Xerox hosts a corporate blog called Information Sanity, with tips on how to cope. As one data point, a search for "Information Overload" on Google returns 2.92 million results in 0.37 second.

The book *Rapt* by Winifred Gallagher reports that many neuroscientists believe attention is a process of either selecting a topic or not. As suggested by the expression "pay attention," we have a limited ability to focus. If this is right, young people who do their homework while on Twitter, the phone, and YouTube may not be engaging deeply enough. "When you're finally forced to confront intellectually demanding situations in high school or college," Ms. Gallagher writes, "you may find that you've traded depth of knowledge for breadth and stunted your capacity for serious thought."

But there's a more optimistic way to think about the issue. Humans adapt, so we'll learn how to live with information overabundance. Young people growing up multitasking are already less anxious about using technology and may well cope better than those of us in older generations. They have no choice but to get more sophisticated at separating the important from the unimportant and the authoritative from the unreliable, even while sampling from among many new kinds of information tools.

Tyler Cowen, an economist and popular blogger, focuses on our broader range of information options in a new book published this month, *Create Your Own Economy*. He says, "When access is easy, we tend to favor the short, the sweet, and the bitty. When access is difficult, we tend to look for large-scale productions, extravaganzas, and masterpieces." Mr. Cowen says, "The current trend—as it has been running for decades—is that a lot of our culture is coming in shorter and smaller bits."

Different kinds of information are useful for different purposes. "Paying attention" means different things for different tasks. As cognitive scientist David Meyer puts it, "Einstein didn't invent the theory of relativity while multitasking at the Swiss patent office." For other kinds of tasks, though, access to blogs and Twitter posts at least gives us the chance to become aware of issues we might want to pursue further, in greater depth.

Technological progress does not reverse, so the trend toward multitasking and consuming many different types of information will only continue. Getting our heads around information abundance will mean becoming more discerning about what information is worth our time and what kinds of tasks require real focus. Tools like on-demand information and smarter filtering will help.

Still, the development of this human software to deal with an overabundance of information will take some time to catch up to the machine technology that made the information abundance possible. Young people will cope first as we all evolve to become more sophisticated, less anxious users of information.

Discussion Questions

1. Why does Crovitz feel that we are in an age of "information overabundance"?

2. According to Crovitz, how will time affect our perception of technology?

3. Why do you think Dwight MacDonald would or would not appreciate the ideas Crovitz presents in this essay?

Why Literature Matters: Good Books Help Make a Civil Society

Essay

DANA GIOIA

Dana Gioia is chairman of the National Endowment for the Arts.

In 1780, Massachusetts patriot John Adams wrote to his wife, Abigail, outlining his vision of how American culture might evolve. "I must study politics and war," he prophesied, so "that our sons may have liberty to study mathematics and philosophy." They will add to their studies geography, navigation, commerce, and agriculture, he continued, so that *their* children may enjoy the "right to study painting, poetry, music. . . ." Adams's bold prophecy proved correct. By the mid 20th century, America boasted internationally preeminent traditions in literature, art, music, dance, theater, and cinema.

But a strange thing has happened in the American arts during the past quarter century. While income rose to unforeseen levels, college attendance ballooned, and access to information increased enormously, the interest young Americans showed in the arts—and especially literature—actually diminished.

According to the 2002 Survey of Public Participation in the Arts, a population study designed and commissioned by the National Endowment for the Arts (and executed by the US Bureau of the Census), arts participation by Americans has declined for eight of the nine major forms that are measured. (Only jazz has shown a tiny increase—thank you, Ken Burns.) The declines have been most severe among younger adults (ages 18–24). The most worrisome finding in the 2002 study, however, is the declining percentage of Americans, especially young adults, reading literature.

That individuals at a time of crucial intellectual and emotional development bypass the joys and challenges of literature is a troubling trend. If it were true that they substituted histories, biographies, or political works for literature, one might not worry. But book reading of any kind is falling as well.

That such a longstanding and fundamental cultural activity should slip so swiftly, especially among young adults, signifies deep transformations in contemporary life. To call attention to the trend, the Arts

Endowment issued the reading portion of the Survey as a separate report, "Reading at Risk: A Survey of Literary Reading in America."

The decline in reading has consequences that go beyond literature. The significance of reading has become a persistent theme in the business world. The February issue of *Wired* magazine, for example, sketches a new set of mental skills and habits proper to the 21st century, aptitudes decidedly literary in character: not "linear, logical, analytical talents," author Daniel Pink states, but "the ability to create artistic and emotional beauty, to detect patterns and opportunities, to craft a satisfying narrative." When asked what kind of talents they like to see in management positions, business leaders consistently set imagination, creativity, and higher-order thinking at the top.

Ironically, the value of reading and the intellectual faculties that it inculcates appear most clearly as active and engaged literacy declines. There is now a growing awareness of the consequences of nonreading to the workplace. In 2001 the National Association of Manufacturers polled its members on skill deficiencies among employees. Among hourly workers, poor reading skills ranked second, and 38 percent of employers complained that local schools inadequately taught reading comprehension.

Corporate America makes similar complaints about a skill intimately related to reading—writing. Last year, the College Board reported that corporations spend some $3.1 billion a year on remedial writing instruction for employees, adding that they "express a fair degree of dissatisfaction with the writing of recent college graduates." If the 21st-century American economy requires innovation and creativity, solid reading skills and the imaginative growth fostered by literary reading are central elements in that program.

The decline of reading is also taking its toll in the civic sphere. In a 2000 survey of college seniors from the top 55 colleges, the Roper Organization found that 81 percent could not earn a grade of C on a high school-level history test. A 2003 study of 15- to 26-year-olds' civic knowledge by the National Conference of State Legislatures concluded, "Young people do not understand the ideals of citizenship . . . and their appreciation and support of American democracy is limited."

It is probably no surprise that declining rates of literary reading coincide with declining levels of historical and political awareness among young people. One of the surprising findings of "Reading at Risk" was that literary readers are markedly more civically engaged than nonreaders, scoring two to four times more likely to perform charity work, visit a museum, or attend a sporting event. One reason for their higher social and cultural interactions may lie in the kind of civic and historical knowledge that comes with literary reading.

Unlike the passive activities of watching television and DVDs or surfing the Web, reading is actually a highly active enterprise. Reading requires sustained and focused attention as well as active use of memory and imagination. Literary reading also enhances and enlarges our humility by helping us imagine and understand lives quite different from our own.

Indeed, we sometimes underestimate how large a role literature has played in the evolution of our national identity, especially in that literature often has served to introduce young people to events from the past and principles of civil society and governance. Just as more ancient Greeks learned about moral and political conduct from the epics of Homer than from the dialogues of Plato, so the most important work in the abolitionist movement was the novel *Uncle Tom's Cabin*.

Likewise our notions of American populism come more from Walt Whitman's poetic vision than from any political tracts. Today when people recall the Depression, the images that most come to mind are of the travails of John Steinbeck's Joad family from *The Grapes of Wrath*. Without a literary inheritance, the historical past is impoverished.

In focusing on the social advantages of a literary education, however, we should not overlook the personal impact. Every day authors receive letters from readers that say, "Your book changed my life." History reveals case after case of famous people whose lives were transformed by literature. When the great Victorian thinker John Stuart Mill suffered a crippling depression in late-adolescence, the poetry of Wordsworth restored his optimism and self-confidence—a "medicine for my state of mind," he called it.

A few decades later, W. E. B. DuBois found a different tonic in literature, an escape from the indignities of Jim Crow into a world of equality. "I sit with Shakespeare and he winces not," DuBois observed. "Across the color line I move arm in arm with Balzac and Dumas, where smiling men and welcoming women glide in gilded halls." Literature is a catalyst for education and culture.

The evidence of literature's importance to civic, personal, and economic health is too strong to ignore. The decline of literary reading foreshadows serious long-term social and economic problems, and it is time to bring literature and the other arts into discussions of public policy. Libraries, schools, and public agencies do noble work, but addressing the reading issue will require the leadership of politicians and the business community as well.

Literature now competes with an enormous array of electronic media. While no single activity is responsible for the decline in reading, the cumulative presence and availability of electronic alternatives increasingly have drawn Americans away from reading.

Reading is not a timeless, universal capability. Advanced literacy is a specific intellectual skill and social habit that depends on a great many educational, cultural, and economic factors. As more Americans lose this capability, our nation becomes less informed, active, and independent-minded. These are not the qualities that a free, innovative, or productive society can afford to lose.

Discussion Questions

1. Why does the author find the comparison between the percentage of young people attending college and the percentage of young people reading books to be strange? How would you explain these statistics?

2. What are some examples of the kinds of activities the author considers to be cultural? If young people are not participating in these activities, how do you think they are spending their leisure time?

3. What are some of the consequences that the article discusses in relation to the decline in reading? Did any of them surprise you? Explain your answer.

4. After reading all the articles in this section, which of them made you want to change your reading habits the most? Why?

Literary Reading in Dramatic Decline, According to National Endowment for the Arts Survey

Fewer Than Half of American Adults Now Read Literature
July 8, 2004

New York, N.Y.—Literary reading is in dramatic decline with fewer than half of American adults now reading literature, according to a National Endowment for the Arts (NEA) survey released today. *Reading at Risk: A Survey of Literary Reading in America* reports drops in all groups studied, with the steepest rate of decline—28 percent—occurring in the youngest age groups.

The study also documents an overall decline of 10 percentage points in literary readers from 1982 to 2002, representing a loss of 20 million potential readers. The rate of decline is increasing and, according to the survey, has nearly tripled in the last decade. The findings were announced today by NEA Chairman Dana Gioia during a news conference at the New York Public Library.

"This report documents a national crisis," Gioia said. "Reading develops a capacity for focused attention and imaginative growth that enriches both private and public life. The decline in reading among every segment of the adult population reflects a general collapse in advanced literacy. To lose this human capacity—and all the diverse benefits it fosters—impoverishes both cultural and civic life."

While all demographic groups showed declines in literary reading between 1982 and 2002, the survey shows some are dropping more rapidly than others. The overall rate of decline has accelerated from 5 to 14 percent since 1992.

Women read more literature than men do, but the survey indicates literary reading by both genders is declining. Only slightly more than one-third of adult males now read literature. Reading among women is also declining significantly, but at a slower rate.

Literary reading declined among whites, African Americans, and Hispanics. Among ethnic and racial groups surveyed, literary reading decreased most strongly among Hispanic Americans, dropping by 10 percentage points.

By age, the three youngest groups saw the steepest drops, but literary reading declined among all age groups. The rate of decline for the youngest adults, those aged 18 to 24, was 55 percent greater than that of the total adult population. The rate of decline in literary reading is calculated by dividing the percentage point drop by the original percentage of literary readers.

Reading also affects lifestyle, the study shows. Literary readers are much more likely to be involved in cultural, sports, and volunteer activities than are non-readers. For example, literary readers are nearly three times as likely to attend a performing arts event, almost four times as likely to visit an art museum, more than two-and-a-half times as likely to do volunteer or charity work, and over one-and-a-half times as likely to attend or participate in sports activities. People who read more books tend to have the highest level of participation in other activities.

The most important factor in literacy reading rates is education, the report shows. Only 14 percent of adults with a grade school education read literature in 2002. By contrast, more than five times as many respondents with a graduate school education—74 percent— read literary works.

Family income also affects the literary reading rate, though not as strongly as education. About one-third of the lowest income group— those with a family income under $10,000—read literature during the survey year, compared with 61 percent of the highest income group— those with family income of $75,000 or more.

According to the survey, the most popular types of literature are novels or short stories, which were read by 45 percent or 93 million adults in the previous year. Poetry was read by 12 percent or 25 million people, while just 4 percent or seven million people reported having read a play.

Contrary to the overall decline in literary reading, the number of people doing creative writing increased by 30 percent, from 11 million in 1982 to more than 14 million in 2002. However, the number of people who reported having taken a creative writing class or lesson decreased by 2.2 million during the same time period.

The survey also studied the correlation between literary reading and other activities. For instance, literature readers watched an average of 2.7 hours of television each day, while people who do not read literary works watched an average of 3.1 hours daily. Adults who did not watch TV in a typical day are 48 percent more likely to be frequent readers—consuming from 12 to 49 books each year—than are those who watched one to three hours daily.

"America can no longer take active and engaged literacy for granted," according to Gioia. "As more Americans lose this capability, our nation becomes less informed, active, and independent minded. These are not qualities that a free, innovative, or productive society can afford to lose. No single factor caused this problem. No single solution can solve it. But it cannot be ignored and must be addressed," Gioia said.

Reading at Risk presents the results from the literature segment of the Survey of Public Participation in the Arts, conducted by the Census Bureau in 2002 at the NEA's request. The survey asked more than 17,000 adults if—during the previous 12 months—they had read any novels, short stories, poetry, or plays in their leisure time, that were not required for work or school. The report extrapolates and interprets data on literary reading and compares them with results from similar surveys carried out in 1982 and 1992.

Discussion Questions

1. What age group shows the greatest decline in the rate of reading? How do you explain this trend?

2. According to this study, how do factors like gender and race correlate with declining rates of reading? What would you interpret these statistics to signify? What are the other factors that, according to this report, affect reading rates? Which of these factors would you have predicted? Which one surprised you? Explain your answers.

3. Why does the number of people now engaging in creative writing seem contrary to the other results of this study? How would you explain this phenomenon?

Is Reading Really at Risk? It Depends on What the Meaning of Reading Is.

Essay

JOSEPH EPSTEIN

Joseph Epstein is a contributing editor to The Weekly Standard *and the author, most recently, of* Fabulous Small Jews *(2003) and* Envy *(2003). This essay appeared in* The Weekly Standard *in 2004.*

"READING AT RISK" is one of those hardy perennials, a government survey telling us that in some vital area—obesity, pollution, fuel depletion, quality of education, domestic relations—things are even worse than we thought. In the category of literacy, the old surveys seemed always to be some variant of "Why Johnny Can't Read." "Reading at Risk"—the most recent survey, carried out under the auspices of the National Endowment for the Arts as part of its larger Survey of Public Participation in the Arts, the whole conducted by the U.S. Census Bureau—doesn't for a moment suggest that Johnny Can't Read. The problem is that, now grown, Johnny (though a little less Jane) doesn't much care to read a lot in the way of imaginative writing—fiction, poems, plays—also known to the survey as literature. For the first time in our history, apparently, less than half the population bothers to read any literature (so defined) at all.

"Reading at Risk" reports that there has been a decline in the reading of novels, poems, and plays of roughly 10 percentage points for all age cohorts between 1982 and 2002, with actual numbers of readers having gained only slightly despite a large growth (of 40 million people) in the overall population. More women than men continue to participate in what the survey also calls literary reading—in his trip to the United States in 1905, based on attendance at his lectures, Henry James noted that culture belonged chiefly to women—though even among women the rate is slipping. Nor are things better among the so-called educated; while they do read more than the less educated, the decline in literary reading is also found among them. But the rate of decline is greatest among young adults 18 to 24 years old, and the survey quotes yet another study, this one made by the National Institute for Literacy, showing that things are not looking any better for kids between 13 and 17, but are even a little worse.

Although the general decline in literary reading is not attributed to any single cause in "Reading at Risk," the problem, it is hinted, may be the distractions of electronic culture. To quote an item from the survey's executive summary: "A 1999 study showed that the average American child lives in a household with 2.9 televisions, 1.8 VCRs, 3.1 radios, 2.1 CD players, 1.4 video game players, and 1 computer." By 2002, to quote from the same summary, "electronic spending had soared to 24 percent [of total recreational spending by Americans], while spending on books declined . . . to 5.6 percent." Up against all this easily accessible and endlessly varied fare—from Palm Pilots to iPods—the reading of stories, poems, and plays is having a tough time competing.

"Reading at Risk" does provide a few not exactly surprises but slight jars to one's expectations. For me, one is that "people in managerial, professional, and technical occupations are more likely to read literature than those in other occupation groups." I would myself have expected that these were all jobs in which one worked more than an eight-hour day and then took work home, which, consequently, would allow a good deal less time for reading things not in some way related to one's work. The survey also claims that readers are "highly social people," more active in their communities and participating more in sports. I should have thought that lots of reading might make one introspective, slightly detached, a touch reclusive, even, but, according to the survey, not so. "People who live in the suburbs," the survey states, "are more likely to be readers than either those who live in the city or the country." Perhaps this is owing in good part to suburbs' being generally more affluent than cities; and, too, to book clubs, in which neighbors meet to discuss recent bestsellers and sometimes classics, and which tend to be suburban institutions.

The one area in which "Reading at Risk" is (honorably) shaky is in its conclusions on the subject of television, which is the standard fall-guy in almost all surveys having to do with education. Only among people who watch more than four hours of television daily does the extent of reading drop off, according to the survey, while watching no television whatsoever makes it more likely one will be a more frequent reader. On the other hand, the presence of writers on television—on C-SPAN and talk shows—may, the survey concedes, encourage people to buy books. No mention is made of those people, myself among them, who are able to read with a television set, usually playing a sports event, humming away in the background. In the end, "Reading at Risk" concludes that "it is not clear from [its] data how much influence TV watching has on literary reading." The survey does suggest that surfing the Internet may have made a dent in reading: "During the time period when the literature participation rates declined, home Internet use soared." But it does not take things further than that. My own speculation is that our speeded-up culture—with its FedEx, fax, email, channel surfing, cell-phoning, fast-action movies, and other elements in its relentless race against boredom—has ended in a shortened national attention span. The quickened rhythms of new technology are not rhythms congenial to the slow and time-consuming and solitary act of reading. Sustained reading, sitting quietly and enjoying the aesthetic pleasure that words elegantly deployed on the page can give, contemplating careful formulations of complex thoughts—these do not seem likely to be acts strongly characteristic of an already jumpy new century.

Like all surveys, "Reading at Risk" is an example of the style of statistical thinking dominant in our time. It's far from sure that statistics are very helpful in capturing so idiosyncratic an act as reading, except in a bulky and coarse way. That the Swedes read more novels, poems, and plays than Americans and the Portuguese read fewer than we do is a statistical fact, but I'm not sure what you do with it, especially when you don't know the quality of the material being read in the three countries. The statistical style of thinking has currently taken over medicine, where it may have some role to play: I am, for example, taking a pill because a study has shown that 68 percent of the people who take this pill and have a certain condition live 33 percent longer than those who don't. Dopey though this is, I play the odds—the pill costs $1 a day—and go along. But I'm not sure that statistics have much to tell us about a cultural activity so private as reading books.

Read any amount of serious imaginative literature with care and you will be highly skeptical of the statistical style of thinking. You will quickly grasp that, in a standard statistical report such as "Reading at Risk," serious reading, always a minority interest, isn't at stake here. Nothing more is going on, really, than the *crise du jour*, soon to be replaced by the report on eating disorders, the harmfulness of aspirin, or the drop in high-school math scores.

Discussion Questions

1. How useful, according to Epstein, is the information provided by the "Reading at Risk" survey, and what conclusions does he draw from it?

2. Do you agree with his evaluation of this survey? Be sure to support your answer with examples. These examples can come from your own observations and readings.

The Future of Books

Essay

KATHY KEETON

Kathy Keeton was a magazine publisher and author. She founded the magazines Viva *(1972),* OMNI *(1979), and* Longevity *(1989), and published two books,* Woman of Tomorrow *(1985) and* Longevity *(1992). She died in her late fifties from complications during surgery.*

For most of us, our first visit to another world comes not through the wonder of television or the joy of travel, but through the simple pleasure of a book. They have served, and will continue to serve, as time machines capable of transporting us back to the past and far into the future.

While television and movies may grab our attention, books require that we join hands with the author and create our own view of characters and places. No one reads a book like Edgar Rice Burroughs' *Tarzan* without bringing to that classic his or her own special vision of the ape-man. The appearance of a movie doesn't replace the need or desire to read; indeed, how many people are inspired to read a novel after seeing the film.

In the realm of education, textbooks will continue to be essential to the learning process. So much of the information basic to the area of science and mathematics, for example, is best imparted through textbooks, which are the work of not one or two teachers, but dozens of experts in a particular field. Access to books by these professionals gives children access to the minds of these individuals.

Through books, we gain admittance to the parlors of the greatest thinkers of all time, from Aristotle to Elie Wiesel. Each time a new strain of intellectual thought enters society, or an observance is made by the psychological community, a series of books ensues, as witnessed by the plethora of books on everything from selecting a mate to coping with death. Books become our therapists, our inspiration, our friends.

Talking books, and video books, will become part of the common fare of reading. Sales for talking books for both adults and children are skyrocketing; in fact, the lost art of storytelling is found again through this medium. Futurists predict that the twenty-first century will bring us increasing amounts of leisure time and I believe, with it, the freedom to pursue what has been and will remain a favorite pastime, reading.

Discussion Questions

1. According to Keeton, how do most of us experience other times and places? Do you think there are more popular ways of mentally traveling to other worlds? If so, what are they?

2. Do you think more people read a book after seeing the movie, or do you think people are more likely to go to a movie if they have read and liked the book?

3. Discuss the importance of textbooks to your education.

4. What are some of the roles Keeton claims books play in our lives? What role do they most often play in yours?

5. Do you think that reading in the twenty-first century will ultimately increase or decrease? Why?

The Sad Decline of Literature

Essay

GEORGE WILL

George Will is a well-known conservative journalist, newspaper columnist, and author. He earned a Ph.D. in politics from Princeton University, and won a Pulitzer Prize for Commentary in 1977. He has appeared as a news analyst for ABC since the early 1980s.

The first modern celebrity—the first person who, although not conspicuous in church or state, still made his work and life fascinating to a broad public—may have been Charles Dickens. Novelist Jane Smiley so argues in her slender life of Dickens, and her point is particularly interesting in light of "Reading at Risk," the National Endowment for the Arts' report on the decline of reading.

A survey of 17,135 persons reveals an accelerating decline in the reading of literature, especially among the young. Literary reading declined 5 percent between 1982 and 1992, then 14 percent in the next decade. Only 56.9 percent of Americans say they read a book of any sort in 2002, down from 60.9 percent in 1992. Only 46.7 percent of adults read any literature for pleasure.

The good news is that "literature," as the survey defined it, excludes serious history, for which there is a sizable audience. The bad news is that any fiction counts as literature, and most fiction, like most of most things, is mediocre. But even allowing for the survey's methodological problems, the declining importance of reading in the menu of modern recreations is unsurprising and unsettling.

Dickens, a volcano of words, provided mass entertainment before modern technologies—electricity, film, broadcasting—made mass communication easy. His serialized novels seized the attention of the British public. And America's: Ships arriving from England with the latest installment of Dickens' 1840 novel *The Old Curiosity Shop* reportedly were greeted by American dockworkers shouting, "Did Little Nell die?"

When journalists in 1910 asked an aide to Teddy Roosevelt whether TR might run for president in 1912, the aide replied, "Barkis is willin'," and he expected most journalists, and their readers, to recognize the reference to the wagon driver in *David Copperfield* who was more than merely willin' to marry Clara Peggotty, David's childhood nurse. Exposure to *David Copperfield* used to be a common facet of reaching adulthood in America. But today young adults 18–34, once the most avid readers, are among the least. This surely has something to do with the depredations of higher education: Professors, lusting after tenure and prestige, teach that the great works of the Western canon, properly deconstructed, are not explorations of the human spirit but mere reflections of power relations and social pathologies.

By 1995—*before* the flood of video games and computer entertainments for adults—television swallowed 40 percent of Americans' free time, up one-third since 1965. Today electronic entertainments other than television fill 5.5 hours of the average child's day.

There have been times when reading was regarded with suspicion. Some among the ancient Greeks regarded the rise of reading as cultural decline: They considered oral dialogue, which involves clarifying questions, more hospitable to truth. But the transition from an oral to a print culture has generally been a transition from a tribal society to a society of self-consciously separated individuals. In Europe, that transition alarmed ruling elites, who thought the "crisis of literacy" was that there was too much literacy: Readers had, inconveniently, minds of their own. Reading is inherently private and hence the reader is beyond state supervision or crowd psychology.

Which suggests why there are perils in the transition from a print to an electronic culture. Time was, books were the primary means of knowing things. Now, most people learn most things visually, from the graphic presentation of immediately, effortlessly accessible pictures.

People grow accustomed to the narcotic effect of their own passive reception of today's sensory blitzkrieg of surfaces. They recoil from the more demanding nature of active engagement with the nuances encoded in the limitless permutations of 26 signs on pages. Besides, reading requires two things that are increasingly scarce and to which increasing numbers of Americans seem allergic—solitude and silence.

In 1940, a British officer on Dunkirk beach sent London a three-word message: "But if not." It was instantly recognized as from the Book of Daniel. When Shadrach, Meshach and Abednego are commanded to worship a golden image or perish, they defiantly reply: "Our God who we serve is able to deliver us from the burning fiery furnace, and He will deliver us out of thine hand, O king. But if not, be it known unto thee, O king, that we will not serve thy gods. . . ."

Britain then still had the cohesion of a common culture of shared reading. The cohesion enabled Britain to stay the hand of Hitler, a fact pertinent to today's new age of barbarism.

Discussion Questions

1. What conclusions can you draw from the results of the recent survey concerning the reading habits of Americans?

2. According to the author, how can this survey be interpreted to present both good and bad news?

3. Why did some societies in the past consider reading to be a dangerous activity? Which do you think poses more danger to our society, reading or the lack of reading by our population?

4. How did the author's example from World War II show that Britain at that time had a "common culture of shared reading"? Do you think we can find a common cultural experience in America today?

Class Discussion

Using the Present Tense

The present tense is normally used to present any information that is factual, scientific, personal, or habitual, as well as for things taking place in the present moment. It is a convention of written English to use the present tense to discuss material you have read.

Which sentences in the following pairs seem right to you? Justify your selection.

1. *Henry Luce, the publisher of* Time *attributes his successful building of a journalistic empire to the national obsession with being well informed.*
2. *Henry Luce said that his empire is built on people's desire to be "well informed."*

1. Time's *readers glance at most sections in the magazine.*
2. Time's *readers scanned the magazine for interesting small bits of information.*

1. *Skimming gave the readers no time to contemplate the material.*
2. *Skimming does not allow readers to think about what they are reading.*

Homework

Blog: IS American Literature in Sad Decline?

Essay

Read the following responses to the above question recently given on an Internet blog site. Then answer the questions that follow.

Brooke Brassell:

What has happened to the high standards that we once used to evaluate American literature? Upon reading a fiction-romance novel recently, I was appalled. I could not quit asking myself how this author's work ever got published. The dialogue between each character was immensely monotonous and lacked any degree of character. If I had been given a list of excerpts from this book and asked to identify each character's statements, I'm not sure that I could have done it. I could get almost no sense of the characters themselves, but I got a great deal of knowledge about the opinions and mental processes of the author herself (which I really didn't care to know about). Also, the background setting was very difficult to understand. This is because the author only used extremely vague descriptions of the characters' surroundings. Thus far, I am at page 44 and I know that it is autumn and that the hero has blue eyes and either brown or blonde hair (I swear to you that this character was described as having both at different points in the book). The sad truth is, it's all too often that I throw a book down in disgust. I am almost forced to read books that are at least fifty years old (preferably older) in order to have my insatiable literary appetite fulfilled. Why are we seeing so many books and pieces of literature out there that are exactly like the one I just described? What's even more troubling is that we are actually taking time out of our lives to read this nonsense. I am certainly not a novelist myself, but I do understand the difference between good and bad writing and an effective piece of work. What happened to having pride in what you write? For that matter, what happened to having pride in what you publish? I hope we will soon see a new generation of writers that will prove me wrong. It is much to my delight that literature and writing in itself is making a comeback, but I hope that the widespread availability of sites that are willing to publish just about anything will not further deteriorate what American writers have been offering in recent years.

John Devera:

American Literature is in decline? First I've heard of it. If you believe that American literature is in decline, you might want to go to a different author. First, American literature is a baby being compared to mature adults. Compared to the literature of Russia or England, America has not developed a Tolstoy or a Shakespeare. But Decline? That presupposes a long past golden age of American literature that really doesn't exist. American Literature begins and ends with a single author. Only one author has any real claim to being the Great American Author: Mark Twain. He is the first genuinely gifted writer who wrote about Americans and about their home. Before Twain, we get a few mediocre authors, like James Fenimore Cooper, who attempt to capture the independence and the "spit in your eye" authority of Americans, but they are almost always laughably inept. Too many early writers are little better than English authors writing from the colonies. Honestly, the best of the pre-Twain authors concerned themselves with political writing, not fiction. Poe and Hawthorne come close at times to hitting greatness, but they never really capture the soul of America. And Irving is just too campy.

After Twain we get a whole bunch of writers who focus on regional or subgroup-specific issues. Fitzgerald's Eastern cities, Faulkner's South, Hemingway's diaspora-American. Cather, London, the Harlem Renaissance, all attempt to capture a snapshot of America, but are never as successful in capturing what Americans are all about.

When Huckleberry Finn decides that he would rather go to hell than be a "good Christian" and turn in Jim, he is the epitome of an American. He is a person who will do what he knows is right regardless of the consequences, regardless of society's posturing. That is closer than anyone had ever come or has ever come to being the Great American Author.

So, have we "declined," since the good old days of Twain? Of course not. The authors of the new millennium are every bit as good as authors have ever been, and just as bad. Compare the most popular authors from any two eras and you get pretty funny and prescient déjà vu. James Fenimore Cooper was as popular, if not more so, than Twain and Harte. I'd compare Stephen King favorably to Cooper. King's writing is even better in many ways, especially his short stories and his non-genre works, like "The Body." I'd also like to re-acquaint or introduce people to a great writer who may be judged by future generations as The Great American Author: Garrison Keillor. This man's folksy humor is reminiscent of Twain. He is sometimes too concerned with a regionality that limits his work, but his insightful characterization, and his masterful skill with circular stories is impressive. Although his essays are exceptional, his short fiction is what will make his name.

I would also like to mention a little-regarded author named Christopher Moore. His humorous fiction is as modern as it comes, usually blending outrageous genre elements like vampires or sea monsters, and social commentary. His works are short and universally broad in their humor, but I think you'll find a finesse in the way he handles delicate moments of tenderness and pathos.

Another great American writer, Harlan Ellison, has said that 98% of all fiction written today is crap. But then he notices that 98% of anything is crap. Even in the time of Twain, 98% of what got published was drivel. And people back then ate up the garbage just as we do today (there is no other explanation for the success of Bulwer-Lytton). But, if you are careful, you can find the gems in the manure. They are there, almost submerged in the detritus of what calls itself popular fiction. But they do shine.

Discussion Questions

1. When Brooke Brassell compares "the high standards" used to judge American literature to today's fiction-romance, what does she conclude? What is the basis of her opinion? Do you think she supports her position effectively? Why or why not?

2. Why does John Devera believe that the opinions of the other blogger are invalid? How do you think his position is relevant to a discussion of the reading habits of present-day Americans?

Reviewing Your Graded Essay

After your essay has been graded by your instructor, you may have the opportunity to revise your paper and raise your grade. Even if you are not submitting a revised version of this essay to your instructor, it is important that you review your work carefully in order to understand its strengths and weaknesses. This sheet will guide you through the evaluation process.

You will want to continue to use the techniques that worked well for you and to find strategies to overcome the problems that you identify in this sample of your writing. In order to help yourself recognize areas that might have been problematic for you, look back at the scoring rubric in this book. Match the numerical/verbal/ letter grade received on your essay to the appropriate category. Study the explanation given on the rubric for your grade.

Write a few sentences below in which you identify your problems in each of the following areas. Then suggest specific changes you could make that would improve your paper. Don't forget to use your handbook as a resource.

1. **Grammar/mechanics**

   My problem:

   My strategy for change:

2. **Thesis/response to assignment**

   My problem:

   My strategy for change:

3. **Organization**

   My problem:

My strategy for change:

4. **Paragraph development/examples/reasoning**

   My problem:

   My strategy for change:

5. **Assessment**
   In the space below, assign a grade to your paper using a rubric other than the one used by your instructor. In other words, if your instructor assigned your essay a grade of *High Fail*, you might give it the letter grade you now feel the paper warrants. If your instructor used the traditional letter grade to evaluate the essay, choose a category from the rubric in this book, or any other grading scale that you are familiar with, to show your evaluation of your work. Then write a short narrative explaining your evaluation of the essay and the reasons it received the grade you gave it.

   Grade:_____

   Narrative:_____

   _____

   _____

   _____

   _____

Assignment 6

Sandra Cisneros's "The Monkey Garden"

This assignment will show you how to recognize arguments in fiction writing. After looking at an example based on an excerpt from Mary Shelley's novel *Frankenstein*, you will be asked to write an essay in response to a writing topic based on the short story "The Monkey Garden." Again in this unit, prewriting pages follow Cisneros's story, and by now, we hope that you have worked out a personal writing process through the prewriting pages in *Write It*'s assignment units.

This assignment is somewhat different from Assignments 1–5 because it asks you to work with a short story rather than a reading selection that overtly makes and supports an argument. In this assignment, you will learn how to recognize an argument made through metaphor, as works of fiction carry messages that readers can recognize, messages that make us think as we test their significance in terms of our own lives. The prewriting exercises that follow "The Monkey Garden" will help you to understand the story's argument—based on your own interpretation of the story—and respond to the writing topic with an effective essay of your own.

Understanding and Responding to Arguments in Fiction

One way to talk about literature is to uncover the arguments it makes, arguments that are presented and supported through the elements of the story it tells. An argument is a kind of discussion in which reasons are advanced for (or against) some value or ethical position, often to influence or change people's ideas and actions. The first step to discussing literature as argument is to understand the way literature works *representationally*. In other words, readers are meant to see a fictional story and its characters as dramatizing general human experiences that all of its readers will recognize and understand. Authors hope to use the devices of fiction to capture a representation of life that is insightful and that rings true for readers.

For example, even though Shakespeare's *Romeo and Juliet* is a centuries-old story of two young lovers in a small town in Italy who cannot marry because of an old feud between their families, readers today understand that it is also about the experience of love and the ethical dilemmas we face when our individual desires conflict with the demands of those who have authority over us. We interpret the argument in *Romeo and Juliet* when we decide what the work is saying about this particular ethical dilemma. Those of you who know this play, what do you think it is arguing? That love is more important than duty? That love put over duty to others leads to tragedy? What details about the plot or characters in this play make you answer the way that you have? As you answer these questions, you begin to see *Romeo and Juliet* as a form of argument. Even though you and your classmates may have different answers, many of your answers may be equally compelling if each of you can bring out the elements in the play that support your interpretation. One of the reasons that we continue to read works such as *Romeo and Juliet* is that they encourage us to discuss and question our experiences and our beliefs as individuals and as members of human society.

Works of fiction contain one or more themes—in other words, ideas very similar to those in prose essays such as "Work in an Industrial Society" and "Reading and Thought." Instead of stating arguments directly as prose essays do, however, fiction takes positions on human concerns indirectly, through the tools of fiction. Sometimes authors will have a narrator present a "thesis statement" in a fairly straightforward manner, but more often the thesis will be implied through the events and characters of the story. Here is a set of strategies that you can use when analyzing the arguments in fiction:

1. List the main characters in the story. Briefly summarize their words and actions. What do these things suggest about their personalities and relationships with each other?
2. Identify the main conflict in the story. What is the subject or issue of the conflict? What more general issue is the story *representing* with this conflict?

3. Identify the two or more sides of the conflict. Looking back at the characters you listed in 1, what does each character contribute to the conflict through his or her words or actions? Look carefully at the evidence that each character (including the narrator) presents, and try to determine how the evidence is being linked to support a position.

4. Look over what you wrote for 2 and 3 and then try to state the argument that the story and its characters are representing. This time, try to state the argument in general terms that readers can apply to their own lives.

5. Identify how the story resolves the conflict. This resolution leads directly to the thesis statement, or the story's position in the argument.

Read the following chapter taken from Mary Shelley's *Frankenstein*. Pay attention to the conflict between Dr. Frankenstein, who is narrating, and his creation, the monster. Then use these five steps to see the chapter as an argument. Remember that these steps are guides and are meant to be used with flexibility. For instance, sometimes you might merge the first two steps or you might want to rearrange the steps in a way that meets your needs.

Chapter IX from Mary Shelley's *Frankenstein*

Essay

The being finished speaking and fixed his looks upon me in expectation of a reply. But I was bewildered, perplexed, and unable to arrange my ideas sufficiently to understand the full extent of his proposition. He continued—

"You must create a female for me, with whom I can live in the interchange of those sympathies necessary for my being. This you alone can do; and I demand it of you as a right which you must not refuse."

The latter part of his tale had kindled anew in me the anger that had died away while he narrated his peaceful life among the cottagers, and, as he said this, I could no longer suppress the rage that burned within me.

"I do refuse it," I replied; "and no torture shall ever extort a consent from me. You may render me the most miserable of men, but you shall never make me base in my own eyes. Shall I create another like yourself, whose joint wickedness might desolate the world? Begone! I have answered you; you may torture me, but I will never consent."

"You are in the wrong," replied the fiend; "and, instead of threatening, I am content to reason with you. I am malicious because I am miserable; am I not shunned and hated by all mankind? You, my creator, would tear me to pieces, and triumph; remember that, and tell me why I should pity man more than he pities me? You would not call it murder, if you could precipitate me into one of those ice-rifts, and destroy my frame, the work of your own hands. Shall I respect man, when he contemns me? Let him live with me in the interchange of kindness, and, instead of injury, I would bestow every benefit upon him with tears of gratitude at his acceptance. But that cannot be; the human senses are insurmountable barriers to our union. Yet mine shall not be the submission of abject slavery. I will revenge my injuries: if I cannot inspire love, I will cause fear; and chiefly towards you, my arch-enemy because my creator, do I swear inextinguishable hatred. Have a care: I will work at your destruction, nor finish until I desolate your heart, so that you curse the hour of your birth."

A fiendish rage animated him as he said this; his face was wrinkled into contortions too horrible for human eyes to behold; but presently he calmed himself, and proceeded—

"I intended to reason. This passion is detrimental to me; for you do not reflect that you are the cause of its excess. If any being felt emotions of benevolence towards me, I should return them an hundred and an hundred fold; for that one creature's sake, I would make peace with the whole kind! But I now indulge in dreams of bliss that cannot be realized. What I ask of you is reasonable and moderate; I demand a creature of another sex, but as hideous as myself: the gratification is small, but it is all that I can receive, and it shall content me. It is true, we shall be monsters, cut off from all the world; but on that account we shall be more attached to one another. Our lives will not be happy, but they will be harmless, and free from the misery I now feel. Oh! my creator, make me happy; let me feel gratitude towards you for one benefit! Let me see that I excite the sympathy of some existing thing; do not deny me my request!"

I was moved. I shuddered when I thought of the possible consequences of my consent; but I felt that there was some justice in his argument. His tale, and the feelings he now expressed, proved him to be a creature of fine sensations; and did I not, as his maker, owe him all the portion of happiness that it was in my power to bestow? He saw my change of feeling, and continued—

"If you consent, neither you nor any other human being shall ever see us again: I will go to the vast wilds of South America. My food is not that of man; I do not destroy the lamb and the kid, to glut my appetite; acorns and berries afford me sufficient nourishment. My companion will be of the same nature as myself, and will be content with the same fare. We shall make our bed of dried leaves; the sun will shine on us as on man, and will ripen our food. The picture I present to you is peaceful and human, and you must feel that you could deny it only in the wantonness of power and cruelty. Pitiless as you have been towards me, I now see compassion in your eyes; let me seize the favorable moment, and persuade you to promise what I so ardently desire."

"You propose," replied I, "to fly from the habitations of man, to dwell in those wilds where the beasts of the field will be your only companions. How can you, who long for the love and sympathy of man, persevere in this exile? You will return, and again seek their kindness, and you will meet with their detestation; your evil passions will be renewed, and you will then have a companion to aid you in the task of destruction. This may not be; cease to argue the point, for I cannot consent."

"How inconstant are your feelings! But a moment ago you were moved by my representations, and why do you again harden yourself to my complaints? I swear to you, by the earth which I inhabit, and by you that made me, that, with the companion you bestow, I will quit the neighborhood of man, and dwell, as it may chance, in the most savage of places. My evil passions will have fled, for I shall meet with sympathy; my life will flow quietly away, and, in my dying moments, I shall not curse my maker."

His words had a strange effect upon me. I compassionated him, and sometimes felt a wish to console him; but when I looked upon him, when I saw the filthy mass that moved and talked, my heart sickened, and my feelings were altered to those of horror and hatred. I tried to stifle these sensations; I thought, that as I could not sympathize with him, I had no right to withhold from him the small portion of happiness which was yet in my power to bestow.

"You swear," I said, "to be harmless, but have you not already shewn a degree of malice that should reasonably make me distrust you? May not even this be a feint that will increase your triumph by affording a wider scope for your revenge?"

"How is this? I thought I had moved your compassion, and yet you still refuse to bestow on me the only benefit that can soften my heart, and render me harmless. If I have no ties and no affections, hatred and vice must be my portion; the love of another will destroy the cause of my crimes, and I shall become a thing of whose existence every one will be ignorant. My vices are the children of a forced solitude that I abhor; and my virtues will necessarily arise when I live in communion with an equal. I shall feel the affections of a sensitive being, and become linked to the chain of existence and events, from which I am now excluded."

I paused some time to reflect on all he had related, and the various arguments which he had employed. I thought of the promise of virtues which he had displayed on the opening of his existence, and the subsequent blight of all kindly feeling by the loathing and scorn which his protectors had manifested towards him. His power and threats were not omitted in my calculations: a creature who could exist in the ice caves of the glaciers, and hide himself from pursuit among the ridges of inaccessible precipices, was a being possessing faculties it would be vain to cope with. After a long pause of reflection, I concluded, that the justice due both to him and my fellow-creatures demanded of me that I should comply with his request. Turning to him, therefore, I said—

"I consent to your demand, on your solemn oath to quit Europe for ever, and every other place in the neighborhood of man, as soon as I shall deliver into your hands a female who will accompany you in your exile."

"I swear," he cried, "by the sun, and by the blue sky of heaven, that if you grant my prayer, while they exist you shall never behold me again. Depart to your home, and commence your labors; I shall watch their progress with unutterable anxiety; and fear not but that when you are ready I shall appear."

Saying this, he suddenly quitted me, fearful, perhaps, of any change in my sentiments. I saw him descend the mountain with greater speed than the flight of an eagle, and quickly lost him among the undulations of the sea of ice.

His tale had occupied the whole day; and the sun was upon the verge of the horizon when he departed. I knew that I ought to hasten my descent towards the valley, as I should soon be encompassed in darkness; but my heart was heavy, and my steps slow. The labor of winding among the little paths of the mountains, and fixing my feet firmly as I advanced, perplexed me, occupied as I was by the emotions which the occurrences of the day had produced. Night was far advanced, when I came to the half-way resting-place, and seated myself beside the fountain. The stars shone at intervals, as the clouds passed from over them; the dark pines rose before me, and every here and there a broken tree lay on the ground: it was a scene of wonderful solemnity, and stirred strange thoughts within me. I wept bitterly; and, clasping my hands in agony, I exclaimed, "Oh! stars, and clouds, and winds, ye are all about to mock me: if ye really pity me, crush sensation and memory; let me become as nought; but if not, depart, depart and leave me in darkness."

These were wild and miserable thoughts; but I cannot describe to you how the eternal twinkling of the stars weighed upon me, and how I listened to every blast of wind, as if it were a dull ugly siroc on its way to consume me.

Morning dawned before I arrived at the village of Chamounix; but my presence, so haggard and strange, hardly calmed the fears of my family, who had waited the whole night in anxious expectation of my return.

The following day we returned to Geneva. The intention of my father in coming had been to divert my mind, and to restore me to my lost tranquility; but the medicine had been fatal. And, unable to account for the excess of misery I appeared to suffer, he hastened to return home, hoping the quiet and monotony of a domestic life would by degrees alleviate my sufferings from whatsoever cause they might spring.

For myself, I was passive in all their arrangements; and the gentle affection of my beloved Elizabeth was inadequate to draw me from the depth of my despair. The promise I had made to the demon weighed upon my mind, like Dante's iron cowl on the heads of the hellish hypocrites. All pleasures of earth and sky passed before me like a dream, and that thought only had to me the reality of life. Can you wonder, that sometimes a kind of insanity possessed me, or that I saw continually about me a multitude of filthy animals inflicting on me incessant torture, that often extorted screams and bitter groans?

By degrees, however, these feelings became calmed. I entered again into the every-day scene of life, if not with interest, at least with some degree of tranquility.

Writing Topic

Explain the moral dilemma that the monster presents to Dr. Frankenstein in this chapter. Do you think Dr. Frankenstein's ultimate choice—to deny rather than provide what the monster asks for—is justifiable? Is he correct when he chooses to satisfy the needs of the monster and to protect his own well being, even if his decision may put others at risk? Be sure to support your response with concrete examples that come from your own experiences, observations, and readings.

Prewriting for a Directed Summary

As in earlier chapters of *Write It*, you will use the answers you fill in here when you write a directed summary in response to the first part of the writing topic for this assignment:

> *first part of the writing topic*: Explain the moral dilemma that the monster presents to Dr. Frankenstein in this chapter.

This question asks you to look at this chapter from a particular point of view. The monster makes specific demands on Frankenstein, demands that force Frankenstein to make a choice. To answer this first part of the writing topic, you will have to summarize the conflicting aspects of the two possible choices he has.

Begin by looking for the elements of argument in this chapter. You will remember from working on the prose essays in the previous chapters that argument works by putting together and linking evidence to support a conclusion. Unlike essays such as "The Uses of Enchantment" or "In Praise of Margins" where writers present their views directly, for this assignment you will have to determine how the story presents an argument and supports it using plot and characters. What position does the monster represent? What evidence does the monster link together to support his demand? What position does Frankenstein ultimately represent? What evidence does he link together to support his decision? We can use, with some flexibility, the five steps we listed above to help isolate and identify the argument.

1. List the main characters in the story. Briefly summarize their words and actions. What do these things suggest about their personalities and relationships with each other?

    In this short excerpt, there are two characters:

    Dr. Frankenstein: He is the scientist responsible for creating the creature. When the creature requests that Dr. Frankenstein make a mate so that he won't be lonely, Frankenstein feels torn. On the one hand, he has compassion for the creature's miserable existence and concludes "that the justice due both to him and my fellow-creatures demanded of me that I should comply with his request." At the same time, Frankenstein worries about the consequences of having two monsters (and possibly their offspring) in the world. Dr. Frankenstein is revealed to be a man capable of reason who wants to make the best decision possible in an impossible situation.

The creature: He is a monster created in a laboratory by Dr. Frankenstein. The creature admits that he is motivated by malice and a thirst for revenge. He both loves Frankenstein as a father and resents him for not loving the creature as a son. The creature argues with Frankenstein and attempts to convince him to comply with his request. The creature seems miserable, desperate, and yet hopeful that Dr. Frankenstein will be willing and able to help him.

2. Identify the main conflict in the story. What is the subject or issue of the conflict? What more general issue is the story *representing* with this conflict?

The moral dilemma in this story is easy to see. Dr. Frankenstein cannot decide whether to grant or deny the monster's request. It is clear that Frankenstein is torn because, while he recognizes compelling aspects to the monster's plea, he also recognizes the interests of society and how they conflict with the interests of the monster. Is it right to consider the needs of the individual when there is the possibility that they conflict with the needs of the group? This is the conflict presented to us *representationally* in this chapter of *Frankenstein*, a conflict that all of us have probably experienced in our lives to some degree. We may find similar situations develop with our family, friends, and authority figures, or in politics, health care, science, business, and law—in fact, it is a conflict that we as a society must struggle with every day.

3. Identify the two or more sides of the conflict.

Looking back at the characters you listed in 1, what does each character contribute to the conflict through his or her words or actions? Look carefully at the evidence that each character (including the narrator) presents and try to determine how the evidence is being linked to support a position.

The monster wants his creator, Victor Frankenstein, to create a mate for him because he is lonely. He is shunned by others because he is different and cannot live happily in isolation. The monster has responded to this treatment with violence, even murder, but insists that his violence has been an unavoidable response to being rejected and shunned because of his ugliness. He wants a mate for companionship, and insists that this will dispel his violent tendencies so that he will no longer be a threat to others. He insists on his right to have a companion and, the story says, the "interchange of those sympathies necessary for [his] being."

Dr. Frankenstein, on one hand, feels responsible for the monster's happiness because he has created him. He understands the suffering of the monster and respects the monster's desire for a solution to his suffering. He finds hope in the monster's claim that, if he has a mate, he will no longer be a threat to anyone. Frankenstein also knows that, if he doesn't grant the monster's request, the monster will "work at [his] destruction" and make his life miserable. On the other hand, Frankenstein also recognizes valid reasons for rejecting the monster's request. He fears the monster's violent tendencies, and he understands the suffering the monster has brought to others. Bringing another into existence may double the threat and will open the possibility for the monsters to reproduce themselves and cause further violence and discord. Frankenstein cannot satisfy both the monster and the larger society of people. He must sacrifice the interests of one or the other. He struggles to resolve this moral dilemma: does he try to provide for the monster, or does he try to provide for the larger community?

4. Look over what you wrote for 2 and 3, and then try to state the argument that the story and its characters are representing. This time, try to state the argument in general terms that readers can apply to their own lives.

How much consideration does Dr. Frankenstein owe his creation, the monster? Should Frankenstein's concern about the monster's potential harm to society outweigh his responsibility for the monster's well being? The monster represents the position that, if individual needs are met, the group will be better, but if they're not met, everyone will suffer. The group has to be willing to make some sacrifice for the needs of the individual. If we don't pay attention to individuals, we might become heartless. After all, groups are made up of individuals.

But if we always decide for the individual, fairness may disappear because those who can demand the loudest or with the most influence could get unfair consideration at the cost of everyone else. As far as possible, we should try to provide everyone with the opportunity for a good life, and this can only be done by making the best decisions for the greatest number of people. Individuals have to see that they must give some things up if we are to live together in harmony.

5. Identify how the story resolves the conflict. This resolution leads directly to the thesis statement, or the story's position in the argument.

We can't tell how the novel as a whole resolves the conflict just by looking at one chapter. We can, however, see a chain of evidence in this chapter that shows both sides of the argument, and we can think of the chapter as a kind of "whole" as we respond to the assignment.

Opinion and Working Thesis Statement

The second part of the writing topic that follows the chapter from *Frankenstein* asks you to take a position of your own:

> *second part of the writing topic*: Do you think Dr. Frankenstein's ultimate choice—to deny rather than provide what the monster asks for—is justifiable? Is he correct when he chooses to satisfy the needs of the monster and to protect his own well being, even if his decision may put others at risk?

Do you agree with Frankenstein's viewpoint, which we've identified to be that the needs of the many outweigh the needs of the few? To answer this, you would simply use the **thesis frame** (which you should recognize from previous chapters of this book) to formulate a thesis statement. As you may have done in previous chapters of *Write It*, if you're not sure what position you want to take, do some prewriting to develop your ideas, and then come back to writing a working thesis statement.

a. What is the subject of the *Frankenstein* excerpt that the writing topic asks you to consider?

   The interest of the individual versus the interest of the group

b. What is Dr. Frankenstein's opinion about that subject?

   He puts the interest of the group before the interest of the individual.

c. What is your opinion about the subject, i.e., will you agree or disagree with Dr. Frankenstein?

_____

_____

_____

The last part of the writing topic asks you to support the argument you put forward in your thesis statement:

   Last part of the writing topic: Be sure to support your response with concrete examples that come from your own experiences, observations, and readings.

   If you had to write this essay, the majority of it would be devoted to supporting the position you take in your thesis statement. You would do some prewriting to explore your ideas and develop your supporting topics, then use an outline to plan and draft your essay. As you can see, even though finding arguments in literature requires you to read with a somewhat different perspective, you can use the same steps of the writing process that you have worked with throughout the writing assignments in *Write It*.

   The *Frankenstein* example is a discussion between two characters that is easily recognizable as a debate, so the argument is fairly clear. But what happens when this is not the case? How do you find the argument when you are asked to look at narration that includes description of characters and setting, but no extended dialogue that carries a debate? Go on to the next pages and try out the five steps using a short story, Sandra Cisneros's "The Monkey Garden."

The Monkey Garden

Essay

SANDRA CISNEROS

Sandra Cisneros is a Mexican-American writer, author, and poet born in Chicago. She earned her B.A. from Loyola University and her M.F.A. at the University of Iowa. She has taught at many colleges and universities, including the University of California and the University of Michigan. "The Monkey Garden" is taken from her best-known novel, The House on Mango Street *(1984).*

The monkey doesn't live there anymore. The monkey moved—to Kentucky—and took his people with him. And I was glad because I couldn't listen anymore to his wild screaming at night, the twangy yakkety-yak of the people who owned him. The green metal cage, the porcelain table top, the family that spoke like guitars. Monkey, family, table. All gone.

And it was then we took over the garden we had been afraid to go into when the monkey screamed and showed its yellow teeth.

There were sunflowers big as flowers on Mars and thick cockscombs bleeding the deep red fringe of theater curtains. There were dizzy bees and bow-tied fruit flies turning somersaults and humming in the air. Sweet sweet peach trees. Thorn roses and thistle and pears. Weeds like so many squinty-eyed stars and brush that made your ankles itch and itch until you washed with soap and water. There were big green apples hard as knees. And everywhere the sleepy smell of rotting wood, damp earth and dusty hollyhocks thick and perfumy like the blue-blond hair of the dead.

Yellow spiders ran when we turned rocks over and pale worms blind and afraid of light rolled over in their sleep. Poke a stick in the sandy soil and a few blue-skinned beetles would appear, an avenue of ants, so many crusty lady bugs. This was a garden, a wonderful thing to look at in the spring. But bit by bit, after the monkey left, the garden began to take over itself. Flowers stopped obeying the little bricks that kept them from growing beyond their paths. Weeds mixed in. Dead cars appeared overnight like mushrooms. First one and then another and then a pale blue pickup with the front windshield missing. Before you knew it, the monkey garden became filled with sleepy cars.

Things had a way of disappearing in the garden, as if the garden itself ate them, or, as if with its old-man memory, it put them away and forgot them. Nenny found a dollar and a dead mouse between two rocks in the stone wall where the morning glories climbed, and once when we were playing hide-and-seek, Eddie Vargas laid his head beneath a hibiscus tree and fell asleep there like a Rip Van Winkle until somebody remembered he was in the game and went back to look for him.

This, I suppose, was the reason why we went there. Far away from where our mothers could find us. We and a few old dogs who lived inside the empty cars. We made a clubhouse once on the back of that old blue pickup. And besides, we liked to jump from the roof of one car to another and pretend they were giant mushrooms.

Somebody started the lie that the monkey garden had been there before anything. We liked to think the garden could hide things for a thousand years. There beneath the roots of soggy flowers were the bones of murdered pirates and dinosaurs, the eye of a unicorn turned to coal.

This is where I wanted to die and where I tried one day but not even the monkey garden would have me. It was the last day I would go there.

Who was it that said I was getting too old to play the games? Who was it I didn't listen to? I only remember that when the others ran, I wanted to run too, up and down and through the monkey garden, fast as the boys, not like Sally who screamed if she got her stockings muddy.

I said, Sally, come on, but she wouldn't. She stayed by the curb talking to Tito and his friends. Play with the kids if you want, she said, I'm staying here. She could be stuck-up like that if she wanted to, so I just left.

It was her own fault too. When I got back Sally was pretending to be mad . . . something about the boys having stolen her keys. Please give them back to me, she said punching the nearest one with a soft fist. They were laughing. She was too. It was a joke I didn't get.

I wanted to go back with the other kids who were still jumping on cars, still chasing each other through the garden, but Sally had her own game.

One of the boys invented the rules. One of Tito's friends said you can't get the keys back unless you kiss us and Sally pretended to be mad at first but she said yes. It was that simple.

I don't know why, but something inside me wanted to throw a stick. Something wanted to say no when I watched Sally going into the garden with Tito's buddies all grinning. It was just a kiss, that's all. A kiss for each one. So what, she said.

Only how come I felt angry inside. Like something wasn't right. Sally went behind that old blue pickup to kiss the boys and get her keys back, and I ran up three flights of stairs to where Tito lived. His mother was ironing shirts. She was sprinkling water on them from an empty pop bottle and smoking a cigarette.

Your son and his friends stole Sally's keys and now they won't give them back unless she kisses them and right now they're making her kiss them, I said all out of breath from the three flights of stairs.

Those kids, she said, not looking up from her ironing.

That's all?

What do you want me to do, she said, call the cops? And kept on ironing.

I looked at her a long time, but couldn't think of anything to say, and ran back down the three flights to the garden where Sally needed to be saved. I took three big sticks and a brick and figured this was enough.

But when I got there Sally said go home. Those boys said leave us alone. I felt stupid with my brick. They all looked at me as if *I* was the one that was crazy and made me feel ashamed.

And then I don't know why but I had to run away. I had to hide myself at the other end of the garden, in the jungle part, under a tree that wouldn't mind if I lay down and cried a long time. I closed my eyes like tight stars so that I wouldn't, but I did. My face felt hot. Everything inside hiccupped.

I read somewhere in India there are priests who can will their heart to stop beating. I wanted to will my blood to stop, my heart to quit its pumping. I wanted to be dead, to turn into the rain, my eyes melt into the ground like two black snails. I wished and wished. I closed my eyes and willed it, but when I got up my dress was green and I had a headache.

I looked at my feet in their white socks and ugly round shoes. They seemed far away. They didn't seem to be my feet anymore. And the garden that had been such a good place to play didn't seem mine either.

Writing Topic

How does the narrator's alienation by the end of the story present us with a critique of gender roles? Do you think this critique is valid? Be sure to support your position with concrete evidence taken from your own experiences, including your observations and readings.

Vocabulary Check

Good writers choose their words carefully so that their ideas will be clear. Therefore, it is important to think about a story's key vocabulary terms and the way they are used by the author. Words can have a variety of meanings, or they can have specialized meanings in certain contexts. Look up the definitions of the following words or phrases from "The Monkey Garden." Choose the meaning that you think gives the most insight to the story. Then explain the way the meaning or concept behind the definition is key to understanding the story's argument.

porcelain

definition: _____

_____

_____

explanation: _____

_____

_____

_____

Rip Van Winkle

definition: _____

_____

_____

explanation: _____

_____

_____

cockscomb

definition: _____

_____

_____

explanation: _____

_____

_____

Questions to Guide Your Reading

Paragraph 1
What are the things that have disappeared, and how does the narrator of the story feel about their absence?

Paragraph 2
What happens to the garden after the disappearance? Why?

Paragraphs 3–4
What natural things occupy the garden now? What things start to appear that seem out of place in a garden?

Paragraph 5
What kinds of things become lost in the garden?

Paragraph 6
If strange things appear and other things get lost in this garden, what reason does the narrator give for its popularity?

Paragraph 7

What rumor is told about the garden? Is there any truth in it? Why do you think this lie is circulated? Why would anyone believe it?

Paragraph 8

What does the narrator try to do in the garden? Is she successful? How does she feel about the garden after that day?

Paragraph 9

What is the relationship between growing up and going to the garden?

Paragraphs 10–14

Who is Sally? What does the narrator want Sally to do? What does Sally do instead? How does the narrator feel about what Sally is doing?

Paragraphs 15–19

Who does the narrator ask for help? What kind of response does she get?

Paragraphs 20–21

What plan does the narrator have next? Does it work? Why? How does she feel then?

Paragraphs 22–23

Then where does the narrator go, and what does she do? What emotions is she experiencing?

Paragraph 24

In the end, what changes have occurred in the way the narrator feels about herself, the garden, and the other children? Has the story established any relationship between her feelings and her age and gender?

Prewriting for a Directed Summary

You will find that providing thorough answers to these questions will help you write a clear and accurate *directed* summary that responds to the first part of the writing topic.

> *first part of the writing topic:* How does the narrator's alienation by the end of the story present us with a critique of gender roles?

For this assignment, you are working with a short story, so you should use the five steps for identifying an argument in literature.

1. List the main characters in the story. Briefly summarize their words and actions. What do these things suggest about their personalities and relationships with each other?

2. Identify the main conflict in the story. What is the subject or issue of the conflict? What more general issue is the story *representing* with this conflict?

3. Identify the two or more sides of the conflict. Looking back at the characters you listed in #1, what does each character contribute to the conflict through his or her words or actions? Look carefully at the evidence that each character (including the narrator) presents, and try to determine how the evidence is being linked to support a position.

4. Look over what you wrote for #2 and #3 and then try to state the argument that the story and its characters are representing. This time, try to state the argument in general terms that readers can apply to their own lives.

5. Identify how the story resolves the conflict. This resolution leads directly to the thesis statement, or the story's position in the argument.

Opinion and Working Thesis Statement

The second question in the writing topic that follows "The Monkey Garden" asks you to take a position of your own:

> *second part of the writing topic*: Do you think this critique is valid?

Now that you have done some careful prewriting and have systematically developed your thoughts, you are ready to formulate a working thesis statement that responds to this part of the writing topic. What argument does the story as a whole make about the subject of gender roles? At this point in your thinking, will you agree or disagree with this argument? In other words, does the message of the story *as you have interpreted it* reflect your own view on gender roles? If not, what position do you want to take on the subject of gender roles and their influence on us?

To formulate your position and thesis statement, keep in mind the way "The Monkey Garden" defines gender roles. For help, review what you discovered in "Questions to Guide Your Reading."

Because these ideas may be new to you, it is possible that you aren't yet sure what position you want to take in your essay. If this is the case, you can explore your ideas on a blank page of this book, or go on to the next section and work on developing your ideas through examples drawn from your experience. Then you will be directed to come back to the working thesis statement you have written here and work on revising it, if necessary, based on the discoveries you made when you explored your ideas more systematically.

1. Use the following **thesis frame** to identify the basic elements of your thesis statement:
   a. What is the subject of "The Monkey Garden" that the first part of the writing topic asks you to consider?

   _____

   b. What is the story's point of view on that subject?

   _____

   c. What is your opinion about the subject, and will you agree or disagree with the story's view?

   _____

   _____

   _____

2. Now use the elements you isolated in 1a, b, and c of the thesis frame to write a thesis statement. You may have to revise it several times until it captures your idea clearly.

   _____

   _____

Prewriting to Find Support for Your Thesis Statement

The last part of the writing topic asks you to support the argument you put forward in your thesis statement:

last part of the writing topic: Be sure to support your position with concrete evidence taken from your own experiences, including your observations and readings.

Use the following questions to help develop examples you might use to support your thesis statement.

Hint

Complete each section of this prewriting activity; your responses will become the material you will use in the next stage—planning and writing the essay.

1. As you begin to develop your own examples, consider the influence of gender roles in your own life. In the space below, list or freewrite about personal experiences (either concerning you, your friends, or your family) when you or someone you know was expected to behave or look a certain way because of gender. Think about your self-identity and your hopes and aspirations to see if they are tied to your own, your family's, or society's expectations based on your gender. Feel free to include any experience, however minor or incidental.

   Once you've written your ideas, look them over carefully. Try to group your ideas into categories. Then give each category a label. In other words, cluster ideas that seem to have something in common and, for each cluster, identify that shared quality by giving it a name.

2. Now broaden your focus; list or freewrite about examples from your studies, your readings, and your knowledge of current events. Think, too, about the readings you have done in some of your other classes or in your free time. Do any of them offer examples of the influence of gender roles that you may be able to use?

   Once you've written your ideas, look them over carefully. Try to group your ideas into categories. Then give each category a label. In other words, cluster ideas that seem to have something in common and, for each cluster, identify that shared quality by giving it a name.

3. Once you've created topics by clustering your ideas into categories, go through them and pick two or three specific ones to develop in your essay. Make sure that they are relevant to your thesis and that they have enough substance to be compelling to your readers. Then, in the space below, briefly summarize each item.

Once you've decided which categories and items on your lists you will use in your essay, take some time to explain below how each category and its items connect to your thesis statement. You will use these details for the next stage, revision.

Revising Your Thesis Statement

Now that you have spent some time working out your ideas more systematically and developing some supporting evidence for the position you want to take, look again at the working thesis statement you crafted earlier to see if it is still accurate. As your first step, look again at the writing topic and then write your original working thesis on the lines that follow it:

> *second part of the writing topic*: Do you think this critique is valid?

your working thesis statement:

_____

_____

_____

Take some time now to see if you want to revise your thesis statement. Often after extensive prewriting and focused thought, the working thesis statement is no longer an accurate reflection of what you plan to say in your essay. Sometimes only a word or phrase must be added or deleted; other times, the thesis statement must be significantly rewritten, as either or both the subject and the claim portions are inaccurate.

After examining your working thesis statement and completing any necessary revisions, check it one more time by asking yourself the following questions:

a. Does the thesis directly identify the argument about gender roles that "The Monkey Garden" presents?

b. Do you make clear your opinion about the way gender roles define us?

If you answered "no" to either of these questions, then rewrite your thesis statement so that it is fully developed.

_____

_____

Planning and Drafting Your Essay

Now that you have examined the argument in "The Monkey Garden" and thought at length about your own views, draft an essay that responds to all parts of the writing topic. Use the material you developed in this section to compose your draft, and then exchange drafts with a classmate and use the peer review that follows to help revise your draft. Don't forget to review Part 1, especially "A Suggested Structure for an Essay That Responds to Another Writer's Work," for further guidance on the essay's conventional structure.

Getting started on the draft is often the hardest part of the writing process because this is where you move from exploring and planning to getting your ideas down in writing and in a unified, coherent shape. Creating an outline will give you a basic structure for incorporating all the ideas you have developed in the preceding pages. An outline will also give you a bird's-eye view of your essay and help you spot problems in development or logic. The form below is modeled on Part 1's "A Suggested Structure for An Essay That Responds to Another Writer's Work," and it is meant to help you create an outline or writing plan before you begin drafting your essay.

Creating an Outline for Your Draft

I. Introductory Paragraph

A. An opening sentence that gives the story's title and author and begins to answer the first part of the writing topic:

_____

B. Main points to include in the directed summary:

1.

2.

3.

4.

C. Look up "Revising Your Thesis Statement," where you wrote a polished and accurate statement of your position on gender roles and their influence on us. Copy it on the line below. It should clearly agree or disagree with the argument in "The Monkey Garden" about gender roles, and it should state a clear position using your own words.

_____

II. Body Paragraphs

    A. Subject of the paragraph: _____

        1. **C**ontrolling idea sentence:

              _____

        2. **C**orroborating details:

              _____

              _____

              _____

        3. **C**areful description of the details' relevance:

              _____

              _____

              _____

              _____

        4. **C**onnection to the thesis statement:

              _____

    B. Subject of the paragraph: _____

        1. **C**ontrolling idea sentence:

              _____

              _____

        2. **C**orroborating details:

              _____

              _____

              _____

3. Careful description of the details' relevance:

_____

_____

_____

_____

_____

4. Connection to the thesis statement:

_____

_____

C. Subject of the paragraph: _____

1. Controlling idea sentence:

_____

2. Corroborating details:

_____

_____

_____

3. Careful description of the details' relevance:

_____

_____

_____

_____

_____

4. Connection to the thesis statement:

_____

   D. Subject of the paragraph: _____

      1. **C**ontrolling idea sentence:

        _____

      2. **C**orroborating details:

        _____

        _____

        _____

      3. **C**areful description of the details' relevance:

        _____

        _____

        _____

        _____

      4. **C**onnection to the thesis statement:

        _____

III. Conclusion

   A. Type of conclusion to be used:

      _____

   B. Key words or phrases to include:

      _____

Peer Draft Review Sheet

Use the following guidelines to give a classmate feedback on his or her draft. Read the draft through first and then answer each of the items below as specifically as you can. Be sure to have a classmate fill out a review sheet for your draft. Look carefully at the responses he or she made to your draft and use them to revise your essay.

Name of draft's author: _____

Name of draft's reader: _____

Introduction

1. Within the opening sentences,
   a. the author is correctly identified by first and last name   yes   no
   b. the short story's title is included and placed within quotation marks   yes   no

2. The opening contains a summary that
   a. explains the narrator's alienation at the end of "The Monkey Garden"   yes   no
   b. explains the story's critique of gender roles   yes   no

3. The opening provides a thesis that
   a. states whether the story's critique of gender roles is valid   yes   no
   b. takes a position on gender roles   yes   no

If the answers to 3 above are yes, state the thesis below as it is written. If the answer to one or both of these questions is no, explain to the draft's writer what information is needed to make the thesis complete.

Body

1. How many paragraphs are in the body of this essay? _____

2. To support the thesis, this number is   sufficient   not enough

3. Do paragraphs contain the 4Cs?

Paragraph 1	Controlling idea sentence	yes	no
	Corroborating details	yes	no
	Careful description of the details' relevance	yes	no
	Connection to the thesis statement	yes	no
Paragraph 2	Controlling idea sentence	yes	no
	Corroborating details	yes	no
	Careful description of the details' relevance	yes	no
	Connection to the thesis statement	yes	no
Paragraph 3	Controlling idea sentence	yes	no
	Corroborating details	yes	no
	Careful description of the details' relevance	yes	no
	Connection to the thesis statement	yes	no
Paragraph 4	Controlling idea sentence	yes	no
	Corroborating details	yes	no
	Careful description of the details' relevance	yes	no
	Connection to the thesis statement	yes	no
Paragraph 5	Controlling idea sentence	yes	no
	Corroborating details	yes	no
	Careful description of the details' relevance	yes	no
	Connection to the thesis statement	yes	no
	(Continue as needed).		

4. Identify any of the above paragraphs that are not fully developed (too short).

5. Identify any of the above paragraphs that fail to support the thesis. _____

6. Identify any of the above paragraphs that are redundant or repetitive. _____

7. Suggest any ideas for additional paragraphs that might improve this essay.

Conclusion

1. Does the conclusion contain any material that should have been developed in the body of the essay?

   a. examples   yes   no

   b. new ideas   yes   no

2. Does the conclusion provide closure (let the reader know
   that the end of the essay has been reached)?   yes   no

3. Does the conclusion leave the reader with an understanding
   of the significance of the argument?   yes   no

State in your own words what the writer considers to be important about his or
her argument.

_____

_____

4. Identify the type of conclusion used (see the guidelines for conclusions in
   Part 1).

Revision

1. During revision, the writer should pay attention to the following problems in
   mechanics:

   comma splices

   comma placement

   fragments

   run-on sentences

   apostrophe use

   quotation mark use

   capital letter use

   spelling

2. During revision, the writer should pay attention to the following areas
   of grammar:

   verb tense

   subject-verb agreement

   pronoun type

   pronoun reference

   pronoun agreement

   irregular verbs

   noun plurals

   dangling or misplaced modifiers

   prepositions

Final Draft Check List

Content

- My essay has an appropriate title.
- I provide an accurate summary of the position on the topic set out by "The Monkey Garden."
- My thesis contains a claim that can be supported with concrete evidence.
- I have a sufficient number of paragraphs and arguments to support my thesis.
- Each body paragraph is relevant to my thesis.
- Each body paragraphs contains the 4Cs.
- I use transitions whenever necessary to connect paragraphs and ideas to each other.
- The final paragraph of my essay (the conclusion) provides the reader with a sense of closure.

Grammar and Mechanics

- I use the present tense to discuss the author's arguments and examples.
- All of my verb tense shifts are correct and necessary to the shifts in time.
- I have verb tense consistency throughout my sentences and paragraphs.
- My sentences are punctuated correctly.
- If I present items in a series (nouns, verbs, prepositional phrases), they are parallel in form.
- If I include material spoken or written by someone other than myself, I have correctly punctuated it with quotation marks and other necessary punctuation.
- I have checked for subject-verb agreement in all of my sentences.

PART 3

Case Studies

Case Study 1

Dave Barry's "It's No Wonder Brides Often Turn into Frankenstein"

The following case study contains an essay, Dave Barry's "It's No Wonder Brides Often Turn into Frankenstein," followed by four timed-writing essays written by students just like you. Read the essay by Barry, and the four student essays that respond to Barry's essay and writing topic. Examine each student essay for its strengths and weaknesses. A set of study questions at the end will help you evaluate its success. Then use the scoring rubric in Part 1 to give each essay a score.

It's No Wonder Brides Often Turn into Frankenstein

DAVE BARRY

Essay

Dave Barry has been a humor columnist at The Miami Herald *since 1983. His column appears in more than 500 newspapers in the United States and abroad. A Pulitzer Prize winner for commentary, he writes about a range of contemporary social issues. Barry has also written a number of books, two of which were used as the basis for the CBS TV sitcom* Dave's World. *He was born in Armonk, New York, in 1947 and went to Haverford College, where he was an English major.*

Every year, as we enter wedding season, I go to the bookstore and pick up a bridal magazine. Then I crumple to the floor with lower-back spasms, because during wedding season, bridal magazines achieve roughly the same mass as Ted Kennedy (D-Mass). They have hundreds of pages of advertisements and articles designed to help the bride, as she gets ready for her Special Day, go completely insane.

She can't help it. Your modern American wedding is more complex, in terms of logistics, than the invasion of Iraq. For one thing, the invasion planners don't have to decide on guest favors; the bride does, and it's not a simple decision. Here is what *Modern Bride* has to say on this topic in its 312-pound March issue:

"Gone are the days of giving guests mixed nuts in little plastic cups as wedding favors.... Brides today have so many options.... Choose unique favor container—tiny tins, clear plastic cones, little gossamer bags—and fill them with your favorite treats. Give each guest a silver frame... Or tie a stack of your favorite cookies together with personalized ribbon. The choices are truly endless!"

And they are! Truly! Endless! Which is why tonight, while you're snoring the snore of the carefree, some stressed-out bride-to-be, who had once hoped (the fool!) to get by with mixed nuts in a cup, will be staring at her bedroom ceiling, asking herself: "Tiny tins? Gossamer bags? Personalized ribbon? Should I maybe personalize the gossamer? What the hell IS gossamer?"

At dawn she's still struggling to make this decision, so she can get on with the other 158,000 critical bridal decisions—decisions she must make by herself, because she stopped talking to her mother weeks ago, following a bitter argument about the cake frosting. The bride, alone, must decide on her dress, shoes, flowers, invitations, place cards, caterer, photographer and all the other wedding elements that must be perfect or her Special Day will be RUINED RUINED RUINED.

And don't tell me that the groom can help. Please. The groom is useless. Statistically speaking, something like 92 percent of all grooms are male. If you let males plan weddings you are going to wind up with Skee Ball at the reception. No, the groom dropped out of the picture minutes after he proposed. For all the bride knows, he has been kidnapped by aliens. It does not matter. The bride must plunge grimly ahead, making decision after decision, day after stressful day, night after sleepless night, until she has, at most, two remaining marbles.

Unfortunately, the bride reaches this state just when she is turning her attention to the most abused victim group in America: bridesmaids. If you've ever wondered why you see so many weddings where the bridesmaids are unrecognizable, the answer is that these poor women were following the fashion orders of a crazed bride who wants all her bridesmaids, regardless of their physical nature, to have exactly the same "look," because otherwise her Special Day would be RUINED RUINED RUINED.

A few years ago my wife was a bridesmaid; the bride was the sweetest, most thoughtful person we know. But she insisted that all her bridesmaids get a certain hairdo, which meant that my wife emerged from the beauty salon with this foot-high thing on her head formed by (1) her hair; (2) a substance that appeared to be either very strong hairspray or Super Glue; and (3) 14 million bobby pins. She had enough steel on her head to make a Cadillac Escalade. Her hairdo was interfering with aircraft compasses. She did not look like my wife. And she wasn't! She was . . . a bridesmaid!

Can anything be done to halt this craziness? Yes. Alert reader Lori Rispoli has come up with a brilliant solution: "Have you ever wondered," she writes, "why it takes a bride months and months to plan a wedding, but a good funeral can be pulled together in two days? The elements are all the same—church, minister, music, flowers, guests, food."

Lori is absolutely right. What we need is a law prohibiting brides from planning their weddings more than, say, a week in advance. A bride caught violating this law would be subject to severe punishment, such as being forced to walk down the aisle to the tune of "I Shot the Sheriff."

Wouldn't that be great? Brides—and their loved ones—would be spared months of insanity. Weddings would be simpler, cheaper and more relaxed. Everybody would win! Except of course the people who put out the bridal magazines. They'd have to find something useful to do. But I'm sure they'll have no trouble. The choices are truly endless.

Writing Topic

Why does Barry say that we need a law that forbids brides from planning their weddings more than a week in advance of the actual event? Do you think there is any validity to his argument? Write an essay responding to these two questions. To develop your essay, be sure to discuss specific examples from your own experiences, observations, or readings.

Student Essay 1

In the essay It's no wonder brides often turn into Frankenstein, by Dave Barry, it talks about how planning a wedding has become more complicated and too extravagant than is necessary. Barry uses the wedding magazine called Modern Bride, in order to show why weddings have become what they are today. The magazine gives the bride way too many options for her wedding which takes up a lot of time and causes way too much stress.

In this essay, Barry says that there should be a law forbidding brides from planning their weddings more than a week in advance. He feels that since people can plan a funeral in less than a week, why can't they plan a wedding in that same amount of time? In reality, a funeral and a wedding are two very different things. A funeral is a way to say goodbye to someone forever and remember what they meant to you while they were alive. On the other hand, a wedding is a joyous celebration of two people wanting to share the rest of their lives together. A wedding is meant to be remembered whereas a funeral isn't. No one wants to celebrate a death but everyone celebrates life and the joining of two lives.

In my opinion, I think that Barry's opinion is wrong because, whose right is it to say how much a person can put into something they are going to celebrate for the rest of their lives? I do agree though that weddings are way too stressful and that people put too much time into something that is only going to last one night, but disagree with his solution. However, in the eyes of the couple getting married, it is going to last forever. It is thought that people only get married once, although not in all cases, so why not make it the best and make it the best?

When my mom married my dad, their wedding was small and only consisted of family and close friends. At the time my parents had gotten married, they didn't have a lot of money, so they had to make due with what they had. When my mom had gotten remarried, years after her divorce from my father, she decided to go all out. She spent a year planning, deciding etc... whatever she needed to do to make this one perfect. She had more money to do this with and a lot more options as well. When I look at the pictures and movies from both weddings, I see that the second one was a lot better. My mother had gotten the chance to put more into it, and that was shown by the excellent planning.

I personally think weddings need a lot of planning. A wedding is supposed to be perfect and throwing a wedding together in a week, one runs the risk of having her entire wedding ruined. Also, every woman dreams of their wedding and how its supposed to be and that takes time and planning for it come out the way they want. Planning a wedding ahead of time is a guaranteed way to make sure it is the best for everyone.

Assessment Questions

1   Does this essay answer the first question in the writing topic?

2.   Does this essay have a thesis that answers the second question?

3.   Does this essay develop the thesis with supporting examples? Evaluate the effectiveness of these examples.

4.   Are there significant errors in grammar that limit the essay's effectiveness? In other words, as you read the essay, did you notice several mistakes in the way the sentences are written?

5.   Using the conventional standards presented in the scoring rubric in Part 1 of this book, what score does this essay deserve? Explain.

Student Essay 2

How hard can it actually be to plan a wedding? In the article by Dave Barry, the point being made is that it has become to difficult to plan a wedding and that brides are becoming overwhelmed by planning a wedding, that they many times cannot sleep or end up arguing with relatives over their wedding decisions. He adds that a law should be made which states that a bride should only have about a week in advance to plan a wedding. However it is not that simple most brides look at their wedding as something that they have been waiting for their own life and would want to remember it years after.

The statement that Barry makes about making a law that allows brides to plan their wedding with only a weeks notice, is absurd. Even if it will be a small wedding the church, hall and guest need to be reserved at least a month and a half before the event. There is also so many weddings in a year that it would be impossible for every wedding to be able get the hall and church and all their guest in one weeks notice.

Barry suggest that passing a law of this kind would reduce the insanity that goes into planning a wedding. Therefore the bride would be more relaxed and not have statement appears any unnecessary arguments with her family because of the stress of the planning. However, this idea is not realistic. Only a small percentage of brides and grooms would like to plan a wedding in a week. I think this would probably cause much more because then everything would have to be done in a week, which means that not much would get done and the bride and groom would not be happy with the results.

From my own experience, I know how much work it takes to plan an event. I Notice that the have never planned a wedding. However, I have planned a baby shower and I plan house parties here and there. I can say that planning a baby shower takes a lot of time not only sending out invitations, but planning the games, buying decorations, to help support buying prizes for the games, choosing and preparing the food. Not to mention making arrangements and changes in the house where the baby shower will take place. Even when I plan parties in my apartment I need at least a weeks notice. And these are just simple gatherings were not much planning is needed.

Barry's argument is to drastic there are steps that a bride could follow to make things run smoother. She can hire a wedding planner or ask family to help with the planning, or simply give herself a good amount of time before the wedding to plan it. Or just simply relax and make the best out of the whole planning experience.

Weddings should be a memorable event. And the planning of a wedding should not be looked at as something dreadful of stressful but something to look forward too and enjoy.

Assessment Questions

1. Does this essay answer the first question in the writing topic?

2. Does this essay have a thesis that answers the second question?

3. Does this essay develop the thesis with supporting examples? Evaluate the effectiveness of these examples.

4. Are there significant errors in grammar that limit the essay's effectiveness? In other words, as you read the essay, did you notice several mistakes in the way the sentences are written?

5. Using the conventional standards presented in the scoring rubric in Part 1 of this book, what score does this essay deserve? Explain.

Student Essay 3

In the article, "It's No Wonder Brides Often Turn into Frankenstein," Dave Barry, the author, states that there should be a law prohibiting brides from planning their wedding more than a week in advance. Barry believes that this would "spare brides and their loved ones months of insanity." He also supports his opinion with the fact that weddings would be simple, cheaper, and more relaxed. As a female and possibly a future bride, I disagree with Barry's beliefs. I just can't imagine not planning for my wedding at least a month in advance. First of all, a wedding is a once in a lifetime event for some people. If anything goes wrong, it would ruin everything, whether it is a relationship or just sentimental memories. Another reason to plan ahead for one's wedding is just the mere fact that things can go bad. Last, but not least, it is just impossible to plan a wedding in one week because there are tons of things to do.

The first reason why I think that if that weddings aren't well planned, some of your guests might get mad at you. Barry might not believe this, but I have personal experience that proves it. I have three older sisters and they have all gotten married within the past couple of years. At my eldest sister's wedding, things got a little bit rusty when my sister, the bride, invited my second eldest sister's ex-boyfriend. You should have seen how angry my second sister got. The girl practically hated her ex boyfriend's guts, but on the other hand, the guy was one of the brides good friends. As one can see, my eldest sister had a lot of decisions to make. Eventually my second sister forgave my eldest sister, but if only she had planned more carefully, things would have been better. She should have sat down and had a talk with my second sister and her boyfriend, and explain to them her dilemma.

Besides saving yourself from arguments and mishaps, planning ahead can help save your wedding ceremony. When my second eldest sister got married, the worst thing in the world had happened. The restaurant where the reception was held at, had mistakenly put down two different weddings for one night. The manager called and apologized my sister for their mishap. This would have been really bad because then the wedding would have been cancelled, but luckily she planned a couple months ahead and could book another location.

Besides preventing this from going bad at the wrong time, planning ahead is needed because there is so much to do. As mentioned in the article the bride has to do most everything from picking the dresses, flowers, gifts, she also has to seat her guest in certain ways to please everyone. She just has so much to do and so little time. Planning ahead will give her less stress because she doesn't have to rush things. As a man, Barry doesn't seem to really understand how women think and feel. He just wants to rush things and get it over with, but if the wedding goes wrong who gets the blame? The bride is at fault if the decoration look tacky or if the bridesmaid's dresses are out of style. She is blamed if her own dress or hair looks ugly.

The bride ends up with all the fault.

Assessment Questions

1. Does this essay answer the first question in the writing topic?

2 Does this essay have a thesis that answers the second question?

3. Does this essay develop the thesis with supporting examples? Evaluate the effectiveness of these examples.

4. Are there significant errors in grammar that limit the essay's effectiveness? In other words, as you read the essay, did you notice several mistakes in the way the sentences are written?

5. Using the conventional standards presented in the scoring rubric in Part 1 of this book, what score does this essay deserve? Explain.

Student Essay 4

Why does Dave Barry say that we need a law prohibiting brides from planning weddings more than a week in advance? Simple: it will save a lot of people a veritable boatload of stress; besides, the whole wedding thing has just gotten way out of hand in my opinion. So, I think Barry's suggestion is quite valid.

To start off, Barry is one-hundred percent right about the excessive content of tone: is it effec-bridal magazines. Every spring, I look around at the lush green foliage and think to myself, "Ah, so beautiful—but what happened to all the trees?"

Then, when I inevitably make a trip to the grocery store, I see where all the trees have gone. They're all part of the magazines that line the rack; and these magazines are so massive that there are stress fractures visible in the rack. Most of the magazines are bridal catalogs.

Flipping one of these magazines open reveals nine-billion advertisements and articles; all of which glorify the "perfect wedding" that people must have. Now, I know from experience that the only thing all the advertisements and articles in those bridal magazines do is whip people into a frenzy. Too many choices (no matter what they pertain to) overloads your brain and you'll go nuts. The whole time you're trying to make a choice among the millions that are possible, this tiny little voice in your brain keeps saying, "Okay, good choice there ... but are you sure it's the right one?" This voice never shuts up, and the longer you have to listen to it, the closer your sanity comes to the edge of the abyss.

Essentially, making those thousands of choices is what wedding planning is all about. It will definitely drive the decision maker insane, but what about the people affected by the decisions? It will drive them crazy too. Case in point: my friend Dena and her wedding plans. weddings are a hassle for all concerned. First, she had to call us all up and convince us to come. After she finally decided on a day, we all had arrangements to make. We've got to get the day off from work; then we've got to make travel plans; then we have to find someone to take care of the kids/cat/dog/whatever; then of course is the painful matter of finding suitable attire; last, but certainly not least, we have to arrange transportation, which is always a pain no matter how you go about it.

Doing all of that junk sent me off the deep-end. As for Dena, she told me that the happiest moment of her wedding was when it ended. I thought that was a pretty sad thing for her to be able to say—and even worse was that I agreed with her. If it hadn't been for all the hassles, we would've both enjoyed the wedding a whole lot more.

I think a time limit on a wedding's planning phase would be wonderful. It's a great idea, but while we're at it, lets cut back on those magazines too. Because frankly, they're ridiculous, and I miss the trees. Trees look nice at weddings you know.

Assessment Questions

1. Does this essay answer the first question in the writing topic?

2. Does this essay have a thesis that answers the second question?

3. Does this essay develop the thesis with supporting examples? Evaluate the effectiveness of these examples.

4. Are there significant errors in grammar that limit the essay's effectiveness? In other words, as you read the essay, did you notice several mistakes in the way the sentences are written?

5. Using the conventional standards presented in the scoring rubric in Part 1 of this book, what score does this essay deserve? Explain.

Case Study 2

Ian Frazier's "In Praise of Margins"

Read Frazier's "In Praise of Margins" again and then see how five college students answered the writing topic that follows it. Use the assessment questions that follow each one to help you identify the essay's strengths and weaknesses. Turn back to the scoring rubric in Part 1 and use it to give each essay a score.

In Praise of Margins

Essay

Ian Frazier

Ian Frazier is an American writer and humorist. He was born in 1951 and grew up in Hudson, Ohio. He attended Western Reserve Academy, and later Harvard University, where he was on the staff of The Harvard Lampoon. *After graduating, he worked as a magazine writer in Chicago, and then later moved to New York City, where he wrote for* The New Yorker. *He has written several books, including* Family *(1994) and* Gone to New York: Adventures in the City *(2005).*

As kids, my friends and I spent a lot of time out in the woods. "The woods" was our part-time address, destination, purpose, and excuse. If I went to a friend's house and found him not at home, his mother might say, "Oh, he's out in the woods," with a tone of airy acceptance. It's similar to the tone people sometimes use nowadays to tell me that someone I'm looking for is on the golf course or at the hairdresser's or at the gym, or even "away from his desk." The combination of vagueness and specificity in the answer gives a sense of somewhere romantically incommunicado. I once attended an awards dinner at which Frank Sinatra was supposed to appear, and when he didn't, the master of ceremonies explained that Frank had called to say he was "filming on location." Ten-year-olds suffer from a scarcity of fancy-sounding excuses to do whatever they feel like for a while. For us, saying we were "out in the woods" worked just fine.

We sometimes told ourselves that what we were doing in the woods was exploring. Exploring was a more prominent idea back then than it is today. History, for example, seemed to be mostly about explorers, and the semi rural part of Ohio where we lived still had a faint recollection of being part of the frontier. Our explorations, though, seemed to have less system than the historic kind: something usually came up along the way. Say we began to cross one of the little creeks plentiful in the second-growth forests we frequented and found that all the creek's moisture had somehow become a shell of milk-white ice about eight inches above the now-dry bed. No other kind of ice is as satisfying to break.

The search for the true meridian would be postponed while we spent the afternoon breaking the ice, stomping it underfoot by the furlong.

Stuff like that—throwing rocks at a fresh mudflat to make craters, shooting frogs with slingshots, making forts, picking blackberries, digging in what we were briefly persuaded was an Indian burial mound—occupied much of our time in the woods. Our purpose there was a higher sort of un-purpose, a free-form aimlessness that would be beyond me now. The woods were ideal for those trains of thought that involved tedium and brooding. Often when I went by myself I would climb a tree and just sit. I could list a hundred pointless things we did in the woods. Climbing trees, though, was a common one. There were four or five trees that we visited regularly—tall beeches, easy to climb and comfortable to sit in. We spent hours at a time in trees, afflicting the best perches with so many carved-in names, hearts, arrows, and funny sayings from the comic strips.

It was in a tree, too, that our days of fooling around in the woods came to an end. By then some of us had reached seventh grade and had begun the bumpy ride of adolescence. In March, the month when we usually took to the woods again after winter, two friends and I set out to go exploring. Right away, we climbed a tree, and soon were indulging in the spurious nostalgia of kids who have only short pasts to look back upon. The "remember whens" faltered, finally, and I think it occurred to all three of us at the same time that we really were rather big to be up in a tree. Some of us had started wearing unwoodsy outfits like short-sleeved madras shirts and penny loafers, even after school. Soon there would be the spring dances on Friday evenings in the high school cafeteria. We looked at the bare branches around us receding into obscurity, and suddenly there was nothing up there for us. Like Adam and Eve, we saw our own nakedness, and that terrible grown-up question "What are you doing?" made us ashamed.

We went back to the woods eventually—and when I say "we," I'm speaking demographically, not just of my friends and me. Millions of us went back, once the sexual and social business of early adulthood had been more or less sorted out. But significantly, we brought that same question with us. Now we had to be seriously doing—racing, strengthening, slimming, traversing, collecting, achieving.

"What are you doing?" The question pursues me still. When I go fishing and catch no fish, the idea that it's fun simply to be out on the river consoles me for not one second. I must catch fish; and if I do, I must then catch more and bigger fish. On a Sunday afternoon last summer I took my two young children fishing with me on a famous trout stream near my house. My son was four and my daughter was eight, and I kidded myself that in their company I would be able to fish with my usual single-minded mania. I suited up in my waders and gear and led my kids from the parking area down toward the water. On the way, however, we had to cross a narrow, shallow irrigation ditch dating from when this part of the valley had farms. Well, the kids saw that little ditch and immediately took off their shoes and waded in and splashed and floated pine cones. I didn't have the heart to drag the kids away, and as I was sitting in all my fishing gear beside that unlikely trickle, a fly fisherman about my age and just as geared-up came along. He took me in at a glance, noticed my equipment and my idleness, and gave a small but unmistakable snort of derision. I was offended, but I understood how he felt as he and his purpose hurried on by.

Here, I'd like to consider a word whose meaning has begun to drift like a caterpillar on a stream. That word is margin. Originally its meaning—the blank space around a body of type or the border of a piece of ground—had neutral connotations. But its adjective form, *marginal*, now has a negative tinge. Marginal people or places or activities are ones that don't quite work out, don't sufficiently account for themselves in the economic world. But especially as the world gets more jammed up, we need margins. A book without margins is impossible to read. And marginal behavior can be the most important kind. Every purpose-filled activity we pursue in the woods began as just fooling around. The first person to ride his bicycle down a mountain trail was doing a decidedly marginal thing. The margin is where you can try out odd ideas that you might be afraid to admit to with people looking on. Scientists have a term for research carried on with no immediate prospects of economic gain: "blue-sky research." Marginal places are the blue-sky research zones of the outdoors.

Writing Topic

According to Frazier, why are "marginal" places and activities valuable? What do you think of his views? To develop your position, be sure to discuss specific examples. Those examples can be drawn from anything you've read—including, if you choose, "In Praise of Margins" itself—as well as from your own observations and experiences.

Student Essay 1   C-

The essay "In Praise of Margins" by Ian Frazier talks about "marginal" spaces. For Frazier a "marginal" space is where you "try out odd ideas that you might be afraid to admit to with people looking on". He is trying to say that every human being needs a place to just escape, forget about the world and explore. Frazier thinks that we need more "marginal" spaces in our lives, whether we are kids or we are adults. He talks about his childhood and also his adulthood. When he was a kid he could go out to the woods and play. He tells us that he did things spontaneously. He did them without a purpose. However, when he got older, things change. He still went to the woods, but only to fish. Now he had a purpose. For Frazier a "marginal" space is not a profit. Is to explore, think, and play. Is to just have fun. Frazier is absolutely correct about "marginal" spaces or activities because a person who has their "marginal" space or activity is more likely to be a more happier, adventurous, and imaginative person.

When someone has their own "marginal" space it is wonderful for them. In their "marginal" space they could have fun and "tedium". For example, when I was young I had my "marginal" space. My marginal space was the backyard of my house. I used to play by myself with dolls. I felt more comfortable playing with my dolls by myself because I could talk to my dolls, and do things without being observed. I loved going there because it was a peaceful place to think and imagine. During that time I did not go to school. However, that was my dream. I remembered that I used to sit in a little chair and think. I used to imagine myself at school playing with more kids and learning new things. I went there without a purpose. I just wanted to play, explore, and imagine different things. I was a really happy girl. I was never sad. My childhood was very fun and interesting. I think that if I would of not have my "marginal" space, I would of been a very sad little girl. When I was young I had no sisters and no brothers until three years after. I think that if I would of not had my "marginal" space my childhood would have been terrible, especially because I had no brothers or sisters to play with. Therefore, "marginal" spaces make a person happier and imaginative. If Frazier knew about my "marginal" space he will be very happy because that place was for me to escape the world and have fun.

"Marginal" activities also help people be more happy, imaginative and adventurous. Whatever kind of activities could make a person feel happy, and make them forget about the world. My mom's happiness was hanging from mango trees, overthere in her town. She lived surrounded with mango trees. She liked hanging from the branches of the trees and swinging from one to another. When she did her "marginal" activity she did not heard her brothers and sisters yelling and fighting. She had always been annoyed from too much noise. However, when she hanged from the trees she forgot about her surroundings. She just imagine she was in the jungle and she was a monkey. For her that was an adventure in the jungle. My mom was happy, always laughing. She always had a smile on her face. She enjoyed her "marginal" activity. "Marginal" activities also work to be a more happier, imaginative, and adventurous because my mom was with her "marginal" activity.

"Marginal" spaces or activities are for everyone, not only for certain people. Children or adults could have their own "marginal" space or acitivity. In the essay

"Hitting Pay Dirt" by Annie Dillard we learned about the "marginal" space and activity a boy/girl had. This child loved being at his/her house basement playing with his being at his/her house basement playing with his/her microscope. He/she used to prepare slides from things that were at hand. Some things that he/she explored was the membrane of the onion's skin, his/her scrapings from her cheek, his/her blood, and ever his/her urine. He/she just had fun exploring and learning new things. The basement was his/her "marginal" space and looking at the different things in his/her microscope was his/her "marginal" activity. He/she did everything without a purpose. He/she just wanted to have fun and explore. However, in "The Dance Within My Heart" by Pat Mora we see the "marginal" space of a women. The museum was her "marginal space". It was her pleausure heavens. For her going from room to room, up and down the stairs was her passion. She liked to explore everything those rooms had. She wander thru the rooms without a purpose. She just wanted to explore and learn new things from the museaum. From this two essays we could see that "marginal" spaces or activities exist for children's and adults. This child and this women had fun being in their "marginal" space. They were really happy with their "marginal" space. Frazier will definetely agree with this two persons having their "marginal" space or activity because they explore and forget about the world.

When someone has their own "marginal" space or activity they are more happier and aimaginative. Like Frazier said it also helps them forget about the world while being at your "marginal" space or doing your "marginal" activity. I hardly recommend persons who are stressed out or have problems to just get their own "marginal" space or activity to get rid off those feelings or things. I am totally sure this will help. I am sure because of my mom telling me about her problem having at home with her siblings. While she did her "marginal" activity she forgot. Everyone follow my advise. Always have in mind Frazier's words, that "marginal" space helps escape from the world and explore.

Assessment Questions

1. Does this essay answer the first question in the writing topic?

2. Does this essay have a thesis that answers the second question?

3. Does this essay develop the thesis with supporting examples? Evaluate the effectiveness of these examples.

4. Are there significant errors in grammar that limit the essay's effectiveness? In other words, as you read the essay, did you notice several mistakes in the way the sentences are written?

5. Using the conventional standards presented in the scoring rubric in Part 1 of this book, what score does this essay deserve? Explain.

Student Essay 2   D/F

In the essay "In Praise of Margins" by Ian Frazier, the author discusses of "Marginal" activities and places. The author believes that the values of "Marginal" activities and places are an asylum where we are not judged by looks of others and actions that are not taken under the consideration of economical gain or loss. The author believes that people should not focus so much on an individual's gain or loss of performing a task, but instead we should enjoy of performing or taking actions of what we do or what we are supposed to do. Also, the author believes that it is just as important to create or live in such places where our "marginal" activities would not be viewed inappropriate to the others.

I agree with Frazier's beliefs of "Marginal activities and places" and believe his ideas should be well supported by the others.

All actions we perform or take in our life are followed by consequences. Some could be good, some could be bad, some could be lucrative or some could be marginal. Regardless of all the choices we have, it is inevitable for us human beings to try achieve the positive results or consequences all the time. But may be we should take a little break from pursuing or focus only on achieving positive results but think about what it is that makes us doing such thing, because trying to achieve best results does not always give us the happy ending. For an example, I had a friend who had ill grandmother. She had multiple heart problem which made her hard to live on her daily life therefore needed a heart surgery from hospital. But it was not easy to get surgery from couple hospitals that she went to, because her health condition was critical and there was a good chance of her not making through her surgery which could lower surgent doctor's medical career. Fortunately, she found a doctor who was willing to do what x doctors are supposed to do and she made it through the surgery as well. Short after she was recovered, she had reported other doctors who'd rejected her and those doctors received probations from the National Doctors" Association along with humiliating reports from the media. In the end, not only they got probation, but it left big flaw on their doctors" record as well. Had they thought more "marginally" like Frazier had stated in his essay they would not have gotten into such a serious consequences.

Ian Frazier discusses of "marginal" places in his essay. But unfortunately we are living in a world where it is to very competitive. It is now hard to live that it was couple decades ago and people's beliefs or opinion of how to live this world has been changing, We began to judge others by what they have, what they can do that make us gain or profit something at the end. By these restrictions, we are not being able to act freely as we are willing to but instead we act based on how other will view us. When a person observes other doing something that is not marginal or can not earn no gain at the end, we usually think of that person dumb, poor, unable or so on. For an example, Frazier had explained his story in essay "In Praise of Margins", about a fishing trip that he went to with is children. He had mistakenly thought that he will be able to fish with his children just as same as without them, he soon found of himself sitting on a rack watching his kids playing in a ditch when he should be fishing. Just as he watches his kids playing, another fisherman just like himself passes by and snorts at him which had offended him as if he was doing something wrong. To Frazier, he was just enjoying his time sitting down on a rock and watch his kids play but to the other fisherman it looked bad because Frazier should be fishing instead of watching his kids. To the fisherman, Frazier is not gaining anything by fishing, but just wasting his time. But to Frazier, he was just enjoying his time just as much as him fishing. How rude it would be to offend someone like that due to different beliefs toward our life? Therefore we should start to change the way we live or think of how our life should be spent or performed and make the world to be more "marginal" place to live. Because in "marginal" place, we are not focused or pressured to live profitable life, but live as freely and happily by doing what we love, enjoy to do.

In conclusion, it will not be easy to creating such places or acting, perform such ways with knowing how the consequences may harm us. But we can no always avoid what is always harmful to us or live in a world where we have to gains in order to be acknowledged by the others. If we have to face consequences, so it be. It will only make us more brave and smart.

Assessment Questions

1. Does this essay answer the first question in the essay topic?

2. Does this essay have a thesis that answers the second question?

3. Does this essay develop the thesis with supporting examples? Evaluate the effectiveness of these examples.

4. Are there significant errors in grammar that limit the essay's effectiveness? In other words, as you read the essay, did you notice several mistakes in the way the sentences are written?

5. Using the conventional standards presented in the scoring rubric in Part 1 of this book, what score does this essay deserve? Explain.

Student Essay 3 C+

In the essay "In Praise of Margins" by Ian Frazier, Frazier says that "as the world gets more jammed up, we need margins." In this essay Frazier talks about the importance of having a marginal space, and also the values of those marginal spaces to us. According to Frazier, when he was young he used to go to the woods with his friends because that was his marginal space. He went there without having a cause or a purpose. He just wanted to play and do childish things like breaking the ice. Frazier says that "our purpose there was a higher sort of un-purpose, a free-form aimlessness that would be beyond me now." That means that Frazier didn't have a purpose to go to the woods, but as he grew older he forgot how to do things without a purpose anymore. Then one day when Frazier took his kids into the woods to fish and saw them playing in a ditch of water and floating pine cones, the importance of having marginal space occurred to him. Frazier realized the value of marginal places and that their importance in a person's life. In the essay, Frazier makes powerful points about marginal values, marginal spaces and their importance in our everyday lives. Marginal places don't have to be in the woods. They can be whatever we choose as long as we feel happy, free, and relaxed being there. It's true that marginal places help us escape from our daily routine and find new, enjoyable experiences.

According to Frazier there are many values attached to marginal places and activities. One of those values is that marginal places help us enjoy life better. Marginal places help us escape from our daily routine by just going to a place where we can clear our minds and not worry about tomorrow or the day before or after that. That is, one of the biggest values in the world is just being able to enjoy ourselves and have alone time with ourselves to release our stress and become like children again. For example, my parents had a marginal place when they were young. Their marginal place was to go to the mountains and hike and play up there, but when they came to United States and worked every day they missed the old days of getting away to the mountains. So they decided to buy a big house in the mountains and let their house be their everyday marginal place. All my brothers and I live there with them and we all see how our parents are always happy and not stressed out as they used to be when we first came to this country. My parents still work hard but when they come home to their house in the mountains they can forget about having to work so hard and they can relax and do what they like to do. This proves that Frazier is right and that having a marginal place is important to all of us because it can help us enjoy life again and appreciate it more as we all grow older everyday.

Another big value of marginal places and activities is that time spent in doing marginal activities makes us better able to do our jobs when we go to work. The daily routine of work makes people stress and hate their jobs, and they think of life in a negative way. Having a marginal place can help us take time for our selves and away from the working world. Most business owners give their employees days off because they want their employees to perform their best in their jobs. For example, my dad owns a company in real estate, and a lot of the people that work there are happy and enjoy their jobs. The pay is just like any other real estate offices, except my dad gives them at least one day off a week and he organizes activities on holidays so that the workers will relax and enjoy themselves. He believes that they will be happier and better employees if they take some time for themselves instead of working every minute of every day like many real estate salespeople seem to do. Just like Frazier said, marginal activities can be the most important kind because having a marginal place can help us be happier people and enjoy our jobs and perform the best in our jobs.

Marginal places don't have to be in the woods. For example, Frazier's marginal place was the woods because that was where he liked to go in his free time and it was the only place for him to escape from the real world. We might find marginal space in different places and in different ways. In the essay "The Dance Within My Heart" by Pat Mora her marginal place was the museum. That was her marginal place, because she enjoyed learning about other people and cultures. Going to a museum made her relax and explore new experiences and ideas and this brought fun into her life. So a marginal place can be wherever you want it to be as long as you feel happy and relaxed being there.

Many people might think that we are too old to have a marginal place, but that is not true. Even if we might think we're too old to have a marginal place, a part of our body is always demanding it. Frazier said that one day his friends and he realized that they are too old to be out in the woods in a tree house, but then when he saw his children playing in the ditch he realized that kind of freedom and fun was missing in his and others life and that it is important no matter what our age. Even retired people need to find time to do things for themselves, things that have no particular purpose but are just for them to enjoy themselves and relax.

In conclusion, we are never too old or too young to have a marginal place. Just like Marie Winn said in her essay "The End of Play," "children's occupations don't differ greatly from adult diversions." That means that we are all maturing too early and that children now want to be older and act older then their age and that we all forget the importance of the values of the marginal places and activities and the good things we can gain out of them.

Assessment Questions

1. Does this essay answer the first question in the writing topic?

2. Does this essay have a thesis that answers the second question?

3. Does this essay develop the thesis with supporting examples? Evaluate the effectiveness of these examples.

4. Are there significant errors in grammar that limit the essay's effectiveness? In other words, as you read the essay, did you notice several mistakes in the way the sentences are written?

5. Using the conventional standards presented in the scoring rubric in Part 1 of this book, what score does this essay deserve? Explain.

Student Essay 4   B

In the passage "In Praise of Margins," Ian Frazier explains what marginal places and activities are. Frazier believes that "the margin is where you can try out odd ideas that you might be afraid to admit to with people looking on." He thinks that people need margins because life can be very stressful and we all need to find marginal space and time where we can do whatever purposeless activities we enjoy doing. When he was a kid, Frazier found his marginal place and activity when he was in the woods exploring nature and playing imaginary games with his friends. He was able to explore and think freely when he was in the woods. Marginal places do not help us economically but personally. He is correct because "marginal" places and activities allow us to get away from the stressful routines of everyday life and experience new things freely and without set goals.

As children, most of us had a place where we liked to go play and be alone sometimes. These places and the activities we did there helped us explore the world by pretending or daydreaming. Frazier and his friends went to the woods to get away and explore whatever came across their path, or sometimes climb a tree and just sit and think. When I was kid I had a couple of marginal places where I could play, pretend, and be alone. My marginal places were the front yard, the back yard, the living room and the family room. No one would disturb me when I was in my marginal places and I was able to pretend to be whatever I wanted. I was a teacher, a cashier, a cook, etc. I didn't have to worry about being embarrassed. I could pretend and imagine what my life might be like in the future. These marginal experiences helped me to explore new ideas and imagine what new experiences would be like.

Marginal places and activities can be relaxing and good for the health, according to the passage "Everyday Playtime for Adults" written by Dulce Zamora. In Zamora's article, she explains how marginal places and activities can relieve stress. Everyday life can sometimes be busy and people forget to make time for themselves. Zamora points out the importance of having free time, time to engage in activities that are fun and satisfying. Zamora tell how experts agree that the best marginal activities are usually simple ones that we freely choose to do because they are fun. A healthy marginal activity can be as simple as talking on a phone to a close friend, doing crosswords, hugging someone, walking, or riding a bike. Zamora states that failing to loosen up and have fun can result in poor health and even sickness. Recent breast cancer patients have talked about their hectic lifestyles prior to being diagnosed with cancer. A person can be happier and healthier if he/she sometimes does things not out of a sense of duty but out of a real desire to do them because they are enjoyable. Zamora's article presents evidence to show that marginal activities are more than just important, as Frazier claims; they are vital to good health and happiness.

Everyone can find good marginal activities. It isn't necessary to go to the woods to find enjoyment and relaxation, all though that is one way to find these things. For instance, take my dad. He is a machinist and he works 40+ hours a week. His job can be very tiring. No matter how tiring his job is or how busy he is he always makes time to fix cars. Fixing cars is his marginal activity. My dad enjoys fixing and working on cars on the weekend. He doesn't see it as a job but as a happy enjoyment. My mom is another example because she loves to cook and her kitchen is her "marginal place." My mom spends a great amount of time in the kitchen. She doesn't work so she has a great amount of time on her hands and she likes to spend it in the kitchen. Being in the kitchen allows her to get away from the cleaning and errands that she has to do every day and focus instead on cooking something just for the enjoyment of it. Marginal places and activities make a person's life less stressful and better for the person's health.

Marginal activities aren't done for a practical purpose, but they can sometime serve an unexpected purpose and be educational. According to the article "Hitting Play Dirt," by Annie Dillard, her marginal activity was an educational one. Dillard always wanted a microscope kit when she was little. One Christmas her parents got her the microscope kit. Every night after dinner she would spend her time in the basement playing with her microscope kit. Her basement was her marginal place where she could be alone and play with her microscope kit. She was able to learn a lot from what the microscope kit had to offer. Dillard marginal place and activity is different from Frazier's because she learned about science from playing with her microscope whereas Frazier would just go out to the woods and find whatever crossed his path. My brother's marginal activity has the same kind of educational aspect. He has recently graduated from college as a mechanical engineer and while he was in school he loved everything about his major. He also enjoyed using what he learned to build automobiles for different competitions. In a way, school was his marginal place where he was able to forget about everything and just focus on mechanical engineering. Therefore, a marginal place or activity can sometimes be educational, as long as the person does the activity for enjoyment rather than out of duty or to pursue a practical goal.

In conclusion, a marginal place or activity should be relaxing, enjoying, and a getaway from everyday tasks. Everyone has a unique marginal place or activity that they enjoy doing just for fun and that can give them relief from stress. As Frazier says, marginal places and activities definitely have a positive affect on our lives.

Assessment Questions

1. Does this essay answer the first question in the writing topic?

2. Does this essay have a thesis that answers the second question?

3. Does this essay develop the thesis with supporting examples? Evaluate the effectiveness of these examples.

4. Are there significant errors in grammar that limit the essay's effectiveness? In other words, as you read the essay, did you notice several mistakes in the way the sentences are written?

5. Using the conventional standards presented in the scoring rubric in Part 1 of this book, what score does this essay deserve? Explain.

Student Essay 5

In the essay of "In Praise of Margins," the author Ian Frazier explains and describes about his marginal space. His marginal space was "The Woods." He spent any times in trees when he climbed a tree. He could think about anything quietly and spend time by himself in his marginal space. At the end of the essay, he writes what is the margin, which is "the blank space around a body of type or the border of a piece of ground." Frazier thinks, if there is no margin, people would not be able to do their work perfectly. He give examples those are a book without margins is hard to read and "marginal behavior can be the most important kind." Therefore, we need margins. Although marginal has a negative tinge in the economic world, people are not able to do quite work without margins. Also margins can give people rest time from the their stresses.

In the world, most people need margins to do their work. People may think that, margins are just blank space and they do not care of margins. However, they can not do quite work without margins. For simple example, people work from the morning to evening in their company. However, if there is not break time while they are working, how do they feel? They will be really tired and get a lot of stresses of their works. People would think, break time is just little party in a day. However, break time, marginal time, is needed to every people to do their work well. Marginal time can give people to relax their works and thoughts. Also in the school, students are taking class and they have break time between classes. It is marginal time to students. Some people ignore the marginal time but it is important to people to have their time.

Marginal space can be my best friend and my best place. Back of my house, there is a garage. My family use it just for stuff storage. Although my family think it is just garage, I do not think like that. It is my best place and it can be my best friend. I decorated garage to my place. I put the title, "Ina's place" in front of garage. Also I put the little sofa and table. When I get stresses from school, family or friends, I go to my place where is only for me. I sit on the sofa and I thinks. I spend hours at a time if I go to my space. I feel really confortable when I am there. My friends and my family may think I look like crazy and strange. But I really like to go to my space.

Assessment Questions

1. Does this essay answer the first question in the essay topic?

2. Does this essay have a thesis that answers the second question?

3. Does this essay develop the thesis with supporting examples? Evaluate the effectiveness of these examples.

4. Are there significant errors in grammar that limit the essay's effectiveness? In other words, as you read the essay, did you notice several mistakes in the way the sentences are written?

5. Using the conventional standards presented in the scoring rubric in Part 1 of this book, what score does this essay deserve? Explain.

Case Study 3

David Denby's "Buried Alive: Our Children and the Avalanche of Crud"

In this case study, you will have the opportunity to read and evaluate four students' essays written in response to the reading selection in Assignment 2 of this book, David Denby's "Buried Alive: Our Children and the Avalanche of Crud." Read Denby's essay, the writing topic that follows it, and the four essays that respond to Denby's argument. Examine each essay for its strengths and weaknesses. A set of assessment questions at the end of each will help you evaluate its success. Then, use the scoring rubric in Part 1 to give each essay a score.

Buried Alive: Our Children and the Avalanche of Crud

DAVID DENBY

David Denby is an American journalist and a film critic for The New Yorker *magazine. He has a B.A. and a Master's degree in journalism from Columbia University. His book* Great Books: My Adventures with Homer, Rousseau, Woolf, and Other Indestructible Writers of the Western World *(1996) is an important study of canonical literature at American universities and was a* New York Times *bestseller. His memoir* American Sucker *(2004) details his investment misadventures in the dot-com stock market bubble, and his latest book,* Snark, *is a polemical dissection of public speech. The following essay is adapted from an essay published in* The New Yorker *(1996).*

To my surprise, I find myself welcoming, or at least not opposing, the advent of the V-chip—the little device that is to be installed in new television sets sold from 1998 on and that will allow parents to block out programs they don't want their children to see. Many parents I know have similar feelings, and quite a few are surprised by the depths of their ambivalence about the way pop culture in all its forms has invaded their homes, and the habits, manners, and souls of their children. My friends are drawn from a small circle of well-educated New Yorkers; we are a fairly compact and no doubt privileged group. Yet our anguish about bringing up children is, I believe, widely shared by parents of all kinds. *Married ... with Children* and the computer game *Doom* are the same in Montana and in Manhattan.

Even parents who enjoy their share of pop are feeling wary and sore, as if someone has made fools of them. And a few parents I know have given themselves over to bitter rage and are locked in an unwinnable struggle to shut out pop culture and the life of the streets—the two are now indistinguishable—from their children's experience.

Someone is bound to say, "It was ever thus," meaning that, as far as their elders are concerned, every generation of children is immersed in something that's no good for them. New York kids in the eighteen-sixties grew up in a rough city with gangs, street violence, and prostitutes, and most of them were no doubt familiar with such raucous and unenlightening entertainments as cockfighting and bare-knuckle boxing. It as ever thus. Someone is bound to say, "after all, many of us watched a good bit of TV as children, yet we wound up O.K., didn't we? What has changed?

It was not ever thus. Our reality has changed. The media have become three dimensional, inescapable, omnivorous, and self-referring—a closed system that seems, for many of the kids, to answer all the questions. The older children teach the younger ones the games and movie references, so they have something to talk about when they're alone. I've just run into a three-year-old girl who knew the names of the characters in *The Hunchback of Notre Dame* before the movie opened. Disney has already claimed her. Pop has also absorbed the edgy, in-your-face tone that teenagers adopt as the sound of independence. That jeering tone has spread like a rash through the whole culture. "It's awesome." "It sucks."

Some sort of commercialized aggression is always putting parents on the defensive—Jim Carrey with ketchup coming out of his ears in movie after movie, or Sylvester Stallone machine-gunning the population of Cleveland, or video arcades with so many shooting games that the noise level exceeds that of the Battle of the Somme. *Beavis and Butthead* is a clever show—it mocks the cruddy teen culture even as it sells it to teens. The show brilliantly sends itself up. Still, it's hard to take. Hip parents may appreciate the wryness of B. & B.'s self-extinction, but it's dismaying that everything on teen TV—even irony—is a commodity.

The kids in the dating-game programs treat each other as commodities, the girls swinging their shoulders and smiling as they show themselves off, the audience whooping as the boys pull off their shirts and reveal their pecs and tattoos. Hardly the end of Western civilization, I admit, but the way the shows force teens to stereotype one another is awful. Children don't understand vulgarity as a concept, and the makers of commercial culture would be happy if they never understood it. Parents have to teach them what vulgarity is somehow. When I have the energy, I argue, I satirize, I get the boys to agree that the shows are stupid. Yet I don't turn off the set, because doing that would only cause them to turn it back on when I'm not there. I want them to turn it off.

Whether the sets are off or on, the cruddy tone is in the air and on the streets. The kids pick it up and repeat it, and every week there are moments when I feel a spasm of fury that surges back and forth between resentment and self-contempt. In those moments, I don't like the way my boys talk—I don't like the way they think. The crude, bottom-line attitudes they've picked up, the nutty obsessive profanity, the echo chamber of voices and attitudes, set my teeth on edge. What American parent hasn't felt that spasm? Your kid is rude and surly, sees everything in terms of winning or losing or popularity, becomes insanely interested in clothes, and seems far, far from courage and selfhood.

Aided by armies of psychologists and market researchers, the culture industries reach my children at every stage of their desires and their inevitable discontent. What's lost is the old dream that parents and teachers will nurture the organic development of the child's own interests, the child's own nature. That dream is largely dead. In this country, people possessed solely by the desire to sell have become far more powerful than parents tortuously working out the contradictions of authority, freedom, education, and soul-making.

Writing Topic

What does Denby think is distinctive and damaging about the way popular culture influences children in the United States today? Do you agree with his view? Be sure to discuss specific examples to support your position; these examples may be taken from your own experiences or observations, or from any of your reading, including the course material we have read and discussed in class.

Student Essay 1

An Ongoing War

In David Denby's "Buried Alive: Our Children and the Avalanche of Crud," Denby feels that pop culture is distinctive and damaging through media. According to Denby, television is a commodity, meaning that it is shown so much on television that it heavily influences children, or teens, to do things based on what they receive from pop culture. Pop culture through media is so big that even people who do not watch television are eventually influenced by it. It's so big on the streets that media has "become three dimensional" according to Denby and aside from possible beneficial shows for children and teens, I agree with Denby that media, because of pop culture, is distinctive and damaging.

First of all, pop culture is very distinctive because unlike other things, media is everywhere. Media is so common in life that Denby says, "Media have become three dimensional, inescapable, omnivorous, and self-referring." It is said to be because teens act according to what they see from media. Even though there are those who do not watch television, some of their friends might already be under the influence of pop culture and eventually, he or she will pick it up from them. For example, even though Sarah does not watch a lot of television, Sarah's friend can easily influence Sarah herself. Because Sarah and her friend are best friends, Sarah will eventually pick it up from her because they hang out a lot. Thus, media is: three dimensional because it becomes alive once it is part of a person, second, inescapable because either you indulge it or you will eventually get caught up with it from your peers, and lastly omnivorous and self-referring because media will consume you and when you become a part of it, you will start referencing from media. Second, media is damaging because there are shows, such as the dating-game program that Denby mentioned, that corrupts teens' way of life. In these dating-game programs, they inspire stereotypes among teens. Denby states, "The girls swinging their shoulders and smiling as they show themselves off, the audience whooping as the boys pull off their shirts and reveal their pecs and tattoos." Teens would (will) adopt this vulgarity from these media and hence, become vulgarity themselves. They will feel like it is the normal to dress a certain way because they are men or women. "Children don't understand vulgarity as a concept, and the makers of commercial culture would be happy if they never understood it." This line, also from Denby's, tells us that along with vulgarity, these people presenting the media do not care for society and the teens, but to make profit. As a product, pop culture through media is corrupting teens because they tend to believe what they see and hear are true.

The only way teens and children can understand pop culture and not be indulged by it, other than the help of their parents, is when they mature and understand that it's only pop culture because they should behave the way they want to behave rather than what is presented to them on television. Parents used to be "primary story-tellers, offering their children their own versions of the world." This quote by Michael Warren from his "Storytellers Shape Spiritual Values," tells us that it used to be parents who taught children the right way, but in today's society, according to Warren, it is now "passed into the hands of those who do not know the child personally and may have at heart interest other than the enrichment of that child's inner life." It has left from the parent's hand to the ones of media. The media does not care for the child and they do what is profitable, which is to sell and advertise pop culture. Since pop culture is a big hit to children and teens, profits are huge and if profits are huge, why would the media stop such an act? Consequently, this vast advertising will reach the children and teens one way another in a way that parents cannot steer them back to what is right, unless—of course—that the parents teach them early on. This theme of pop culture through media is "shaping" children's life is rather common.

When I look back to when I was younger, it seems to make sense after reading Denby and Warren's essay. I once was under the same influence of pop culture. At the time, I thought wearing baggy jeans and a white tee would make me feel "cool." All the ideal guys were doing it and on television, all the cool and popular boys wore that attire, and just to add it on, they did their hair in a "slick fashion." Eventually, I grew out of it, of course, because I stopped watching television and started to not care what the common fashion was. I wore what I felt was comfortable and not care for the slightest bit on how I looked to other people. Now that I grew out of it, I feel like I'm one of those parents that Denby mentioned because I am ambivalent about it. Maturity is all it takes to understand what you are doing rather than just copying `pop culture' and become part of it. It felt like if people who don't understand pop culture will get consumed by it and as a product, they will become a part of pop culture.

When Denby was showing examples with the dating-game program, he was trying to show how destructive and damaging pop culture is through media. He also shows how distinctive it can be by showing how big media is. Along with Denby, Warren shows us that "storyteller" is the primary way a children will learn what is right. Media in today's society is so influential that pop culture can spread with or without watching television. It goes around influence one person at a time to the next. Like David Denby, I agree with him that media is distinctive and damaging to children and teen.

Assessment Questions

1. Does this essay answer the first question in the writing topic?

2. Does this essay have a thesis that answers the second question?

3. Does this essay develop the thesis with supporting examples? Evaluate the effectiveness of these examples.

4. Are there significant errors in grammar that limit the essay's effectiveness? In other words, as you read the essay, did you notice several mistakes in the way the sentences are written?

5. Using the conventional standards presented in the scoring rubric in Part 1 of this book, what score does this essay deserve? Explain.

Student Essay 2

Negative Culture

Many people are immersed in popular culture through the mens of movies, television shows, music, and any other media in modern day society. As a result, parents worry that popular culture negatively influences their children tremendously. In David Denby's essay, "Buried Alive: Our Children and the Avalanche of Crud," Denby illustrates how the influence of popular culture is actually damaging, but unique, on children in today's society through many examples he has witnessed, this confirming parents' fear. He believes that popular culture is damaging as well as distinctive because it changes children; especially in terms of their attitudes. Popular culture has deterimental effects on children through the instances stated in Denby's essay, along with examples from the real world.

Music is a believed to be form of popular culture that people cannot live without, including kids and adolescents. Why is it that today every song that comes on the radio has to do with partying, sex, or drinking? Denby states in his essay that "the jeering tone [of music] has spread like a rash through the whole culture." Obviously a rash is a sign of something virulent and if it is spreading through the whole culture, everyone must therefore become aware of it and absorbed by it. Denby uses this simile to show what pop culture is doing in order to show its impact on children. Today's singers have lyrics like " before I leave, brush my teeth, with a bottle of jack" or "let's have a toast for the douche bags" or even "your sex is on fire." These songs are usually written because the singers have experiences they want everyone to know about. However, teens who listen to these songs are going to use the words they hear or try some of the stuff stated in the songs which is not the right thing for them to do. The singers need to realize this.

Parents are not going to be able to deal with their twelve year old daughter when she comes home and tells them she wants a bottle of jack to brush her teeth with or wants to have "hot" sex. This type of music is distinctive to today's culture because radio stations don't have strict limits about songs they play and the type of people listening to them, with most listeners being teenagers. All these songs will be songs teens will never be able to forget. The "in your face… sound[s] of independence" Denby states in his essay is what teenagers will adapt.

Television dating shows are a typical example of harmful popular culture. Denby states "the people in dating-game programs treat each other as commodities…" in his essay. Parents can agree that they wouldn't want to see their son come in and rip his shirt off and have drawn on tattoos and abs on his chest because as he saw the girl rip it off the guy on *The Bachelorette*. It's damaging for a parent to see their child do it when they are only 10 years old. The children should be taught that other people are not someone else's commodity.

Children have the naive tendency to mimic anything they see. Stereotyping occurs in every dating show, however children don't need to be stereotyping other people they may see. Usually when I go to the beach in the summer, there are the girls whose bodytypes do not fit the standards of what guys want, and then there are the guys who do not fit the standards of the girls. Many times when I go with my friends, they are always saying that 'this girl wants to get all the guys simply because of her bathing suit' or 'this girl is anorexic.' They stereotype them based on what they deduct from their outward appearances. Denby denounces this behavior and I agree because it's not something young adults should be doing. Nevertheless, it's distinctive in today's culture because kids are growing up around everyone stereotyping and judging every other person as a result of the media. Like Denby stated, the children need to understand that it is bad and learn that it isn't something they should do on their own and not by having someone repeatedly tell them its bad. These dating shows are damaging to the youth but it's further damaging when the kid doesn't understand it's bad.

Why is it that all shows on television have to be about pretty people? And the richest? Laguna Beach, Newport Harbor, 90210, and others all have the "hot" and "filthy rich" types of people portrayed in them. Children usually want to emulate these types of people they see in these shows. It is not healthy for kids to try to act like someone they are not at such young ages. "Culture industries reach my children at every stage of their desires and their inevitable discontent," Denby states. According to him, children are affected by the cultural industries, in this sense, the television shows they watch. The point is not to have the children be reached in a bad intent, but in a good kind. Its best to have a diverse selection of people in the television shows and to have them not be about being the wealthiest and attractive.

It is apparent that today's children would dream of looking good or asking to have the newest Blackberry smartphone because they saw a person have it on a television show. Instead, they should be saying they are happy with the way they are and with what they have. Denby would agree with this point because he states that he doesn't like the way his boys talk and pick everything up. He argues, all the kids are interested in the clothing, or possessions that the "desirable" people have.

Popular culture has the most influence on children's attitudes. Parents usually want their child's attitude to be positive and un-problematic, however, since today's popular culture only deals with spoiled teens who have horrible attitudes and children usually watch the shows, they will inevitably absorb everything they see and repeat it. The attitudes and "obsessive profanity," Denby states, set him into fury. If Denby is furious about this, many parents must feel this way also. Most children don't have attitudes from the get-go but develop these traits as a result of the media, and that's why the popular culture is distinctive, it creates the attitudes children have.

The statement children "… [see] everything in terms of winning or losing popularity, [become]insanely interested in clothes…" shows what attitude does to them. Today's generation of children are so intrigued by their social status and the way people portray them that they don't care about the way they act. They will behave the same way all the time because they understand it gets them noticed by people, and has become really prominent in middle schools and high schools. There are always the "popular" kids who want everyone to be like them and do everything that they do. I have seen this on a personal account when I was still in middle school. It is really damaging because, like Denby says, it is rude to everyone around them and the children will become selfish.

Pop culture is really distinctive and damaging to today's generation of children and adolescents. It is generally focused on having the best of everything because everyone on television has it or attitudes that children have. The popular culture's influence on children is negative. All the media being put out today have some influence on the young. David Denby, the author of the essay "Buried Alive: Our Children and the Avalanche of Crud" agrees that popular culture has a negative influence on children. Why can't popular culture be a little more un-bias and not make children want to change?

Assessment Questions

1   Does this essay answer the first question in the writing topic?

2. Does this essay have a thesis that answers the second question?

3. Does this essay develop the thesis with supporting examples? Evaluate the effectiveness of these examples.

4. Are there significant errors in grammar that limit the essay's effectiveness? In other words, as you read the essay, did you notice several mistakes in the way the sentences are written?

5. Using the conventional standards presented in the scoring rubric in Part 1 of this book, what score does this essay deserve? Explain.

Student Essay 3

Pop Culture as Corruption

"Pop culture in all its forms has invaded their homes, and habits, manners, and souls of their children." In "Buried Alive: Our Children and the Avalanche of Crud" David Denby states that pop culture is damaging and inescapable to children and is changing their attitudes. Pop culture consists of media such as television shows, movies, and music, almost everything that is in the form of entertainment. Children are surrounded by the media everywhere they go, it is what they do and see. Children are like sponges, they absorb everything, in this case what they watch and hear. In "Buried Alive: Our Children and the Avalanche of Crud" by David Denby, pop culture harmfully affects children's attitudes by displaying rude behavior through television shows. I agree with the author's point of view that pop culture is negatively affecting children.

Media portrays many negative concepts to children which they grasp and repeat. Television shows are everywhere and most children spend their time watching them. What they probably do not notice is all the "bottom-line attitudes they've picked up" or "the nutty obsessive profanity" they're listening to. This is what Denby is worried about. The media is everywhere, it is "inescapable" and it truly is harming the way children are acting. They watch television shows with their favorite reality stars and they look at the way they are acting and talking and hold on to what they see and mimic it. Today, there are shows with constant use of profanity. This bad language takes a toll on children who may not be as familiar with it and who may think it is cool, therefore, repeating it. Aside from profanity, there are icons that display bad attitudes. They act rude toward someone or something and come off as being aggressive to others, but to their young watchers they are only drawn by it. These damaging behaviors portrayed by media are harming children and their way of acting.

Reality shows today are very popular, but they also undesirably influence children's attitudes. One reality show that many people watch is *Jersey Shore*, it is everywhere. Yes, this show may be interesting to watch, but what draws a lot of watchers is how violent the cast is and the obsessive profanity they use. The cast members are constantly cursing at each other and fighting in clubs with strangers. The only things they do all day is cause trouble and swear like if it is part of everyone's daily language. All these attitudes they show are harmful to children viewers, they are sending out the wrong way to behave with each other. "Whether the sets are off or on, the cruddy tone is in the air and on the streets." Even when kids are not watching the show they are talking about it with their friends, and they are talking about how "Jwow" and "Sammie", two rivals in the show, got into a fight. They admire this kind of behavior. This is a problem. Children then think that it is okay to be violent and use bad words in their daily lives. Denby is worried that the way people are acting in media is harming children's minds and actions, and the worst part is that there is no way to escape it.

Many celebrities in pop culture have their own television shows and display harming attitudes. One example would be Kim Kardashian who comes out in *Keeping up with the Kardashians*. Kim is famous and idolized by many. She does have a downfall though, her attitude. In the reality show if she does not get things done her way she acts impolite, which many children are watching. She has even used profanity toward her own mother. Does this mean that children can refer to their parents with bad language? Well they are watching the way she acts and since they may look up to her they might think that it is okay to act the way she does. This foul attitude is harming children and their ways of acting toward friends and even family. Denby states, "I don't like the way my boys talk—I don't like the way they think." Children are drawn by the way she acts and therefore grasp it and display it in their actions. Their minds are being corrupted by ill-mannered celebrities on television today.

There are also television shows which display overall bad concepts. Take for example the show *My Super Sweet Sixteen*. This show is based on girls who are turning 16 and just have to have the best party in their whole city. If the girls do not get what they want they throw tantrums and whine until it is done their way. This show has it all, rude behaviors, profanity, bad attitudes; you name it this show has it. Young girls love watching this show because they feel they can relate to it, but all they are watching are examples of the ways they should not act. "Your kid is rude and surly, sees everything in terms of winning or losing popularity, becomes insanely interested in clothes, and seems far, far from courage and selfhood." Denby in this quote stresses how children today just want to be better in everything they do, and they do it through displaying "rude" behaviors. The girls in *My Super Sweet Sixteen* want the newest car, the biggest party, the prettiest dress, anything that will out do any party their friends had. They are spoiled misbehaved girls who are expressing a bad message to young viewers everywhere. Parents do not want their children throwing tantrums because they cannot get what they want, and they certainly do not want them using profanity and whining to get it. Television shows with misbehaved spoiled teens are harmfully affecting children's ways of acting.

Pop culture today, is everywhere and it is damaging children's daily behavior. There are many contributors to this damage, television shows, music, movies etc. In these types of pop culture the concepts being portrayed are not only being damaging to kids but are also being mimicked. This idea of seeing something and repeating it worries Denby for the sake of children's mind. The media should not be a corruption to children but a form of entertainment; this is what seems to be forgotten by children viewers.

Assessment Questions

1. Does this essay answer the first question in the essay topic?

2. Does this essay have a thesis that answers the second question?

3. Does this essay develop the thesis with supporting examples? Evaluate the effectiveness of these examples.

4. Are there significant errors in grammar that limit the essay's effectiveness? In other words, as you read the essay, did you notice several mistakes in the way the sentences are written?

5. Using the conventional standards presented in the scoring rubric in Part 1 of this book, what score does this essay deserve? Explain.

Student Essay 4

Society Is Going Down the Drain?

Our world and sense of life is changing dramatically. Mass Media has taken over our society here in the United States and all over the world. Everywhere you look, you can see its expanding power. From the comfort from our own homes, to the schools and workplaces that we reside, it's literally everywhere. But is Mass Media a good thing in our society today? Does it have an impact on our children and how they will grow up? David Denby wrote the essay "Buried Alive: Our Children and the Avalanche of Crud". In it he states that pop culture is having a negative impact on our society and our kids. After reading his essay and finding other research online to compare them with my life experiences, I would have to agree with Denby that pop culture is having a negative effect on our kids, but not all media is necessarily bad. A small portion is actually very beneficial for the child to create a healthy mindset.

As I said in the thesis, not all media is a bad thing. However the given majority of it is actually bad on children's minds. But there are some good healthy television shows and advertisements that promote certain material that is above the influence. For example, there are a huge variety of ads and commercials that promote not doing drugs or alcohol because they can ruin your life. Smoking ads are another big one, they usually show some teen smoking in some dark alley way acting like he is very cool and hip, then the next scene shows him in a hospital and the doctor says that he has lung cancer and his life is totally ruined. These ads really help out children make the right decisions in order to do well in life and succeed. But these are just ads and commercials, these are 30 seconds long, not enough time to get the message across. Well, there are some shows and programs out there for children and teens that are healthy. For children you have Nickelodeon shows like Dora the Explorer and Go Diego Go which are considered educational programs that are interactive in which kid's problem solve certain situations and work their minds out. For teens, there is the Extreme Home Makeover show in which needy families get help from volunteers to make a new household for them. This can rub off towards the teens by having them possibly volunteer and work with different kinds of organizations where they live. In context, these shows are very limited, but they are still out there if you look deep.

The majority of pop culture and media is very unhealthy for children and teens. It makes them in Denby's mind seem, "rude or surly, sees everything in terms of winning or losing popularity, makes them becomes insanely interested in clothing, and seems far, far from courage and selfhood". When Denby was a child, the mindsets of his peers were nothing like they are today. The reason, Industrialization and the improvement of technology along with the expansive powers of media. Just look at television today. MTV, VH1, all the shows in which teens are getting knocked up pregnant, all the parties, drinking, drugs, sex and so on. There everywhere. An example would be all the bachelorette shows in which there is one girl and twelve men, each man gets eliminated until there is a winner. In those shows you see the competitive nature of the men, always trying to find deviant ways to either harass or embarrass each other so that they possibly will lose. When this kind of behavior is seen by adolescents, they them bring that kind of behavior into our community, and that's a bad thing. Something that is meant purposely for entertainment is actually brought into real life. Luckily and hopefully it's not something more life threatening.

Denby also gave us the impressions on how parents react and deal with the crudeness of their children. In "Buried Alive" he writes, "The crude, bottom line attitudes they've picked up, the nutty obsessive profanity, the echo chamber of voices and attitudes, set my teeth on edge". Parents have a lot of stress now since media has taken over as basically the teacher of the children. Gone is a dream in which parents and teachers at schools will develop a child's mind and relate it to a child's own interest and nature. Pop culture has taken over. Another example is music videos. Today, hip hop and rap music is at an all time high in popularity. Some artists try certain beats and rhyme in order to create some sort of flow in their music. By doing this, they might express certain lyrics and visuals that are very inappropriate and misunderstandable. They can include a variety of certain drug relations or alcohol relations. The number one tool that I see in music videos that can have an impact on our society is broken relationships. There are too many references in the videos that will ruin relationships such as cheating on other women or treating each other disrespectfully.

When young minds see these kinds of things, they believe that it is appropriate when actually it is the exact opposite of what they believe. Music videos might sound cool and nice, but once you dissect it little by little it is actually a terrible thing that has effected a whole age group in believing what they say is actually true and okay to do.

Self-esteem is defined as a psychological term to reflect someone's overall evaluation or appraisal for their own worth. Basically, if somebody sees someone or something better than their own being in any aspect, they will feel bad because they want to be just like that someone or have that something. Pop Culture today is known for sugar coating everything in order for things to look good. The example, Magazines. These are considered booklets of advertising for media. They want the public to purchase their product and will do just about anything in order to make that happen. So let's say the product that their selling is clothing. Media officials get some very attractive models to wear the cloths that they are trying to sell. The models are perfect in every aspect, and when the public sees and views the images of these models in magazines, they just think, I want to be just like them. If they cannot be just like them, then their self-esteem is gone. Young teenage girl in high school view the magazines and want to be cool and hip, or possibly be in the popular gang. They have to have the product or they consider themselves misfits in their society. Magazines are a huge marketing tool for the media, that's basically all it's meant for. They use it for the money and popularity, and we use it to raise our self-esteem and have the top of the line best materials that the marketers have to offer. Magazines might seem pretty and nice, but once you look intently and actually see what the images actually mean in another perspective from the suppliers point of view, you can tell that they are just trying to get your money or self-esteem.

So in conclusion, I agree with Denby's point of view in his writing "Buried Alive: Our Children and the Avalanche of Crud". He states the effect of pop culture on our society is a bad thing for our children and teens. I agreed but also stated that not all media is necessarily bad, and yet some media is actually a great thing for a given population. This sort of media is very rare, the majority however is actually very bad. After reading his work and doing prior research on the subject, I do believe media has taken over our society in a brutal way. Its everywhere and we have ourselves to blame because behind the camera or screen, there is a person who is creating this sort of dilemma in our society. The vast improvements of technology and industrialization are the cause. The future seems foggy, we don't really know if us as a whole will revolt against this type of behavior, or just let it come at us with more intensity. We know what the media and pop cultures goal is, to market and deteriorate our society until it has full control on how we live, we must not let this happen, because if it does, they win.

Assessment Questions

1. Does this essay answer the first question in the essay topic?

2. Does this essay have a thesis that answers the second question?

3. Does this essay develop the thesis with supporting examples? Evaluate the effectiveness of these examples.

4. Are there significant errors in grammar that limit the essay's effectiveness? In other words, as you read the essay, did you notice several mistakes in the way the sentences are written?

5. Using the conventional standards presented in the scoring rubric in Part 1 of this book, what score does this essay deserve? Explain.

Case Study 4

Dwight MacDonald's "Reading and Thought"

The following case study uses MacDonald's essay "Reading and Thought," which you will remember from Part 2. The essay is reproduced here, followed by five timed-writing essays written by students just like you. Read MacDonald's essay and the five student essays that respond to the topic that follows it. Examine each student essay for its strengths and weaknesses. A set of study questions at the end will help you evaluate its success. Then use the scoring rubric in Part 1 to give each essay a score.

Reading and Thought

Dwight MacDonald

Dwight MacDonald (1906–82), was a part of the New York intellectuals of his time, and became famous for his attacks on middlebrow culture. He frequently carried on his debate in essays published in magazines such as The Partisan Review, The New Yorker, Esquire *(for which he wrote a dyspeptic movie column), and the magazine he edited in the 1940s,* Politics.

Henry Luce [the publisher of *Time* magazine] has built a journalistic empire on our national weakness for being "well informed." *Time* attributes its present two-million circulation to a steady increase, since it first appeared in 1925, in what it calls "functional curiosity." Unlike the old-fashioned idle variety, this is a "kind of searching, hungry interest in what is happening everywhere—born not of an idle desire to be entertained or amused, but of a solid conviction that the news intimately and vitally affects the lives of everyone now. Functional curiosity grows as the number of educated people grows."

The curiosity exists, but it is not functional since it doesn't help the individual function. A very small part of the mass of miscellaneous facts offered in each week's issue of *Time* (or, for that matter, in the depressing quantity of newspapers and magazines visible on any large newsstand) is useful to the reader; they don't help him make more money, take some political or other action to advance his interests, or become a better person. About the only functional gain (though the *New York Times*, in a recent advertising campaign, proclaimed that reading it would help one to "be more interesting") the reader gets out of them is practice in reading. And even this is a doubtful advantage. *Time*'s educated people read too many irrelevant words—irrelevant, that is, to any thoughtful idea of their personal interests, either narrow (practical) or broad (cultural).

Imagine a similar person of, say, the sixteenth century confronted with a copy of *Time* or the *New York Times*. He would take a whole day to master it, perhaps two, because he would be accustomed to take the time to think and even to feel about what he read; and he could take the time because there *was* time, there being comparatively little to read in that golden age. (The very name of Luce's magazine is significant: *Time*, just because we don't have it.) Feeling a duty—or perhaps simply a compulsion—at least to glance over the printed matter that inundates us daily, we have developed of necessity a rapid, purely rational, classifying habit of mind, something like the operations of a

Mark IV calculating machine, making a great many small decisions every minute: read or not read? If read, then take in this, skim over that, and let the rest go by. This we do with the surface of our minds, since we "just don't have time" to bring the slow, cumbersome depths into play, to ruminate, speculate, reflect, wonder, *experience* what the eye flits over. This gives a greatly extended coverage to our minds, but also makes them, compared to the kind of minds similar people had in past centuries, coarse, shallow, passive, and unoriginal.

Such reading habits have produced a similar kind of reading matter, since, except for a few stubborn old-fashioned types—the handcraftsmen who produce whatever is written today of quality, whether in poetry, fiction, scholarship, or journalism—our writers produce work that is to be read quickly and then buried under the next day's spate of "news" or the next month's best seller; hastily slapped-together stuff that it would be foolish to waste much time or effort on either writing or reading. For those who, as readers or as writers, would get a little under the surface, the read problem of our day is how to *escape* being "well informed," how to resist the temptation to acquire too much information (never more seductive than when it appears in the chaste garb of duty), and how in general to elude the voracious demands on one's attention enough to think a little.

Writing Topic

According to MacDonald, what is the nature of the "printed matter that inundates us daily," and what connection does this kind of reading have with thought? What do you think about the position he takes here? Be sure to support your argument with specific examples based on your observations and experiences; you may also draw on your reading, including the supplementary readings in this unit.

Student Essay 1

Henry Lace, publisher of time magazine, says that educated people have developed a "functional curiosity" that compels people who think they are educated to read. Henry Luce go on by saying that news, print, articles, novels, etc. intimately affect our daily lives and those who compose of it. But, according to Dwight MacDonald in "Reading and Thought" the only advantageous gain we receive when reading an article, passage, novel, etc. is simply the practice of reading. Dwight continues and states that the connection between reading and thought is time. Dwight concludes saying that we read it and then it becomes irrelevant, old news, instead of thinking about it or challenging ourselves with it. And that is why reading is only practice.

I agree with Dwight MacDonald, reading today is only practice. A lot of the time all we do is read it and then put it on the shelf, dump it, and repeat that process. I realize that I do the same thing, read & dump, with readings, that I could care less about. I am assigned in some of my classes. Reading without mediation is just reading, meaningless. But when we read and think or think throughout the reading, we finish with meaning. The next couple of paragraphs will be example of reading without thought and then reading with thought.

This last summer I took a Sociology class. In eight weeks I had to read two books, the text book and "Lies My Teacher told me." To say the least it was a little overwhelming, but in the end I was able to read the two books. Read, all I did was quickly read through the two books, which caused an absence of the real meaning in the two books. All I gained was practice and the practice was beneficial, but meaning is far more enhancing to the reader. Meaning gives us perspective and broadens our narrow point of views. Because we can attach meaning to life, not practice.

Reading with thought is far more beneficial to us. For example, I love the book of Ecclesiasties in the Bible. It is full of depressing poetry and in the end it gives the meaning of life. I have read Exxlesiasties on numerous occasions. I have attached value to it and believe that no matter how many time I read it, I will catch something new or will be reminded of something important. for me reading Ecclesiasties is far more than practice, instead it has importance and meaning to it. I can't read it without thinking about. Reading is important to us but when we think and mediate on the reading it turns into something else. Something meaning full.

Reading without thought is merely practice. But when reading and thought are combined the result is meaning. It puts value on reading. I think that everyone should think about the reading, and they should read Ecclesiasties.

Assessment Questions

1. Does this essay answer the first question in the writing topic?

2. Does this essay have a thesis that answers the second question?

3. Does this essay develop the thesis with supporting examples? Evaluate the effectiveness of these examples.

4. Are there significant errors in grammar that limit the essay's effectiveness? In other words, as you read the essay, did you notice several mistakes in the way the sentences are written?

5. Using the conventional standards presented in the scoring rubric in Part I of this book, what score does this essay deserve? Explain.

Student Essay 2

According to Dwight MacDonald in Reading and Thought, he talks about the difference of reading from old ages to today, and how in the past people had the time to read and think and imagine what the person was reading. Whereas, today we don't have time to take a book and really get in depth of the story. Dwight says that how we read is functional curiosity. He said that we only read because of what is happening in todays life and us wanting to inquire information. What we read today only is to receive information. We read with ease. However, a person from the older ages would take much longer because of their reading skill and wanting to experiance their reading material, Dwight also says that people now only wright to be read quickly and then thrown away never to be seen again. He makes a point to say that the problem we have is we want to be well informed and we need to resist that, so as we read we can think, experience, and reflect.

Reading styles have changed from old times to today. According to Dwight MacDonald we read alot, but only to inquire information, and we don't ruminate, reflect , or even experience what we read and we give no thought to our readings. In materials that I have read I have only read them because I had to or else because I wanted to get some information. I understand Dwight, because many people read for those few reasons. It's even fewer who read to imagine, experience, and visuallize themselves there. An example of this is, In high school many of the books I read were because I had to, and even while I read I skimmed over the material. Another example of this is when I have had a project were it required me to gather information I only read the important parts just to wright it down on my paper. Finally, I would read, but I would the newspaper only because something had happen near by my city and I wanted to know what was going on.

In high school I read many materials such as Raisin in the Sun, How to Kill a Mocking Bird, Mice of Men, but although I read those stories I never thought of myself as a character or even to be there. I read the story, but most of my time skimmed over the material. The reason for that is like Dwight said only to inquire information. I remember very little from the stories. I only read enough and only thought enough to be able to answer the questions ons on the test.

A second example, is that I only pick up a book or a magazine to read when I'm looking for information. Also in highschool I only read when it required me to have resources or get answers to a question. Many of my readings were long so I would look for only the part I needed, so I never took the time to imagine myself there. Many of my fellow classmates would do the same There was really not one person that would take their time and effort to read and enjoy the book.

Finally, any material that I would read would be in my spare time, and the material I would read was not for my enjoyment. It would be like Dwight said to know whats happing like he called it to be well informed. I would get the newspaper and read what was going on. The section that I would read more often would be the local. Only because I cared more about what was going on in my city or near by. Reading the newspaper does not give us the affect of experiencing something it just gives us the information, and numbers of people read for that same exact reason.

In conclusion, I understand what Dwight MacDonald is saying that many people now and day do not care to take their time and read something enjoyable, and not just to read but see themselves there or be involved with the story. Now when we read, we do not have any thought in our reading only the purpose to know more and be well informed, So in my next reading I will enjoy what I'm reading and become one of the main characters.

Assessment Questions

1. Does this essay answer the first question in the writing topic?

2. Does this essay have a thesis that answers the second question?

3. Does this essay develop the thesis with supporting examples? Evaluate the effectiveness of these examples.

4. Are there significant errors in grammar that limit the essay's effectiveness? In other words, as you read the essay, did you notice several mistakes in the way the sentences are written?

5. Using the conventional standards presented in the scoring rubric in Part 1 of this book, what score does this essay deserve? Explain.

Student Essay 3

In Dwight MacDonald's essay, "Reading and Thought," Dwight states that because our society no longer has the time to read, our minds are becoming similar to that of people in the past centuries. Meaning, although we have advanced far beyond the people in the past, the limitation we set upon our reading time is holding the advancement of our thought process back because we no longer take the time to think about what we have read. Dwight also states that the problem with today's people is that we tend to avoid long readings, and we do not hold enough attention to even think the slightest bit.

Personally, I agree with Dwight because I do feel our society is becoming less intelligent due to the fact we do not read as much. Over time the less we read the more stagnant our minds become, and the more stagnant our minds become the less original intellect is outputted. Most people today have replaced their reading time with other various types of stimuli, such as watching television or playing video games; however, such stimuli does not produce one's own vision or original thought, thus limiting their own power of thoughts and opinions.

Based on my personal experience, I also noticed the decrease in my intellectual capacity because of the lack of reading. After I graduated high school in 2004, I decided to take a couple years off in order to focus just on my businesses. While running my businesses, such as my liquor stores and my clothing line, I realized after awhile that my mind was not working as effieciently as it had before. At times, I even found myself just staring into space without a single thought on my mind. It turns out while running my business, I was always so occupied that I never took the time to do any decent reading. Even when I would go over contracts, it would usually be a quick skim over what I deemed important and I just ignored the rest. Then I even found it incredibly difficult to produce new and original marketing campains, which completely shocked me because I was known for producing amazing marketing ideas. I soon realized that my lack of thought in general was due to the fact that my brain was not being stimulated as it should be by way of reading. I knew this to be true because when I realized my thought process was becoming stagnant, I immediately started to pick up research journals on business and marketing, and I began to read through them diligently. After a couple days of constant and thoughtful reading, I noticed a huge difference in the way I thought because I was filled with so many new ideas about business and marketing campaigns.

Another example of how reading and thought go hand in hand is one pertaining to my ex-girlfriend's mom's foster kids. My ex-girlfriend's mom, Emma, constantly takes in and raises foster kids for a living. I remember two foster kids specifically whom I helped take care of Eric and Jessika. Eric and Jessika are brother and sister who grew up in many broken homes. Because they were raised under such harsh conditions, they rarely focused on their education. One activity they hated to do the most was reading. I noticed, because their lack of reading, that they hardly ever came up with their own original ideas or opinions. In fact, when we asked them what they wanted to do for leisure, they both kept saying, "whatever he/she wants to do." When we got into details about asking them of their likes and dislikes, one sibling would respond the same as the other sibling, again no original thought. Because reading helps stimulate one's own thoughts and opinions, Eric and Jessika did not seem to have either.

In essence, reading has a direct influence over one's thoughts. If an individual were to go without reading for a good amount of time, there is a real high possibility that their minds will become stagnant and vapid. If we want our society to keep progressing with new and original ideas, we must then continue to make time for reading. Especially with the younger generation of kids, we must keep them reading. Since the younger generation is our future, we want to make sure that life as we know it does not become so dull and unoriginal due to lack of new ideas brought on by the lack of reading.

Assessment Questions

1. Does this essay answer the first question in the writing topic?

2. Does this essay have a thesis that answers the second question?

3. Does this essay develop the thesis with supporting examples? Evaluate the effectiveness of these examples.

4. Are there significant errors in grammar that limit the essay's effectiveness? In other words, as you read the essay, did you notice several mistakes in the way the sentences are written?

5. Using the conventional standards presented in the scoring rubric in Part 1 of this book, what score does this essay deserve? Explain.

Student Essay 4

The Loss of Reading

In "Reading and Thought," by Dwight MacDonald, MacDonald states that reading is not the same as it was in the past eras. MacDonald states that reading should involve deep analysis of what had been read, reflection, and experience what the eye flits over (MacDonald). MacDonald directly quotes the publisher of Time Magazine Henry Luce, when he says that, "Functional curiosity grows as the number of educated people grows," but MacDonald contradicts this statement saying that curiosity isn't functional because it does not help the individual function (MacDonald). MacDonald also explains that one of the reason why we do not embrace the gift of reading is because we simply do not have the time. Another reason given is that the writers of newspapers, magazines, and other forms of literature that are not of the academy, actually produce work that are meant to be read quickly and set aside (MacDonald).

I agree on MacDonald's claim that reading has been neglected. A reader should embrace the gift of reading, and be humble that there are so many things available to be read. In the past times, there wasn't anything to be read. A library did not exist in the colonial times, the internet was not invented, and there weren't books produced everyday for the average people. I believe that many people have forgotten that reading is a gift and a privelage. Analyzing, reflecting, and just breaking down a piece of Literature in order to find the true hidden message in a book is what makes life important. Now, all that is produced in the newspapers and magazines are gossip and "How to's." In my opinion, I think the celebrity magazine sells more than the actual newspapers. I also believe that most adults read newspapers to find deals on merchandise and coupons rather than to find out the polls in elections.

With all the gossip and scandals going around on celebrities, there isn't anything to be analized and reflected on what has been read. Whenever I talk with my friends they always seem to know whether or not Brad Pitt and Angelina Jolie adopted a new child, but they didn't seem to know what the local news headline was. Except for a few, most of my friends didn't even know what the local newspaper was called. The fact that gossip is more popular than world news shows how low the academic level has dropped for the average people.

Coupons and deals are always a great find, they save you a lot of money and teach you to spend money unwisely. My friend Angela Bae used to search for coupons every Sunday in her newspapers. She would bring the newspaper to work and just cut out coupons and throw everything else away. By everything, I mean everything, even the actual newspaper. She would never read about what was going on in the world, but she would always read about what was on sale this week. She wouldn't even be able to tell you if we were in war, or with what country. It has been forgotten that reading is a gift and also that having a lot of things to read is a gift.

I believe that both the publishers and readers have forgotten what reading and analizing means. Most that are produced are work that are to be buried under gossip and coupons, instead of what is of importance like world news, politics, and local news. MacDonald specifically states that our mind asks one question, "read or not read?" necaise we tell our selves that we do not have time to read and give thought (MacDonald). Reading has been dumped into the vast black hole along with the one-hit wonders, poodle skirt, shoulder pads, and many other things that are not useful in today's daily life. Gossip, scandals, and coupons seem to be more important than political issues. This shows how uneducated the world is becoming because we have forgotten the true meaning of reading, that reading is to break down the book or article and produce deep thoughts and reflection.

Assessment Questions

1. Does this essay answer the first question in the writing topic?

2. Does this essay have a thesis that answers the second question?

3. Does this essay develop the thesis with supporting examples? Evaluate the effectiveness of these examples.

4. Are there significant errors in grammar that limit the essay's effectiveness? In other words, as you read the essay, did you notice several mistakes in the way the sentences are written?

5. Using the conventional standards presented in the scoring rubric in Part 1 of this book, what score does this essay deserve? Explain.

Student Essay 5

The Time It Takes for Reading and Thought

According to Dwight MacDonald's "Reading and Thought," he believes the connection between reading and thought is time. That it takes time to read and to think no matter what someone is looking at. Books, magazines, and even newspapers will always take time to look over to understand what it says.

I believe that MacDonald is taking the right position here. I do agree that it takes time to read and think. When I open a book, I want to know what I am getting myself into. When I start to write the perfect essay, I have to think a lot about what I am going to write. In this essay, I am going to discuss how much time it takes me to read and think.

Reading opens my eyes to so many different things. For example, in one book I can be an airline pilot flying to Africa or a young boy on a desert island. But before I can go to those places, I have to take the time to read the book. I have to take the time to understand what I am reading. If I do not understand the book, then I will have no idea what is going on in the book. Another thing that takes time when reading is looking up words I do not understand. I have to get a dictionary and look up a word so I can understand what the author is trying to say. If I do not take the time for that, then I will not understand that part in the book. Finally, it takes time to put it in my own words. If I ever wanted to tell my mother about the book, I would have to put it in words that she would have to read the book herself. This is why I believe it takes time to read because I have to understand whay I am reading, I have to look up the words I do not know to find what they mean, and put it into my own words so I can understand the book or story better.

Another thing that takes time is writing the perfect essay. The essay has a lot of steps to it that will take a lot of time. It only takes a lot of time to write the perfect essay. One step is called brainstorming. During my brainstorming phrase, I have to think about what I going to write. I would also take the time to think about the questions I need to answer. Last, I have to write down my ideas before they leave my brain. Another step is outlining my essay. I have to take the time to see what order I will write the information in. it also takes time to list the ideas down. That's for me to know what things I am going to write about. Another step is writing the essay down onto the paper. Al the time it takes to put it into my own words. It takes a lot of time to think about what words I would want to use. Last, it takes a lot of time to check my essay for mistakes. I have to make sure my grammar is correct. I have to make my spelling is correct. If I messed up anytime in the essay, I have to change it to make it make sense. That is why I believe it takes a lot of time to think when I want to write the perfect essay.

That is why I agree with MacDonald. I believe time is the connection between reading and thought. There are so many things I need to think about reading and thinking. No matter what, everyone takes time in life to think about the choices he is going to make and the time to read to get ahead in life.

Assessment Questions

1. Does this essay answer the first question in the essay topic?

2. Does this essay have a thesis that answers the second question?

3. Does this essay develop the thesis with supporting examples? Evaluate the effectiveness of these examples.

4. Are there significant errors in grammar that limit the essay's effectiveness? In other words, as you read the essay, did you notice several mistakes in the way the sentences are written?

5. Using the conventional standards presented in the scoring rubric in Part 1 of this book, what score does this essay deserve? Explain.

A Glossary of Key Terms

annotation
a comment, underline, or other marking made on or in the margins of a reading to help critically evaluate the text

conclusion
the closing section of an essay that may restate the thesis and its supporting points, or offer the reader an emotional appeal or interesting anecdote that gracefully signals the end of an essay

drafting
a stage of the writing process where a writer develops and organizes the ideas in a paper in an effort to present the essay's points with clarity and effectiveness

editing
the stage in the writing process where work is checked for grammatical and mechanical errors

freewriting
an activity in which the writer quickly puts down on paper random thoughts and ideas on a topic as a method of discovery

handbook
a text that guides the writer through the various stages of writing and provides complete information on the grammar, mechanics, and conventions of written English

index
an alphabetical list of all subjects mentioned in the text, followed by the page numbers on which those subjects appear

introduction
the opening paragraph(s) of an essay that provide a context for the material that follows

outline
a brief list of an essay's thesis statement, main points, main supporting ideas, and specific details

paragraph
related sentences grouped around a central idea or thought

peer review
an activity structured by a set of criteria for students to evaluate one another's writing during the writing process in an effort to guide revision

post-grade evaluation
a process where a writer, after receiving instructor feedback on a paper, determines patterns of weakness and strength in his or her writing and formulates a plan for improvement

prewriting
invention techniques or strategies—such as clustering, freewriting, or listing—for exploring ideas about a topic

revising
the process of rethinking and rewriting the initial draft

scoring rubric
a guide for evaluating the strengths and weaknesses of an essay

summary
a short presentation in the writer's own words of the argument and main points of a reading

table of contents
a topical list at the beginning of a text that shows at a glance the text's chapters and subjects and the pages on which they are located

thesis statement
a sentence (or sentences) found in an essay's introduction that gives the essay's central argument, the perspective or idea that locks the other components of the essay together

timed essay
usually a response to a question or topic written in a supervised setting in a designated amount of time

topic sentence
the sentence in a paragraph that states the paragraph's main point

transition
a word, phrase, or device used to provide a connection between sentences or paragraphs

Index